American English
Idioms and Slang

A bridge to successful communication

by J.D. Hunter

Copyright 2014 by J.D. Hunter

ISBN 13   978-1493744336
ISBN 10   149374433X

Printed in the United States of America

About the Author

J.D. Hunter developed the first ESL (English as a Second Language) course at The Boeing Company in Seattle, Washington. She discovered that while the students caught on fast to normal English words and phrases, there were many idiomatic phrases and slang words that "threw them for a loop". She started collecting these words and phrases, and when she retired, she kept her dictionary handy and kept adding to it. There are now 5,000 idioms and slang words in this dictionary.

Acknowledgements

First of all I would like to acknowledge my Mother, who bought my very first computer for me. I so enjoyed it because I could edit so fast and efficiently.

Next I would like to acknowledge my Father, who was from Oklahoma. He delighted in using the Midwest vernacular, and was quick to eye a plump woman as "sixteen ax handles across." I picked up his habit of using lots of slang words.

A huge acknowledgement goes to my husband, Gerald, who has always supported my dedication to this project.

Last, but certainly not least, I would like to acknowledge and dedicate this book to the millions of students of "English as a Second Language" for their courage and perseverance in learning an extremely complex and challenging language. I have loved teaching students of ESL, and learning a great deal about their various cultures.

Introduction

Vocabulary Entries – Main entries follow one another in alphabetical order, and are cross-referenced.

Abbreviations, acronymns, prefixes – are listed before the regular alphabetic order.

Example (Ex:) Some word or phrase definitions have an example sentence for further clarification of the word or phrase, but some do not when just the definition is adequate.

Parts of speech are abbreviated in some cases – adj (adjective), adv (adverb), prep (preposition), and spelled out for "verb" and "noun"; "phr" is used for "phrase", and "conj" for conjunction.

Clichés - There is also a smattering of popular clichés that English speaking people use a lot.

A.O.K. [abbrev] all OK. Ex: I just passed my driving test. Everything is *A.O.K.*

A.S.A.P. [abbrev] (business) *As soon as possible.* Ex: I want that memo done A.S.A.P.

AZT [abbrev] Zidovudine, a drug used in the treatment of AIDS. Ex: We are using AZT with very good results.

A pop [adj] each. Ex: Those candy bars cost 50 cents *a pop.*

About face [prep phr] turn completely around. Ex: a popular military command is "About Face" which results in everyone marching in the opposite direction from which they came.

About the size of it [prep phr] the true facts. Ex: We didn't play well and lost the game. That's *about the size of it.*

About time [adv phr] past the deadline or expected time . Ex: It's *about time* he proposed to Jean. They've been dating four years.

Above all [adv phr] most importantly. Ex: *Above all*, I want you to finish your homework tonight.

Above and beyond the call of duty (See *Beyond the call of duty*)

Above board [prep phr] open and honest with no ulterior motives. Ex: All the policies at the company are *above board*.

Above your head [prep phr] beyond your mental capability. Ex: Don't try to do that Calculus problem. It's *above your head.*

Absence makes the heart grow fonder

Absence makes the heart grow fonder [cliché] loving someone more when they're gone. Ex: Jim has been gone for three weeks and I really miss him. *Absence makes the heart grow fonder.*

According to Hoyle [prep phr] following the standard rules. Ex: Working on Sunday isn't exactly *according to Hoyle.*

Ace him out [verb phr] gain an advantage. Ex: I *aced him out* and won the race. (See *Beat him to the punch*)

Ace in the hole [noun phr] an advantage that you use at an opportune time. Ex: I've got a great follow up plan that is my *ace in the hole.* (See *Ace up his sleeve)*

Ace up his sleeve [noun phr] (See *Ace in the hole)*

Aced [verb] received an "A" on a test. Ex: I *aced* the test in English today.

Across the board [prep phr] (business) includes everyone or applies universally. Ex: The raises this year will be *across the board.*

Act out [verb] misbehave. (said about children) Ex: The Smith children are always *acting out.* (See *Act up*)

Act up [verb] (See *Act out)*

Act your age! [expression said to children] behave. Ex: Don't pop your gum. *Act your age!*

Actions speak louder than words [cliché] what you do has more credibility than what you say.

Active hormones [noun] puberty; experiencing a heightened sense of sexuality. Ex: John is dating three girls. He really has *active hormones.*

Add fuel to the fire [verb phr] escalate a disagreement. Ex: When you tell Jody her opinion is wrong, it really *adds fuel to the fire.*

Add insult to injury [verb phr] show a lack of respect for someone by adding to their troubles. Ex: Don't tell Hal he needs to pay you money he owes you right after he has just lost his job. That is *adding insult to injury.* (See *Pour salt in the wound*)

Afraid of your shadow [verb phr] #1 jumpy, nervous. Ex: Just tell the teacher you don't understand the question. Don't be *afraid of your shadow.* #2 shy. Ex: George will not ask anyone to the dance because he is *afraid of his own shadow.*

After a fashion [prep phr] similar to. Ex: "Do you think Sam looks like his brother?" "*After a fashion.* They both have long noses."

After a while crocodile [part of a 1950's goodbye expression] The first person says "See you later alligator" and the reply is, "*After a while crocodile.*"

After all [adv] #1 finally. Ex: I got a "B" on my test *after all.* #2 [prep phr] nevertheless. Ex: *After all*, we want Bill to finish college.

After all is said and done [adv phr] in the final analysis. Ex: *After all is said and done*, Jack still has the fastest time in the race.

After my own heart [prep phr] having the same interests and values. Ex: Tom is a man *after my own heart*. He likes to play golf on Saturday also.

Age before beauty [noun phr] meant figuratively, not literally; said jokingly when you let a friend go before you through an entrance.

Ages ago [adv] sometime in the past. Ex: I took that history class *ages ago.*

Ahead of the game [prep phr] #1 prepared and informed in a situation.   Ex: You will do well in your presentation because you are *ahead of the game*. #2   (business) being ahead of schedule on a project. Ex: When the boss asked how we were doing on the project, I told him we were *ahead of the game.*

Aim at the moon [verb phr] set high goals. Ex: He is ambitious and *aims at the moon.*

Aim to please [verb phr] try to satisfy. Ex: What do you want for dinner? I *aim to please* your appetite.

Air ball [noun] (sports - basketball) totally miss the basket when making a shot.   Ex: Roy is not a very good basketball player and shoots a lot of *air balls.*

Air dirty laundry in public [verb phr] discuss private matters publicly.   Ex: Printing information about the candidate's affair is *airing dirty laundry in public*.

Air guitar [noun] pretend to play a guitar without really having one. Ex: You really play a great *air guitar!*

_____

Airhead [noun] not too intelligent. (Said more about women than men) Ex: That comment really proves she is an *airhead.* (See *Bimbo*)

Alive and kicking [verb phr] recover from a setback full of energy. Ex: He came back from his illness *alive and kicking.*

All adrift [adj phr] confused and disorganized mentally. Ex: Don't ask him what the answer is. He is *all adrift.*

All along [adv phr] from the beginning. Ex: The teacher knew *all along* who had the best study habits.

All-American [adj] #1 America's best. Ex: Here are the *All-American* football players for this year. #2 [adj] made exclusively with American resources. Ex: The line of clothes was exclusively *all-American.*

All-around [adj] excel in many related activities. Ex: Jim is an *all-around* athlete, participating in swimming, track and football.

All at once [adv phr] immediately. Ex: *All at once* the deer jumped out of the woods.

All booked up [adj phr] busy. Ex: I'd like to come to the play, but I'm *all booked up.* (See *All tied up*)

All but [adj phr] nearly. Ex: She *all but* fainted when she won the contest.

All charged up [adj phr] enthusiastic or excited. Ex: I'm *all charged up* about winning the race. (See *All fired up*)

_____

All decked out [adj phr] dressed up in formal clothes. Ex: When you go to the opera, you get *all decked out*. (See *dressed to the hilt*)

All downhill from here [adj phr] #1 things will be *all downhill from here*. The hardest part of the task is done. #2 refers to age. When you are 40, people say, "It's *all downhill from here*", meaning the best years of your life are over.

All ears [adj phr] listening attentively. Ex: Tell me now; I'm *all ears*.

All elbows [adj phr] awkward. Ex: Watch it John. You are *all elbows*.

All eyes [noun] watch with great interest. Ex: *All eyes* were on the Olympic runner.

All fine and good [adj phr] O.K. (usually used with the conjunction "but") Ex: Sure, you got close to hitting a home run. That's *all fine and good*, but you struck out!

All fired up [adj phr] excited. Ex: He is *all fired up* about his new car. (See *All charged up*)

All for naught [adj phr] useless effort. Ex: The engineer's work was *all for naught*, when the rain washed out the bridge.

All for the best [adj phr] basically good. Ex: It was *all for the best* that Jack did not get that promotion, because he got a better job offer later.

All get out [adj phr] extremely. Ex: He's as popular as *all get out*.

All hands meeting [noun] (business) includes everyone. Ex: The *all hands meeting* is Monday, January 13 at 8:00 A.M.

All Hell's broken loose [expression of concern] a crisis situation is occurring. Ex: The dam broke and the water is flooding the valley. *All Hell's broken loose.*

All in [adj phr] exhausted. Ex: I worked all day loading heavy boxes. I'm *all in*. (See *Dead on your feet*)

All in a day's work [adj phr] A modest reply to a compliment. Ex: "You did a great job on that presentation!" "It's *all in a day's work.*"

All in all [adj phr] considering everything. Ex: *All in all,* it was a good basketball game.

All in good time [adv phr] after an indeterminable amount of time. Ex: You will be able to operate the skill saw *all in good time.*

All's fair in love and war [cliché] Everything is equal. Ex: "You shouldn't date Mark's girlfriend." "Why not, *all's fair in love and war.*"

All of [adj phr] about. Ex: It's *all of* ten miles to my house.

All of a sudden [adv phr] something unexpected happens. Ex: *All of a sudden* the car swerved in my path.

All or nothing at all [adj phr] either give 100% to a project or 0%. Ex: I expect *all or nothing at all* from the troops in my division.

All out [adj phr] #1 giving 100% of your energy. Ex: In the last big battle, our troops went *all out* to end it quickly. #2 [adj phr] having none. Ex: We're *all out* of butter.

All over but the shouting

All over but the shouting [adj phr] some activity is about to
end successfully. Ex: The last batter is up and it's the
ninth inning in baseball. I guess it's *all over but the
shouting.*

All present and accounted for [adj phr] nothing or no one is
missing. Ex: We're ready to leave on our trip, now
that the kids are *all present and accounted for.*

All right! [expression of excitement] #1 agree with someone.
(emphasize "all") Ex: <u>All</u> right. I'll go to the movies
with you. #2 congratulations. (emphasize "right") Ex:
All <u>right</u>! He hit a home run! #3 stop what you are
doing or saying. (emphasis on "right") Ex: *All <u>right</u>!*
You kids stop fighting and get to sleep!

All show, no go [adj phr] all talk and no action. Ex: Josh never
carries through with his ideas. He is *all show, no go.*

All sown up [adj phr] the deal or negotiation is complete. Ex:
We agreed on a price for the house and the deal is *all
sown up.*

All sweetness and light [adj phr] everything is wonderful and
life is going well. Ex: Janice thinks everything is *all
sweetness and light,* and doesn't face problems.

All tapped out [adj phr] #1 exhausted every way to solve a
problem. Ex: I'm *all tapped out.* You try to come up
with another solution. #2 have no money. Ex: I can't
loan you $5.00. I'm *all tapped out.* *(*See *On his last
legs)*

All that jazz [adj phr] everything in a group of related objects.
Ex: I'm taking English, Math and *all that jazz* this
quarter at school.

All the bells and whistles [adj phr] (See *Bells and whistles*)

All the king's men [adj phr] unlimited number of people. Ex: *All the king's men* could not put out that fire.

All the live long day [adv phr] every moment of the day. Ex: I've been studying *all the live long day*!

All things being equal [adj phr] consider all parts as having equal value or importance. Ex: *All things being equal,* I still think Matt is the best person for the job.

All things considered [adj phr] examining all parts. Ex: *All things considered*, this has turned out to be a pretty good summer.

All thumbs [adj] clumsy. Ex: Don't let David carry that glass bowl. He's *all thumbs* today.

All tied up [adj phr] busy. Ex: I can't go to the play with you. I'm *all tied up.* (See *All booked up)*

All told [noun expression] total count. Ex: *All told,* there were 1400 volunteers at the rally.

All work and no play makes Jack a dull boy [cliché] Comment made to one who is working too much, and needs to relax.

Along for the ride [prep phr] join in an activity without a specific reason for doing so. Ex: I didn't want to rob the bank. I was just *along for the ride.*

Along the way [prep phr] in the future. Ex: I hope to take sailing lessons *along the way*.

Also ran [noun] a loser in a political or horse race. Ex: Abraham Lincoln was an *also ran* many times before he became President of the United States.

Am I blue? [noun phr] Am I depressed?

And the like [noun phr] similar or related items. Ex: The little
        shop sells coffee, tea, spices, *and the like*.

Another day, another dollar [expression said at the end of a
        typical workday]

Ante up [noun phr] #1 put up your share of money for a bet.
        Ex: Come on. It's time to *ante up* and I will deal the
        cards.   #2 [noun phr] pay back what you owe. Ex:
        You've owed me $5.00 for two weeks. It's time to
        ante up.

Ants in your pants [noun phr] excitable and nervous. Ex: That
        child must have *ants in his pants.* He is so active.

Antsy [adj] impatient. Ex: Economics class is so boring that I
        get *antsy* before it is over.

Any port in a storm [noun phr] when you are having a lot of
        difficulties, any solution is worth trying. Ex: "Have you
        talked to Phil about a loan?" "No, but I will. *Any port
        in a storm*, you know."

Any way, shape or form [noun phr] no way. Ex: He's no match
        for me in *any way, shape or form.*

Any way you slice it   [noun phr]   however you analyze the
        situation. Ex: *Any way you slice it*, Ken will be the new
        first baseman.

Anything worth doing is worth doing well [cliché] put your
        best effort into any endeavor.

Apart from [prep] except for. Ex: *Apart from* running out of gas
        once, the trip was a lot of fun.

Apple knocker [noun] rural person. Ex: He is a real *apple knocker.* He grew up on a farm.

Apple of my eye [noun phr] one of his favorite people. Ex: She is the *apple of her Father's eye.*

Apple pie order [noun phr] everything arranged perfectly. Ex: Just as I got everything in *apple pie order,* the kids came in with their muddy boots.

Apple polisher [noun] person who tries to gain favor by flattery. Ex: She is a real *apple polisher.* She wants the teacher to like her best. (See *Brown nose*)

Are we having fun yet? [noun expression] When you are working hard and things are not going well, a co-worker may jokingly say, "*Are we having fun yet?*" to lighten up the mood.

Are you slumming? [noun phr] Used in a kidding manner when you see someone of high class in a lower class establishment. Ex: *Are you slumming?* I didn't expect to see you at this discount store.

Are your ears burning? [noun phr] talking about someone and he/she appears. You ask the question, "*Are your ears burning?*" to let the third party know you were talking about him/her.

Arm and a leg [noun phr] (See *Cost an arm and a leg*)

Arm in arm [adv phr] #1 affectionately. Ex: They went *arm in arm* through life together. #2 together, supportive. Ex: The committee went to see the mayor *arm in arm*.

Armed to the teeth [verb phr] going into battle with plenty of weapons. (old expression; still used.) [Origin: When pirates boarded a ship they held their cutlasses in their teeth so they could grasp the ship's rigging.] Ex: The boys were *armed to the teeth* with excuses about why they were late.

Around the clock [prep phr] without ceasing. Ex: We have worked on this project *around the clock*.

Around the corner [prep phr] will happen shortly. Ex: My good luck is just *around the corner*.

Artful dodger [noun] skillfully evade something or someone. Ex: When the subject of race relations is brought up, he is an *artful dodger*.

As a matter of course [adv phr] regular order of the day. Ex: *As a matter of course* we eat dinner at 5:00.

As a matter of fact (See *Matter of fact*)

As all get out (See *All get out*)

As easy as pie (See *Easy as pie*)

As far as I know [conj] the limit of my information. Ex: *As far as I know,* we're going to the beach this weekend, but it depends on the weather.

As far as it goes [conj] up to a certain point. Ex: That advertising idea is O.K. *as far as it goes.* We have a lot more work to do on it.

As fit as a fiddle [cliché] in good shape. Ex: I feel *as fit as a fiddle* after running five miles.

As follows [adv] preface to a list of items. Ex: Pack your kit *as follows*: one each plate, bowl, cup, set of eating utensils, can opener, and box of matches.

As God is my witness [prep phr] preface to telling the entire truth about something. Ex: *As God is my witness*, Jack never stole the candy.

As good as it gets [conj] there probably will not be another time or moment equal to this one. Ex: I am having a wonderful time. This is *as good as it gets*.

As good as new [conj] when something broken gets fixed, it is said to be "*as good as new*". Ex: I glued the bowl together and it is *as good as new*.

As I live and breathe [prep phr] in actuality. Ex: When you see someone you have not seen for a long time and are surprised, you say, "Well, if it isn't Joan, *as I live and breathe*."

As is [prep phr] in its present condition with no warranties. Ex: I bought the used Datsun *as is*.

As it is [prep phr] considering present circumstances. Ex: I'd like to take a vacation, but *as it is*, I can barely afford my car payments.

As luck would have it [prep phr] relating an unfortunate circumstance. Ex: *As luck would have it*, I ran out of gas on the freeway.

As old as Adam [conj] information known for a long time. Ex: I knew a long time ago that Julie was adopted. That news is *as old as Adam.*

As plain as day [conj] evident. Ex: It is *as plain as day* that the grass needs mowing.

As plain as the nose on your face [conj] obvious. Ex: Can't you see that he wants to go to University? It should be *as plain as the nose on your face.*

As the crow flies [adv phr] a straight line from one geographical place to another. Ex: I live ten miles from Ray, *as the crow flies.*

As the twig is bent, so grows the tree [cliché] as children are taught, so they will behave in the future.

As we speak [prep phr] right now. Ex: *As we speak,* Saul is getting ready for his trip.

As well [prep phr] also. Ex: I am inviting Joyce to the party *as well.*

Ashes to ashes and dust to dust [Biblical expression] death; finality.

Ask for it [verb phr] #1 deserve punishment. Ex: He is really *asking for it* by throwing a temper tantrum. #2 request for something. Ex: Do you want that cookie? Just *ask for it.*

Asleep at the switch [verb phr] not paying attention. (See *Asleep at the wheel*)

Asleep at the wheel [verb phr] not paying attention.

At a clip [prep phr] at one time. Ex: He can pound nails *at a fast clip.*

At a loss for words [prep phr] shocked or surprised and not know what to say. Ex: I didn't know Ann had cancer. I am *at a loss for words.*

At a snail's pace [prep phr] extremely slow. Ex: There is so much discussion about this project that it is moving *at a snail's pace.*

At a tender age [prep phr] as a child. Ex: He was read to *at a tender age.*

At all [adv phr] definitely not. Ex: I can't understand these test questions *at all.*

At any rate [prep phr] concludes a point. Ex: *At any rate,* you are not going to the beach.

At cross purposes [prep phr] having opposing views. Ex: Those two are always *at cross purposes.*

At death's doorstep [prep phr] extremely ill, very close to death. Ex: Kay's father is *at death's doorstep.*

At each other's throats [prep phr] arguing violently. Ex: The two brothers were *at each other's throats* most of the time.

At his expense [prep phr] #1 done to embarrass or ridicule someone. Ex: They were laughing *at his expense.* #2 make someone pay. Ex: Lunch is *at his expense.*

At large [prep phr] missing or escaped. Ex: The ape is still *at large* from the zoo.

At least [prep phr] minimal amount of effort. Ex: *At least* you can sweep the floor while I am gone.

At liberty [prep phr] permitted, free. Ex: I'm not *at liberty* to disclose the cost yet.

At long last [prep phr] finally. Ex: *At long last* my overtime check has come.

At loose ends [prep phr] indecisive. Ex: I am *at loose ends.* I cannot decide whether to go to the movie or the play.

At my wit's end [prep phr] frustrated. Ex: I am *at my wit's end.* Our team has not won a game for 4 weeks. (See *At the end of my rope*)

At odds with [prep phr] in disagreement. Ex: I am *at odds with* my neighbor over the height of his fence.

At the drop of a hat [prep phr] do something impulsively. Ex: We decided to go to the movie *at the drop of a hat.*

At the end of my rope [prep phr] frustrated. Ex: I am *at the end of my rope.* The kids have been so naughty today. (See *At my wit's end*)

At the expense of [prep phr] do something worthwhile that has a negative aspect. Ex: I went to choir practice *at the expense of* not doing my homework.

At the mercy of [prep phr] #1 in debt to someone. Ex: He is *at the mercy of* Frank because he owes him money. #2 under threat from. Ex: All of south Florida was *at the mercy of* the hurricane.

At the same old game [prep phr] repeated manipulation. Ex: I thought you had changed, but I see you are *at the same old game.*

At the top of his lungs [prep phr] loudest he can yell. Ex: The baby yelled *at the top of his lungs* because he was hungry.

At this stage of the game [prep phr] present status on a project, or activity. Ex: *At this stage of the game*, I think we will have to hire more people to get the project done.

At your earliest convenience [prep phr] as soon as you can. (usually used when writing a letter and requesting a prompt reply to the letter) Ex: Could you please answer my request *at your earliest convenience.*

At your fingertips [prep phr] close by, readily available. Ex: I have many computer games *at my fingertips.*

Athletic bag [noun] similar to a suitcase; made of nylon or leather and carries clothes for whatever sport you are participating in. Ex: His *athletic bag* contains several pairs of shoes.

Attitude adjustment [noun] having a couple of drinks to relax after work. Ex: I need an *attitude adjustment.* How about joining me at Sam's Grill?

Avenue is closed [noun phr] solution is not possible. Ex: I'd like to get the Sales Department to finance this project, but that *avenue is closed.*

Aw shucks #1 expression of disappointment. Ex: "I can't go downtown." "*Aw shucks.*" #2 modest reply to answer a compliment. Ex: You think I did a good job? *Aw shucks*, t'weren't nothin'.

Ax to grind [noun phr] #1 have a bad attitude and always be negative. Ex: He is always cranky. He must have an *ax to grind.* with someone. #2 have a selfish and hidden motive. Ex: He seems to have an *ax to grind* with Harry. Wonder what has happened in the past.

Ax will fall [noun phr] something unpleasant will happen. Ex:
If I don't get the dishes done fast, the *ax will fall* and
Mom will get mad.

B&B [abbrev] *Bed and Breakfast*. Having rooms available in your home for tourists to stay in. Ex: We stayed at a great *B&B* in Vancouver, Canada.

BFF [abbrev] *Best friend forever*. 2013 cell phone texting abbreviation.

BLT [abbrev] bacon, lettuce and tomato sandwich. Ex: Order a *BLT* for me please.

B.Y.O.B. [abbrev] bring your own bottle. When written on an invitation to a party, it means you bring a bottle of whatever liquor or non-alcoholic beverage that you want to drink at the party. Ex: Come to my party. BYOB.

Babe [noun] (2013 casual, informal) #1 good looking girl with a shapely figure. Ex: Hey, look at that *babe!* #2 Used in conversation between a man and woman who know each other well. Ex: Hey *Babe*, want to watch TV tonight. (can refer to either a man or woman)

Babe in the woods [noun phr] inexperienced. Ex: Don't put Jack on that project. He's just a *babe in the woods*.

Baby boomers [noun] babies born between 1946 and 1964; the post-World War II babies. Ex: *Baby boomers* seem quite aggressive in the business world.

Baby bump [noun] (2014 slang) pregnant. Ex: Did you notice Brenda has a *baby bump*? (See *Bun in the oven*)

Back 40 [noun] #1 the furthermost fields on a farm. Ex: We planted corn on the *back 40*. #2 Any place that is an inconvenient distance. Ex: I had to park in the *back 40* when I went to the shopping mall.

Back against the wall [noun phr] pressured to make a decision. Ex: My *back is against the wall* and I'm not ready to buy that house. (See *Backed into a corner*)

Back and forth [adv phr] one way and then the other way. Ex: Julie is running *back and forth* from the kitchen to the living room.

Back burner [noun] (business) of secondary importance. Ex: Let's put this project on the *back burner* and work on it next week.

Back by popular demand [verb phr] return to an activity because many people want you. Ex: Here's Archer, *back by popular demand*, to work on our project.

Back down [verb] concede a point or argument. Ex: He *backed down* because his Father was right.

Back in circulation [verb phr] available to date. Ex: Jodie is *back in circulation again.* Why don't you call her?

Back in the day [verb phr] (2012 slang) in the past. Ex: *Back in the day* Moms stayed home and didn't work outside the home.

Back in the saddle [verb phr] return to regular activities. Ex: She is *back in the saddle* after her operation. (See *Back into the swing of things*)

Back into the swing of things [verb phr] return to regular activities. (See *Back in the saddle*)

Back off [verb] said when you are getting angry and want the other person to go away. Ex: *Back off.* I'm tired of you being a bully.

_____

Back on track [verb phr] back to a predictable routine after taking corrective action. Ex: Tony is *back on track* after failing school first semester. He's getting all A's.

Back out [verb] withdraw from a commitment. Ex: You should not *back out* or we will lose money on the deal.

Back pedal [verb] renege on a decision. Ex: He always *back pedals* and we can't depend on him.

Back porch philosopher [noun] someone who espouses common sense ideas or plans. Ex: Will Rogers was a *back porch philosopher*.

Back stabber [noun] someone who says cruel things about others when they are not around. Ex: *Back stabbers* hurt other people's feelings.

Back talk [noun] rude answers by children to adults. Ex: *Back talk* is usually punished.

Back to square one [verb phr] back to the beginning. Ex: This plan is not working out – *back to square one* (See *Back to the drawing board)*

Back to the drawing board [verb phr] (See *Back to square one*)

Back to the salt mines [verb phr] return to work after a break. Ex: Our 15 minutes are up. *Back to the salt mines*.

Back up [verb] support. Ex: You need the sales figures to *back up* your projected profits. #2 [noun] verification. Ex: Be sure to keep a copy of the report for *back up*.

Back-handed compliment [noun] criticism using a compliment. Ex: When someone says "You did a good job on the presentation, but it could have been shorter", it is a *back-handed compliment*.

_____

Backed into a corner [verb phr] left with no other alternatives. Ex: They were *backed into a corner* and made the wrong decision. (See *Back against the wall*)

Backed the wrong horse [verb phr] supported the wrong person. Ex: We *backed the wrong horse* in the last Presidential election.

Backseat driver [noun] person who gives constant advice and criticism to the driver of a car. Ex: Don't be a *backseat driver*. It irritates the driver.

Backup system [noun] #1 alternate plan or operation. Ex: We have a generator as a *backup system* for our emergency lighting. #2 method of securing copies of data on a computer. Ex: I use a tape *backup system* for all my computer files.

Bad blood [noun] ill feelings. Ex: They can't work on the same project. There's *bad blood* between them.

Bad form [noun] not acceptable. Ex: You shouldn't call the director "boss". It's *bad form*.

Bad karma [noun] bad luck, supposedly brought on by wrongdoings in a former life. Ex: I have had three accidents this week. Must be *bad karma*.

Bad mouth [noun] criticize. Ex: Don't *bad mouth* the plan until you execute it.

Bag and baggage [noun] includes everything. Ex: I am moving in with you, *bag and baggage*.

Bag it [verb] forget it. Ex: Are you going to the store? No, I'm *bagging it* for today.

Bag lady [noun] poor homeless woman who carries all her possessions in a huge purse or bag. Ex: There are many *bag ladies* in New York City.

Bag of bones [noun phr] skinny person. Ex: The survivors from Auschwitz were just a *bag of bones.*

Bag of tricks [noun phr] unusual or creative ideas that you save for an opportune moment. Ex: He has jokes and card games in his *bag of tricks.*

Bah humbug   [exclamatory expression of dissatisfaction] (popularized by Scrooge in Charles Dickens' book <u>A Christmas Carol</u>) Ex: *Bah humbug*, I don't like the Christmas season.

Bail out [verb] #1 decide not to go along with whatever the group is doing. Ex: Don't *bail out* until you find a replacement.   #2 abandon an investment or project. Ex: He *bailed out* before it cost him too much.

Baited breath [noun] anxiously awaiting. My mother-in-law is coming to visit and I am waiting with *baited breath*.

Baker's dozen [noun] thirteen. Ex: This store sells a *baker's dozen* doughnuts.

Balderdash [1940's exclamatory expression of disbelief] (See *Baloney*)

Bald-faced lie [noun] blatant and obvious falsehood. Ex: I can't believe she told such a *bold-faced lie*.

Ball game's changed [noun phr] a new set of rules applies. Ex: Since we got a new boss, the *ball game's changed*.

Ball is in your court [noun phr] action is required by you. Ex: I completed my part of the project; the *ball's in your court* now.

Ball of fire [noun phr] person of great energy. Ex: Fran was just a *ball of fire* raising the money for the shelter.

Ball of wax (See *Whole ball of wax*)

Ball park figures [noun] best estimate of the amount . Ex: In *ballpark figures*, will it cost $10,000 or $20,000?

Ballooned [verb] grew unexpectedly. Ex: The interest on the loan really *ballooned*. (See *Mushroomed*)

Baloney [exclamatory expression of disbelief] Ex: "I am getting a huge increase in my allowance." "*Baloney,* you are not." (See *Balderdash*)

Bamboozle [verb] deceive. Ex: I thought he was going to hit the ball to the left but I was *bamboozled*. He hit it to the right.

Banana belt [noun] area having uncharacteristically warm weather. Ex: The Northwest is in the *banana belt* this fall.

Banana Republic [noun] countries in Central America. Ex: There is political unrest in some *Banana Republic* countries.

Bandy words about [verb phr] friendly argument or discussion. Ex: The two brothers were *bandying words about*.

Bane of his existence [noun phr] stumbling block to success. Ex: The keyboard on my new computer is so stiff that it has become the *bane of my existence*.

Bang heads [verb phr] disagree with someone. Ex: He and I always *bang heads* on that topic. (See *Bump heads)*

Bang-up job [noun] excellent work. Ex: George did a *bang-up job* fixing his boat.

Bank on it [verb phr] depend on someone. Ex: Greg will be on time. You can *bank on it.*

Baptism by fire [noun phr] put into a position of responsibility in a difficult situation without prior experience. Ex: Going to fight in the war was *baptism by fire.*

Bar fly [noun] person who spends a lot of time in a tavern. Ex: George Wendt on <u>Cheers</u> TV show was a *bar fly.*

Bar none [prep phr] without exception. Ex: It's the tastiest fish I've eaten, *bar none.*

Bare bones [noun] essentials. Ex: This project is down to the *bare bones.* We have no more budget.

Bare essentials [noun] only what is needed; without luxuries. Ex: I am taking only the *bare essentials* on my camping trip.

Barefoot and pregnant [adj phr] perceiving women as being totally ignorant and dependent. Ex: Chuck would never marry a career-woman. He likes them *barefoot and pregnant.*

Barely scratched the surface [verb phr] given superficial treatment. Ex: We *barely scratched the surface* of possibilities for the new product line. (See *Tip of the iceberg*)

Bark at the moon [verb phr] #1 voice useless complaints or criticism of people in powerful positions. Ex: He's just *barking at the moon* when he says the CEO should resign. #2 do something without a good reason; literally, refers to dogs who *bark at the moon* for no reason.

Bark is worse than his bite [noun phr] talk or yell loudly, but be a nice person underneath the gruff exterior. Ex: The new boss's *bark is worse than his bite.*

Barking up the wrong tree [verb phr] #1 request assistance from the wrong people. Ex: You are *barking up the wrong tree.* The Sales Department can't help you with that problem. #2 under the wrong impression. Ex: You are *barking up the wrong tree* if you think the Knicks will make the playoffs.

Barrel of laughs [noun phr] something funny or entertaining. Ex: That roller-coaster was just a *barrel of laughs.*

Basic Fundamentals [noun phr] #1 (education) Reading, writing and arithmetic. (See *Three R's)* Ex: All schools should teach the *basic fundamentals.* #2 (sports) main rules of the game. Ex: Here are the *basic fundamentals* of playing soccer.

Basic garden variety [adj phr] combination of breeds. Ex: Our dog is a *basic garden variety* dog.

Basket case [noun] exhausted mentally and emotionally. Ex: I was a *basket case* after working all that overtime.

Bat an eye [verb phr] react with surprise or resistance. Ex: He didn't *bat an eye* when Julie told him her mother was coming to visit.

Bats in his belfry [noun phr] acting crazy. Ex: The old man has *bats in his belfry*. He is walking around shouting about the end of the world.

Batting a thousand [verb phr] totally accurate repeatedly. Ex: He picked the winner in every race so far. He's *batting a thousand* today.

Battle of the bulge [noun phr] fighting the gain of weight around your waist. Ex: "Looks like you are doing well at fighting the *battle of the bulge*." "Yes, I've lost five pounds this week."

Battle of wits [noun phr] compete mentally. Ex: It was a *battle of wits* to see who would win the Scrabble game.

Bawl out [verb] loudly chastise. Ex: She *bawled out* the child for running into the street. (See *Give him an earful*)

Be a slave driver [verb phr] pressure someone to work much harder or longer hours for an extended period of time. Ex: The old plantation owners were real *slave drivers*.

Be a sport [verb phr] #1 concede to someone's request. Ex: I'll *be a sport* and go to the baseball game with you. #2 accept defeat graciously. Ex: The team *was good sports* and congratulated the team that won.

Be at a stand-still [verb phr] not productive. Ex: Without funding for construction, the project will *be at a stand-still*.

Be hard pressed [verb phr] pressured to do something, but unlikely to have the resources to accomplish it. Ex: I am *hard pressed* to get my garden planted before summer, because I am working lots of overtime at the office.

Be in hot water [verb phr] in trouble. Ex: He *was in hot water* for not calling his wife when he was late. (See *Deep do do*)

Be my guest [verb phr] go ahead and try something out. Ex: *Be my guest* and see how my new computer game works.

Be real [verb phr] say something realistic. Ex: "I think the Sonics will win the championship." "*Be real* - the Lakers will win."

Be that as it may [verb phr] whatever happens. Ex: *Be that as it may*, we still have a deadline to meet on that contract.

Bean counters [noun phr] (business) accountants. Ex: Big companies hire lots of *bean counters.*

Bear down on [verb phr] approach quickly. Ex: The truck was *bearing down* on the car.

Bear in mind [verb phr] remember. Ex: *Bear in mind* that you will be in New York next summer.

Bear with me [verb phr] be patient. Ex: *Bear with me* while I look for the tickets.

Beat a dead horse [verb phr] futile effort. Ex: Trying to find the tickets is *beating a dead horse*.

Beat a hasty retreat [verb phr] leave quickly. Ex: He beat a *hasty retreat* from the alley when he saw the gang.

Beat around the bush [verb phr] be vague. Ex: Tell me the whole story. Don't *beat around the bush.*

Beat back [verb] fight to restrict or contain. Ex: The rangers worked hard to *beat back* the forest fire.

Beat down the door [verb phr] act aggressive. Ex: I'd *beat down the door* for a chance to work with him.

Beat feet [verb] move or exit rapidly. Ex: *Beat feet* before the store owner comes.

Beat him to the punch [verb phr] gain an advantage. Ex: I *beat him to the punch* and got the best piece of watermelon. (See *Ace him out*)

Beat the bushes [verb phr] search extensively. Ex: I had to *beat the bushes* to find a new part for my old stereo.

Beat the clock [verb phr] accomplish something in less than the given time limit. Ex: I *beat the clock* and got my car in to be fixed an hour before they closed.

Beat the gun [verb phr] start before the signal or approval has been given. Ex: The runner *beat the gun* and had to begin again.

Beat the living daylights out of him [verb phr] hit someone repeatedly. (usually said as a threat only) Ex: If that boy spits on me again, I will *beat the living daylights out of him.*

Beat the odds [verb phr] be successful in spite of overwhelming obstacles. Ex: Maybe you will *beat the odds* and win the game.

Beat the pants off [verb phr] win handily and decisively. Ex: Team A *beat the pants off* Team B.

Beater car [noun] an older model car, usually at least 10 years old. Ex: I got another flat tire on my old *beater car*.

Beating on the pearly gates [verb phr] dead. Ex: If he doesn't stop smoking soon, he'll be *beating on the pearly gates*.

Become of [verb] happened to. Ex: What's *become of* Virginia? I haven't seen her lately.

Bed down [verb] #1 prepare to sleep. Ex: The Boy Scouts began to *bed down* around the campfire. #2 (business) develop relationships with. Ex: Our buyers try to *bed down* with several vendors to get the best prices.

Bed of roses [noun phr] something pleasant. Ex: The clean-up job was no *bed of roses,* but the pay was good.

Bee in her bonnet [noun phr] agitated. She got a *bee in her bonnet* when her husband went on a business trip.

Beef up [verb] enhance. Ex: We better *beef up* the presentation so it will last an hour.

Beefcake [noun] good looking man with great physique. Ex: What a *beefcake.* He works out all the time.

Beemer [noun] BMW car. Ex: Mostly upper middle class people drive *Beamers.*

Been around [verb] experienced. Ex: Eric has *been around* long enough to not be cheated by the car dealer.

Bees knees [noun phr] (1930's slang) cute. Ex: Sharon's new baby is just the *bees knees*!

Before he was a twinkle in his Father's eye [prep phr] (1950's phrase) before he was conceived. Ex: We knew what name we were going to give him *before he was a twinkle in his Father's eye.*

Before the cows come home [prep phr] (country western) before dark. Ex: Said to someone leaving the house. "Now you be back *before the cows come home."*

Beggars can't be choosers [cliché] a free offering that you are not in a position to refuse. Ex: I didn't like the hot dogs at the picnic, but *beggars can't be choosers*.

Behind his back [prep phr] saying something negative about someone in secret. Ex: Everyone is talking about Ted *behind his back.*

Behind the eight ball [prep phr] not up to expectations. Ex: George was *behind the eight ball* on that idea.

Behind the scenes [prep phr] surreptitiously. Ex: Ralph negotiated with management *behind the scenes* to get our new equipment.

Behind the times [prep phr] outdated, unfashionable. Ex: Her dress is way *behind the times.* It has a dropped waistline.

Bells and whistles [noun phr] all the luxurious options. Ex: My new car came with all the *bells and whistles* such as heated seats, electronic plug ins and a GPS system.

Belly up [verb] #1 go bankrupt. Ex: His business went *belly up.* #2 walk up to the bar or table for a drink. Ex: Dale *bellied up* to the bar. #3 take responsibility. Ex: He should *belly up* and finance the project.

Belt out [verb] sing loudly. Ex: That movie star can *belt out* a song and dance as well.

Bend over backwards [verb phr] exhaust every effort; do everythihg possible. Ex: I will bend over backwards to get him into the best university.

Bend your ear [verb phr] tell you something. Ex: Have you got time to let me *bend your ear*?

Benefit of the doubt [noun phr] extend trust . Ex: I don't know if Bob cheated on the exam or not, but I gave him the *benefit of the doubt*.

Bent out of shape [verb phr] upset or hurt. Ex: When she wasn't invited to the party, she got all *bent out of shape*. (See *Get your nose out of joint*)

Benzo [noun] Mercedes Benz car. Ex: Did you see Jack's new *Benzo*?

Beside himself [prep phr] distraught. Ex: He was *beside himself* when his son was killed in the war.

Beside the point [prep phr] not crucial to the discussion. Ex: Whether or not you have the money to go is *beside the point*, since you don't have the time off. (See *Beside the question*)

Beside the question [prep phr] (See Beside the point)

Best foot forward (See *Put your best foot forward*)

Best laid plans of mice and men [noun phr] something attempted fails, regardless of planning. Ex: "How did the project go?" "It didn't. The *best laid plans of mice and men* you know."

Bestie [noun] (2014 slang) best friend.

Bet on the come [verb phr] spend money, assuming that there will be enough income later to meet expenses. Ex: The company expanded their operations, *betting on the come.*

Bet the farm [verb phr] wager everything you have. Ex: He *bet the farm* that the Chicago Cubs would win the game.

Bet your bottom dollar [verb phr] be assured. Ex: You can *bet your bottom dollar* the teacher will have an essay exam.

Better late than never [cliché] preferable to arrive late than not at all. Ex: Here comes Harry ten minutes late to the meeting. *Better late than never.*

Better left unsaid [verb phr] a comment should not have been made. Ex: Why did you ask Ben about his ex-wife. That was *better left unsaid.*

Better luck next time [noun phr] encouragement to win at the next opportunity. Ex: It's too bad you lost the game. *Better luck next time.*

Between a rock and a hard place [prep phr] caught in the middle of a conflict and no alternative looks positive. Ex: The boss wants me to work overtime and my wife wants me to be home with her. I am *between a rock and a hard place.* (See *Catch 22*)

Between the sheets [prep phr] in bed. (supposedly having sex) Ex: The couple was *between the sheets.*

Between you, me, and the gatepost [prep phr] confidentially. Ex: *Between you, me, and the gatepost,* I think the mayor should resign from office.

Bewitching hour [noun] 12:00 A.M. Ex: I want you to be home by the *bewitching hour*.

Beyond his reach [prep phr] unattainable. Ex: The goal is *beyond your reach*.

Beyond me [prep phr] not understandable. Ex: Why we ever moved to the desert is *beyond me*.

Beyond measure [prep phr] excessive. Ex: He has riches *beyond measure*.

Beyond the call of duty [prep phr] provide a service or put forth more effort than was expected. Ex: The group saved $200,000 on the project, which was *beyond the call of duty*.

Beyond the shadow of a doubt [prep phr] absolutely. Ex: You have the ability to do it *beyond the shadow of a doubt*.

Bible belt [noun] Midwestern and Southern United States-- areas considered conservative and religious. Ex: The *Bible Belt* folks usually vote Republican.

Biding his time [verb phr] slow to act. Ex: He sure is *biding his time* finishing his work.

Big as life [adj phr] #1 in person. Ex: I wanted to see you this afternoon, and here you are, *big as life*. #2 actual size. Ex: The model of the new car was *big as life*.

Big Brother [noun] authoritarian government. Ex: *Big Brother* is controlling more of our lives every day.

Big cheese [noun] the boss. *Ex:* The *big cheese* just called a meeting. (See *Big enchilada*)

Big enchilada (See *Big cheese*)

Big fat hairy deal [1960's slang expression] That's not important - so what? Ex: "The boss said we're not going to spend any more time on project x". *"Big fat hairy deal."*

Big fish in a small pond [noun phr] have a lot of importance, but in a small group of people. Ex: He's a *big fish in a small pond*, because he works for a small company.

Big hearted [adj] generous, kind. Ex: I know he is a *big hearted person* because he donated time and money to the homeless.

Big House [noun] prison. (See *Pokey*)

Big picture [noun] (business) the overall business goals of a company. Ex: The *big picture* is that we expect to increase our sales force by 15%.

Big shot [noun] important person. Ex: The mayor sure is a *big shot* in city hall. (See *Head Honcho*)

Big stink [noun phr] controversy or unpleasantness. Ex: There was sure a *big stink* when the vice president resigned.

Big ticket item [noun phr] expensive object. Ex: My new couch is a *big ticket item.*

Big time [adv phr] on a large scale. Ex: James closed a sale *big time* this afternoon.

Bigger fish to fry [adj phr] more important activities. Ex: I know Nancy wants me to type her letter, but I have *bigger fish to fry*.

Bigger than a breadbox [adj phr] quantitative size used to describe something, assuming a breadbox as being approximately two feet by six inches square. Also used sarcastically to describe the importance of something. Ex: How important is the project at the central office? Well, it's *bigger than a breadbox*!

Bigger than both of us [adj phr] extremely impressive and expensive. Ex: That new TV Phil bought is *bigger than both of us.*

Bigwig [noun] important person. (See *Big Cheese*)

Bimbo [noun] superficial and not too intelligent woman. Ex: That girl acts so silly. She is a real *bimbo.* (See *Airhead)*

Biological clock is ticking [noun phr] limited time to reproduce. Ex: Women over 35 who do not have children and have a limited number of years in which to get pregnant have an invisible *biological clock that is ticking* the years away.

Bird brain [noun] idiot. Ex: Kevin flunked the test today. He is a real *bird brain.* (See *Bozo)*

Bird in the hand is worth two in the bush [cliché] Don't leave a certain situation such as a job or relationship for something that is uncertain.

Birds and bees [noun phr] human reproduction. Ex: I learned more about the *birds and the bees* from my friends than my parents.

Bird's eye view [cliché] see the whole picture from a distance. Ex: When I am up in this hot air balloon, I have a *bird's eye view* of the city.

Birds of a feather flock together (cliché)   People with similar interests or avocations will be attracted to each other or spend time together.

Birthday suit [noun] naked. Ex: Don't run around outside in your *birthday suit*!

Bite off more than you could chew [verb phr] take on more responsibilities than you can handle. Ex: With that extra project, I really *bit off more than I can chew.*

Bite the bullet [verb phr] accomplish something unpleasant but necessary. Ex: I've just got to *bite the bullet* and get this report typed instead of watching TV.

Bite the dust [verb phr] #1 died. (usually not referring to a person) Ex: I stepped on the spider. It *bit the dust.* #2 a relationship ends, or a situation has come to a dead halt. Ex: Project X just *bit the dust* today.

Bite the hand that feeds you [verb phr] (See *Don't bite the hand that feeds you*)

Bite your head off   [verb phr] respond angrily. Ex: Don't talk to Bill today. He'll *bite your head off* if you bother him!

Bite your tongue [verb phr] do not say anything. Ex: I wanted to offer my niece advice, but I *had to bite my tongue.* (See *Hold your tongue)*

Bitter pill to swallow   [noun phr]   event that has a negative effect on you. Ex: Losing his job was a *bitter pill for Joel to swallow.*

Black and white [noun phr] attitude that is limited in perspective. Ex: He should let his son decide whether or not he wants to go to college, but he sees everything in *black and white.*

Black book [noun] (outdated) a small book single people, usually men, keep with names and phone numbers of eligible dates. (This list is now kept on a person's cell phone) Ex: Doug has some really cute girls in his *black book.*

Black cloud is following me [noun phr] having continuous bad luck. Ex: I got in a car wreck yesterday. That *black cloud is following me.*

Black day [noun] a time of misfortune. Ex: It was a *black day* when the stock market fell.

Black heart [noun] cruel, merciless person. Ex: Rasputin had a *black heart.*

Black sheep of the family [noun phr] family member who has done something to discredit or shame the other family members. Ex: Peter is the *black sheep of the family*. He is in prison now.

Black strap [adj] rum and molasses; also any bad whiskey. Ex: During prohibition a lot of *black strap liquor* was produced.

Black thumb [noun] lack of talent for growing plants. Ex: I have a *black thumb*; everything I plant dies.

Blackball [verb] exclude from a group. Ex: Sam was *blackballed* from joining the country club.

Blackout [noun] without electricity. Ex: We had a blackout in January due to a heavy snowfall.

Blank out [verb] forget (e.g. a bad experience). Ex: I want to *blank out* everything my ex-wife said.

Blaze a trail [verb phr] #1 be the first to walk along a path in the wilderness. Ex: The early settlers *blazed a trail* to the West. #2 be a pioneer in any venture. Ex: Lots of computer geeks are *blazing new trail*s in the world of computing.

Blaze away [verb phr] fire without stopping. Ex: The robber's gun *blazed away*.

Bleeding edge of technology [noun phr] pun on "leading edge of technology", where someone is taking more risk than necessary to promote new technology. Ex: That company is likely to fail because they are on the *bleeding edge of technology.*

Bleeding him dry [verb phr] #1 using or wasting all his money or resources. Ex: The contractors were *bleeding him dry* when they were building his house. #2 extortion or blackmail. Ex: They were *bleeding him dry*, so he could keep his past a secret.

Bless your pea-pickin' heart [verb phr] (1930's country western) you are wonderful. Ex: *Bless your pea pickin' heart* for helping me fix dinner.

Blew a mainspring [verb phr] become upset. Ex: He *blew a mainspring* when he lost the contract.

Blind as a bat [adv phr] not see well. Ex: Without my glasses I am *as blind as a bat.*

Blind date [noun] go out with someone you have never met. Ex: My sister arranged a *blind date* for me with her co-worker.

Blind leading the blind [noun phr] neither the leader or his followers are experienced. Ex: We're all learning Windows 8 together. It's the *blind leading the blind*.

Blind-sided [adj] totally surprised by some new aspect or problem. Ex: The manager was *blind-sided* when he found out one of his employees was an alcoholic.

Block party [noun phr] people in a neighborhood get together to have a meal or work on a project. Ex: Everyone in Timberlane is having a *block party* Saturday night.

Blockbuster [noun] a movie that attracts sell-out crowds from the first day it opens. Ex: <u>Man of Steel</u> was a real *blockbuster*.

Blood and thunder [noun] movies full of violence. Ex: Quentin Tarantino movies are full of *blood and thunder*.

Blood bath [noun] violent situation in which two groups of people are killing each other. (either literally or figuratively) Ex: In some African countries a *blood bath* is happening.

Blood is thicker than water [noun phr] direct family relationships are more important than others. Ex: She left her estate to her children, but nothing to her step-children, since *blood is thicker than water*.

Blood out of a turnip (See *Can't get blood out of a turnip*)

Blood pact [noun] promise two people keep until death by cutting their fingers and mixing the blood. Ex: The two boys made a *blood pac*t to be friends forever.

Blood relation [noun] in the family; related to each other. Ex: He is my second cousin, a *blood relation*.

Blow a fuse [verb phr] lose your temper. Ex: Jim *blows a fuse* easily.

Blow blue smoke [verb phr] casual talk that is meaningless. Ex: Don't believe him. He *blows a lot of blue smoke.* (See *Blow hot air*)

Blow him away [verb phr] amaze him. Ex: When Eric sees this new car, it will *blow him away*.

Blow hot air [verb phr] (See *Blow blue smoke*)

Blow hot and cold [verb phr] changing greatly in opinion or attitude. Ex: I can never figure her out. She *blows hot and cold.*

Blow it [verb] fail completely. Ex: Don't *blow it* when you go for your job interview.

Blow it out your ear [verb phr] Sarcastic expression meaning "I don't care what you said - forget it." (See *Stick it in your ear*)

Blow off steam [verb phr] angry and shouting. Ex: The boy *blows off steam* quite often. He needs to control himself.

Blow-out [noun] #1 a tire on a car going flat suddenly. Ex: The accident was caused because of the *blow-out* on his tire. #2 a wild party. Ex: The party at Marcia's lasted all night. It was a real *blow out.*

Blow out of proportion [verb phr] exaggerate. Ex: Whenever he gets upset, he will *blow* all the problems *out of proportion.*

Blow out of the water [verb phr] get control of or win an event decisively. Ex: John will *blow* Tim *out of the water* in the next 100-meter race.

Blow over [verb] will pass. Ex: This storm will *blow over* by tomorrow.

Blow someone off [verb phr] ignore someone. Ex: She *blew off* her ex-boyfriend.

Blow sky high [verb] explode. Ex: That warehouse will *blow sky high* if we don't control the flames.

Blow the whistle on [verb phr] expose wrong doing or illegal activity. Ex: She *blew the whistle on* the company because it was disposing of waste material illegally.

Blow your brains out [verb phr] commit suicide, by shooting yourself in the head with a gun. Ex: No one expected Larry to *blow his brains out.*

Blow your cookies [verb phr] throw up. Ex: He had the flu and *blew his cookies.*

Blow your mind [verb phr] difficult to comprehend. Ex: All those people starving in Somalia really *blows my mind*.

Blow your own horn [verb phr] self-praise, to bring attention to your own successes. Ex: I had to *blow my own horn* since he didn't appreciate my work.

Blow your top [verb phr] angry and explosive. Ex: Why do you *blow your top* whenever I am late coming home? (See *Hit the ceiling*)

Blow your wad [verb phr] spend all the money you have in your pocket. Ex: I *blew my wad* yesterday and can't go to the movies today.

Blowhard [noun] braggart. Ex: Joe is such a *blowhard*. He is always bragging about how much money he makes.

Blue blood [noun] aristocrat. Ex: He is related to the blue-blooded Vanderbilts.

Blue book [noun] book denoting fair market value of a car. Ex: You better check the *blue book* before you sell your car.

Blue in the face [adj phr] exhausted and out of breath. Ex: He yelled till he was *blue in the face*.

Blue jeans affair [noun] informal gathering. Ex: The party is a *blue jeans affair*.

Blue light special [noun] special sale at a department store. Ex: I got in on the *blue light special* and got this TV for half price.

Blue plate special [noun] specialty dish in a restaurant. Ex: The *blue plate special* for the day is meat loaf.

Blue ribbon [adj] excellent; first rate. Ex: Mary's blackberry pie was truly *blue ribbon*.

Blue skies [noun] everything is wonderful. Ex: It will be *blue skies* from now on, because I got a promotion.

Blue sky [noun] conceptual. Ex: John's company is just *blue sky* now. He doesn't even have an approved loan yet.

Blue-collar worker [noun] factory or construction employee; low to middle income earner. Ex: *Blue collar workers* can wear jeans to work.

Blushing bride [noun] a new bride, traditionally said to be shy and blushing. Ex: George took Sally as his *blushing bride.*

Boarding house reach [noun phr] reach across the table for food without asking for it to be passed. Ex: Eric has a real *boarding house reach* and will get the food first.

Bodacious [adj] (2013 slang) superb. Ex: That guy sure has *bodacious* muscles.

Bogged down in the detail [verb phr] spend so much time on small issues that the activity does not progress. Ex: The engineers got *bogged down in detail* and didn't submit the final plans.

Boggle your mind [verb phr] overcome from the complexity or grandeur of something. Ex: The new computer network capability will *boggle your mind.*

Boiled in oil [verb phr] empty threat. Ex: If you don't get tickets for Saturday's game, I'll have you *boiled in oil.*

Boilerplate stuff [noun] (business) usual way of operating. Ex: The plan for the shopping center is just *boilerplate stuff.*

Boils down to [verb phr] condense. Ex: What my complaint *boils down to* is if I don't get the raise, I'm leaving.

Bombed out [verb] #1 drunk. Ex: He got *bombed out* and had to take a taxi home. (See *Three sheets to the wind*) #2 failed. Ex: I *bombed out* on that last presentation.

Bone of contention [noun phr] unsettled issue. Ex: The *bone of contention* between the two managers is how many people to assign to each project.

Bone to pick [noun phr] issue of conflict to discuss. Ex: John, you said you would be home at 9:00. It's now 10:30. I have a *bone to pick* with you.

Bong [noun] used to smoke marijuana.

Boob Tube [noun] Television set. Ex: Most people watch the *boob tube* too much.

Boogie Board [noun] short surfboard suited for skimming the waves. Ex: *Boogie boards* are more popular than surfboards now.

Boogie on down here [verb phr] hurry over to my place. Ex: Can you *boogie on down here* tonight? (See *Let's boogie*)

Boonaroonie [noun] playful synonym for a child. Ex: The *boonaroonie* is climbing the walls today. Since it is raining, he can't play outside.

Boot him out [verb phr] remove someone from office or prohibit re-election. Ex: Let's *boot the governor out* the next election.

Booty Call [noun phr] (2013 slang) invitation to have sex. Ex: You've got a 9:00 p.m. *booty call* with me.

Bootylicious [adj] (2012 slang) very sexy and desirable. Ex: Beyoncé is a *bootylicious* entertainer.

Booyah! [verb] Originated from Louisiana as a shout out for the Saints football team.

Born under a lucky star [verb phr] said about someone who appears to be very fortunate through little effort of his own. Ex: She was *born under a lucky star* and got that promotion without any hard work.

Born with a silver spoon in his mouth [verb phr] said about someone with inherited wealth. Ex: Cornelius Vanderbilt's children were *born with a silver spoon in their mouths.*

Born yesterday [verb phr] naive. Ex: I thought he would see Shannon was after his money, but I guess he was *born yesterday*.

Bosom buddies [noun phr] best of friends. Ex: Hannah and Dave are *bosom buddies.*

Both sides of the fence [noun phr] support two differing opinions. Ex: Frank always rides *both sides of the fence* in an argument.

Bottleneck [noun] anything that causes a slowdown. Ex: Getting the well dug has become a real *bottleneck* for us because we can't get our building permit.

Bottom line [noun] (business) #1 the actual motivation behind a decision. Ex: The *bottom line* is that the company is losing money and people have to be laid off. #2 the profit or loss line of a company financial statement. Ex: The *bottom line* is we had a 35% loss last quarter.

Bottom of the barrel [noun phr] the last choice anyone could have made. Also refers to people not very attractive or desirable. Ex: She was the *bottom of the barrel* pick for the softball team.

Bottom of the rung [noun phr] Having the least power or authority. Ex: Don't ask me to change the office policy - I'm at the *bottom of the rung*.

Bottom out [verb phr] reach the end of problems or trials. Ex: I think the financial difficulties of the company are about to *bottom out* and we can start hiring again.

Bottomless pit [noun] never getting full of food. Ex: His stomach is a *bottomless pit*.

Bottoms up [verb phr] A toast. Ex: Let's all drink to Mary's graduation. *Bottoms up!* (See *Cheers*)

Bought it hook, line, and sinker [verb phr] tell someone a story that was not true and they believed it entirely. Ex: He told her he was playing golf all day and she *bought it hook, line, and sinker.*

Bought the farm [verb phr] died. Ex: He *bought the farm* yesterday. After all he was 87 years old.

Bounce a check [verb phr] not have enough money in your bank account to cover the amount of the check you wrote. Ex: *Bouncing checks* is not good financial planning.

Bounce back [verb phr] recover from a setback. Ex: He *bounced right back* after his back operation.

Bouncing off the walls [verb phr] hyperactive, uncontrollable. [used to describe some children's behavior.] Ex: The kids just *bounced off the walls* today. I put them down for a nap early.

Bound and determined   [verb phr]   put every effort into accomplishing a goal. Ex: I am *bound and determined* to get an "A" in Spanish next term.

Bow and scrape routine [noun phr] subservient to gain favor with someone. Ex: If he does the *bow and scrape routine*, perhaps his wife will let him play poker with his friends.

Bow out [verb] cancel or reject. Ex: I'm going to have to *bow out* of the vacation plans. I have to work that week.

Bowl over [verb phr] pleasantly surprise. Ex: The anniversary party will *bowl* Paul *over*.

Boy toy [noun] sexy and provocative female. Ex: Lots of men look at models as *Boy Toys*.

Bozo [noun] idiot. (See *Bird brain*)

Brain dead [noun phr] not pay attention and act stupid. Ex: He didn't know the answer to that question. Is he *brain dead*?

Branch water [noun) clear fresh water from a mountain stream. Ex: The *branch water* is very cold.

Brand spanking new [adj] from the factory. Ex: Dad bought a *brand spanking new* car last night.

Brave it out [verb phr] stay and wait through some difficult experience. Ex: You have to *brave it out* until our company shows a profit. (See *Tough it out)*

Breadwinner [noun] person who provides financially for the family. Ex: My Dad is the *breadwinner* of our family.

Break a leg! [verb phr] A well-wishing to a performer or speaker before performing. Ex: The play is tonight. *Break a leg!*

Break away [verb] #1 escape from a routine. Ex: Let's *break away* and go out to dinner tonight. #2 pull ahead of everyone in a race. Ex: The runner *broke away* from the others and won the race.

Break bread [verb phr] #1 have a meal, usually with company. Ex: Let's *break bread* with the neighbors tonight. #2 Christian ritual celebrating the Last Supper. The disciples *broke bread* for the last time.

Break camp [verb phr] pack and go home. Ex: Since it's raining, let's *break camp.*

Break cover [verb] come out of hiding or disclose true identity. Ex: The Marines *broke cover* when the enemy left.

Break even [verb phr] finish no better or worse than at the start. Ex: I will *break even* on my stock investment.

Break ground [verb] start a new building or project. Ex: They will *break ground* Monday for the new restaurant.

Break in #1 [noun] commit burglary. Ex: There was a *break in* last night next door to my home. #2 [verb] Train someone to do a task. Ex: We have to *break in* Ron on the new software we got while he was on vacation.

Break loose [verb phr] set aside some time. Ex: If I can *break loose* tonight, we'll go to a movie.

Break my neck [verb phr] use great speed and effort to accomplish something. Ex: I had to *break my neck* to get to school on time. (not literally!)

Break off [verb] #1 discontinue. Ex: The union decided to *break off* negotiations with the company. #2 dissolve an engagement of marriage or other close relationship. Ex: She will have to *break off* the engagement because Duane drinks too much.

Break out the good stuff [verb phr] offer expensive alcohol. Ex: My brother is coming to visit. Let's *break out the good stuff.*

Break the habit [verb phr] stop doing some objectionable or addictive behavior, such as smoking tobacco or drinking alcohol. Ex: Cigarettes are not healthy, so he has to *break the habit.*

Break the ice [verb phr] #1 conquer being uncomfortable meeting someone new. Ex: After we *broke the ice,* I found she was lots of fun. #2 start a conversation on a difficult subject. Ex: Jack *broke the ice* by talking about his recent divorce.

Break the news [verb phr] relay information. Ex: I can hardly wait to *break the news* that my stock just went up.

Break your heart [verb phr] An emotional event causing great sorrow. Ex: The kidnapping of that child is enough to *break your heart.*

Breakdown #1 [noun] lose control mentally. Ex: JoAnn had a *breakdown* after her husband died. #2 [noun] (business) the details. Ex: Can you give me the *breakdown* on the Jones contract?

Breakneck pace [noun] as fast as possible. Ex: Get that story to the paper at *breakneck pace*.

Breakthrough thinking [noun] (business) a paradigm shift in thinking about business processes. Ex: Our company needs some *breakthrough thinking* to keep our market share.

Breathe down your neck [verb phr] #1 standing close behind you. Ex: Don't *breathe down my neck*. It makes me nervous. #2 have someone else scrutinize your work closely or to push to get the work done quickly. Ex: The contractors are *breathing down the necks* of the architects.

Breathe easy [verb phr] relax. Ex: *Breathe easy*. Mom says we can go to the picnic.

Breeze through it [verb phr] do it easily. Ex: I'll just *breeze right through* the housework so I can go swimming.

Brew-Ha-ha [noun] fuss or temper tantrum. Ex: Don't cause a big *brew-ha-ha* over a little disagreement. (See *To-do)*

Bridge the gap [verb phr] find a common understanding. Ex: We *bridged the gap* in our different languages by using sign language.

Bright-eyed and bushy tailed [cliché] alert, especially early in the morning. Ex: "You sure are *bright eyed and bushy tailed* this morning. " "Yes, I begin vacation today."

Bring him down a peg [verb phr] humbled him. Ex: When his project failed, it sure *brought him down a peg*.

Bring home the bacon [verb phr] support your family. Ex: Today, many mothers *bring home the bacon*.

Bring the house down [verb phr] receive applause and praise from the entire audience when performing in a play. Ex: When he imitated that comedian, it *brought the house down.*

Bring to bear [verb phr] take into account. Ex: There are a lot of aspects that *bring to bear* on his decision.

Bring to light [verb phr] expose, particularly a problem. Ex: It was *brought to light* that he hadn't paid his taxes in 2002.

Bring to the table [verb phr] #1 offer a new suggestion . Ex: I'm *bringing to the table* a new plan for the heat outlet. #2 (business) add skills or talents to a project. Ex: John and Larry have database experience to *bring to the table.*

Bring up [verb phr] #1 rear (as children). Ex: *Bring up* your children to be polite. #2 recall (as an issue). Ex: Don't *bring up* the fact that he failed his driver's test.

Bring up to speed [verb phr] #1 train someone to be as proficient as you. Ex: I need to *bring* Marcia *up to speed* on the new computer. #2 inform someone of the details prior to their involvement. Ex: Jane was on vacation for the first meeting. Please *bring* her *up to speed.*

Broad minded [adj] tolerant. Ex: That person is *broad minded* and accepts people from other religions as friends.

Broke up [verb] decide to go separate ways after dating or being married. Ex: Sally and Mike *broke up* yesterday. They had dated for 4 years.

Bromance [noun] (2013 slang) romance between two men.

Brought on board [verb phr] (business) hired or transferred someone into the business organization. Ex: We *brought* four new salespersons *on board* yesterday.

Brown as a berry [adj phr] have a beautiful suntan. Ex: Lots of people who live in Florida are *brown as a berry*.

Brown bag it [noun take a sack lunch to work or school. Ex: My husband likes to *brown bag it* because he gets homemade cookies.

Brown bag lunch [noun] (business) business meeting where everyone brings his own lunch to eat during the meeting or lunches are delivered packed in brown bags. Ex: We'll have *brown bag lunches* at the noon meeting.

Brown nose [noun] someone who flatters a person in a powerful position to get ahead. (See *Apple polisher*)

Brown out [noun] lose electrical power to a certain area of a city. Ex: Last month Denver had two *brown outs.*

Brownie points [noun] tally of favors earned. Ex: If you make coffee each morning, you will win a lot of *brownie points* with the boss.

Brush off [noun] ignore someone. Ex: Since he got his promotion he gives his old friends the *brush off.*

Brush up on [verb phr] review or refresh (as a skill). Ex: I need to *brush up on* my Spanish before I travel to Mexico.

Buck the trend [verb phr] act independently, against current popular ideas or opinions. Ex: I'm going to *buck the trend* and decorate my home in Early American. (See *Swim against the tide*)

Bucks [noun] money.   Ex: It costs six *bucks* for the movie. (See *Moola*)

Buck up [verb]cheer up. Ex: *Buck up!* Your luck will improve.

Bucket list [noun] list of activities you want to experience before you die. Ex: Hang gliding is next on my *bucket list.*

Buckle down [verb] get to work! Ex: Come on students - *buckle down!*

Buckle under [verb] become subservient, or give up. Ex: He *buckled under* when his boss demanded overtime.

Buffalo someone [verb phr] (country western) #1 fool someone. Ex: I thought he knew a lot about computers but he *buffaloed me.*

Bug him [verb] irritate someone until you make the person really angry. Ex: That small child *bugs* his mother by whining for cookies. (See *Get in your hair*)

Bug in your ear [verb phr] get an idea from someone. Ex: She got a *bug in her ear* to go to Hawaii.

Bug out [verb] #1 leave quickly.   Ex: Got to *bug out* - my wife is waiting.   #2 bulge or open wide (as eyes).   Ex: When he saw his new bike, his eyes *bugged out.*

Bugging [verb] #1 placing secret listening devices. Ex: When Nixon was President, the Watergate Hotel was *bugged*. #2 have anal sex.

Build castles in the air [verb phr] have unrealistic ideas or goals. Ex: Dan *builds castles in the air*. His ideas are not backed up by many facts.

Bull in a china shop [noun phr]   awkward and clumsy. Ex: That small boy was like a *bull in a china shop* in his grandmother's home. He broke several dishes.

Bum rap [noun] situation that was unfair to a person. Ex: Some people go to jail on a *bum rap.*

Bummed out [verb]   disappointed. Ex: I am bummed out that I didn't make the baseball team.

Bummer   [exclamation of disappointment]   Ex: I heard you failed your exam - *bummer!*

Bump heads [verb] disagree. Ex: We always *bump heads* over politics. (See *bang heads*)

Bump into   [verb]   #1 encounter someone you know. Ex: I *bumped into* my friend Brad at the store.   #2 physically touch someone accidentally. Ex: I *bumped into* someone when the bus stopped suddenly.

Bump on a log [noun phr] useless. Ex: Get busy. Don't be a *bump on a log.*

Bumper to bumper traffic   [noun]   extremely slow-moving traffic. Ex: Freeway traffic this morning is *bumper to bumper.*

Bun in the oven [noun phr] pregnant. (See Baby bump)

Bunch of baloney [expression of disbelief]   not credible. Ex: Sam's new operating plan is a *bunch of baloney.*

Bundle up [verb] dress warmly. Ex: *Bundle up* or you will catch cold when you go outside.

Buoy up [verb] #1 keep afloat. Ex: That new life jacket will *buoy you up.* #2 support (as for a sad person). Ex: We have to *buoy up* Ted's spirits since his wife died.

Burn a hole in your pocket [verb phr] refers to spending money very fast. Ex: Every time I get my paycheck it *burns a hole in my pocket.*

Burn out [verb] being exhausted from working too hard or too many hours. Ex: I am *burned out.* I worked 30 hours of overtime this week.

Burn the midnight oil [verb phr] stay up very late, usually used in conjunction with preparations for the next day. Ex: I had to *burn the midnight oil* last night before my final exam.

Burn up the road [verb phr] travel at great speed and for a great distance. Ex: The two boys *burned up the road* getting to the basketball game.

Burn your bridges [verb phr] destroy relationships when you leave people with whom you have lived or worked. Ex: Don't *burn your bridges.* You may have to work with these people again.

Burned to a crisp [verb phr] burn food while cooking it so it is black. Ex: My bacon *burned to a crisp* when I answered the phone.

Burning question [noun] one that cannot be delayed. Ex: Does anyone have that *burning question* before I continue the lecture?

Burning up [verb] #1 having a fever. Ex: The little girl is *burning up* and has the flu. #2 angry. Ex: I am still burning up over that remark she made. (See *Had it up to here*)

_____

Burr under his blanket [noun phr] cranky. Ex: Ever since he was transferred to another job he has had a *burr under his blanket.*

Burst your bubble [verb phr] destroy your idea or dream. Ex: I hate to *burst your bubble,* but Rob just isn't that into you.

Burst your buttons [verb phr] so proud about something or someone that your chest puffs out with pride. Ex: When his son got an "A" on his test, his Dad nearly *burst his buttons.*

Bury the hatchet [verb phr] reconcile. Ex: The two brothers *buried the hatchet* and are now good friends again.

Bury your head in the sand [verb phr] ignore reality. Ex: He *buries his head in the sand* and can't see that David is failing school.

Bush league [noun] #1 not acting in an ethical manner. Ex: Stealing Brad's girlfriend was real *bush league.* #2 not first-rate. Ex: That hotel was sure *bush league.*

Busier than a one armed paper hanger [verb phr] having many activities. Ex: I can't go to the store with you, because I'm *busier than a one armed paper hanger today.*

Business as usual [noun phr] (business) no change in the process. Ex: I thought we might promote new ideas with the new manager, but it's *business as usual.*

Busybody [noun] someone interested in what other people are doing and saying. Ex: The next door neighbor is a real *busybody.*

Busywork   [noun]   marginally productive or unnecessary activity. Ex: Re-arranging my kitchen shelves is *busywork.*

But for the life of me   [conj]   not recalling an event. Ex: *But for the life of me* I don't know where I put my keys.

Butt in   [verb]   #1 interrupt. Ex: Pardon me for *butting in,* but I know the answer to that question. #2   get involved where not wanted.   Ex: Diane is always *butting in* when we are working on our project.

Buttinski   [noun]   person who interrupts.

Butt out   [verb]   stop interfering. (impolite) Ex: *Butt out* Diane! This is not your problem to solve.

Butter him up   [verb phr]   flatter someone.   Ex: We need to *butter up* the boss to get a raise. (See *Brown nose)*

Butter wouldn't melt in his mouth.   [cliché]   Someone is so strict and harsh (cold) that there is no warmth at all. Ex: Did you meet the new neighbor? *Butter wouldn't melt in his mouth.*

Butterfingers   [adj]   clumsy. Ex: I have dropped my fork twice. What a *butterfingers!*

Butterflies in my stomach   [noun phr]   terribly nervous. Ex: Whenever I speak in front of a crowd, I get *butterflies in my stomach.*

Button-holed   [verb]   stereotyped. Ex: She has been *button-holed* as a secretary and cannot get a management position.

Buy into   [verb]   agree to and support. Ex: I hope Alan will *buy into* the new plan.

Buzz around [verb]   acting flighty.   Ex: Danielle is always *buzzing around* the boys.

Buzz off [verb] leave. Ex: I don't want you around. *Buzz off!*

Buzz word [noun] (business) a very popular word that all persons in a certain group know and use. Ex: "Rightsizing" is a current *buzz word* in U.S. companies.

By all counts [prep phr]   considering every fact. Ex: *By all counts* we should be arriving in Toronto by 3:00 p.m.

By all means [prep phr] certainly. Ex: *By all means* you can borrow my lawnmower.

By and by [prep phr]   a future time. Ex: *By and by* I will learn to ski.

By and large [prep phr] generally or mostly. Ex: *By and large* there are some talented students in the class.

By any chance [prep phr] perhaps, possibly. Ex: *By any chance*, did you see Rebecca at the mall?

By any means [prep phr] at all. Ex: We are not through *by any means*.

By hook or by crook [prep phr]   accomplish a task successfully using every effort (implies by honest or dishonest method). Ex: We'll get our new business funded *by hook or by crook.*

By leaps and bounds [prep phr] rapidly. Ex: Your swimming ability has improved *by leaps and bounds* since last year.

By the same token [prep phr]   using the same measurement.
Ex: I know it takes him longer to do the job, but *by the
same token,* he hasn't had as much training. (See *On
the other hand*)

By the seat of his pants   [prep phr]   barely accomplish
something. Ex: He made the train, but only *by the
seat of his pants.*

By the short hairs [prep phr] have someone at a disadvantage.
Ex: When he negotiated for his new car, the salesman
had him *by the short hairs.*

By the way [prep phr] incidentally. Ex: *By the way*, do you
want to go to the movies tomorrow?

By the wayside [prep phr] disappeared. Ex: My dreams of a
new car went *by the wayside* when I lost my job.

_____

CEO [abbrev] (business) *chief executive officer* – the top ranking person in a company.

CFO [abbrev] (business) *chief financial officer* – person in charge of all the major financial decisions of the company.

CISC [abbrev] (computer) *complex instruction set computing. CISC* is a microprocessor design that is found in most desktop computers that can handle powerful instructions.

CYA (abbrev) (business) *cover your ass.* Keep written records so you can back up your actions later if someone questions you. Ex: I always keep a copy of the customer's requests. *CYA* you know.

Cabin fever [noun] restless and irritable. Ex: When stormy weather keeps you inside the house for a long time, you get *cabin fever.*

Calculated risk [noun] an impending risk that is well thought out so the risk element is minimized. Ex: He took a *calculated risk* to invest in the stock.

Call a spade a spade [verb phr] speaking frankly. Ex: I don't think George can do that job. I'm just *calling a spade a spade.*

Call at [verb] visit. Ex: Serena *called at* her Mother's house on Friday night.

Call him names [verb phr] use a racial or physical slur. Ex: The schoolchildren *call him names* because he is so fat.

_____

Call his bluff [verb phr] #1 challenge him. Ex: We were playing poker and when Sam kept betting, I *called his bluff.* #2 make him prove what he just said. Ex: George said he could jump 5 feet. I decided to *call his bluff.*

Call in [verb] #1 notify. Ex: Please *call in* if you are ill. #2 demand payment. Ex: The bank may *call in* our loan.

Call it a night [verb phr] end an enjoyable activity. Ex: Let's *call it a night.* I have to get up early in the morning.

Call it quits [verb phr] stop trying. Ex: I *called it quits* after trying five times to swim across the river.

Call off [verb] cancel. Ex: They *called off* the meeting since everyone was sick.

Call off the dogs [verb phr] quit pestering someone. Ex: *Call off the dogs.* I am working on this project as fast as I can.

Call on [verb] #1 visit. Ex: The pastor will *call on* the hospital patients once a week. #2 request an answer. Ex: I was hoping the teacher would *call on* me since I knew the answer.

Call out [verb] yell. Ex: When he broke his leg, he *called out* for help.

Call the shots [verb phr] take charge. Ex: The leader of the expedition always *calls the shots.*

Call to mind [verb phr] remember. Ex: He *called to mind* every vacation he had taken.

Call to task [verb phr] reprimand. Ex: The boy was *called to task* for breaking the window.

Call up [verb] #1 enlist . Ex: During the Gulf war, the Army Reserves had to *call up* a number of men and women. #2 reach by phone. Ex: My sister will *call* me *up* whenever she gets a chance.

Called on the carpet [verb phr] held accountable for an action. He was *called on the carpet* for coming home late.

Calm before the storm [noun phr] period of quiet before problems begin to surface or things get very busy. Ex: It's 7:00 o'clock. The show starts at 8:00. The *calm before the storm* will end when the audience starts arriving.

(The) camera never lies [cliché] shows all physical faults. Ex: I wish I were thinner, but *the camera never lies.*

Can it [verb] forget it. Ex: " Are you going to the movies?" "Let's *can it.* I am not feeling well."

Can you top that? [noun phr] Can you do better than that? Ex: I can juggle 6 balls at a time. *Can you top that?*

Cancer stick [noun] cigarette.

Can't carry a tune in a bucket [verb phr] tone deaf. Ex: That child can't carry a tune in a bucket.

Can't get blood out of a turnip [cliché] can't get money from someone who is poor. Ex: I want that $5.00 I borrowed from Jim, but he is unemployed. *Can't get blood out of a turnip!*

Can't help himself [verb phr] loses control. Ex: Adam would like to stay on his diet, but when he's around chocolate, he *can't help himself.*

Can't see the forest for the trees   [verb phr]   pay so much attention to the details of a situation that you miss the overall view. Ex: The employees need to team more, but they *can't see the forest for the trees*. They all are working individually.

Can't spend both sides of your dollar   [verb phr]   can't spend more than the actual amount of money you have. Ex: I sure would like that new sweater but I *can't spend both sides of my dollar.*

Can't teach an old dog new tricks   [cliché]   unable to train someone experienced to adapt to a new method of doing something. Ex: We wanted Jan to learn this new method, but you *can't teach an old dog new tricks.*

Capitalize on   [verb]   use to an advantage; use to make money. Ex: He *capitalized on* the low interest rate and bought a new house.

Captive audience   [noun]   people in the audience who are required to be there, instead of choosing to be there. Ex: The President gave a speech to a *captive audience.*

Card him   [verb]   verify his age for legal purchase of alcohol or tobacco. Ex: I have to *card him*. He is buying beer and looks younger than 21.

Carried away   [verb]   over-react. Ex: Darcy gets *carried away* every time she sees a mouse.

Carried it too far   [verb phr]   over-zealous. Ex: It's fine to want to help Dad chop wood, but you *carried it too far.* Now we have enough wood for six families!

Carries a lot of weight [verb phr] impressive or having clout. Ex: The fact that he has a Master's Degree *carries a lot of weight* in applying for jobs.

Carry a grudge [verb phr] not forget an injustice that has been done to you. Ex: Carl has *carried a grudge* ever since he wasn't chosen for the basketball team.

Carry a heavy load [verb phr] #1 burdened with many troubles. Ex: He has *carried a heavy load* since his Father died. #2 take many hours of classes or difficult subjects in school. Ex: I am *carrying a heavy load* this term with 19 hours.

Carry a torch [verb phr] not forget a former lover or friend. Ex: Sam is still *carrying a torch* for his ex-girlfriend.

Carry it off [verb phr] fool or deceive. Ex: Do you think you can *carry it off* and pretend you are Santa Claus at the Christmas party?

Carry on [verb] #1 continue. Ex: *Carry on* with your presentation. #2 converse. Ex: The two girls were *carrying on* for two hours. #3 misbehave. Ex: The child got a spanking because he was *carrying on* something awful. #4 date secretly. Ex: He was *carrying on* with Lynn six months before he married her. #5 portable luggage. Ex: When I went to the airline counter, the stewardess asked me how many *carry on's* I had.

Carry out [verb] #1 complete (as a promise). Ex: I have to *carry out* my promise to get better grades. #2 remove. Ex: *Carry out* the garbage. #3 [noun] fast food. Ex: Why don't we have some *"carry out"* food tonight instead of cooking?

Carry over [adj] (business) work left from the day before. Ex: How many *carry over* caseloads do you have?

Carry through [verb] complete. Ex: He *carried through* on that new project.

Carrying a spare tire [verb phr] overweight and have a bulge of fat around your waist. Ex: He gained 20 pounds since he stopped smoking and now is *carrying a spare tire.*

Cart it off [verb phr] dispose of it. Ex: Would you *cart that extra box off* to the dump?

Carve out [verb] create (as a business position). Ex: He *carved out* a position as head quality inspector.

Carve up [verb] split (as an estate). Ex: By the time the two brothers *carved up* the estate, there was nothing left for their sister.

Case of the heebie-geebies [noun phr] nervous about an impending event. Ex: I get a *case of the heebie geebies* whenever I have to speak in front of a crowd. (See *Case of the jitters*)

Case of the jitters [noun phr] (See *Case of the heebie-geebies*)

Case of the willies [noun phr] (See *Case of the heebie-geebies*)

Case the joint [verb phr] check out a situation or place. Ex: Burglars are known for *casing a joint* before they actually rob it.

Cash in your chips [verb phr] #1 gambling term meaning the game is over and you can trade in the chips you won for money. Ex: I'm through playing blackjack. I'm going to *cash in my chips*. #2 to die. Ex: Joe *cashed in his chips* yesterday. The funeral is tomorrow. (See *Bought the farm*)

Cash or credit [noun phr] method of payment. Ex: A salesperson will ask you, "*Cash or credit?*" (Are you paying by *cash, or with a credit card?*)

Cash rolls in [noun phr] quick accumulation of money, usually from donations. Ex: We'll be able to do more work with the homeless when the *cash rolls in* from our telethon.

Cast in cement [verb phr] unchangeable. Ex: His decision was *cast in cement.*

Cast out [verb] #1 dispose of. Ex: They *cast out* the bad peaches that were in the box. #2 person who is forced to leave. Ex: The *cast out* left town yesterday.

Castoffs [noun] used clothing. Ex: Please take these *castoffs* down to the recycle station.

Cat got your tongue [cliché] said to someone who needs to respond but is silent. Ex: I asked you a question and you didn't say anything. What's the matter? *Cat got your tongue?*

Cat house [noun] house of prostitution. Ex: There is a *cat house* located in the bad part of town.

Cat out of the bag (See *Let the cat out of the bag*)

Cat that swallowed the canary [noun phr] looking guilty. Ex: Did you eat that last cookie? You look like the *cat that swallowed the canary.*

Catch 22 [noun] have two choices in a situation, neither one of which is desirable. Ex: I need my degree to get a good job but I have no money to go to school. I am in a *Catch 22.* (See *Between a rock and a hard place*)

Catch a lot of flak [verb phr] get criticized heavily. Ex: He is going to *catch a lot of flak* for the way he handled the problem.

Catch as catch can [verb phr] #1 flexible and accept whatever is available. Ex: When we go to the beach we'll eat *catch as catch can.* We might find a burger place or just dig for clams. #2 use any method to get all that you can get. Ex: There are so many fish in this lake. It is *catch as catch can.* Some people are using worms for bait and some are using marshmallows.

Catch big air [verb] (sports - mountain biking) go airborne. Ex: You need to keep your balance when you *catch big air.*

Catch his eye [verb phr] get his attention. Ex: Can you *catch the waiter's eye* and tell him we want our bill now.

Catch it [verb] be punished. Ex: You're going to *catch it* for breaking that window.

Catch more flies with honey than with vinegar [cliché] If you approach people in a positive manner, they will respond positively. Ex: " I'm surprised you got that contract. Mr. Smith is difficult to deal with. " "Well, you can *catch more flies with honey than with vinegar.* "

Catch on   [verb] #1   become fashionable or popular. Ex: Those knit leggings are *catching on* in the fashion world. #2 understand. Ex: He *catches on* to that math problem easily.

Catch the drift   [verb phr] understand the main idea of what the group is discussing. Ex: I can *catch the drift* of what the discussion is all about. They want funding for a new art museum.

Catch the tail end [verb phr] (See *Tail end*)

Catch you later [verb phr] Bye for now. See you later.

Catch your breath   [verb phr] rest briefly. Ex: I have been running hard and have to *catch my breath.*

Cat's meow   [noun] (1940's slang) girl who is cute, fun and desirable. Ex: Susie is just the *cat's meow*. She is wearing one of those pink jumpsuits today.

Cat's pajamas   [noun] (1940 's slang) trendy and stylish. Ex: The bell-bottomed pants sure are the *cat's pajamas.*

Cattywampus [adj] confused; disorganized. Ex: Everything is so *cattywampus* in my bedroom. I have to re-arrange things.

Caught flat-footed [verb phr] unprepared in a situation. Ex: I was *caught flat footed* by my son's decision to leave college.   (See *Caught napping)*

Caught in a bind [verb phr] not have a solution to a problem that will be positive for all involved. (See *Catch-22)*

Caught in the middle [verb phr] see the value in two opposing arguments and under pressure to side with each.

___

Caught napping [verb phr] unprepared. (See *Caught flat-footed*)

Caught off-guard [verb phr] surprised by an unexpected remark or action. Ex: She really *caught me off guard* when she said she was pregnant.

Caught red-handed [verb phr] caught in the act of wrong-doing. Tom was caught *red-handed* stealing car parts from the dealer.

Caught with his pants down [verb phr] being found at a great disadvantage. Ex: He was *caught with his pants down* when he was found cheating on the exam.

Cave in [verb] #1 fail. Ex: My plans for a picnic began to *cave in* when a storm was predicted. #2 surrender to pressure. Ex: He *caved in* and went to the concert with his friends.

Ceiling fell in [noun phr] the plan collapsed, failed. Ex: I was ready to go to Europe but the *ceiling fell in* when the snowstorm hit and my plane could not take off.

Cellular [adj] telecommunications technology in which areas are divided into cells and have stations receiving and sending signals. The signal from a mobile phone switches from cell to cell as the phone moves from one area into another. Ex: I just bought a new *cellular* phone the other day.

Chalk it up [verb phr] attribute. Ex: Well, we lost this game, but we'll *chalk it up* to inexperience.

Change hands [verb] get a new owner. Ex: The store will *change hands* tomorrow.

Change his tune [verb phr] change his opinion. Ex: He will *change his tune* when he finds out his favorite singer will be at the concert.

Change horses midstream [verb phr] change your mind halfway through a project. Ex: Don *changed horses midstream* when the budget was cut on his project.

Change of heart [noun phr] relent or change your mind. Ex: My Mom had a *change of heart* and let me go to the dance.

Change of pace [noun phr] different routine. Ex: I need a *change of pace*. I'm not going to stay out late every night.

Change of scene [noun phr] different environment. Ex: I'm going to go back to school next year for a *change of scene.*

Changed color [verb] blushed. Ex: She *changed color* when he made that crude remark.

Changing of the guard [verb phr] #1 reorganizing business. Ex: There's been a *changing of the guard* and Mr. Smith is now the Vice President. #2 Official guards of a monument change places with a new group on a set number of hours. Ex: It is time for the *changing of the guard* at Buckingham Palace in London, England.

Channel surf [verb] changing TV channels. Ex: Give me the remote so I can *channel surf.*

Charley horse [noun] a cramp in your leg. Ex: Ouch! I've got a *Charley Horse* and I can't run any more.

Charm the pants off someone [verb phr] ingratiate yourself to gain favors. Ex: Emily can *charm the pants off anyone*. She is a smooth talker. (See *Suck up*)

Charting new waters [verb phr] #1. inexperienced at what you are doing. Ex: *I'm charting new waters* here trying out my new computer program. #2. try something no one else has tried before. Ex: The man is *charting new waters* attempting to sky dive over that mountain.

Chase his tail [verb phr] do worthless activity. Ex: He's really *chasing his tail* providing those sales figures for Project X. I hear that project is going to be dropped.

Chat [noun] (computer) #1 a feature that lets people talk to each other on the Internet by exchanging messages in real time. Ex: I can *chat* with my granddaughter on Facebook. #2 talk casually with someone. Ex: The two friends have fun *chatting* when they get together.

Cheap shot [noun] critical remark made to demean someone. Ex: He called her a "dumb blonde". What a *cheap shot.*

Check his membership card in the human race [verb phr] Someone's behavior is overly harsh or unreasonable. Ex: Why did that jury find him guilty? *Check out their membership in the human race.*

Check in #1 [verb] arrive at a hotel and be assigned your room. Ex: I will be *checking into* the Hilton Hotel at 2:00 P.M. #2 [adj] Appropriate arrival time. Ex: *Check-in* time for the seminar is 7:00 A.M. #3 [verb] Notify or contact someone. Ex: *Check in* from time to time while you are on your trip and pick up your messages.

Check it out [verb phr] #1 verify that information is accurate. Ex: I heard that new car cost $10,000.   Would you *check it out?* #2 see if a situation is safe or suitable. Ex: Dad, my car tire looks low. Would you *check it out* and see if it's o.k.? #3 borrow a book or material on signature from the library. Ex: Did you *check out* that new romance novel at the library?

Check off [verb] scan a list of items to see if everything is correct. Ex: Would you quickly *check off* all the items in our grocery cart ?

Check out [verb] be absorbed in thoughts and not aware of reality. Ex: He has really *checked out.* I asked him if he had studied for the test on Tuesday, and he asked, "What test? "

Checkup [noun] #1 a doctor's examination. Ex: I'm getting my *check up* tomorrow to see if I'm o.k. to sign up for aerobics.   #2 [verb] contact someone to see if the person is alright. Ex: Would you *check up* on Joan tonight? She hasn't been feeling well lately.

Checked out [verb] #1 died. Ex: Roy *checked out* yesterday. The funeral is Monday. #2 left the hotel after paying the bill. Ex: We *checked out* this morning at 10:00.

Cheer up! Things will get better. [expression of well-wishing] (said to people who have had a lot of bad luck)

Cheers! [verb] popular expression for a toast. Ex: Let's lift our *glasses and toast Ray's promotion. Cheers! (See Bottoms up)*

Cheesecake [adj] (informal) posing for a picture in a bathing suit or other revealing attire. Ex: What a great *cheesecake* photo of that movie star.

Cheesy [adj] tacky. Ex: Don't wear that shirt. It is *cheesy.*

Chest bump [noun] (2012 slang) two guys will *bump chests.* It is a "high five" gesture of good will. (See *Fist bump*)

Chew him up one side and down the other [verb phr] thoroughly chastise someone. Ex: He was late so she *chewed him up one side and down the other.* (See *Chew his ear off)*

Chew his ear off [verb phr] scold harshly. Ex: Mom really *chewed his ear off* for losing his homework. (See *Chew out*)

Chew out [verb phr] scold.

Chew the fat [verb phr] talk casually with someone. Ex: Sam and Phil are *chewing the fat* out in the back yard. (See *Shoot the breeze*)

Chicken feed [noun] a small sum of money. Ex: You only get paid $5.00 an hour. That's *chicken feed.* (See *Chicken scratch*)

Chicken hearted [adj] cowardly. Ex: He's so *chicken-hearted* that he cannot kill that injured bird.

Chicken scratch [noun] small amount of money. (See *Chicken feed*)

Chicken out [verb] afraid to participate. Ex: Are you going bungee jumping? No, I *chickened out.*

Chicken shit [noun phr] (<u>crude</u>) insignificant. Ex: I got paid *chicken shit* for mowing his yard. (insignificant amount of money)

_____

Chief cook and bottle washer [noun phr] someone who is responsible for all the details as well as the overall success of something. Ex: What do you do in this restaurant? Well, I'm _chief cook and bottle washer._

Chillax [verb] (2014 slang) chill and relax.

Chill out [verb] calm down. Ex: You need to _chill out_ when someone criticizes you.

Chime in [verb] Speak up. Ex: If you think of a new idea, just _chime in._

Chin up [verb] have a positive attitude. Ex: _Chin up._ Your luck could be worse.

Chinaman's chance [noun phr] no chance. He doesn't have a _Chinaman's chanc_e of making the ball team.

Chinese fire drill [noun phr] (business) totally unorganized random activity. Ex: We have another _Chinese fire drill_ today. We're all supposed to project future product gains by noon.

Chip away at [verb phr] work steadily and slowly on a project. Ex: He _chips away at_ finishing his deck every weekend.

Chip in [verb] add your money or assistance to a group project. Ex: Sam has a birthday today. Could you _chip in_ for a cake?

Chip off the old block [noun phr] appears or acts like his father. Ex: Brad is a _chip off the old block._ He even walks like his father.

_____

Chip on your shoulder [noun phr] defensive. Ex: Some people
always have a _chip on their shoulder_ and don't trust
people.

Chips are down (See _When the chips are down_)

Chit chat [verb phr] Talking casually. _(See Idle chit chat)_

Chock full [adj phr] completely full of. Ex: This sweater is _chock
full of_ moth holes.

Choke up [verb] #1 (sports - baseball) hold the bat further up.
Ex: When he _choked up_ on the bat he hit a home run.
#2 be close to tears. Ex: She was _all choked up_ when
her cat died.

Cholo [noun] person who has Native American and Spanish
ancestry. A derogatory term.

Chomping at the bit [verb phr] impatient. Ex: Hurry up. Dad is
chomping at the bit to leave.

Choose up [verb] pick team players. Ex: Let's _choose up_ sides
and play a game of basketball.

Chop Chop [verb] hurry. (See _Shake a leg_)

Chosen few [noun] favored. Ex: Only a _chosen few_ get to be
President of the United States.

Church key [noun] can opener. Ex: I can't find my _church key_
and I need to open this bottle.

Chunky [adj] slightly overweight. Ex: Don't you think Denise is
chunky since she returned from her trip?

Churn out [verb] create repeatedly without difficulty . Ex:
Many romance novels are _churned out_ in a short time.

Clam [noun] dollar. (See Samolean)

Clamp down [verb] become strict. Ex: You need to *clamp down* on the rowdy child.

Clean bill of health [noun phr] everything is O.K. (Said by doctors to patients after an examination) Ex: I checked your lab work and you have a *clean bill of health*.

Clean cut [adj] having a trim neat appearance. Ex: Arie certainly is a *clean cut* boy. He always wears a pressed shirt.

Clean his clock [verb phr] beat up someone. Ex: If he teases me again, I will *clean his clock.*

Clean mind [noun] thinking pure thoughts. Ex: He has such a *clean mind* and never tells dirty jokes.

Clean out [verb] #1 go through stuff and throw old things away. Ex: He *cleaned out* his closet. #2 win everything (as in card games). Ex: George *cleaned out* his pals and had lots of money.

Clean out the cobwebs [verb phr] clear the mind to concentrate, or stop day-dreaming. Ex: It is time to *clear out the cobwebs* so we can get something accomplished.

Clean slate [noun] start over and try to improve your reputation. Ex: He left prison with a *clean slate.*

Clean up your act [verb phr] correct your behavior. Ex: That child needs to *clean up his act* and respect his parents.

Clear as a bell [adj phr] easy to understand. Ex: Those instructions are *clear as a bell.*

Clear as mud [adj phr] unclear. Ex: Those directions were *clear as mud.*

Clear conscience [noun] without guilt. Ex: The boy has a *clear conscience* because he did not tell a lie.

Clear cut [verb] #1 cutting a wide area of trees to the ground. Ex: The loggers *clear cut* the forest. #2 [adj] obvious. Ex: It was a *clear cut* case of dishonesty.

Clear head [noun] rational. Ex: The professor always has a *clear head* and explains everything logically.

Clear himself [verb phr] prove his innocence. Ex: After he was arrested, he needed to *clear himself* of the accusation.

Clear the air [verb phr] resolve a disagreement or misunderstanding. Ex: I am upset with you and we need to *clear the air.*

Clear the decks [verb phr] #1 leave. Ex: Time to *clear the decks*. It is late. #2 put everything aside to prepare for a new project. Ex: Let's *clear the decks* so we can begin the next project.

Clear the table [verb phr] remove all the dirty dishes from the table after a meal. Ex: Please *clear the table* Jeff.

Cliffhanger [noun] a suspenseful story. Ex: That new mountain climbing novel sure is a *cliffhanger.*

Clock is ticking [noun phr] time is limited. Ex: You're nearly forty. If you want to have a child, remember the *clock is ticking*. (See *Biological clock is ticking.)*

Clock watcher [noun] one who spends the day looking at the clock. Ex: Sherman has always been a *clock watcher.* He is the first one out the door at the end of the day.

Close but no cigar [verb phr] guess at an answer and almost get it right. Ex: "I thought you came from New York." "No, New Jersey. *Close, but no cigar.*"

Close call [noun] narrow escape. Ex: He had a *close call* when he slipped on the mountain. (See *Close shave*)

Close down [verb] go out of business. Ex: If we don't get more contracts we will have to *close down.*

Close enough for government work [verb phr] (business) The work performed may not be exactly perfect, but it will generally be accepted. Ex: "What do you think of the work statement? " "*It's close enough for government work.*"

Close in on [verb] #1 surround. Ex: The Indians *closed in on* the group of settlers. #2 suffocate. Ex: The walls seem to *close in on* him after being bed-ridden for two weeks.

Close shave [noun] narrow escape. Ex: That was a *close shave.* Your mother almost caught us eating a handful of cookies. (See Close call)

Close up [verb] #1 [pronounced <u>cloze up</u>] lock up your business and go home. Ex: Will you *close up* at 5:30 tonight? #2 [pronounced <u>close up</u>] view from a short distance. Ex: I like to see the photographs *close up.*

Close up and personal [adv phr] affect intimately. Ex: When he got laid off it affected his family *close up and personal.*

Clothes horse [noun] person who buys a lot of the latest style clothes. Ex: Vicky has six new dresses. She is a real *clothes horse.*

Cloud (The) [noun]   Computer file storage that is not on your hard drive. Ex: I keep all my photos on *The Cloud*.

Cloud up [verb] #1 become overcast. Ex: The sky *clouded up.* #2 become tearful. Ex: Her face *clouded up* and she began to cry. #3 confuse (as purpose). Ex: Don't *cloud up* the issue.

Clueless [adj] not understanding what is going on. Ex: That boy is *clueless*. He always sleeps in class.

Clutch at straws [verb phr] try desperately. Ex: They *clutched at straws* to find out why the car wouldn't run.

Coast is clear [noun phr]   indication that it is safe to proceed. Ex: You can bring the trailer up the ramp. The *coast is clear*.

Cobwebs in the attic [noun phr]   not think clearly. Ex: I must have had *cobwebs in the attic* when I let the dog loose this morning.

Cock-a-meemie [adj] absurd. Ex: Taking your lawnmower on vacation is a *cock-a-meemie* idea.

Cock and bull story [noun] not true. Ex: His story about flying saucers sounds like a *cock and bull story* to me.

Cocked an eye at [verb phr] viewed suspiciously. Ex: When she asked her father if her girlfriends could spend the night with her, he *cocked an eye at her.*

Coffin nail [noun] a cigarette.   Ex: Don't smoke those *coffin nails.* (See *Cancer stick*)

Coin a phrase [verb phr] invent a phrase. Ex: Ben Franklin *coined the phrase* "A penny saved is a penny earned."

Coked [verb] drugged. (1960's slang) Ex: He was *coked* so bad he passed out.

Cold call [noun] knocking on prospective customers' doors without phoning first - done by salespersons. Ex: To sell insurance you have to make a lot of *cold calls.*

Cold/hot enough for you? [verb phr] (hello greeting)

Cold feet [noun] lack courage to proceed in an activity. Ex: He got *cold feet* and did not go sky diving.

Cold fish [noun] lacking personality or warmth. Ex: Alice is a real *cold fish.* She doesn't speak to anyone.

Cold hard cash [noun] have the money in hand. Ex: I have *cold hard cash* to buy the car.

Cold hearted [adj] not show any empathy for your fellow man. Ex: Clyde seemed *cold hearted* when he refused to help the man in the wheelchair.

Cold shoulder [noun] purposely slight or ignore someone. Ex: She gave him the *cold shoulder* because she was mad at him.

Cold turkey [adv] quit something altogether without assistance, such as stop smoking. Ex: I quit smoking *cold turkey* last month.

Colder than a well digger's nose (1950's country western expression) extremely cold. Ex: I can't plant those crops yet. It's *colder than a well digger's nose.*

Collect call [noun] call a person long distance on a land line phone and tell the operator the other person is paying for the call. The operator asks the other if he/she is willing to accept a *"collect call".*

Come about

Come about [verb] happen. Ex: Our move to a new apartment will *come about* in July.

Come across [verb] #1 find. Ex: I *came across* your watch yesterday. It was in the car. #2 meet unexpectedly. Ex: I *came across* Jean yesterday at the store. #3 pass over (as a bridge). I *came across* the bridge at 7:00 today. #4 communicated. Ex: He *came across* loudly and clearly. #5 perceived as. Ex: You *come across* as being a very happy person.

Come again? [verb phr] What did you say? Ex: Roy did not hear his wife and said, "*Come again?*"

Come and go [verb phr] in and out of style. Ex: Clothing styles, games and toys just *come and go*.

Come around [verb] #1 visit. Ex: *Come around* 8:00 to my house. #2 begin to understand or agree. Ex: He'll *come around* to my viewpoint. #3 become conscious. Ex: It took me two hours after surgery to *come around*.

Come away from [verb phr] left. Ex: I *came away from* the meeting with more projects.

Come back to haunt you [verb phr] a negative situation in your past that is brought up again. Ex: The fact that he had a juvenile record *came back to haunt him*.

Come by [verb] acquire with some effort. Ex: Has he *come by* that land he was trying to buy?

Come by it naturally [verb phr] a trait you were born with. Ex: He *comes by his outgoing personality naturally*.

Come clean [verb phr] tell the truth. Ex: *Come clean* now. Did you leave the door unlocked?

Come crashing down around his ears [verb phr] totally fail in a plan, project or course of action. Ex: They invested all the money in Project X and it came *crashing down around their ears.*

Come down on [verb phr] #1 punish. Ex: He *came down on* the child for lying. #2 reduce price. Ex: The salesman *came down on* the car price so we could afford to buy it.

Come down with [verb phr] catch. Ex: I hope you don't *come down with* the flu.

Come from good stock [verb phr] descend from a reputable or noteworthy family. Ex: He *comes from good stock.* All his family went to Harvard.

Come full circle [verb phr] faced again with a problem that you had given to someone else to resolve, who had also delegated the responsibility, etc. until it got back to you. Ex: The decision about how much to spend on advertising has *come full circle.*

Come Hell or high water [verb phr] determined to carry through with an action no matter what happens. Ex: I will go to Europe *come Hell or high water.*

Come into money [verb phr] inherit or win lots of money. Ex: He *came into lots of money* when his Father died.

Come into play [verb phr] are examined. Ex: A lot of factors *come into play* in this business deal.

Come off [verb] accomplish successfully. Ex: The play *came off* very well.

Come off it [verb phr] don't belabor a point. Ex: *Come off it;* I don't want to sell the house any more than you do.

Come on [verb] (Be sure to emphasize the correct word for the correct meaning to be understood) #1 not entirely agree with what someone says. (Emphasize <u>on</u>) Ex: You say I really like Gina. *Come <u>on,</u>* you know I don't. #2 act in a sexually provocative manner. (Emphasize <u>come</u>) Ex: Bridgett's short dress sure is a *<u>come</u> on.*

Come on strong [verb phr] be aggressive. Ex: Some liberated women *come on too strong.*

Come out in the wash [verb phr] everything will be all right. Ex: Don't worry about missing the deadline. It will all *come out in the wash.*

Come out of his shell [verb phr] an introvert who becomes more extroverted. Ex: He has *come out of his shell* since he joined that club.

Come out of the closet [verb phr] disclose hidden traits. Ex: Maynard came *out of the closet* and declared he was gay.

Come out of the woodwork [verb phr] appear from nowhere. Ex: Desi just *came out of the woodwork* and wants to attend the meeting.

Come out with it [verb phr] tell the truth immediately. Ex: Well, *come out with it.* Did you do your homework?

Come rain or shine [verb phr] in any event. Ex: *Come rain or shine* we will go to the beach.

Come through [verb] succeed. Ex: He *came through* on his exam and got an "A".

Come to [verb] #1 become conscious. Ex: He *came to* after being hit on the head. #2 amount to. Ex: The bill didn't *come to* much money.

Come to a bad end [verb phr] be ruined. Ex: The homeless man *came to a bad end.*

Come to a head [verb phr] at a crisis point in a situation. Ex: The conflict *came to a head* and he left the room.

Come to blows [verb phr] start fighting. Ex: The two men were so angry they almost *came to blows.*

Come to find out [verb phr] discover. Ex: *Come to find out* I am the same age as you.

Come to grips with [verb phr] struggle to accept. Ex: He *came to grips with* the fact that he had cancer.

Come to pass [verb phr] happen. Ex: It *came to pass* that he became famous.

Come to terms with [verb phr] accept. Ex: He *came to terms with* the contract provisions.

Come to the point [verb phr] what is the main idea you are trying to explain? Ex: *Come to the point* - do you want to go to the movies or not?

Come to the well [verb phr] (business) ask for more resources. Ex: We need to *come to the well* for additional computers.

Come to your senses [verb phr] be realistic, objective. Ex: *Come to your senses* and finish college.

Come unglued [verb] become extremely upset. Ex: Don't *come unglued* just because I was out late. (See *Come unhinged*)

Come unhinged [verb] very upset. (See *Come unglued*)

Come up against [verb phr] meet with opposition. Ex: He *came up against* someone who played ball better than him.

Come up empty handed [verb phr] not get the response you wanted. Ex: I asked for a raise, but *came up empty handed.*

Come up roses [verb phr] have a good result. Ex: Everything is *coming up roses.* I just got a raise.

Come up short [verb phr] #1 insufficient. Ex: I *came up short* on money and could not buy the dress. #2 fail to attain. Ex: Joan *came up short* and did not get an "A" on her test.

Come up smiling [verb phr] retain a good attitude. Ex: He *came up smiling* after his bout with the flu.

Come up to [verb phr] equal. Ex: She will have to work harder to *come up to* Rob's score.

Come upon [verb] find unexpectedly. Ex: We *came upon* Grandma's wedding dress in the attic.

Come what may [verb expression] whatever happens. Ex: *Come what may*, I am going to the beach in June.

Comes down to [verb phr] final decision. Ex: It *comes down to* the fact that we are going to the store whether you want to go or not.

Comes with the territory [verb phr] associated with, good or bad. Ex: James always brings his dog with him. It *comes with the territory*.

Comfort zone [noun] familiar territory. Ex: We tend to choose our friends from our own *comfort zone.*

Comfortable as an old shoe [adv phr] relaxed. Ex: Her husband feels *comfortable as an old shoe* when he watches TV in the evening.

Coming apart at the seams [verb phr] #1 have a tear in your clothing. Ex: The boy is *coming apart at the seams.* His mother needs to mend his shirt. #2 be distraught. Ex: Melina is *coming apart at the seams* since Jose left.

Common ground [noun] compromise or mutual understanding. Ex: The two friends covered a lot of *common ground* when they planned their trip.

Communications satellite [noun] (communications) a relay system for TV and radio signals orbiting above the earth's surface. Ex: We are getting a weak signal from our *communications satellite.*

Company buyout [noun] (business) the ownership of a company is acquired by someone with a great deal of money and leverage. Ex: After the *company buyout* many people were laid off.

Consider the source [verb phr] question the objectivity of the person who tells you something. Ex: "He said Philip was a coward." "Well, you have to *consider the source.*"

Conspicuous by your absence [verb phr] draw attention to yourself by being absent. Ex: The employee was *conspicuous by his absence* at the staff meeting.

Consumed by it [verb phr] addicted to. Ex: He was *consumed by the games* on the computer.

Cook your goose [verb phr] be disadvantageous to you. Ex: He disagreed with the boss and *cooked his goose.*

Cool as a cucumber [adj phr] self-controlled, especially in difficult situations. Ex: When the driver cut in front of him, he remained *cool as a cucumber.*

Cool it [verb] Calm down. (See Cool your heels)

Cool your heels [verb phr] needing to calm down and be patient. Ex: *Cool your heels.* The traffic will clear up soon.

Cool million [noun] exactly a million dollars. Ex: He inherited a *cool million* from his aunt.

Cop a plea [verb phr] admit to a lesser crime to avoid a more serious punishment if convicted for the original crime. Ex: Many criminals *cop a plea* to avoid a long prison sentence.

Cop out [verb] relinquish responsibility. Ex: He *copped out* by playing sick so he wouldn't have to do dishes.

Corner market [noun] small, locally owned grocery. Ex: You can get eggs at the *corner market.*

Corner the market [verb phr] (business) capture the majority of support for a product. Ex: That company has *cornered the market* on computer software.

Corporate raider [noun] (business) greedy businessman who buys out financially solvent companies and uses their profits to buy other companies, eventually bankrupting all companies. Ex: There were a lot of good companies ruined by *corporate raiders* in the 1980's.

Cost an arm and a leg [verb phr] expensive. Ex: That diamond ring must have *cost an arm and a leg.*

Cotton Kingdom [noun] Southern United States. Ex: In the *Cotton Kingdom* the summers are hot and humid.

Cotton pickin' [adj] (country western) darn. Ex: Keep your *cotton pickin'* hands off my guitar.

Cotton to [verb] fond of. Ex: I don't *cotton to* the idea of driving so far.

Couch commander [noun] a TV remote control. Ex: I've got my *couch commander* and am ready for an evening of TV.

Couch potato [noun] someone who is sitting doing absolutely nothing, or wasting time watching television. Ex: Darin is nothing but a *couch potato.* He never even eats at the dinner table.

Cougar [noun] #1 an animal in the cat family. #2 Older women who are attracted to much younger men.

Cough up [verb] return something you owe. Ex: *Cough up* my stapler you borrowed last week.

Coughed his head off [verb phr] have a fit of coughing and not be able to stop. Ex: I *coughed my head off* in the meeting this morning.

Could sink your teeth into [verb phr] something that you can become very involved in.   Ex: This novel is so interesting that I could *sink my teeth into it.*

Count calories [verb phr] diet. Ex: I have to *count calories* after that big dinner tonight.

Countdown [adj] period before a rocket takes off.   Ex: *Countdown* time at is 6:00 A.M.

Count for [verb] mean. Ex: My college education has to *count for* something.

Count me out [verb phr] don't want to participate in the activity. Ex: I don't want to go to the store. *Count me out.*

Count off [verb] divide a group of individuals by having them take turns counting off "1", "2", "3", "4" successively. Ex: Let's *count off* for our school spelling teams.

Count on me [verb phr] rely on my help. Ex: You can *count on me* when you need a good friend.

Count the minutes [verb phr] wait impatiently for an activity to end. Ex: He was *counting the minutes* until school was out.

Count up [verb] total. Ex: *Count up* the number of vacation days you have left.

Count your blessings [verb phr] Encouraging phrase when life is not going well. Ex: You should *count your blessings.* You have good health.

Counting our pennies [verb phr] watching the budget. Ex: We'd like to go to Hawaii with you, but we're *counting our pennies* with two kids in college.

Counting sheep [verb phr] trying to fall asleep by actually picturing sheep and counting them. Ex: The small child is *counting sheep* to help fall asleep.

Cover all your bases [verb phr] leave nothing to chance; consider all options. Ex: Be sure to *cover all bases* in your presentation.

Cover ground [verb phr] work hard. Ex: We have to *cover* a lot of *ground* if we are going to meet the schedule.

Cover up [verb] #1 pull the covers over you when you go to bed. Ex: Mom will *cover* you *up* tonight. #2 hide an illegal activity. Ex: The store is just a *cover-up* for a drug distribution center.

Cow-puncher [noun] (country western) a cowboy or rodeo rider. Ex: That *cow puncher* has a new saddle.

Coyote ugly [adj] (1990's slang) be drunk and sleep with a girl and wake up with your arm around her in the morning. You discover she is really ugly. You would rather chew your arm off and leave quickly than wake her. Ex: The new girl sure is *coyote ugly.*

Cozy up to [verb phr] #1 snuggle. Ex: Want to *cozy up to* me in my sleeping bag? #2 try to please. Ex: She sure likes to *cozy up to* the boss.

Crack a bottle [verb phr] open a bottle of wine or other liquor. Ex: Let's *crack that last bottle* of Scotch.

Crack a smile [verb phr] smile shyly. Ex: The shy girl barely *cracked a smile* at the joke.

Crack down on [verb phr] get tough. Ex: Let's *crack down on* illegal drug smuggling.

Crack me up [verb phr] laugh a lot. Ex: That joke *cracks me up.*

Crack the books [verb phr] study hard for an exam. Ex: I need to *crack the books* tonight so I can pass my History exam.

Crack the whip [verb phr] demand certain behavior. Ex: Mother really *cracked the whip* and we had to clean our rooms.

Crack up [verb] #1 lose mental control. Ex: When her mother died, she *cracked up.* #2 have a car accident. Ex: The teenager *cracked up* his Dad's car. #3 laugh uncontrollably. Ex: I *cracked up* when I heard that joke.

Cracked up to be [verb phr] an expectation of someone. Ex: Alex was all he was *cracked up to be* - intelligent, fun and witty.

Cracker barrel [adj] home-spun philosophy. Ex: Will Rogers was a *cracker barrel* philosopher.

Crackerjack [adj] excellent. Ex: He is a *crackerjack* baseball player.

Crawl into a hole and die [verb phr] embarrassed. Ex: When I fell down, I could have *crawled into a hole and died.*

Crawling out of the woodwork [verb phr] appear unexpectedly. Ex: When I wanted help picking out a dress, the saleswomen came *crawling out of the woodwork.*

Crazier than a coot   [verb phr]   (1940's country western) unstable behavior. Ex: That drunk wanders around singing to himself all day long. He is *crazier than a coot.*

Cream of the crop   [noun phr]   the best. Ex: These new students are the *cream of the crop.*

Cream skimmer   [noun]   someone who takes the best from a situation and moves on. Ex: A lot of ambitious people are *cream skimmers.*

Creature comforts of life   [noun phr]   average necessities like food, clothes and shelter. Ex: We need the *creature comforts of life* to be satisfied.

Croaked   [verb]   died. Ex: My pet bird *croaked* yesterday. (See *Bit the dust*)

Cropping up   [verb phr]   becoming plentiful. Ex: Fast food places are *cropping up* all over town now.

Cross his palm with silver   [verb phr]   bribe someone. Ex: If you *cross his palm with silver*, he will fix the TV.

Cross my heart   [verb phr]   make a promise and say, "*Cross my heart and hope to die.*" (Used by children)

Cross that bridge when you come to it   [verb phr]   handle a situation when it arises. Ex: "What about the marketing of our product?" "We will *cross that bridge when we come to it.*"

Cross your fingers   [verb phr]   (gesture) #1 Actually cross your fingers hoping for good luck. Ex: Keep your *fingers crossed* for me that I will get the promotion. #2 tell a lie. (used by children) Ex: If you *cross your fingers* behind your back when you tell a lie, it makes it o.k.

Crossed my mind [verb phr] thought briefly about it. Ex: Didn't it *cross your mind* to invite Renee?

Cruising for a bruising [verb phr] ask for trouble, or look for a fight. Ex: You are *cruising for a bruising* if you argue with the local bully.

Crumb snatchers [noun] children. Ex: I can come for dinner but I will have to bring the *crumb snatchers.* (See *curtain climbers*)

Cry crocodile tears [expression of exaggerated or faked sadness] Ex: She *cried crocodile tears* when she broke her sister's toy.

Cry wolf [verb phr] call for help when you really do not need it; then no one believes you when you really do need help. Ex: He *cried wolf* one too many times so we will not help him now.

Crying in your beer [verb phr] being self-pitying. Ex: Stop *crying in your beer*. You will find a better job.

Crying my heart out [verb phr] weeping uncontrollably from extreme sadness. Ex: She *cried her eyes out* when her boyfriend left.

Crying need [verb] dire necessity. Ex: There's a *crying need* for more foster parents in the community.

Crystal clear [adj] extremely clear. Ex: It's *crystal clear* that we need to control our costs. (See *Clear as a bell*)

Curiosity killed the cat (cliché) If you are too inquisitive, you may get into trouble.

Curl his lip [verb phr] show displeasure. Ex: The dog *curled his lip* and growled at the intruder.

Curtain climbers [noun] children. (See *Crumb snatchers)*

Curtains for me [noun phr] my downfall. Ex: If I don't get this report done, it will be *curtains for me.*

Cut a long story short [verb phr] be brief. Ex: To *cut a long story short,* I got lost and didn't get home until midnight.

Cut a rug [verb phr] (1940's slang) dance. Ex: That older couple sure can *cut a rug.*

Cut above [verb] better than. Ex: The service at the Empress is a *cut above* the rest of the restaurants in the area.

Cut and dried [adj phr] already decided upon. Ex: Looks like your decision to get married is *cut and dried.*

Cut and run [adj phr] escape or leave suddenly. Ex: Hey look. I've got to *cut and run.*

Cut corners [verb] take a shorter way or cheaper method to do something. Ex: If you *cut corners* and buy less food, we will have more money for savings.

Cut him down to size [verb phr] humble him. Ex: That cruel remark really *cut him down to size.*

Cut his eye teeth [verb phr] got his first experience in an activity. Ex: He *cut his eye teeth on* fixing airplanes.

Cut his losses [verb phr] abandon a project or investment when sensing defeat or having a negative cash flow. Ex: That company must *cut its losses* in the next quarter.

Cut it short [verb phr] say it quickly. Ex: *Cut it short.* I have to leave now.

Cut me some slack [verb phr] don't be critical. Ex: Hey *cut me some slack*. I was too tired to do the dishes. (See *Gimme a break*)

Cut me to the quick [verb phr] hurt my feelings. Ex: When you made fun of me, it *cut me to the quick.*

Cut off your nose to spite your face (See *Don't cut off your nose to spite your face*)

Cut offs [noun] jeans that have been cut off right above the knee and are not hemmed so they are ragged. Ex: "What are you wearing biking?" "My *cut-offs.*"

Cut out for [verb phr] naturally suited. Ex: He was *cut out for* banking since he is so good with numbers.

Cut rate [noun] below market value for a product. Ex: Cottage cheese is on sale at *cut rate* prices this week.

Cut the apron strings [cliché] leave home and take control of your life. Ex: Jack needs to *cut the apron strings* and get his own apartment.

Cut the mustard [verb phr] meet expectations. Ex: He didn't *cut the mustard* so we let him go.

Cut through the red tape [verb phr] handle a situation without taking the usual bureaucratic steps. Ex: You have to *cut through a lot of red tape* to order supplies in the company.

Cut to the chase [verb phr] get to the main point. Ex: Let's *cut to the chase.* Where was the suspect last night?

Cut up [noun] Someone who likes to joke around. Ex: I always invite Peter to my parties since he's such a *cut up.*

Cut you off [verb phr] interrupt your discussion, or no longer allow you to argue. Ex: I hate to *cut you off,* but I must leave now.

Cuter than a bug's ear [verb phr] (1930's slang) appealing. Usually said about children or women who are small in stature. Ex: My granddaughter is *cute as a bug's ear.*

Cuts both ways [verb phr] behavior expected to be reciprocated. Ex: It *cuts both ways.* If I do you a favor, I want you to do one for me.

Cyberbully [noun] bullying using electronic devices and equipment. Ex: *Cyberbullying* has caused some of those who were bullied to commit suicide.

Cyberspace [noun] (computer) out in the atmosphere where computer commands electronically sent are transmitted. Ex: Messages on the Internet travel through *cyberspace.*

DINKS [acronym] *double income, no kids*. Ex: They take expensive vacations because they're *Dinks*.

DIY [abbrev] *do it yourself*. Ex: Lots of people involve themselves in *DIY* projects because it is cheaper.

D.L. [abbrev] [2014 slang] *down low*. (See On the DL)

D.O.A. [abbrev] *dead on arrival*. (a designation used mostly by hospitals when patients are brought in by ambulance)

D.U.I. [abbrev] *driving under the influence* or drunk driving. Ex: Jack got a *DUI* last night. (See *D.W.I.*)

D.W.I. [abbrev] *driving while intoxicated*.

Dadgummit [1940's expression of disappointment (See *Dadratit)*

Dadratit [1940's expression of disappointment]

Daily constitutional [noun] whatever keeps your bodily functions working properly (such as a walk, or a drink of juice, etc.) Ex: He walks three miles for his *daily constitutional*.

Daily grind [noun] everyday routine. Ex: Nice talking with you, but I've got to get back to the *daily grind*.

Damned if you do, damned if you don't [verb phr] (impolite) in a negative position regardless of your actions. Ex: If I work overtime I will upset the family. If I don't work overtime, I will upset my boss. I'm *damned if I do and damned if I don't. (*See *Between a rock and a hard place)

Dangle a carrot [verb phr] offer an incentive to accomplish a task. Ex: If I *dangle a carrot,* my son will finish his homework.

Dark ages [noun phr] #1 the past. Ex: I wore that pink sundress back in the *dark ages*. #2 referring to a time of ignorance or uncivilized behavior. Ex: Dropping science from our school curriculum might put us back in the *dark ages*.

Dark horse [noun] relatively unknown candidate in a competitive race or election. Ex: The senator was a *dark horse* in the last election.

Day in and day out [adv phr] constantly. Ex: When Harry was ill, his wife was with him *day in and day out*.

Day in the sun [noun phr] time of honor or recognition. Ex: After winning the race, Jim deserves his *day in the sun*.

Day late and a dollar short (proverb) unorganized. Ex: He is always a *day late and a dollar short* and will never be admired.

Day of reckoning [noun phr] time when you will be held accountable for your mistakes or misbehavior. Ex: When your *day of reckoning* comes, you will be sorry you were mean to that person.

Dead ahead [adv] directly in front of. Ex: The stop sign is *dead ahead* of you.

Dead as a doornail [verb phr] being quite dead. Ex: I stepped on the ant and it was *dead as a doornail.* (See *Bought the farm*)

Dead drunk [verb] extremely drunk. Ex: The two boys got *dead drunk* last night. (See *Sloshed*)

Dead duck [noun] unable to function. Ex: When Ken lost that contract, he was a *dead duck*.

Dead end [noun] no more options. Ex: I am at a *dead end* and can think of no solution to this problem.

Dead giveaway [noun] obvious indication. Ex: It's easy to see that Marie got her raise. Her new car is a *dead giveaway*.

Dead heat [noun] tie among participants at the end of a competition. Ex: The swim race was a *dead heat*.

Dead in the water [verb phr] unable to move or progress - like a sailboat on a windless day. Ex: Without funding the banking project is *dead in the water*.

Dead lost [verb] totally lost. Ex: I am *dead lost*. We will have to find a gas station and ask where Bob's house is.

Dead meat [noun] exaggerated threat of death. Ex: If you don't get the oil changed in the car today, you'll be *dead meat*!

Dead on your feet [verb phr] exhausted; tired. Ex: I am *dead on my feet* since I worked as a grocery store clerk all day. (See *Dead tired*)

Dead reckoning [adj] faultless intuition . Ex: When it comes to management politics, Eric has *dead reckoning*.

Dead right [adj] turn exactly 45 degrees to the right. Ex: To get to Joe's house you take a *dead right* at the grocery store.

Dead ringer [noun] looking exactly alike. Ex: He's a *dead ringer* for his brother.

Dead serious [adj] not frivolous. Ex: I am *dead serious*. We must stick to our budget.

Dead set on [adj phr] decided unconditionally. Ex: He was d*ead set on* getting a bicycle for Christmas.

Dead tired [adj] exhausted. Ex: After running in the marathon, he was *dead tired.* (See *Dead on your feet)*

Dead to rights [adj phr] undeniably. Ex: I caught him *dead to rights*, lying to me about the money he stole.

Dead to the world [verb phr] in deep sleep. Ex: The baby was so tired that he was *dead to the world* after we put him down for his nap.

Dead weight [noun] #1 burden not worth the effort to carry or resolve. Ex: The two other parts of the project are just *dead weight* and should have been dropped months ago. #2 person who contributes nothing, but uses others' resources. Ex: Don't ask Denise to carry responsibility. She is just a *dead weight.*

Dead wrong [verb] totally incorrect. Ex: When he presented the sales figures for July, he was *dead wrong.*

Deaf as a post [verb phr] ignore what is being said completely. Ex: When I tell the girls to clean up the kitchen they become *deaf as a post*.

Dealy-which-it [noun] silly name for something when you can't think of the real name for it.   Ex: Take that *dealy-which-it* off the couch. (See *Thingy)*

Dear John letter [noun] a letter ending a relationship. Ex: He is upset because he received a *Dear John* letter.

Death march [noun] During World War II prisoners were marched until they dropped dead. Ex: The Bataan *death march* during World War II killed many men.

Death of me [noun phr] ultimate frustration. Ex: Bart will be the *death of me* yet. He has spilled his juice five times today.

Deep do do [noun] in trouble. Ex: If Mom finds out you ate a piece of the cake she is serving tonight, you will be in *deep do do*. (See *Your name is mud*)

Deep pockets [noun] wealthy, or having many resources. Ex: Billionaires of computer fame have very *deep pockets*.

Deep six something [verb] get rid of it. Ex: *Deep six* that old telephone book.

Deep South [noun] Alabama, Louisiana, Mississippi, Arkansas, Georgia, Tennessee, and Florida. Ex: Jimmy is from the *deep South* - Alabama to be exact.

Den of thieves [noun phr] place of business with questionable reputation. Ex: That appliance store may have a good sale, but they're really a *den of thieves*.

Designing woman [noun] one who plots to get married or involved romantically. Ex: *Designing women* are generally avoided by men.

Devil of a time [noun phr] difficulty. Ex: I'm having a *devil of a time* tying my necktie.

Devil to pay [noun phr] be liable for the consequences of your actions. Ex: The boy broke the window and he will have the *devil to pay*.

Devil's advocate (See *Play the devil's advocate*)

Devil's bedpost [noun] (card games) four of clubs. Ex: Isn't it about time for you to play the *devil's bedpost?*

Devil-may-care attitude [noun expression] cavalier and reckless. Ex: Javier is not the serious type. He has a *devil-may-care attitude*.

Diamond in the rough [noun phr] A person who has undeveloped talent and ability. Ex: The homeless boy is just a *diamond in the rough*. I can tell he is very smart.

Dibs on [noun] (informal- usually used by children) speaking first and claiming ownership of an item. Ex: I get *dibs on* the last cookie.

Dicey [verb] risky. Ex: Don't you think that project is a little bit *dicey* for us? (See *Sketchy*)

Did away with [verb phr] #1 abolished (as a law). Ex: They did away with prohibition in 1930. #2 killed. (as a sick animal) Ex: We had to *do away with* the horse because he broke his foot.

Did I hear my name taken in vain? [verb expression] you say this when joining a group realizing they have been talking about you.

Diddly squat [noun] almost nothing. Ex: That jacket didn't cost *diddly squat*.

Didn't pull any punches [verb phr]   specific and blunt in communicating with someone. Ex: The teacher didn't *pull any punches* and told the student he was failing math.

Didn't set well [verb phr] #1 upset. Ex: His attitude about single parenthood *didn't set well* with me. #2 made me sick. Ex: That last piece of pie *didn't set well* on my stomach.

Die for [verb] greatly desire. Ex: That new blue dress is to *die for.*

Die is cast [noun phr] decision is unchangeable. Ex: The *die is cast.* We are getting a new gym next year. (See *Set in cement*)

Die like a dog [verb phr] without dignity, as in a war. Ex: Many Marines *died like dogs* during the Vietnam War.

Die off [verb] Lose one after another, until extinct. Ex: The ancient dinosaurs have all *died off.*

Died a thousand deaths [verb phr] be acutely embarrassed. Ex: Phil saw me without my make-up. I could have *died a thousand deaths.*

Died laughing [verb] laughing a lot for a long time. Ex: When he told that joke, I nearly *died laughing.*

Die-hards [noun] #1 people who persevere. Ex: She is a real *die-hard* and is still researching that paper. #2 the last people at a party. Ex: The Smiths are real *die-hards.* They are so much fun.

Different as day and night [adj phr] not alike. Ex: I don't know why Jan and Bill get along so well; their interests are as *different as day and night.*

Different strokes for different folks [cliché] everyone is unique. Ex: He doesn't like to play the piano. She loves music and plays the piano. *Different strokes for different folks,* you know.

Dig deep [verb] summon resources deep within you. Ex: I know you can win that race if you *dig deep.*

Dig his own grave [verb phr] be responsible for his own downfall. Ex: Be nice to your fellow co-workers or you can *dig your own grave.*

Dig in [verb] proceed with great energy. Ex: *Dig in.* We have to have the cost estimates done by 10:00.

Digs [noun] home or apartment. Ex: Come over to my *digs f*or dinner.

Dilly dally [verb] (1940's slang) waste time. Ex: Don't *dilly dally* or we will be late to the movies.

Dime a dozen [noun phr] abundant; easy to acquire. Ex: Those ski jackets are a *dime a dozen.*

Dimwit [noun] unintelligent person. Ex: What a *dimwit!* I forgot my car keys again. (See *Dweeb*)

Ding someone [verb phr] find fault with him. Ex: Frank gets a *ding* for being late to the meeting.

Dingleberry [noun] (1950's slang) odd person. Ex: That *dingleberry* is swimming in that cold lake in December. (See *Dweeb*)

Dink around [verb phr] spend leisure time doing nothing. Ex: We just *dinked around* yesterday and watched the game on TV. (See *Fool around*)

Dink shot [noun] (sports - tennis) a weak shot that barely goes over the net. Ex: The tennis player hit a *dink shot* and his opponent missed it.

Dipshit [noun] (<u>crude</u>) undesirable person. (See *Dweeb*)

Dipstick [noun] loser. Ex: Larry is such a *dipstick.* He asked four girls to the Prom and no one accepted.

Dire straits [noun] difficult financial situation. Ex: He is in *dire straits* since he was laid off at work.

Dirt bike [noun] lightweight motorcycle, good for riding trails. Ex: Lots of people ride *dirt bikes* on the weekend for relaxation.

Dirt cheap [adj] inexpensive. Ex: Those dishes are *dirt cheap*. They are on sale.

Dirt poor [adj] extremely poor. Ex: Abe Lincoln's parents were *dirt poor.*

Dirty deal [noun] unfair to someone. Ex: Taking credit for someone's ideas is a *dirty deal*.

Dirty dog [noun] rascal. Ex: That *dirty dog* took my last dollar and spent it on a cola.

Dirty jokes [noun] jokes that have sexual connotations. Ex: Most people do not like *dirty jokes.*

Dirty look [noun] frown. Ex: Don't give me a *dirty look* when I am talking to you.

Dirty mind [noun] lecherous. Ex: That politician has a *dirty mind.*

_____

Dirty money [noun] wealth acquired by illegal means. Ex: Drug cartels are known for laundering *dirty money*.

Dirty rotten rat [noun] unscrupulous. Ex: He stole my girlfriend. What a *dirty rotten rat.*

Disappeared into thin air [verb phr] vanished. Ex: My keys have *disappeared into thin air.* Have you seen them?

Discretion is the better part of valor [cliché] behave prudently, making decisions carefully. Ex: Don't tell your friend about your affair. After all, *discretion is the better part of valor*.

Dispense with [verb] discard or eliminate. Ex: Let's *dispense with* the minutes of the last meeting and get down to the issues.

Ditsy [adj] flighty; disorganized. (usually said about women) Ex: That woman is really *ditsy.* (See *Airhead)*

Dive into [verb phr] begin an activity with vigor. Ex: He *dove into* his new app program.

Divide and conquer [verb phr] fragmenting on issues allowing a third party or group to gain control. Ex: The principle of *divide and conquer* was used by the Bolsheviks to gain control of the Soviet Union.

Divvy up [verb] divide up. Ex: Let's *divvy up* the money left in the poker game.

Dizzy dame [noun phr] (1930's slang) unthinking or illogical woman.

Do a 180 [verb phr] change your mind and have an opposite opinion of what you originally had. Ex: It is confusing when he *does a 180*. We don't know what to believe.

_____

Do a 360 [verb phr] change your mind and then reverse to your original decision. Ex: That policy implementation *did a 360*.

Do a double take [verb phr] not believe what you see and take a second look. Ex: I did a *double take* when I saw Marie. She had lost so much weight.

Do a good turn [verb phr] do a favor. Ex: If you *do a good turn* for someone else, they will do one for you.

Do a handshake [verb phr] a verbal agreement sealed by shaking hands. Ex: They won't draw up a new contract; they'll just *do a handshake*.

Do a number on [verb phr] #1 cheat. Ex: The company officer really *did a number on* the employees. #2 outsmart. Ex: Fred *did a real number on* the opposition and got the contract. Ex: #3 beat physically or in some sport. Ex: Team A *did a number on* Team B and beat them in the game.

Do an about face [verb phr] change your mind. Ex: He did an *about face* and went to the movie anyway.

Do an end run [verb phr] (business) bypass immediate authority to appeal to higher authority. Ex: We may need to do *an end run* to the director if our manager won't agree to the project.

Do away with [verb phr] eliminate. Ex: I *did away with* the old magazines.

Do handsprings [verb] be overjoyed. Ex: When Mike gets his promotion, he'll *do handsprings*.

Do I have to spell it out for you? [verb phr]   Can't you understand? (said with impatience)   Ex: "Why do I have to be home by midnight?" "*Do I have to spell it out for you?*"

Do it [verb] have sex. Ex: Let's *do it* after the kids are asleep tonight. (See *Fly me*)

Do it in style   [verb phr] do something lavishly and with elegance. Ex: The Smiths always *do it in style.* They rented a limousine to take them to the airport.

Do it in your head [verb phr] mentally calculate or formulate, not using pen and paper. Ex: It's an oral exam, so for each math problem, you'll have to d*o it in your head*.

Do lunch [verb phr] have lunch together. Ex: Let's *do lunch* on Friday.

Do me [verb] have sex with me. (See *Fly me*)

Do or die [adj] total effort. Ex: Hiking to the top of that mountain is a real *do or die* effort.

Do out of [verb phr] cheat. Ex: The old woman will *do* her daughter *out of* her inheritance.

Do tell [verb] #1 Request to hear gossip. Ex: "Guess what I heard about Mindy!" "*Do tell!*" #2   Sarcastic reply to a statement that everyone already knows.   Ex: "The team lost another baseball game." "Do tell!"

Do the honors [verb phr] be the host, or take the job. Ex: When it comes to carving turkey at our house, my dad will always *do the honors*.

Do the leg work [verb phr] investigate or research something. Ex: I'll do the *leg work* for your research paper.

Do the paperwork

Do the paperwork [verb phr] (business) create the documentation. Ex: Have you *done the paperwork* for the new project?

Do the trick [verb phr] accomplish the task. Ex: I glued it. That should *do the trick.*

Do up [verb] decorate or embellish. Ex: I need to *do up* the house for the party Saturday.

Do without [verb] manage without something. Ex: We manage to *do without* new shoes every year.

Do you mind? [noun phr] (said irritatingly) leave me alone. Ex: I'm trying to get dinner. *Do you mind?*

Do your own thing [verb phr] pursue activity independent of other people's influence or ideas. Ex: Tom is always *doing his own thing.* He is in Europe hiking now.

Do yourself proud [verb phr] make a good effort. Ex: You *did yourself proud* on that essay.

Doctor something [verb] #1 falsify. Ex: The accountant *doctored* the books before the auditor came. #2 change for the better, or to disguise its faults. Ex: If there is too much salt in the soup, you can *doctor* it by adding a couple of potatoes.

Does a chicken have lips? [rhetorical remark] made when someone says something that is obvious to everyone. Ex: Did you pass the test?" *"Does a chicken have lips?"*

Does that ring a bell? [noun phr] do you remember that? Ex: We went to school together in 1982. *Does that ring a bell?*

Does your Mother know you're out? [noun phr] snide remark, implying someone is acting childish.

Doesn't carry any weight [verb phr] is not important or influential. Ex: He may be the president of his own company, but he *doesn't carry any weight* in the courthouse.

Doesn't have a leg to stand on [verb phr] the argument or point of view has no validity. Ex: That politician *doesn't have a leg to stand on* .

Doesn't have the sense he was born with [verb phr] acting foolishly. That boy *does not have the sense he was born with.*

Doesn't hold water [verb phr] has no credibility. Ex: Your theory *doesn't hold water.*

Doesn't know his right hand from his left [verb expression] confused. Ex: Don't ask him for directions. He *doesn't know his right hand from his left.*

Dog and pony show [noun phr] (business) a demonstration or presentation of a new idea or concept, usually presented with visuals, such as view foils, graphs, charts, etc. Ex: The boss wants me to do a *dog and pony show* on the new engineering process.

Dog days [noun] the hot days of late summer. Ex: I love to swim during the *dog days* of summer.

Dog-eared [adj] worn. Ex: The pages of the book are *dog-eared.*

Dog eat dog world [adj phr] competitive and aggressive. Ex: The company bid was undercut. It's a *dog eat dog world* out there.

Dog tired [adj phr] exhausted. Ex I am *dog tired* after working 12 hours painting the house. (See *Done in*)

Doggie bag [noun phr] The bag/sack a restaurant packages leftover food for you to take home. (done only upon request) Ex: Could you put the rest of my steak in a *doggie bag*?

Doggone it! [exclamatory expression of disappointment] Ex: *Doggone it!* I wanted to go to the movies.

Doing time [verb phr] serving a jail sentence. Ex: The convict is *doing time* for forgery.

Dollar for dollar [noun phr] worth the money. Ex: *Dollar for dollar*, you can't find a better buy on washing machines.

Dollars to doughnuts [noun phr] quite sure of your opinion and make a bet with someone. Ex: I'll bet you *dollars to doughnuts* that Rick will get an A on the test tomorrow.

Domino effect [noun phr] When one item falls, another will fall, etc.   Ex: These countries will all become Socialist because of the *domino effect*. (See *Ripple effect*)

Done deal [noun phr] certainty. Ex: You want me to pick you up for work tomorrow? It's a *done deal*.

Done in [verb phr] #1 exhausted. Ex: The boy was *done in* after the race. (See *Dog tired*) #2 killed. Ex: The Mob has *done in* my brother.

Done nothing [verb] #1 lazy. Ex: I have *done nothing* all day. #2 innocent. Ex: Don't convict him. He has *done nothing*.

Done squat [verb] accomplished nothing. Ex: The child has *done squat* all day.

Done to a "T" [verb phr] perfect. Ex: The steak is *done to a "T"*.

Don't air the dirty laundry [verb phr] some family secrets are better not discussed with others. Ex: "Did you tell Mary about Joe's divorce?" "No, I *don't* think we should *air the dirty laundry.*"

Don't be a wet blanket (See *Wet blanket)*

Don't bite the hand that feeds you [cliché] Always show respect for the person or company that enables you to survive. Ex: He always says bad things about the company. You *shouldn't bite the hand that feeds you.*

Don't box me in [verb phr] don't leave me without options. Ex: "I expect that design to be done by Friday." "*Don't box me in.* I need more time than that."

Don't bust a gasket [verb phr] don't get so excited or upset. Ex: Just because I broke your CD, *don't bust a gasket.* (See *Don't have a cow)*

Don't count your chickens before they hatch [cliché] Plans may not work out the way you anticipate, so be cautious. Ex: *Don't count your chickens before they hatch.* You might not get that job you want.

Don't cut off your nose to spite your face [cliché] take action that will backfire on you. Ex: The company laid off too many workers. They *cut off their nose to spite their face.*

Don't do anything that I wouldn't do ! [goodbye expression] said in jest to a friend when you are departing.

Don't drag your feet [verb phr] do not procrastinate. Ex: *Don't drag your feet.* Mow the lawn now.

Don't fart around [verb phr] (impolite) Get busy.

Don't give a hoot [1950's slang] don't care. (See *Don't give a rat's ass*)

Don't give a rat's ass [verb expression] Currently popular 2013 slang phrase, although it is considered impolite by the older generation. (See *Don't give a hoot*)

Don't give me any lip! [verb phr] (usually said to a child) be quiet and do not talk back.

Don't have a cow [verb phr] don't get upset. (See *Don't bust a gasket*)

Don't hold your breath [verb phr] skeptical about what you heard. Ex: *Don't hold your breath.* I really do not think we will get a pay raise this month.

Don't kick 'em when they're down [verb phr] make allowances for someone's misfortunes. Ex: The team just lost the game. *Don't kick 'em when they're down* by yelling at them. (See *Add insult to injury*)

Don't know beans about it [verb phr] do not know anything.

Don't know if I'm coming or going [verb phr] So overworked or under pressure that everything becomes confused. Ex: I am working two jobs and *don't know if I am coming or going.*

Don't let it go to your head [verb phr] don't become egotistical. Ex: Just because you won the lottery, *don't let it go to your head.*

Don't let the door hit you in the back [verb phr] leave now. (said sarcastically) Ex: "I guess I'll be going now." "*Don't let the door hit you in the back.*"

Don't let the grass grow under your feet [cliché] #1 don't procrastinate. Ex: *Don't let the grass grow under your feet.* Wash the windows now. #2 move to another place. Ex: The Jacksons never let the *grass grow under their feet.* They are moving again to Tennessee.

Don't lift a finger [verb phr] do not exert yourself. Ex: My husband *doesn't lift a finger* around the house.

Don't look a gift horse in the mouth [cliché] if someone offers you something free, accept it. Ex: I really didn't want that extra doughnut, but you *can't look a gift horse in the mouth.*

Don't lose your cool [verb phr] (See *Lose your cool*)

Don't monkey around [verb phr] don't behave in an improper manner. Ex: *Don't monkey around.* Someone will get hurt if you keep tripping people.

Don't pass the buck [cliché] take responsibility for handling a difficult situation. Ex: President Harry Truman always said "The buck stops here. " He never *passed the buck.*

Don't push your luck [verb phr] Don't take undue advantage of someone's good nature. Ex: Don't ask me to take care of your cat. That's *pushing your luck.*

Don't put the cart before the horse [cliché] take things one step at a time. Do not try to do the last thing first. Ex: He hasn't taken driving lessons yet. I don't want him to drive my car. You can't put the *cart before the horse.*

Don't put yourself out [verb phr] don't exert extra effort. Ex: *Don't put yourself out.* I will take a cab home.

Don't reinvent the wheel [verb phr] (See *Reinvent the wheel*)

Don't rock the boat [verb phr] (See *Rock the boat*)

Don't shoot the messenger [verb phr] Don't criticize the person delivering an unpopular message.

Don't spit in the wind [verb phr] (See *Spit in the wind*)

Don't spread it around [verb phr] Don't tell others a secret you just found out. Ex: Ted got an "F" on his test, but *don't spread it around.*

Don't stand on ceremony [verb phr] (See *Stand on ceremony*)

Don't throw the baby out with the bath water [cliché] Do not throw out all the old ways of operating or planning and start with only brand new ideas, plans, or operating procedures. Keep some of the old to mix in with the new and temper the new.

Don't upset the apple cart [verb phr] Don't do or say something in opposition to the main way of thinking. Ex: Just go along with the new rules. *Don't upset the apple cart.*

Don't want to see hide nor hair of him [verb phr] want no further contact with a person.

Don't waste your breath [verb phr] don't try to explain to me. Ex: "Let me tell you where I was last night." "*Don't waste your breath.* I won't believe you anyway."

Doom and gloom [noun phr] negative thinking. Ex: I wish he would not spread his *doom and gloom* around here every day.

Dotted line [noun] (business) someone who reports to you for project-related business activities, but you are not responsible for them budget-wise. Ex: Frances has three *dotted lines* reporting to her.

Double back [verb] travel back along the same route trying to locate something. Ex: I *doubled back* two times before I found Janie's house.

Double boxed [verb phr] (business) Having two people who share the responsibility for a managerial position. Ex: Harrison is in charge of the Accounts Payable department, but he is *double boxed* with Johnson in Accounts Receivable.

Double dare [verb] Try to entice someone to take a risk. Ex: I *double dare* you to swim across this river.

Double dealing [noun] Deceive people by working both sides of a situation to your advantage. Ex: I wouldn't work with Harry. He will just *double deal* with you.

Double dipping [verb] taking advantage in a retirement situation. Ex: Government employees can *double dip* and get government retirement in addition to Social Security.

Double duty [noun] serve two purposes at the time. Ex: This plastic wrap serves *double duty.* It wraps my lunch and it protects my homework from the rain.

Double edged sword [noun] A situation that has positive and negative aspects to it. Ex: Accepting his help is a *double edged sword.* Then he will expect me to repay him in some way.

Double speak [noun] use words or phrases that mean the opposite of what they appear. Ex: To call a missile a "Peacekeeper" is an example of *double speak.*

Double standard [noun] Two sets of rules that conflict are applied to the same situation. Ex: It is a *double standard* that men expect their wives to be faithful, while they are not.

Double talk [noun] say one thing and mean exactly the opposite. Ex: The company is full of *double talk.* They talk of cost cutting, but the executives are having their offices redecorated.

Double up [verb] #1 fold. Ex: *Double up* the blanket. It will be cold tonight. #2 bend over in laughter or in pain. Ex: That joke was so funny I *doubled up* with laughter. #3 share space in a room. Ex: Let's *double up* and share this hotel room so we won't have to pay for the cost of another room. #4 line up with a partner, as in a dance. Ex: Let's *double up* and be partners for this dance.

Dough [noun] money. (See *Bucks*)

Down a piece [adv] (country western) not very far. Ex: He lives *down* the road *a piece* .

Down and out [adj] #1 have bad luck and no money. Ex: Poor Dan, he is really *down and out.* When he lost his job, his wife left him also. #2 a vagrant. Ex: That old man is *down and out.* He is homeless.

Down home [adj] practical, ordinary. Ex: I am very fond of Linda. She is so *down home.*

Down in the dumps [prep phr] discouraged. Ex: He is *down in the dumps* since he flunked his driver's test.

Down in the mouth [prep phr] negative. Ex: She can't say anything nice about anyone. She is so *down in the mouth.*

Down memory lane [prep phr] recall an event from the past. Ex: Let's take a trip *down memory lane* and eat in the same restaurant where we first met.

Down on his luck [prep phr] unlucky and short of resources. Ex: He is *down on his luck.* He just wrecked his car.

Down pat [prep phr] memorized perfectly. Ex: I'm sure she will do well in the play because she has her lines *down pat.*

Down the drain [prep phr] abandoned. Ex: The Smith/Jones project is sure *down the drain.*

Down the garden path [prep phr] course of action which looks positive with no problems, but may deceptive. Ex: She was led *down the garden path* and lost all her money on bad investments. (See *Down the primrose path)*

Down the hatch [prep phr] said as a toast when you drink a beverage. Ex: You raise your glass and say, "*Down the hatch!*" (See *Cheers!*)

Down the pike [prep phr] in the future. Ex: We will build a new highway *down the pike.*

Down the primrose path [prep phr] (See *Down the garden path*)

Down the road [prep phr] ahead, in the future. Ex: I know we will have lots of children *down the road.*

Down the tubes [prep phr] no longer operable; a failure. Ex: That new construction plan is *down the tubes.*

Down time [noun] (business) time during which business employees or machinery are not working. (e.g. weekends, holidays)

Down to brass tacks [prep phr] basics. Ex: Let's get *down to brass tacks.* Can we afford a vacation or not?

Down to earth [prep phr] #1 without pretense. Ex: George is a real *down to earth* person. #2 realistic. Ex: Let's get *down to earth* and find out exactly how much it will cost.

Down to the wire [prep phr] no more time left to complete something. Ex: The project due date is tomorrow. We are *down to the wire* and have to work overtime.

Down under [noun] country of Australia. Ex: I am thinking about making a trip *down under* this year.

Down with him [prep phr] get rid of him; vote him out of office or cause him to resign. Ex: *"Down with him"* shouted the crowd of people about the candidate.

Down play [verb] reduce the significance. Ex: We don't want to upset the kids. *Down play* the effect of losing your job.

Downer [noun] something depressing. Ex: Watching the TV news every night is a real *downer.*

Downshifting [verb] return to a simpler and more economic life style. (See *Voluntary Simplicity*)

Downside [noun] the negative aspect(s). Ex: The *downside* is that we can't afford to hire any more employees.

Downsize [verb] (business) reduce manpower. Ex: One of the options from the bankruptcy was to *downsize* the company. (See *Rightsize*)

Downturn [noun] (business) when business gets worse. Ex: With this latest cancelation of orders, the *downturn* for the company is certain.

Drag his feet [verb phr] procrastinate. Ex: It's a good idea, but Oliver is *dragging his feet.*

Drag in [verb] #1 exhausted. Ex: He was so tired he looked like something the cat *dragged in*. #2 force someone to participate. Ex: Derek was *dragged in* to give his opinion.

Drag on [verb] pass slowly . Ex: This day is really *dragging on*.

Drag out [verb] #1 relate slowly or in great detail. Ex: He *dragged out* the story to get the children more excited. #2 remove someone from an activity. Ex: We had to *drag* Lonny *out* of the room because he was disorderly.

Drag the bottom [verb phr] look for a possible drowned person. (as in a river) Ex: We need to *drag the bottom* of the river. I think this is the place Josh fell in.

Draw a blank

Draw a blank [verb phr] can't remember something. Ex: I *drew a blank* when he asked me what Tom's mother's name was.

Draw a line in the sand [verb phr] Make a final decision. Ex: We're going to *draw a line in the sand* and not spend more than $10,000 for home improvements.

Draw him out [verb phr] get someone to express his opinions. Ex: Jack's ideas are good. Let's *draw him out* and see what he says.

Draw the line [verb phr] set the standards or rules. Ex: I am *drawing the line* here. You cannot borrow any more money from me.

Draw straws [verb phr] a game where each person draws a straw from one person's hand. One of the straws has been cut shorter than the others. The person who draws the short straw is selected for whatever task was agreed upon at the outset or for whatever prize is available. Can be good or not so good!

Dream on [verb] What you want or desire is not likely to become a reality. Jennifer would like to be a famous movie star. I told her *"Dream on"*. (See *You wish*)

Dream up [verb] imagine. Ex: I *dreamed up* a great vacation.

Dress up [verb] wear formal clothes. Ex: We always *dress up* for church. (See *Glad rags*)

Dressed down [verb] severely scolded. Ex: The Marine sergeant *dressed down* his recruits.

Dressed fit to kill [verb phr] dressed elegantly. Ex: The movie star was *dressed fit to kill*. (See *Dress up*)

Dressed to the hilt [verb phr] (See D*ressed fit to kill)*

Dressed to the nines [verb phr] (See D*ressed fit to kill)*

Dressed to the nth degree [verb phr] (See Dressed fit to kill)

Dressed to the teeth [verb phr] (See D*ressed fit to kill)*

Dribble in [verb] receive in small amounts over a period of time. Ex: The insurance checks from the hurricane just *dribbled in.*

Drink down [verb] finish your drink. Ex: *Drink* your juice *down.*

Drink in [verb] see and enjoy (as a view). Ex: Just *drink in* that sunset. It's so beautiful!

Drink up [verb] drink what you are served. Ex: *Drink up*. We have a lot to celebrate tonight.

Drive a hard bargain [verb phr] being tough to negotiate with. Ex: The real estate agent *drove a hard bargain* when he sold their home.

Drive a nail into your coffin [verb phr] do something dangerous or unhealthy that could shorten your life. Ex: Driving fast just *drives a nail into your coffin*.

Drive me nuts [verb phr] irritated by either someone's actions or words. Ex: You *drive me nuts* when you pick your teeth. (See *Drive me over the edge*)

Drive me over the edge [verb phr] (See *Drive me nuts*)

Drive me to distraction [verb phr] frustrate or confuse. Ex: That active child is *driving me to distraction*.

Drive me up the wall [verb phr] (See *Drive me nuts*)

Drive safely [verb] [a common goodbye phrase]

Drive-by [adj]   done from a vehicle, as a shooting. Ex: There's another *drive-by* shooting in our neighborhood.

Drive-in [noun] #1 A movie theater that is outside. Cars park in a large lot and people watch the movie from their cars. #2 a restaurant where you can stay in your car and are served from a tray that clips to your car window.

Drop back and punt [verb phr] abandon the current process or change the method of action. Ex: The new promotion process isn't working so we need to *drop back and punt*.

Drop by [verb]   visit - usually to check on someone's progress. Ex: I'll *drop by* the hospital and see how Renee is doing.

Drop dead [verb] (<u>impolite</u>)   quit bothering me. Used many times by siblings.

Drop dead gorgeous [adj]   pretty. (said about women) Ex: That movie star is *drop dead gorgeous.*

Drop his drawers [verb phr] took his pants down. Ex: He had to *drop his drawers* for his physical examination.

Drop in   [verb] #1 visit unexpectedly. Ex: We need to clean up the house in case company *drops in*. #2 to attend a class in school without first registering. Ex: Be sure your teacher counts the *drop-ins* the first day.

Drop in the bucket [noun phr] small amount. Ex: My salary is just a *drop in the bucket* compared to the CEO.

Drop it [verb] forget it. Ex: *Drop it.* I am tired of your complaints. (See *Stuff it*)

Drop like a hot potato [verb phr] stop immediately. Ex: That project was doomed to fail and I dropped it like a *hot potato.*

Drop like flies [verb phr] faint from exhaustion. Ex: It was so hot at the game that people were *dropping like flies.*

Drop off [verb] #1 removed. Ex: His name was *dropped off* the membership list at the club. #2 deliver something. Ex: I'll *drop off* the letter at the mailbox. #3 go to sleep. Ex: He was so tired that he *dropped right off.* #4 [noun] sharp descent. Ex: There is a bad *drop off* on the Cascade Trail.

Drop out [noun] #1 someone who does not complete a task. Ex: He is a high school *dropout.*   #2 [verb] quit an activity. Ex: I *dropped out* of soccer because I needed to study more.

Drop out of sight [verb phr] #1 became obscure. Ex: The luxury cars *dropped out of sight* for a few years during gas shortage. #2 lose contact. Ex: Don't *drop out of sight* just because you're moving to Florida.

Drop over [verb]   #1 disappear from view. Ex: The sun *dropped over* the mountains. #2 visit. Ex: *Drop over* sometime for dinner. #3 fall from exhaustion. I was so tired after studying for my test that I *dropped over* from exhaustion.

Drop the ball [verb phr]   neglect a responsibility or fail to complete an assignment. Ex: The boss wanted the project done by June 20th and the group *dropped the ball.*

Drop through the cracks [verb phr] get lost or forgotten. Ex: Don't let any of the details of the agreement *drop through the cracks. (*See *Fell through the cracks*)

Drop through the floor [verb phr] #1 react dramatically when you are surprised. Ex: If he buys a car for me, I'll *drop through the floor*! #2 lose much of its value. Ex: If I'm lucky, I'll sell my stock before it *drops through the floor*.

Drop you a line [verb phr] write a short note or letter to someone after you have visited that person. Ex: When you leave you say, "Bye now. I'll *drop you a line* as soon as I get home."

Drown his sorrows [verb phr] drink to forget troubles or unhappiness. Ex: When his mother died, he drank a lot to *drown his sorrows*.

Drum up [verb] solicit. Ex: We have to *drum up* a lot of business if we're going to be profitable.

Drummed out [verb] evicted or pressured to leave. Ex: The mayor was *drummed out* of office after he overran the budget for two years.

Drunk as a skunk [cliché] extremely inebriated. (See *Wiped out*)

Dry as a bone [verb phr] extremely dry weather conditions. Ex: My garden is *dry as a bone*. I will have to water it.

Duck soup [noun] easy to accomplish. *Ex:* Riding a bike is *duck soup* for the boy. (See *Easy as pie*)

Ducks in a row [cliché] Everything is organized. Ex: All his *ducks are in a row* and he is ready to give the presentation.

Dude/hey Dude [noun] (2013 slang) " Hello" greeting to a friend.

Due in [adj] expected time of arrival. Ex: The plane is *due in* at 4:00.

Due to [prep] because of. Ex: *Due to* the hurricane, the power is out.

Dug in his heels [verb phr] unyielding. Ex: He *dug in his heels* and would not change his mind.

Duke it out [verb phr] fight. Ex: He wants to *duke it out* with his brother over the football game.

Dumb as a doornail [verb phr] Acting as if you have no brains. Ex: That bird is *dumb as a doornail*. It keeps flying into the window. (See *Dumb as a post*)

Dumb as a post [verb phr] (See *Dumber than a rock*)

Dumber than a rock [verb phr] (See D*umb as a doornail)*

Dump on [verb] #1 relate many problems or troubles to someone. Ex: I am tired of being *dumped on* by you. #2 berate someone. Ex: The manager *dumped on* the employee for being late.

Dumped him [verb] one person in a relationship ends the relationship. Ex: When LaVonne *dumped* Sergei, he was depressed.

Dumpster diving [noun] looking for hidden treasures by going methodically through dumpsters.

Dust off [verb] #1 use something that has been unused for a long period. Ex: Let's *dust off* the sled. The snow is great for sledding. #2 finish. Ex: I'm going to *dust off* this English paper in two hours.

Dutch treat [noun] each party pays his/her own way on a date. Ex: Let's go *Dutch treat* to the movie tonight.

Dutch uncle [noun] (1940's slang) someone who has a lot of advice. Ex: My *Dutch uncle* tells me what stock to buy.

Dweeb [noun] undesirable person. (See *Dimwit*)

Dyed in the wool [verb phr] unchanging; rigid. Ex: Rudy is a *dyed in the wool* Republican. He never votes for a Democrat.

E- [prefix] a prefix meaning *electronic*.

E.R. [abbrev] emergency room in a hospital. Ex: The *E.R.* is full.

E-mail [noun] electronic messages sent and received from one computer to another computer linked with it. Ex: Did you read your e-mail messages yesterday?

Eager beaver [noun] energetic, enthusiastic worker. Ex: Mark is such an *eager beaver*. He is here at 6:00 A.M. every morning.

Eagle eye [noun] #1 sharp eyesight. Ex: She discovered the mistake because of her *eagle eye*. #2 watches or supervises closely. Ex: The father kept an *eagle eye* on his son swimming nearby.

Ear to the ground [noun phr] eavesdrop on conversations to pick up information that can be useful to you. Ex: Keep your *ear to the ground* and see what you can find out about the new neighbor.

Early bird [noun] someone who accomplishes something before everyone else. Ex: Dan got up at 5:00 A.M to mow his lawn. He is a real *early bird*.

(The) early bird catches the worm [cliché] If you are aggressive and take the initiative, you will reap the most rewards.

Earn an honest dollar [verb phr] work hard for your wages. Ex: He is a plumber and *earns an honest dollar* every day.

Earnest money [noun] (real estate term) money put down as evidence you are serious about negotiating a loan for a house. Ex: We put $1,000 *earnest money* down to buy our new home.

Earth calling Mars [noun phr] get someone's attention. Ex:
Earth calling Mars. Don't you know that meeting has
been cancelled? (See *Pilot to Bombardier*)

Earth shattering [adj] shocking. Ex: I received some *earth
shattering* news yesterday that my aunt had died.

Earth station [noun] (communications) ground terminals used
for reception and transmission of information to or
from a communications satellite. Ex: We get our
video hookups via an *Earth Station*.

Ease on down [verb phr] move at a comfortable pace. Ex: I'm
going to *ease on down* tonight and just watch TV all
evening.

Ease up [verb] #1 slow down. Ex: The rain is beginning to *ease
up*. #2 be less strict. Ex: *Ease u*p and let the child stay
up until 8:00.

Easier said than done [adj expression] sounds easy, but is
difficult to accomplish. Ex: To move the greenhouse
to the backyard is *easier said than done*.

Easin' [verb] relaxing. Ex: The two friends are just *easin'* and
watching a movie. (See *Veg out*)

East is East and West is West [noun expression] We all have
different customs. Ex: Easterners speak with clipped
tones and Westerners kind of drawl their words. *East
is East and West is West*!

Easy as pie [adj phr] not difficult. Ex: The last test was *easy as
pie*. (See *Piece of cake*)

Easy come, easy go [verb expression] be flippant about a loss. Ex: You win the lottery. You go to collect the money, and find the ticket was dated for the previous week! *Easy come, easy go!*

Easy does it [noun phr] #1 go slowly. Ex: *Easy does it*. We have to lower him down slowly from the mountain because he has a broken leg. #2 keep calm. *Easy does it.* Don't cry over your lost dog. I am sure we will find him.

Easy going [adj] relaxed and casual. Ex: Brad is so *easy going* that most problems do not upset him.

Easy money [noun] money won on a bet. Ex: Did you bet on the game yesterday? That was *easy money.*

Easy on the pocketbook [adj phr] inexpensive. Ex: Since that sweater is on sale, it is *easy on the pocketbook.*

Easy peasy [adj] (2014 slang) very simple. Getting insurance is *easy peasy.*

Eat crow [verb phr] embarrassed and forced to apologize. (See *Eat humble pie*)

Eat humble pie [verb phr] (See *Eat crow)*

Eat it up [verb phr] enjoy being flattered. Ex: He told his girlfriend how pretty she was and she just *ate it up*.

Eat like a bird [cliché] eat small portions of food. Ex: The two year old child *eats like a bird*.

Eat me out of house and home [verb phr] said to someone who eats a lot. Ex: You are *eating me out of house and home*. Last night you had four pork chops!

Eat my dust [verb phr] drive or ride a horse very fast, leaving a trail of dust for those behind you. Ex: He was the first rider and the others were *eating his dust.*

Eat out [verb phr] dine away from home. Ex: We need to *eat out* more often.

Eat your heart out [verb expression] people are jealous of your good fortune. You acknowledge it to friends by saying "*Eat your heart out*" meaning that you recognize they are envious.

Eat your words [verb phr] say something you regret and have to apologize. Ex: I said something unkind to my brother and had to *eat my words.* (See *Eat crow*)

Eating out of his hand [verb phr] have someone under your influence. Ex: He had Jeff *eating out his hand* when I told him he only had to invest $2,000 in the venture.

Economically challenged [noun] poor. Ex: It is politically correct these days to say you were *economically challenged* when you were a child.

Egg in your beer [noun phr] wanting the best of everything. Ex: I suppose you want *egg in your beer* also!

Egg on my face [noun phr] embarrassed. Ex: I really had *egg on my face* when I didn't know the sales figures.

Elbow grease [noun] hard work. Ex: You will have to use a lot of *elbow grease* to clean your room.

Elbow in [verb phr] #1 join an activity when not invited. Ex: He *elbowed in* to play cards with the group. #2 push into a line in front of other people. Ex: She *elbowed in* front of the other people.

Electronic Bulletin Board [noun] (computer) information offered on a group of networked computers. Ex: You can find all those addresses on the *electronic bulletin board*.

Electronic copy [noun] the version of a document on a computer system or other electronic media. Ex: Send me an *electronic copy* of that memo.

Elevator music [noun] bland music piped into offices and elevators in office buildings. Ex: I wish we could listen to jazz instead of that *elevator music*.

Eleventh hour [noun] last possible time. Ex: It is the *eleventh hour* and we must decide whether to buy the house or not.

Empty nest syndrome [noun phr] when children are grown and leave home, many parents feel lonely and useless. Ex: When her children graduated from college and moved away from home, she was depressed, which is the *empty nest syndrome*.

End of my rope [noun phr] totally frustrated with a difficult situation, idea or person. Ex: I am at the *end of my rope*. I have applied for fifty jobs and don't have one yet. (See *Last straw*)

End over end [noun phr] tumbling. Ex: He went *end over end* down the mountain.

Endo [noun] (sports; bicycling) crash headlong. Ex: Jim took a bad *endo* over the weekend.

Enjoy it while it lasts [verb phr] take pleasure now, because the situation will change to be less comfortable or calm. Ex: *Enjoy the sun while it lasts* before the rain comes.

Etched in stone [verb phr] unchangeable (as an opinion or decision) Ex: That procedure is *etched in stone* and will be difficult to update. (See *Set in cement*)

Even Steven [adj phr] everything is equal. Ex: The two boys had each won two races and were *even steven*.

Even the score [adj phr] retaliate. Ex: He was mean to me and I am going to *even the score*.

Ever so often [adv phr] occasionally. Ex: *Ever so often* we eat dinner out.

Every bit as [adj phr] equal in ability. Ex: Nick is every bit as athletic as Matt.

Every cloud has a silver lining [cliché] A negative situation has some redeeming aspect. Ex: Cheer up. *Every cloud has a silver lining*. You will win the game next week.

Every dog has his day [noun phr] every person will have opportunities to be recognized for an accomplishment. Ex: He is working so hard and will be successful someday. *Every dog has his day.*

Every living soul [noun phr] all inclusive. Ex: I can't get supper on the table. *Every living soul* has called me this evening. (See *Every Tom, Dick, and Harry*)

Every man for himself [noun expression] make an individual effort. Ex: Remember, in the swimming race, it's *every man for himself*.

Every mother's son [noun phr] every male person. Ex: *Every mother's son* said that he wanted to go to Europe.

Every now and then [adv phr] occasionally. Ex: *Every now and then* I think of you.

Every other one [noun phr] alternate. Ex: The first boy in the lineup and *every other one* is on team one.

Every particular [noun] all the details. Ex: Please give me *every particular* of the game.

Every time I turn around [adv phr] often. Ex: *Every time I turn around,* he's gone golfing again.

Every Tom, Dick, and Harry [noun phr] includes everyone. Ex: *Every Tom, Dick, and Harry* wants lower taxes. (See *Every living soul*)

Every which way [adv phr] All directions. Ex: The wind blew the snow *every which way.*

Everybody and his brother [noun phr] everyone in a group. Ex: *Everybody and his brother* is going to the movies tonight. (See *Every Tom, Dick, and Harry*)

Everything but the kitchen sink [noun phr] entire amount Ex: You packed *everything but the kitchen sink* for the camping trip. (See *Everything from A to Z*)

Everything from A to Z [noun phr] (See *Everything but the kitchen sink*)

Everything is hunky-dory [1950's slang phrase]   OK. (reply to "How are you") Ex: "How are things?" "*Everything is hunky dory.*"

Excuse my French [verb phr] apology after you have sworn aloud, or used vulgar or profane language. Ex: $$**8#@. Excuse my French, but I am really angry about my flat tire.

Exist on a shoestring [verb phr] live on very little money. Ex: The college student *exists on a shoestring.*

Expecting [verb] pregnant. Ex: She is *expecting* in April. (See *Baby bump)*

Explain yourself [verb phr] give your reasons for your actions. Ex: *Explain yourself* Ricky. Where were you last night?

Extract his/her pound of flesh [verb phr]   get even with someone. Ex: I expect Vicki will *extract her pound of flesh* from Greg after he told those lies about her.

Eye for an eye (biblical expression] retaliate. Ex: He drew a gun on the robber because the robber had drawn a gun on him last week. *An eye for an eye.*

Eye for it [noun phr] knack for it. Ex: He has an *eye for carpentry.*

Eye on the ball [noun phr] pay close attention to the ball, in a baseball game or other game, such as golf. Ex: If you just keep your *eye on the ball*, you will hit a home run.

Eye to eye [noun phr] agree. Ex: We see *eye to eye* on everything.

Eyeballed it [verb] measure something by carefully looking at it. Ex: He cut the board by *eyeballing it.*

Eyes are bigger than his stomach [noun phr] take more than you can eat. Ex: Look at Bill. His plate is still full after everyone else has finished. His *eyes were too big for his stomach.*

Eyes in the back of her head [noun phr] having intuition. Ex: How did Mother know that I was taking a cookie from the cookie jar? She must have *eyes in the back of her head.*

Eyes pop out [noun phr] register surprise by opening your eyes wide. Ex: He was so surprised when he caught that fish that his *eyes popped out.*

FYI [abbrev] (business) *for your information.* Written on correspondence that someone wants you to read for general information, but not requiring action.

F bomb [noun] (2014 slang) refers to f_ _ _, which is not socially acceptable to say.

Facebook [noun] social networking computer site.

Face off [noun] (sports; hockey, soccer) At the beginning of a game and after every goal opposing players try to gain possession of the puck/ball. Ex: I was surprised that the Green Team got the ball after the *face off.*

Face the music [verb phr] accept the consequences of an action. Ex: He robbed a store and must *face the music.*

Fade from public view [verb phr] no longer newsworthy. Ex: The actor has *faded from public view.*

Fade into oblivion [verb phr] disappear. Ex: Childhood memories *fade into oblivion.*

Fair and square [adv phr] win without cheating. Ex: He won the foot race *fair and square*.

Fair game [noun] can be taken advantage of Ex: Be sure to keep your purse close to you so you won't be *fair game* for a thief.

Fair haired boy [noun] the favorite. Ex: Frank is the *fair haired boy* of the math teacher.

Fair sex [noun] women. Ex: The *fair sex* always complains they are not treated equally.

Fair to middlin' [verb phr] (1930's country western expression) O.K. a reply when someone asks, "How are you?" You reply, "*Fair to middlin'*."

Fair weather friends [noun] people who are only your friends when everything is going well. If you have any hardships or problems in your life, they will leave. Ex: Now that Luke has lost his job, many of his *fair weather friends* no longer call him.

Fake me out [verb phr] fool me. Ex: You really *faked me out*! I didn't know you could run that fast.

Fal de ral [noun] nonsense. Ex: That's a lot of *fal de ral*. Where are the facts?

Fall into line [verb phr] conform to what is expected. Ex: You better *fall into line* and do what your Father says.

Fall in love [verb phr] realize that you have deep feeling for someone. Ex: You might f*all in love* more than once.

Falling apart [verb phr] emotionally upset. Ex: She is *falling apart* since her purse was stolen.

Falling like flies [verb phr] succumbing rapidly. Ex: The enemy is *falling like flies*.

Falling out [noun] argument. Ex: I had a *falling out* with my girlfriend yesterday.

Famous last words [noun phr] make a statement, but no one believes the statement will be true. You reply, "*Famous last words*".

Fancy that! [1940's exclamation of amazement] (See *Lord love a duck*)

Fanny pack [noun] a small nylon or leather pouch that straps around your waist in which you can carry money, band aids, sunscreen, Kleenex, etc. Used by both men and women especially when hiking or bicycling. Ex: I think I have some band aids in my *fanny pack*.

Far and away [adj phr] absolutely. Ex: That car has *far and away* the best warranty.

Far be it for me [noun expression] not my opinion or what I would endorse. Ex: *Far be it for me* to say that politicians are truthful.

Fallback position [noun] (business) second plan for action if the first proposal is unacceptable. Ex: I think you will have to retreat to a *fallback position* and come up with another plan.

Far cry from [noun] opposite from an acceptable or valued thing. Ex: This hotel sure is a *far cry from* the Hilton.

Far out [adj phr] #1 great. Ex: The new convention rooms are *far out!* #2 weird. Ex: His behavior has been *far out* since he returned from Africa.

Fast and furiously [adv phr] rapidly. Ex: We were painting *fast and furiously* before it rained.

Fast food [noun] quick meals prepared at a restaurant . (Usually hamburgers, french fries and a drink) Ex: Many people lead busy lives and eat a lot of *fast food*.

Fast lane [noun] living with a lot of risk and sometimes danger in your life. e.g. driving too fast, drinking a lot, etc. Ex: I am not surprised that he was arrested for speeding. He has been living in the *fast lane* for a long time.

Fast shuffle [noun] elude someone. Ex: Let's give Linda the *fast shuffle.* (See *Give someone the slip*)

Fast talker [noun] someone who manipulates others verbally. Ex: He is such a *fast talker* he could sell people worthless land.

Fast track [noun] (business) promoted rapidly. Ex: She is on the *fast track* and is now a director.

(The) faster I go, the behinder I get (cliché) it is best not to hurry through tasks, because quite often you have to re-do them.

Faster than greased lightning. [adj phr] extremely fast. Ex: Jeff won that race because he was *faster than greased lightning.*

Fat cat [noun] wealthy. Ex: The CEOs are *fat cats.*

Fat chance [noun] unlikely. Ex: "Ron is going back to college next year." "*Fat chance* he is. He has no money."

Fat city [noun] having lots of money. Ex: If I get this contract, I will be in *fat city.*

Fat, dumb, and happy [adj phr] ignorant of or deliberately ignoring reality. Ex: Even with the other layoffs, Jack will be *fat, dumb, and happy* as long as his project is not canceled.

Fat farm [noun] an expensive resort for wealthy people to diet. There are regulated exercises and meals. Ex: I lost 14 pounds at the *fat farm.*

Fat is in the fire [noun phr] escalate an already volatile situation so it is likely to explode. Ex: When you made that last remark, I knew the *fat was in the fire.*

Fat of the land [noun phr] ecological resources available to you. Ex: Many Eskimos live off the *fat of the land.*

Fate worse than death [noun phr] unpleasant future. Ex: Running out of our natural resources would be a *fate worse than death.*

Feast or famine [noun phr] there is a lot of something or nothing. Ex: Either I have a lot of work or none - it's *feast or famine.*

Feather his nest [verb phr] use situations and people to accumulate more wealth. Ex: He used Don's connections with his company to *feather his own nest.*

Feather in his cap [noun phr] achieve an admirable feat. Ex: Being elected President of his class was a *feather in his cap.*

Fed up [verb] totally disgusted. Ex: I am *fed up* with your behavior.

Feed you a line [verb phr] flatter someone. Ex: Can't you tell he is just *feeding you a line?*

Feel him out [verb phr] try to ascertain how someone feels about a situation. Ex: *Feel him out* and see if he would be willing to go in with us on the deal.

Feel it in my bones [verb phr] intuition that something is going to happen. Ex: I think we're going to sell the house today. I *feel it in my bones.*

Feel small [verb phr] be humiliated. Ex: When I asked him to pay for his part of the meal, he had no money and *felt small.*

Feel the pinch [verb phr] be short of money. Ex: The college student was *feeling the pinch* and had to get a part time job.

Feel your oats [verb phr] live recklessly. Ex: He is really *feeling his oats* since he moved away from home.

Feeling no pain [verb phr] quite drunk. Ex: Hal was *feeling no pain* after he drank a six pack of beer.

Feeling run down [verb phr] feeling tired. Ex: I *feel run down* ever since I had the flu.

Feet of clay [noun phr] not able to take action rapidly. Ex: I should have bought that stock right away but I had *feet of clay.*

Fell by the wayside [verb phr] choose the wrong path of action to take. Ex: When she started taking drugs, she *fell by the wayside.*

Fell flat [verb] #1 was rejected. Ex: I presented my idea to management but it f*ell flat.* #2 failed. Ex: I thought that project would *fall flat.* Not enough resources were allocated.

Fell for it [verb phr] be gullible and someone takes advantage of you. Ex: David really *fell for the scheme* and got swindled out of all his money.

Fell from grace [verb phr] not popular or the favorite any more. Ex: My sister *fell from grace* when she did not finish college.

Fell into place [verb phr] things are working out smoothly. Ex: Everything *fell into place* for him after he graduated and found a job right away.

Fell on deaf ears [verb phr] not listened to. Ex: His words *fell on deaf ears.*

Fell on hard times [verb phr] become poor. Ex: The couple *fell on hard times* last year when he lost his job.

Fell on your face [verb phr] do something embarrassing. Ex: I could not remember my speech and *fell on my face.*

Fell off the turnip truck [verb phr] naïve about a situation.

Fell off the wagon [verb phr] begin drinking alcohol again after abstaining. Ex: Ron *fell off the wagon* and is going to Alcoholics Anonymous again.

Fell short of [verb phr] did not meet expectations. Ex: He *fell short of* the record set by his brother in the high jump.

Fell through the cracks [verb phr] an important part of a situation was ignored. Ex: That information *fell through the cracks* and that was why the plan did not work out.

Fender bender [noun] an auto accident where little damage occurs to either vehicle. Ex: "I heard you got into an automobile accident." "Oh, it was just a *fender bender.*"

Fer sure [prep phr] affirmation of what someone has just said. Ex: "I sure like Joyce's new hairdo." "*Fer sure.*"

Fess up [verb] tell the truth, confess. Ex: Come on, *'fess up.* Did you eat all of the chips?

Few and far between [adj phr] sparse. Ex: Vegetables are *few and far between* in my garden.

Few bricks short of a full load [noun phr] acting illogical. Ex: His behavior indicates that he is a *few bricks short of a full load.*

Few tricks up his sleeve [noun phr] keep secrets from people so you can outsmart them. Ex: I still have a *few tricks up my sleeve* when it comes to stretching the budget.

Fiddle around [verb phr] waste time. Ex: Don't *fiddle around.* Start your homework now. (See *Dilly dally*)

Fiddle faddle [1940's slang] Ex: Oh *fiddle faddle.* I can't get the lid off this jar. (See *Fiddlesticks*)

Fiddlesticks [1940's slang] (See *Fiddle faddle*)

Fifth wheel [noun] someone in a group who is unwanted or not liked. Ex: Janet felt like a *fifth wheel* when they all decided to go to the beach and did not invite her.

Fifty lashes with a wet noodle [1950's slang expression] joking but mildly irritated with someone. Ex: What do you mean you spilled your coke in my car? *Fifty lashes with a wet noodle.*

Fight fire with fire [verb phr] return aggressive behavior with aggression. Ex: It is necessary to *fight fire with fire* to get him to understand our position.

Fight like cats and dogs [verb phr] not getting along well. Ex: The brother and sister *fight like cats and dogs.*

Fight tooth and nail [verb] fight physically with someone. Ex: Jerome fought *tooth and nail* to win the boxing championship.

Fill 'er up [verb phr] said to the operator of a full service gas station when you want your car gas tank completely filled.

Fill his shoes [verb phr] an adequate replacement for someone. Ex: Fred was such a great person. It will hard to *fill his shoes,* but I will try.

Fill in [verb] substitute. Ex: Can you *fill in* for me at the card game tonight?

Fill in the gaps [verb phr] give needed information to someone. Ex: I was late to the meeting, so will you *fill in the gaps* for me?

Fill me in [verb phr] let me know what the plan is. Ex: *Fill me in* when I get back from vacation.

Fill the bill [verb phr] an adequate solution. Ex: Marty's idea does not quite *fill the bill.*

Finders keepers [noun] (children's saying. "*Finders keepers,* losers weepers") keep something you find and not try to return it to the owner.

Fine how-do-you-do [noun phr] things did not turn out as you expected. You say, "*That's a fine how-do-you-do.*" (See *Fine kettle of fish*)

Fine kettle of fish [noun phr] unexpected problems. (See *Fine how-do-you-do*)

Fingers in the pie [noun phr] too many people are involved in a situation and completely confuse the issue. Ex: Too many people have their *fingers in the pie* so it is difficult to make a decision. (See *Flies in the ointment*)

Fingered him [verb]   pointed him out as the guilty party.   Ex: The victim *fingered the person* who robbed him.

Finish off [verb]   #1 eat it all.   Ex: Why don't you *finish off* the rest of the potatoes?   #2 kill.   Ex: The murderer *finished off* his victim.

Fire drill [noun] (business)   having to take action immediately on an item without being given proper time to gather data.   Ex: We have another *fire drill* this morning.   Be prepared to work through lunch.

Fire power [noun] (business)   how much influence you have.   Ex: The other organization has more *fire power* than we do.

First and foremost [adv]   first and most important.   Ex: *First and foremost* we must have a clear goal.

First come, first served [cliché]   the first person arriving at an event gets the best choices of whatever is offered.   Ex: We better get to the picnic early.   *First come, first served*, you know.

First hand [adv]   experience directly.   Ex: I tried skating and found out how it felt *first hand*.

First things first [noun phr]   the very first item to consider.   Ex : I know we have to paint the boat, but *first things first.* The seats have to be re-covered.

Fish out of water [noun phr]   feel uncomfortable doing something.   Ex: I feel like a *fish out of water* when I have to give a speech.

Fishing for compliments [verb phr]   trying to get someone to give you a compliment.   Ex: He is always *fishing for compliments.* He seems to be insecure.

Fist bump [noun phr] (2012 slang) a "high-five" gesture made by two people bumping right fists together. (See *High five*)

Fit as a fiddle [verb phr] in good physical shape. Ex: Tom runs a mile a day to stay *fit as a fiddle*.

Fit to be tied [verb phr] angry or upset. Ex: When I got a flat tire, I was *fit to be tied*. (See *Go ballistic*)

Fits like a glove [verb phr] fits exactly right . Usually refers to clothing. Ex: My new jacket *fits like a glove*. (See *Fits to a T*)

Fits to a "T" (See *Fits like a glove*)

Fix up [verb] #1 arrange a date. Ex: Would you like me to *fix you up* with my sister for the dance? #2 repair or decorate. Ex: I'm going to *fix up* the extra bedroom and make an office out of it.

Fix your wagon [verb phr] prevent you from doing something. Ex: I'm going to *fix your wagon* so you won't irritate him anymore.

Fixed for [verb] supply. (as cash) Ex: How are you *fixed for* going out Saturday night?

Flappin' in the breeze [verb phr] an idea expressed freely and without constraints. Ex: "She said she was going to leave him." "Yes, well her mouth was just *flappin' in the breeze.*"

Flash mob [noun] (2013) group that comes together spontaneously and performs either a dance or song and disperses.

Flash in the pan [noun phr] an idea or person that is bold and flamboyant and sounds good initially, but fades over time. Ex: I thought that idea would work, but it was just a *flash in the pan.*

Flat broke [verb] no money at all. Ex: I would like to go to the movies with you, but I am *flat broke.*

Flatbacking your way to success [verb phr] (business) giving sexual favors in return for promotions is "*flatbacking your way to success.*"

Flatline [verb] #1 no change in growth. Ex: The company's stock *flatlined* last quarter. #2 dead. Ex: When I felt for his pulse it was clear he was *flatlined.*

Flatter than a pancake [adv phr] extremely flat. Ex: I smashed that ant *flatter than a pancake.*

Flavor of the month [noun phr] (business) popular concept. Ex: Empowering employees seems to be *the flavor of the month.*

Flea market [noun] collection of used items sold at bargain prices. Ex: I got this great tea set at the *flea market* on Saturday.

Flesh and blood [noun] relatives. Ex: I can't believe those people are his own *flesh and blood.* They are so different from him.

Flesh out [verb] enhance a document or story with more detail. Ex: If you *flesh out* this story, it will be easier to understand.

Flex your muscles [verb] show your strength or superiority. Ex: The body builder *flexed his muscles.*

Flick your Bic [verb] light a cigarette lighter. Ex: Let me *flick my Bic* so we can see in this cave.

Flies in the ointment [noun phr] Too many people involved in the situation. (See *Fingers in the pie*)

Flip out [verb] become angry. Ex: He *flipped out* when I told him that his car had a dent. (See *Fully edged)*

Flip over [verb] (teen) fall in love. Ex: When he saw the cheerleader, he *flipped over* her.

Flip someone off [verb phr] #1 not take someone seriously; show a lack of respect. Ex: She just *flipped off* her ex-boyfriend. #2 make an obscene hand gesture. Ex: Those teenagers just *flipped off* someone in that car.

Flip your lid [verb phr] lose your temper. Ex: I *flipped my lid* when the kids spilled tomato juice on my carpet. (See *Blow your top*)

Floating around [verb] freely distributed. Ex: That directive is *floating around* the office everywhere.

Fluff and stuff [noun phr] meaningless trivia added in conversation or in a proposal to make it appear more important. Ex: That proposal is pretty good if you eliminate all the *fluff and stuff.*

Fly ball [noun] (sports, baseball) a ball that does not hit the ground when hit. Ex: The batter hit a *fly ball* which was caught by the shortstop.

Fly-by-night [verb phr] not a reputable or trustworthy endeavor. Ex: It was a fly-by-night operation and was raided by the police.

Fly by the seat of your pants [verb phr] improvise. Ex: I didn't have a plan so had to *fly by the seat of my pants.*

Fly in the face of [verb phr] an idea that will be accepted in spite of all opposition. Ex: I think this idea is good enough to *fly in the face of* all negative comments.

Fly me [verb] (impolite) Have sex with me. (See *Do me)*

Fly off the handle [verb phr] lose your temper. Ex: He *flew off the handle* and punched Ken. (See *Flip your lid*)

Fly the bird [verb phr] make an obscene hand sign to someone. (See *Flip someone off*)

Fly the coop [verb phr] leave and not tell anyone where you have gone. Ex: He *flew the coop* and we have not seen him for six months.

Flyaway hair [noun] hair that is not smooth and silky. It sticks out here and there, usually because it has static electricity in it. Ex: I have to use a lot of hairspray because I have *flyaway hair* today.

Flying high [verb phr] excited, optimistic and enthusiastic. Ex: He was *flying high* after getting a promotion.

Foggiest idea [noun] slightest notion. Ex: I haven't the *foggiest idea* where I put my sunglasses.

Fold down [verb phr] prepare bed covers for sleeping. Ex: Please *fold down* the covers for the children.

Fold in [verb] #1 reluctantly concede to someone else's wishes or decision. Ex: I knew he would *fold in* if we all disagreed with him. #2 gently add ingredients in a recipe, turning the mixture with a spoon. Ex: *Fold in* two eggs before pouring the brownies into a greased pan.

Fold up [verb] collapse. Ex: Please *fold up* the bleacher seats when the game is over.

Follow in his Father's footsteps [verb phr] adopting the same occupation as your Father. Ex: He *followed in his Father's footsteps* and became a lawyer.

Follow suit [verb] #1 in card games, play a card of the same suit. Ex: You forgot to *follow suit*. You were supposed to play a diamond. #2 take the same action. Ex: When the bank lowers its rates, the other banks will *follow suit* or lose business.

Follow the crowd [verb phr] conform to whatever the group is doing. Ex: Why do you always *follow the crowd?* You should learn to think for yourself.

Follow through [verb] complete an action. Ex: You need to *follow through* on your batting swing.

Follow your nose [verb phr] smell something very delectable and try to find the origin of that smell. Ex: He *followed his nose* and found the bread Mother had just baked.

Food for thought [noun phr] information that makes one think. Ex: Larry's speech on family values was *food for thought.*

Food insecurity [noun phr] Politically correct term for anyone who does not know where their next meal will come from. Ex: There are some children in my school who have *food insecurity.*

Fool around [verb] #1 wasting time. Ex: You kids stop *fooling around* and clean up your room. (See *dilly dally*) #2 promiscuous or unfaithful. Ex: I sure didn't know that Dan was *fooling around* with his secretary.

Foot in his mouth [noun phr] say something that is embarrassing to yourself and others. Ex: When I said we didn't need any more budget cuts, I really put my *foot in my mouth.*

Foot in mouth disease [noun phr] have a bad habit of speaking impulsively without thinking of the consequences. Ex: Be careful of what you say. You've had *foot in mouth disease* before!

Foot in the door [noun phr] create the opportunity to achieve a personal goal for yourself. Ex: You have a *foot in the door* to being successful.

Foot the bill [verb phr] pay for. Ex: My daughter expects me to *foot the bill* when she goes to college.

Footloose and fancy free [verb phr] have no responsibilities and be free to do as you wish. Sometimes said by a person just getting a divorce: "Now I will be *footloose and fancy free.*"

Footsie [noun] (See *Play footsie*)

For all the tea in China [prep phr] something of great magnitude. Ex: You couldn't change her mind *for all the tea in China.*

For crying in the beer [exclamation of amazement] (See *For crying out loud)*

For crying out loud [exclamation of amazement] (See *For goodness sakes*)

For good [prep phr] permanently. Ex: I gave Margaret my book on house plants *for good*. (See *For keeps)*

For good measure [prep phr] a little bit extra. Ex: I put a list of references in the manual *for good measure.*

For goodness sakes [exclamation of amazement] (See *For crying out loud*)

For keeps [prep phr] permanently. (See *For good)*

For love nor money [prep phr] not likely to occur. Ex: I wouldn't run five miles *for love nor money.*

For old time's sake [prep phr] repeat an action you used to do with old friends for sentimental reasons. Ex: Let's have another beer *for old times' sake.*

For Pete's sake [exclamation of amazement] Ex: *For Pete's sake,* take off those muddy boots in the house! (See *For crying out loud*)

For short [prep phr] abbreviated form of the word. Ex: My name is Robert, Bob *for short.*

For the asking [prep phr] free upon request. Ex: You can have a free tape with your new DVD player, *just for the asking.*

For the birds [prep phr] not desirable. Ex: That dress is *for the birds.*

For the long haul

For the long haul [prep phr] lengthy duration of time. Ex: He
        planned to be a plumber *for the long haul.* (See *For
        the long term*)

For the long term [prep phr] permanently. (See *For the long
        haul*)

For the most part [prep phr] mainly. Ex: *For the most part,* I
        like eggs. Of course I don't like them scrambled.

For the record [prep phr] what actually happened. Ex: Just *for
        the record*, I had nothing to do with the missing tools.

For the time being [prep phr] now. Ex: *For the time being* you
        will get no more favors.

For two cents [prep phr] close to taking an impulsive negative
        action. Ex: *For two cents,* I would punch him.

Force his hand [verb phr] provoke an action or reaction from
        another person. Ex: If I *forced his hand*, he would
        probably back down from his position.

Forclempt [verb] all choked up. Ex: Some of the actors on
        Saturday Night Live did a skit in which they are
        forclempt over many situations.

Fore-runner [noun] an idea or product which is outstanding in
        its field. Ex: The model A car was the *fore-runner* of
        the powerful sedans of today.

Foregone conclusion [noun] already decided upon. Ex: It was
        a *foregone conclusion* that the boy and the dog would
        become best friends.

Forever and a day [adv phr] exaggeration of forever. Ex: I will
        love you *forever and a day.*

Forge ahead [verb] keep trying to make progress. Ex: We must *forge ahead* with our plans for our new home.

Fork over [verb phr] give something to someone else. Ex: I know you have my ball. Come on, *fork it over.*

Forty winks [noun] a nap. Ex: I've got to get *forty winks* before the party tonight.

Foul up [verb] make a mistake. Ex: Don't *foul up* and miss the ball. (See *Screw up*)

Found a gold mine [verb phr] discover a potentially lucrative situation. Ex: I *found a gold mine* when I hired Sally. She has lots of computer experience.

Found himself [verb phr] realizing a desire. Ex: He *found himself* wanting to buy a new car.

Four bits [noun] 50 cents. Ex: Bubble gum costs *four bits.*

Four wheeler [noun] a vehicle with all-wheel drive, good for driving on ice or snow. Ex: If you go to the mountains in the winter you need to have a *four wheeler.*

Fox in the hen house [noun phr] (country western) doing something sneaky or dishonest; making trouble. Ex: When those two boys got together, I knew there was a *fox in the hen house.*

Freak him out [verb phr] #1 frighten him. Ex: If Cindy watches the late-night terror movie, it will *freak her out.* #2 experience something absurd. Ex: Bill says the punk haircuts *freak him out.*

Free and easy [adj phr] #1 carefree. Ex: He was *free and easy* after his divorce. #2 no moral issues. (See *Play fast and loose*)

Free as a bird [verb phr] totally unencumbered. Ex: I can go shopping with you Saturday. I'm *free as a bird* then.

Free for all [noun phr] many people engaged in raucous behavior. Ex: It was a *free for all* at the tavern.

Free for the asking [verb phr] readily available at no cost. Ex: Pamphlets on drug abuse are *free for the asking*.

Free loaders [noun] not paying for food or lodging, but mooching off other people. Ex: His family sure has a lot of *free loaders*.

Free meal ticket [noun] invitation to dinner. Ex: I have a *free meal ticket* at my Mom's every Tuesday night.

Free spirit [noun] independent thinker; non-conformist. Ex: He is going to live in a Tibetan monastery. He is a real *free spirit*.

Freewheeling [verb] no rules or guidelines. Ex: Internationally competing companies are quite often *freewheeling*.

Freebies [noun] favors not expected to be repaid. Ex: I'll buy your lunch today. It's a *freebie*.

Freeze [verb] #1 <u>stop!!</u> a command used when someone is pursuing you with a weapon. <u>To be taken very seriously</u> . #2 turn to ice.

Frenemy [noun] (2013 slang) someone who pretends to be your friend, but is really an enemy.

Fresh as a daisy [adv phr] energized and looking neat and tidy. Ex: Joyce looks *fresh as a daisy* today.

Fresh out of [verb] usually said in a store where they have just depleted a product. Ex: We are f*resh out of* tomatoes.

Freudian slip [noun] make a sexual remark accidentally and cover your embarrassment by saying "I made a *Freudian slip.*"

Fried [verb] angry. Ex: I was really *fried* when he put a dent in my car. (See *Fly off the handle)*

Fritter away [verb phr] (country western) waste time. Ex: Do not *fritter away* the day. It is time to study.

Frog in your throat [noun phr] have phlegm in your throat and have to clear your throat by coughing before you can speak. Ex: I'm sorry. I have a *frog in my throat* this morning.

From all four corners of the earth [prep phr] from everywhere possible in the entire world. Ex: They came from *all four corners of the earth* to hear the famous rock star sing.

From cover to cover [prep phr] entire book. Ex: I read the book *from cover to cover.*

From scratch [prep phr] #1 from the basic elements. Ex: Ellen baked this cake *from scratch*, not from a cake mix. #2 from the beginning. Ex: When the dog tore up his composition, John had to create a new one *from scratch.*

From soup to nuts [prep phr] includes everything about the subject. Ex: This book includes everything *from soup to nuts.* (See *Everything but the kitchen sink*)

From the Black Lagoon [prep phr] undesirable or dreadful place. Ex: The new carpet in the lobby came *from the Black Lagoon.*

From the bottom of my heart [prep phr] sincere. Ex: I care for you *from the bottom of my heart.*

From the frying pan into the fire [prep phr] go from a risky situation to an even more risky one. Ex: When I went to work for that new company I went *from the frying pan into the fire.*

From the get go [prep phr] beginning. Ex: The candidates did not disclose their issues *from the get go.* (See *From the top*)

From the horse's mouth [prep phr] (See *Straight from the horse's mouth)*

From the sublime to the ridiculous [prep phr] from one extreme to another. Ex: His poetry ranged *from the sublime to the ridiculous.*

From the top [prep phr] beginning. Ex: Let's take it *from the top.* What is our first step? (See *From the word go*)

From the word go [prep phr] (See *From the top)*

From time to time [prep phr] occasionally. Ex: *From time to time* I like to go sailing.

From way back [prep phr] distant past. Ex: I remember Shelly *from way back* in high school.

From womb to tomb [prep phr] (business) from beginning to end. Ex: This project has been difficult *from womb to tomb.*

Frontload [verb] (business) provide advance information before a meeting. Ex: Be sure to *frontload* Bob before he comes to the meeting since he has been on vacation.

Front room [noun] (1950's slang) living room. Ex: We have two sofas in our *front room*.

Front-runner [noun] person who is in the lead in a competition.

Frou-frou [adj] fancy. Ex: I see you are wearing your *frou frou* dress today.

Frosted [verb] irritated. Ex: I was *frosted* when he got home late. (See *Get your dander up*)

Frosting on the cake [noun phr] something extra or unexpected in an already successful situation. Ex: Giving us a raise for getting the project done on time was *frosting on the cake*.

Frown on [verb] disapprove. Ex: The boss will *frown on* your taking more than an hour for lunch.

Frumpy [adj] unkempt. Ex: That girl is frumpy. She hasn't even combed her hair.

Fry your brains [verb phr] ruin your memory by taking drugs. Ex: Many college students in the 1960's *fried their brains* on drugs.

Fuddy Duddy [noun] (1950's country western) old fashioned person with outdated ideas. Ex: My grandmother is such a *fuddy duddy*. She even irons her sheets!

Fuel to the fire [noun phr] (See *Add fuel to the fire*)

Full blast [adv] top level of speed. Ex: Don't turn on the heater *full blast*.

Full blown [adj] completely developed. Ex: He has a *full blown* case of AIDS.

Full bore [adv] giving an action 100% of your energy. Ex: He ran the race *full bore* the whole way.

Full of beans [verb phr] not credible; full of nonsense. Ex: I don't believe that Rod is going to get a Mercedes. He is *full of beans*. (See *Full of bull*)

Full of bull [verb phr] not believable. (See *Full of beans*)

Full of himself [adj phr] arrogant and proud. Ex: Sam is sure *full of himself*.

Full of hot air [verb phr] not credible. (See *Full of beans*)

Full of it [verb phr] (See *Full of beans*)

Full steam ahead [adv phr] proceed aggressively. Ex: I think we should undertake the project full steam ahead.

Full tilt [adv phr] giving 100%. (See *Full bore*)

Fully edged [verb] angry. (See *Fly off the handle*)

Fumbling in the dark [verb phr] working at something without adequate training or skill. Ex: You're just *fumbling in the dark* and don't really know enough about building this cabinet.

Fun and games [noun phr] something enjoyable and not serious. Can apply to relationships. Ex: I thought we were just having *fun and games*. I didn't know you were serious.

Fundage [noun] money. I hope to have enough fundage to go to Spain this summer.

Funkmobile [noun] (1970's slang) unique old car. Ex: That 1950 Chevrolet is a cool funkmobile.

Funnier than a rubber crutch [adj phr] (1940's slang) extremely funny. Ex: That joke was *funnier than a rubber crutch*.

Funny farm [noun] mental institution. Ex: If I don't get away from this stress, they will have to send me to the *funny farm*.

Fuss budget [noun] (1950's slang) picky person.

Fussing and feuding [verb]   complaining and arguing. Ex: You
kids stop *fussing and feuding* and come to dinner.

GN [abbrev] *good night* or *get naked.* (whichever applies!) cell phone texting abbreviation.

Gad about [noun] someone who is very social and enjoys visiting many people. Ex: Marcie is such a *gad about.* She knows everyone.

Gadzooks [1950's exclamation of amazement] (See *Good grief*)

Gag me with a spoon [1960's expression of disgust] Ex: He just burped out loud. *Gag me with a spoon.*

Gained his second wind [verb phr] recover energy and not be tired. Ex: He *gained his second wind* and finished the race in record time.

Gaining ground [verb phr] closing in on the competition. Ex: The Bears team is *gaining ground* on the Cardinals team.

Galloping trots [noun] diarrhea. Ex: When I had the flu, I had the *galloping trots.* (See *Montezuma's Revenge*)

Gang up on [verb phr] act as a group to persuade someone to change his mind. Ex: We had to *gang up on* Charlie to get our tools back.

Gangsta rap [noun] popular rap music whose lyrics idolize crime and violence and devalue police. Ex: Some *gangsta rap* musicians are idolized by teenagers. Pioneered by Ice T.

Gas guzzler [noun] an older car that does not get good gas mileage. Ex: My old car is a *gas guzzler.*

Gathering dust [verb phr] neglected; unused. Ex: My piano is *gathering dust.* I haven't played it for a year.

Gee whiz [1950's exclamation of surprise] Ex: *Gee whiz,* I got an "A" on the test. (See *Gee whilikers*)

Gee whilikers [1950's exclamation of surprise] (See *Gee whiz*)

Geez [exclamation of surprise] Ex: *Geez,* I didn't know you had a sailboat! (See *Gee whiz*)

Geek [noun] very intelligent person who is a genius at computer programs. Ex: Those two *geeks* are always playing computer games.

Generation X [noun] people born in the 1960's and 1970's. Ex: The *Generation X* kids work to live, rather than living to work.

Generous to a fault [verb phr] give away anything you have. Ex: Bob is *generous to a fault.* He gave his new jacket to his son.

Get a break [verb phr] #1 obtain an opportunity or advantage unexpectedly. Ex: He *got a lucky break* and is now vice-president of the company. #2 rest period. Ex: The musicians will *get a break* in 15 minutes.

Get a charge out of it [verb phr] be amused. He *got a charge out of the antics* of his granddaughter.

Get a do [verb phr] get your hair styled professionally. Ex: After work today I'm going to the hairdressers to *get a new do.*

Get a grip [verb phr] control your emotions. Ex: *Get a grip* before you yell at your son. (See *Get a hold of yourself*)

Get a handle on [verb phr] understand it. Ex: Tell me more about the problem so I can *get a handle on* it.

Get a hold of yourself [verb phr] control yourself. (See *Get a grip*)

Get a kick out of it [verb phr] enjoy it. Ex: I *get a kick out of* playing with my children.

Get a leg up [verb phr] have an advantage.

Get a life! [verb phr] Be actively interested in living. Said sarcastically to someone who needs to be more involved or have more fun.

Get a move on [verb phr] hurry up. Ex: *Get a move on* or you will miss the bus. (See *Get off your dime*)

Get a pink slip [verb phr] be fired. Ex: The entire editorial department got *pink slips* today.

Get a rise out of [verb phr] reaction from someone irritating you. Ex: He can always *get a rise out of* his sister by pulling her hair.

Get all your ducks in a row [verb phr] #1 arrange and manage your life properly. Ex: When I *get all my ducks in a row,* I can retire. #2 (business) organize your presentation and have your ideas well backed up. Ex: You better have *all your ducks in a row* before you give out those sales figures.

Get along [verb] be compatible. Ex: Stop arguing! Can't you and your sister *get along* for five minutes? #2 manage. Ex: I don't know how I will *get along* when Don is on vacation. #3 leave. It's getting dark, so you kids *get along* home now.

Get an earful [verb phr] hear something secretive or controversial. Ex: I *got an earful* about the new contract when I met with Darrin.

Get anywhere [verb phr] accomplish something. Ex: He is not going to *get anywhere* unless he practices the piano every day.

Get away with murder [verb phr] take advantage of people and not be reprimanded. Ex: Some people say the boss's son *gets away with murder.*

Get down on all fours [verb phr] crawl. Ex: *Get down on all fours* with the baby.

Get down to brass tacks [verb phr] the basics of a situation. Ex: Let's *get down to brass tacks.* Do you plan to contribute to the charity or not?

Get even [verb phr] avenge a wrong done to you. Ex: He *got even* with his brother.

Get him pegged [verb phr] determine his motivation. Ex: Once we *get him pegged*, we can work better with him.

Get his back up [verb phr] become angered. Ex: Don't *get your back up.* I was not talking about you. (See *Get your dander up*)

Get his comeuppance [verb phr] get what you deserve. Ex: You will *get your comeuppance* when you have children of your own.

Get his goat [verb phr] annoy him. Ex: Why do you want to *get his goat* by teasing him? (See *Grates on my nerves*)

Get in gear [verb phr] start working. Ex: Let's *get in gear* and get this car fixed by noon.

Get in on the ground floor   [verb phr]   participate at the beginning of a venture. Ex: We need to *get in on the ground floor* of this project so we know what is really happening.

Get in your hair   [verb phr]   annoy you. Ex: Don't let him *get in your hair* by making fun of you.

Get into shape   [verb phr]   condition your body. Ex: I'm going to exercise and *get into shape.*

Get it   [verb]   #1 fetch. Ex: *Get the juice* from the refrigerator. #2 understand.   Ex: I told my husband about the problem twice, but he didn't *get it.*

Get it off your chest   [verb phr]   talk about it. Ex: You need to *get it off your chest.* Why don't you tell your sister how you feel?

Get it on   [verb phr]   have sex. (See *Get laid)*

Get it together   [verb phr]   be organized. Ex: I need to *get it together* and clean out my bedroom.

Get laid [verb]   have sex. (See *Get it on)*

Get lost!   [verb]   go away. Ex: He is always telling his little brother to *get lost.*

Get lucky   [verb]   a sexual favor is granted to you. Ex: Maybe you will *get lucky* tonight.

Get more mileage   [verb phr]   lasts longer. Ex: This hairspray *gets more mileage* than my old brand.

Get nailed down   [verb phr]   get a final decision made. Ex: Let's *get* the plan *nailed down.*

Get off my back! [verb phr] stop putting pressure on me. Ex: *Get off my back.* I have enough to do already. (See *Get off my case*)

Get off my case! [verb phr] quit hounding me! (See *Get off my back*)

Get off on the wrong foot [verb phr] make a poor first impression. Ex: When you go for your job interview don't *get off on the wrong foot.*

Get off Scot-free [verb phr] escape punishment or payment. Ex: He *got off scot-free* after robbing the grocery store.

Get off the ground [verb phr] get a project started. Ex: Once we *get* this project *off the ground* we can relax.

Get off your butt [verb phr] (impolite) get busy. Ex: You need to *get off your butt,* and get your homework done. (See *Get off your dime*)

Get off your dime [verb phr] get busy. (See *Get off your butt*)

Get on his calendar [verb phr] (business) schedule a meeting with him. Ex: When I *get on his calendar,* I will explain our position to him.

Get on his case [verb phr] chastise. Ex: I have to *get on his case* every night to get his homework done. (See *Jump on*)

Get on his good side [verb phr] be in favor with someone. Ex: You need to spend time with him to *get on his good side.* (See *Get on his good list*)

Get on his good list [verb phr] (See *Get on his good side*)

Get on the bandwagon [verb phr] join the group. Ex: You need to *get on the bandwagon.* We're all going to the beach.

Get on the horn [verb phr] call someone on the telephone. Ex: Let's *get on the horn* to Betty and ask her to go camping with us.

Get on the stick [verb phr] get busy. Ex: Let's *get on the stick* and get this wood chopped.

Get on your nerves [verb phr] irritate you. Ex: When Janelle bites her fingernails, it *gets on my nerves.* (See *Drives me to distraction*)

Get out of bed on the wrong side [verb phr] be cranky when you arise in the morning. Ex: I think you *got out of bed on the wrong side* this morning.

Get outta here! [exclamatory expression] said to someone who exaggerates a point. Ex: "I'm going to run the marathon in under three hours." *"Get outta here!"*

Get over [verb] #1 release emotional attachment. Ex: I bought my son a new puppy to help him *get over* losing his cat.

Get real! [expression of disbelief] said after someone says something that is mostly fantasy and not reality. Ex: "I think I will win the lottery." *"Get real!"*

Get rolling [verb] #1 leave. Ex: I better *get rolling.* I have to cook dinner tonight. #2 begin an activity. Ex: If I'm going to get the laundry done today I need to *get rolling* with it.

Get screwed [verb] #1 have sex. (See *Get laid*)

Get skunked [verb] (sports) not make any points in a game Ex: The soccer game score was 3 to 0. My team really *got skunked*. (fishing) I *got skunked*. I did not catch any fish.

Get soaked [verb] be cheated or over-charged for something. Ex: That's the last time I'll shop there and *get soaked*.

Get the ball rolling [verb phr] begin a project. Ex: Let's *get the ball rolling* by drawing up some plans. (See *Get with it*)

Get the chair [verb phr] be executed or sentenced to die by electrocution. Ex: The judge declared he would *get the chair* for his crime.

Get the drop on [verb phr] take advantage of an opportunity when it appears. Ex: Let's *get the drop on* the others by going to the lake to fish at 4:30 A.M. That's when the fish are really biting.

Get the gist of it [verb phr] a general understanding of the basic principles. Ex: I think I *get the gist of* the algebra problem.

Get the goods on him [verb phr] collect evidence of wrongdoing. Ex: The police detective *got the goods on* the criminal.

Get the hang of it [verb phr] master it. Ex: I think I *get the hang of* how to roller skate.

Get the lead out [verb phr] hurry. *Ex: Get the lead out* or you will miss your appointment. (See *Hot foot it)*

Get the nod [verb phr] received approval. Ex: The second company *gets the nod* to complete the contract.

Get the picture [verb phr] understand the main problem. Ex: She needs help with her science project. Do you *get the picture?* (See *Get the point*)

Get the point [verb phr] understand the main problem. (See *Get the picture*)

Get the sack [verb phr] fired. Ex: Lots of employees are *getting the sack* in that company. (See *Get a pink slip*)

Get the show on the road [verb phr] begin an activity. Ex: Let's *get the show on the road* and go to the beach.

Get the upper hand [verb phr] get the advantage. Ex: He *got the upper hand* in the bidding of the project.

Get to the bottom of it [verb phr] the actual truth of a situation. Ex: Let's *get to the bottom of it* and find out who took your wallet.

Get to the gist of it [verb phr] find the main point . Ex: After we *got to the gist of it,* we could solve the problem. (See *Get to the heart of the matter*)

Get to the heart of the matter [verb phr] find the main point. (See *Get to the gist of it*)

Get under your skin [verb phr] irritate you. Ex: Whenever you yell, it *gets under my skin.* (See *Get on your nerves*)

Get underfoot [verb phr] become an annoyance to someone. (Usually said about children or pets) Ex: That dog *gets underfoot* whenever I am preparing a meal.

Get up and go has got up and went [verb phr] loss of energy. Ex: "Why aren't you coming to the movie?" "My *get up and go has got up and went.*"

Get up to speed [verb phr] familiarize yourself with the task at hand. Ex: When I get *up to speed,* I will contribute more ideas. (See *Playing catch up)*

Get up with the chickens [verb phr] wake up early in the morning. Ex: I always *get up with the chickens.* You can accomplish more that way.

Get what's coming to you [verb phr] be treated exactly the way you have treated someone else. Ex: He will *get what's coming to him* for mistreating that dog. (See *Get your comeuppance)*

Get while the getting's good [verb phr] take advantage of a good situation before it changes. Ex: If we *get while the getting's good,* we can surf for two hours.

Get wind of [verb phr] found out about. Ex: They *got wind of* the impending merger of the two companies.

Get with it [verb phr] pay attention. Ex: *Get with it.* The movie starts in 15 minutes. (See *Get with the program)*

Get with the program [verb phr] (See *Get with it)*

Get your act together [verb phr] (See *Get with it)*

Get your brains fried [verb phr] unable to think clearly as a result of taking drugs. Ex: He was studying to be a doctor before he *got his brains fried.*

Get your dander up [verb phr] rile or irritate you. Ex: It *gets my dander up* when she is late. (See *Sets my teeth on edge)*

Get your ears lowered [verb phr] get a haircut. Ex: Looks like you *got your ears lowered* today.

Get your just desserts [verb phr] (See *Get what is coming to you*)

Get your nose out of joint [verb phr] be hurt. Ex: Every time we don't invite him, he *gets his nose out of joint.* (See *Bent out of shape)*

Get your rear in gear [verb phr] hurry up. Ex: *Get your rear in gear.* We have to be there in 15 minutes.

Gets in my hair [verb phr] irritates me. (See Get your dander up)

Getting cold feet [verb phr] cautious and hesitant. Ex: They *got cold feet* about jumping into the lake.

Getting rummy [verb phr] tired and unable to concentrate. Ex: Driving all night makes you *rummy.*

Gift of gab [noun phr] ability to communicate easily. Ex: Nancy has a real *gift of gab.* She can talk to anyone.

Gimme' a break [verb phr] give me some leeway. Ex: *Gimme' a break.* I have been skiing for only two months. That's why I fall down a lot. (See *Cut me some slack*)

Girl Friday [noun] indispensable female assistant. Ex: Susie is our *Girl Friday* and we couldn't run this office without her.

Give a hard time [verb phr] harass. Ex: He *gave her a hard time* about gaining weight.

Give a rip [verb phr] care. Ex: I don't *give a rip* about the score of the game.

Give a song and dance [verb phr] give an excuse that is not very credible. Ex: She *gave a real good song and dance,* but her Mother did not believe her.

Give and take [verb] compromise. Ex: It takes a lot of *give and take* to have a good marriage.

Give him a bad name [verb phr] say something that damages someone's reputation. Ex: The rumor someone started *gave him a bad name.*

Give him a hand [verb phr] help him. Ex: Could you *give him a hand*? He needs to move this lumber.

Give him a piece of your mind [verb phr] chastise someone. Ex: If he tracks mud in the house once more I will *give him a piece of my mind.* (See *Give him what for*)

Give him a run for his money [verb phr] compete aggressively. Ex: I will *give him a run for his money* on the basketball court tonight.

Give him a wedgie [verb phr] reach down someone's pants and pull their underwear up tightly. (usually involves teen boys) Ex: I gave Chris a wedgie yesterday and he really got mad.

Give him an earful [verb phr] chastise someone. Ex: Bennett was late to practice and *got an earful* from his coach. (See *Give him a piece of his mind*)

Give him an inch; he'll take a mile

Give him an inch; he'll take a mile [cliché] If you are lenient, someone will take advantage of you.

Give him enough rope to hang himself [verb phr] unscrupulous people will eventually get what they deserve. Ex: I am going to *give him enough rope to hang himself.*

Give him free rein [verb phr] give someone total freedom. Ex: I *gave him free rein* to decide what time he was coming home.

Give him the benefit of the doubt [verb phr] (See Benefit of the doubt)

Give him the bum's rush [verb phr] ignore the person.

Give him the creeps [verb phr] make someone uncomfortable. Ex: That new teacher *gives me the creeps.* He is always staring at me.

Give him the elbow [verb phr] #1 nudged him. Ex: I *gave him the elbow* when I saw that pretty girl. #2 encouraged him to speak. Ex: Joan *gave Jack the elbow* encouraging him to voice his opinion.

Give him the gate [verb phr] fire someone. (See *Get a pink slip*)

Give him the heave-ho [verb phr] fire someone. (See *Give him the gate*)

Give him the once over [verb phr] look at someone carefully to see if she is physically attractive to you. Ex: He *gave her the once over* and decided to ask her out.

Give him the raspberry [verb phr] boo someone. Ex: The player shoved his opponent and the fans *gave him the raspberry.*

Give him the run of the house [verb phr] treat as a family member. Ex: We *give* our dog *the run of the house* when we are gone.

Give him the slip [verb phr] (See Fast shuffle)

Give him the third degree [verb phr] question someone relentlessly. Ex: His father *gave him the third degree* when he wrecked the family car.

Give him the time of day [verb phr] give time and attention to someone. Ex: He doesn't *give me the time of day* since he got his promotion.

Give him what for [verb phr] chastise someone. (See *Give him a piece of your mind)*

Give it a face lift [verb phr] renovate it. Ex: Our house needs a *face lift.* I am going to paint it.

Give it a once over [verb phr] clean something superficially and not thoroughly. Ex: Just *give the car a once over* and we will go.

Give it a rest [verb phr] forget it. Ex: *Give it a rest.* I am tired of hearing about your problems. (See *Stuff it)*

Give it the gun [verb phr] make a car go faster. Ex: *Give it the gun* when we get to the passing lane.

Give it the old college try [verb phr] attempt to master it. Ex: I will *give it the old college try* and see if I can snowboard.

Give it to me in black and white [verb phr] in writing. Ex: You need to *give the report to me in black and white* so we will have a clear record.

Give it up [verb phr] (See *Give it a rest)*

Give me a break [verb phr] Don't make assumptions if you don't know the whole story. Ex: *Give me a break.* The reason I didn't do well on the test is that I had to take care of my brother last night. (See *Cut me some slack*)

Give me a buzz [verb phr] call me. Ex: *Give me a buzz* and we will talk about it. (See *Give me a jingle)*

Give me a jingle [verb phr] (See *Give me a buzz*)

Give me a ring [verb phr] (See *Give me a buzz)*

Give me five [verb phr] (gesture - Slap right hands together with someone when you agree heartily with them. (See *High five*)

Give me the whole scoop [verb phr] tell me everything about a situation. Ex: *Give me the whole scoop* about what happened yesterday.

Give my eye teeth [verb phr] an exaggeration of how much something is desired. Ex: She would *give her eye-teeth* for a chance to go to the Olympics. (See *Give my right arm*)

Give my right arm [verb phr] (See *Give my eye-teeth*)

Give the devil his due [verb phr] give credit to someone you dislike. Ex: Tom is really hard to work with, but I'll have to *give the devil his due*; he did get the job done on time.

Give the go-ahead [verb phr] gave permission. Ex: I *gave the go-ahead* to have the house remodeled.

Give up [verb] #1 stop eating or using something. Ex: I have to *give up* drinking colas if I want to lose weight. #2 surrender or concede. Ex: I *give up;* I can't work this cross-word puzzle.

Give up the ghost [verb phr] die. Ex: Our old dog finally *gave up the ghost.* (See *Pushing up daisies)*

Give you an earful [verb phr] #1 relate gossip. Ex: I can *give you an earful* about Jack's new girlfriend. #2 reprimand. Ex: He *gave the child an earful* for running out into the street.

Give you the brush-off [verb phr] ignore you. Ex: She *gave her ex-husband the brush-off.* (See *Give you the cold shoulder)*

Give you the cold shoulder [verb phr] (See *Give you the brush-off)*

Give you the shirt off his back [verb phr] so generous you would literally give a needy person your own shirt. Ex: Vern would *give you the shirt off his back.*

Glad rags [noun] dressy clothes, usually formal. Ex: Put on your *glad rags* tonight. We're going out to dinner. (See *Dressed to the hilt)*

Glass ceiling [noun] (business) Seemingly invisible barrier keeping women from becoming top executives. Ex: The *glass ceiling* exists at some of our top companies in the U.S.

Gloss over [verb] treat a problem lightly or avoid discussing the details of it. Ex: He *glossed over* the fact that the company had a cash flow problem.

Glutton for punishment [noun phr] taking on too much responsibility. Ex: She is a *glutton for punishment*. After she raised her own children she is now taking care of her grandchildren.

Gnarly [adj] (1990's slang) #1 cool, groovy. Ex: That car of yours is *gnarly*. #2 (mountain biking) difficult, challenging. Ex: The trail on the North Fork is really *gnarly*. (See *Really rad*)

Gnawed at the back of your mind [verb phr] bothered you. Ex: The fact that he cheated on the test *gnawed at the back of my mind.*

Go against the grain [verb phr] not take the natural course of action. Ex: He *went against the grain* and started a business in Costa Rica.

Go along with [verb phr] #1 cooperate/agree with. Ex: He will *go along with* whatever you say. #2 accompany. Ex: I will *go along with* you to the store.

Go ape over [verb phr] excited about. Ex: I *went ape over* his new car. (See *Revved up*)

Go around in circles [verb phr] active but accomplishing little. Ex: I have been *going around in circles* this morning and need to focus my attention this afternoon.

Go back on your word [verb phr] reverse your decision or withdraw your previously committed support. Ex: Ginny *went back on her word* and did not finish the financial statement.

Go ballistic [verb] become upset rapidly. Ex: My mother will *go ballistic* when she sees the dent in the fender of her car. (See *Blow sky high*)

Go bananas [verb] enthusiastic or highly excited. Ex: He *went bananas* over his new car. (See *Go ape over*)

Go by the book [verb phr] always abide by the rules. Ex: That teacher always *goes by the book*. You have to turn in your homework on time.

Go cold turkey [verb phr] quit smoking, drinking, etc., immediately. Ex: I'm going to quit smoking *cold turkey* this Friday.

Go far [verb] be successful. Ex: I always knew the class president would *go far* in the world.

Go far afield [verb phr] not staying on the subject. Ex: He is *going far afield* of the main agenda.

Go figure [verb] no logic to someone's actions. Ex: Dave dropped out of school. *Go figure.*

Go fly a kite [verb expression] leave. (when you want someone to go) (See *Take a flying leap in a rolling doughnut*)

Go for a dip [verb phr] go swimming. Ex: Let's *go for a dip* tonight.

Go for broke [verb phr] make every effort. Ex: We ought to *go for broke* and bet all our money on that horse.

Go for it [verb phr] try it. Ex: *Go for it!* I think you can make the team.

Go for the brass ring [verb phr]   Try for the greatest success. Ex: Linda *went for the brass ring* and became a famous actress. (See *Go for the gusto*)

Go for the gusto [verb phr] (See *Go for the brass ring)*

Go for the jugular [verb phr]   act vicious. Ex: Steve *went for the jugular* and hurt his friend's feelings.

Go from 0 to 60 [verb phr]   become angry quickly. Ex: I *go from 0 to 60* when my kids borrow my DVD's. (See *See red*)

Go-getter [noun] someone who is enthusiastic and ambitious. Ex: Missy is real *go-getter*. She is in the office by 6:00 every morning.

Go gung-ho [verb] enthused and energetic. Ex: Max is *going gung-ho* learning to sail. (See *Wired)*

Go halvsies [verb] (See *Dutch treat)*

Go in lowball [verb phr] submit the low bid on something. Ex: Our company did not get the bid because we did not *go in lowball.*

Go into orbit [verb phr] become highly upset. (See *Go ballistic*)

Go it alone [verb phr] by yourself. Ex: After his wife died he had to *go it alone.*

Go jump in the lake [verb expression] leave. (when you want someone to go) (See *Go fly a kite)*

Go like gangbusters [verb phr] hurry through a task. Ex: We are *going like gangbusters* trying to finish waxing the car before it rains.

Go off the deep end [verb phr] not make decisions rationally. Ex: Taking drugs made him *go off the deep end*.

Go one better [verb phr] #1 tell a more exciting story. Ex: Tim will always *go one better* when someone tells a story. #2 a greater accomplishment. Ex: Julie *went one better* than her sister and got all A's in school.

Go out of your way [verb phr] make an extra effort. Ex: He *went out of his way* to pick up the people in his van pool.

Go over it with a fine tooth comb [verb phr] look at all the details. Ex: *Go over the contract with a fine tooth comb* before you sign it.

Go over like a lead balloon [verb phr] be unpopular. Ex: I suggested that we go to the beach, but the idea *went over like a lead balloon*. (See *Go over like a pregnant pole vaulter*)

Go over like a pregnant pole-vaulter [verb phr] (See *Go over like a lead balloon*)

Go overboard [verb phr] overdo something to excess. Ex: He always *goes overboard* when he tackles a new sport.

Go places [verb phr] become famous or successful. Ex: I knew she was *going places* when I heard her sing five years ago.

Go public with [verb phr] disclose to the media. Ex: The politician *went public with* the story of his divorce.

Go soak your head [verb expression] (informal – only said to a good friend) reply to a ridiculous remark. (See *Go suck eggs*)

Go suck eggs [verb expression] (informal) (See *Go soak your head*)

Go the extra mile [verb phr] exceed what is required. Ex: He *went the extra mile* and got the award.

Go through the motions [verb phr] be uninvolved mentally or emotionally. Ex: She *went through the motions* after her husband died.

Go to any length [verb phr] try a variety of ways to succeed at something. Ex: He will *go to any length* to get on the hockey team.

Go to extremes [verb phr] take extraordinary measures to acquire something. Ex: The company *went to extremes* to hire the talented producer.

Go to Hell in a handbasket [verb phr] a deteriorating situation. Ex: The company is *going to Hell in a handbasket* unless their financial situation improves.

Go to pieces [verb phr] emotionally distraught. Ex: She *went to pieces* when her dog died.

Go to the John [verb phr] said by men. Means "go to the bathroom."

Go to your head [verb phr] become conceited. Ex: Just because you won the prize, don't let it *go to your head.*

Go toe to toe [verb phr] compete equally with someone. Ex: The two athletes *went toe to toe* in the contest.

Go under [verb] #1 pass beneath. Ex: The boat *goes under* the bridge. #2 Use a pseudonym. Ex: He *goes under* the name John Brown. #3 approaching financial ruin. Ex: That car business *is going under*.

Go under the knife [verb phr] have surgery. Ex: The doctor will *go under the knife* himself tomorrow.

Go up in smoke [verb phr] evaporates. Ex: I thought I was going to get a promotion, but it *went up in smoke.*

Go whole hog [verb phr] be totally committed. Ex: He is *going whole hog* on cleaning his room.

Go with the flow [verb phr] be flexible. Ex: Just *go with the flow* and you will get along with everyone.

Goes without saying [verb phr] something everyone already knows. Ex: *It goes without saying* the Congressman will be re-elected.

Gofer [noun] someone who is always running errands for more important people. Ex: Derek was a *gofe*r for the company last year, but now he is a manager.

Going down for the third time [verb phr] #1 drowning. Ex: That boy is *going down for the third time*. Save him!! #2 (business) declaring bankruptcy. Ex: We have to get a loan or we are *going down for the third time.*

Going great guns [verb phr] running smoothly. Ex: My career is *going great guns* since I got that new position.

Going like a bat out of Hell [verb phr] in a big hurry.

Going nowhere fast [verb phr] not motivated to be successful. Ex: The boy is *going nowhere fast* since he dropped out of school.

Going nuts [verb] going crazy. Ex: I am *going nuts* since I am doing the work of two people.

Going steady [verb phr] dating only one person. Ex: That couple has been *going steady* for six months.

Going to be a scorcher [verb phr] (weather) extremely hot. Ex: It's *going to be a scorcher* in Phoenix, Arizona today.

Going to be the death of me [verb phr] challenged to the utmost by someone. (sometimes said about children) Ex: The twins are *going to be the death of me* yet.

Going to beat the band [verb phr] moving fast. Ex: Those two boys are *going to beat the band* picking up their toys. (See *Going to town*)

Going to town [verb phr] (See *Going to beat the band*)

Goings on [noun] what is happening. Ex: What are the *goings on* at your house these days?

Gold mine [noun] an opportunity to make a lot of money. Ex: That new stock deal is a real *gold mine*.

Golden handshake [noun] forced retirement for older employees in companies. Can be accompanied by a cash settlement. Ex: Sometimes the *golden handshake* is financially beneficial. (See *Golden parachute)*

Golden parachute [noun] (See *Golden Handshake*)

Gomer [noun] undesirable person. (See *Dweeb*)

Gone for good [verb phr] gone forever. Ex: His nephew is *gone for good.*

Gone to pot [verb phr] deteriorated. Ex: Tim didn't water his garden and it has *gone to pot*. (See *Gone to the dogs)*

Gone to the dogs [verb phr] deteriorated. (See *Gone to pot*)

Gone to the happy hunting ground [Indian saying] died. Ex: Chief Blackfoot's ancestors have *gone to the happy hunting ground.*

Good as done [adj. phr] #1 almost completed. Ex: My new woodshed is *good as done*. I just have to paint it. #2 assured completion. Ex: When Bruce volunteered to do the painting, it was *good as done*.

Good as gold [cliché] behaving extremely well. Ex: Those children are *good as gold.*

Good chemistry [noun] mutually attracted to each other. Ex: Briana and Connor have *good chemistry.*

Good egg [noun] a dependable friend. Ex: Scott is such a *good egg.* He helped me change my flat tire.

Good grief [expression of surprise] (See *Good Heavens*)

Good Heavens [expression of surprise] (See *Good Grief)*

Good old boy network [noun phr] (business) executives who take care of each other, politically, monetarily, and otherwise. Ex: The *good old boy network* is very supportive.

Good old days [noun phr] remembrances of the past that are very pleasant. Ex: In the *good old days* you could get your windows washed at the gas station.

Good vibes [noun] positive feelings about someone. Ex: We had *good vibes* from the day we met.

Goodie Two Shoes [noun phr] person who has high behavior expectations. Ex: She is such a *goodie two shoes* and won't have a glass of wine at the party.

Goof around [verb] Having a good time doing nothing in particular. (See *Hang out*)

Goof off [verb] Acting silly and just having fun. Ex: The guys were *goofing off* playing water polo.

Goof up [verb] make a mistake. Ex: I sure *goofed up* when I told Jack he could play catcher in the game. (See *Screw up*)

Goose egg [noun] a score that is "zero." Ex: In our last hockey game we got a *goose egg*.

Goose is cooked [noun phr] caught doing something wrong. Ex: *Your goose is cooked.* Mom caught you eating cookies before dinner.

Got a tiger by the tail [verb phr] a situation that is out of control. Ex: He's *got a tiger by the tail* trying to work with the inner city kids.

Got an eyeful [verb phr] saw more than you should have. Ex: The boy *got an eyeful* when he saw his sister undressing.

Got him pegged [verb phr] figured out someone's behavior or motives. Ex: I've *got him pegged.* He never takes a risk.

Got his sea legs [verb phr] able to walk aboard ship without getting queasy. Ex: Now that I've *got my sea legs* I am having a good time on the cruise.

Got ice water in his veins [verb phr] in control and low key. Ex: He's *got ice water in his veins.* He had his cut stitched up with no anesthetic.

Gotrocks [noun] someone who is rich. Ex: Ask Mrs. *Gotrocks* for a donation.

Got saltwater in his veins [verb phr] love of the sea - usually pertains to fishermen. Ex: He's got a 27 foot boat, and has *saltwater in his veins.*

Got the best of me [verb phr] overtook, conquered. Ex: I had to go to bed when my cold *got the best of me.*

Got the goods on him [verb phr] have incriminating evidence against someone. Ex: The detective *got the goods on him* and he was arrested.

Got the hots for him [verb phr] excited sexually by someone. Ex: Mary's *got the hots for Jack* and wants to go out with him.

Got the munchies [verb phr] hungry for a snack. Ex: I've *got the munchies.* Do you have any chips around?

Got the short end of the stick [verb phr] someone was unfair to you. Ex: He got the *short end of the stick* and had to set the table three nights in a row while his brother didn't have to help.

Got the world on a string [verb phr] be lucky and have everything going your way. Ex: He's *got the world on a string* since he won the science award.

Got to the bottom of it [verb phr] found out the truth. Ex: He *got to the bottom of it* and found out his neighbor was stealing from him.

Got wind of [verb phr] found out. Ex: She *got wind of* the fact that her daughter was pregnant.

Got your drift [verb phr] understand what you are saying. Ex: I've *got your drift.* I know you can't go to the movies tomorrow.

Gotcha [verb] fool someone and then tell the person *"Gotcha"* so they know it was a joke.

Gotta boogie [verb phr] (1990's slang) have to leave. Ex: *Gotta boogie.* Going to play cards tonight.

Grab the brass ring [verb phr] try to make the most of every opportunity. Ex: You should *grab the brass ring* since you only go around once.

Grand Central Station [noun] busy place. Ex: My kitchen becomes *Grand Central Station* every time my son brings his teammates home.

Grand poobah [noun] leader of a group. Ex: The *grand poobah* is calling a meeting today. (See *Head honcho*)

Grande finale [noun] most important part of a presentation or play, which is at the end. Ex: For the g*rande finale*, the choir will sing the Hallelujah Chorus.

Grandstanding [verb] doing something to be the center of attention. Ex: Ever since he was three years old he *grandstands* to get people to pay attention to him.

Granny flats [noun] rooms in your home that are rented to older persons. Ex: Since my children moved out, I have enough space to have *Granny flats.*

Granny glasses [noun] round, wire rimmed glasses. Ex: Those *granny glasses* look good on you.

Granola   [adj]   #1 homespun.   Ex: She is an old fashioned *granola* girl. #2 {noun} a topping for yogurt which is made of oats, honey, brown sugar and nuts.

Grass grows greener on the other side   [cliché]   other peoples' situations and relationships seem better than yours.

Grass roots   [adj]   starting at the bottom.   Ex: There is a *grass roots* movement to clean up the environment.

Grates on his nerves   [verb phr]   irritates him.   Ex: When you chew your fingernails, it *grates on his nerves*.   (See *Gets in my hair*)

Gravy train   [noun]   road to wealth.   Ex: We're on the *gravy train* since we made those good stock investments.

Gray area   [noun]   not clearly defined.   Ex: There is a lot of *gray area* in these project plans.

Gray markets   [noun]   When foreigners buy U.S. products at discount prices and, in turn, sell the goods back home at lower prices.

Grease his palm   [verb phr]   give him some money for a favor.   Ex: Charlie will give you a ride if you *grease his palm.*

Grease the skids   [verb phr]   smooth the way.   Ex: If I *grease the skids* for you, I am sure you will get the job.

Greased lightning   [noun]   moving extremely fast.   Ex: That deer moves like *greased lightning.*

Greaser   [noun]   (1950's slang)   a teenage boy who smoked, rode motorcycles and wore his hair long.   Most of the time he wore white T-shirts and jeans.

Greasy spoon [noun] inexpensive restaurant serving hamburgers, hot dogs and french fries. Ex: Meet you at the *greasy spoon.*

Green around the ears [noun phr] inexperienced. Ex: Don't let Parker cut down that tree. He is *green around the ears* when it comes to using a power saw.

Green around the gills [noun phr] sick. Ex: That boy looks a little *green around the gills* today. Perhaps he should see the school nurse.

Green eyed monster [noun] jealousy. Ex: Don't let the *green-eyed monster* get you.

Green thumb [noun] talent for growing plants. Ex: My mother's *green thumb* keeps her house in flowers.

Green with envy [adj phr] jealous. Ex: I am *green with envy* because you got a new car.

Greenbacks [noun] dollar bills. Ex: How many *greenbacks* do you have? (See *Dough*)

Greens [noun] salad. Ex: Are we having *greens* for lunch?

Grey matter between the ears [noun phr] brains. Ex: She acts like she has no *grey matter between the ears.*

Gridlock [noun] when no cars can move on the freeway because it is too crowded. Ex: In several years we will have *gridlock* unless we build a rapid transit system.

Grim reaper [noun] death. Ex: The *grim reaper* catches up with everyone.

Grin and bear it [verb phr] handle an adverse situation without complaint. Ex: My car broke down but I suppose I can *grin and bear it*.

Grind it up a little finer [1940's country western] explain it to me more clearly. Ex: *Grind up the new plan a little finer* for me. (See *Run it by me again*)

Grind to a halt [verb phr] stop. Ex: Production will *grind to a halt* if the workers are on strike another month.

Groddy to the max [adj phr] (1960's slang) disgusting and revolting. Ex: When he eats with his fingers, it is *groddy to the max*.

Groovy [verb] (1960's slang) fabulous. (See Rad)

Groppin' [verb] having sex. (See *Do it*)

Gross out [verb phr] something that is disgusting. Ex: Don't *gross me out* by picking your teeth at the table.

Ground rules [noun] basic procedures. Ex: *Ground rules* say you should be staying within your budget.

Grounded [verb] teenagers who have not abided by their parents' house rules do not get to participate in any activities with their friends for a determined amount of time. Ex: You are *grounded* for two weeks for coming home late last night.

Groundswell [verb] unexpected outpouring. Ex: There is a *groundswell movement for* women's rights.

Groupies [noun] people who hang around a famous person(s) and literally worship them. Ex: Many rock stars have *groupies* who follow them wherever they go.

Grow by leaps and bounds [verb phr] uncontrolled growth. Ex: Our city has *grown by leaps and bounds.*

Grow to like [verb phr] become fond of someone or something as time passes or as it is used. Ex: I know you don't like squash now, but you will *grow to like* it, since our garden is full of it!

Grow up [verb phr] Act like an adult. Ex: Those boys are acting too silly. They need to *grow up.*

Growing like a weed [verb phr] said about children. Ex: We haven't seen Johnny for a while. He is *growing like a weed.*

Gruesome twosome [noun] a pair of unusual people whose physical attributes and/or behavior is unique. (sometimes said in jest to friends) Ex: Look, here comes the *gruesome twosome.*

Grunge [adj] [1990's slang] dress with several layers of clothing. Ex: The *grunge* look is popular on the West Coast.

Grungy [adj] icky, messy. Ex: I really look *grungy* after pulling up weeds in my garden.

Grunt work [noun] work considered at the low end of the economic scale. Ex: Cleaning out bathrooms at the restaurant is *grunt work.*

Guessing game [noun] not providing facts. Ex: Tell me where you were last night. I don't like a *guessing game*!

Gum up [verb phr] cause to be inefficient. Ex: You are going to *gum up* the project by constantly arriving late.

_____

Gum up the works [verb phr] make a mistake. Ex: I really *gummed up the works* by installing my software wrong on my computer. (See *Goof up*)

Gun shy [adj] reluctant to take a chance. Ex: We are *gun shy* about diving in the lake because it is so cold.

Gung ho [adj] enthusiastic. Ex: I am really *gung ho* about that new computer class. (See *All fired up)*

Gussied up [verb phr] (country western) dressed very nicely. Ex: I am all *gussied up* to go to the Opera. (See *Dressed to the hilt*)

Gutless wonder [noun] someone who is bold. Ex: Anyone who feeds the lions in their cage is a *gutless wonder!*

HIPC [abbrev] *Health Insurance Purchasing Cooperative;* pools of consumers who will join together to buy insurance. Ex: Does the government support *HIPC?*

HIV virus [noun] AIDS virus - sexually transmitted disease that can be fatal. Ex: People contracting the *HIV virus* are vulnerable to other infections.

HMU [abbrev] *Hit me up* – cell phone texting abbreviation for "Get in touch with me".

HOV Lane [abbrev] *High Occupancy Vehicle lane;* highway lane to be used only by cars with at least 2 people riding in them. Ex: Sometimes only cars with 3 persons riding in them can use the *HOV lanes.*

Hacked off [verb phr] upset. Ex: When he passed my idea off as his own, I was *hacked off.* (See *Come unglued*)

Had it up to here [verb phr] angry. (See *Hacked off*)

Have the last word [verb phr] end the argument. Ex: Why do you always have to *have the last word?*

Have words with him [verb phr] argue with someone. Ex: I *had words with him* yesterday over his dogs barking all night. (See *At odds with*)

Hair stand on end [noun phr] something that surprises or shocks you will literally make your hair stand up straight. Ex: When he told me the ghost story it made my *hair stand on end.*

Hairball [noun] undesirable person. (1960's slang) (See *Loser*)

Hair-trigger temper [noun] quick temper. Ex: Her father has a *hair-trigger temper*.

Hakuna Matata [noun] no worries. Ex: It's best to take life as it comes - *Hakuna Matata*. (from the movie Lion King) (See *Happy as a clam*)

Half a loaf is better than none (cliché) having a little of something is better than having nothing.

Half-baked idea [noun phr] not well thought out; has little chance of success. Ex: I thought his business would fail, because it was a *half-baked idea* to begin with.

Half pint [noun] small child. (See Pipsqueak)

Half the battle [adj phr] part of a challenge. Ex: Convincing Evan to do the project is *half the battle.*

Half-cocked [adv] without thinking. Ex: He always goes off *half-cocked* before we can explain it to him.

Ham it up [verb phr] be silly. Ex: The boy *hammed it up* and made the class laugh.

Hand in glove [adv] closely associated or cooperative. Ex: They worked *hand in glove* to get the new building financed and built.

Hand in hand [adv] in a friendly manner. Ex: They walked *hand in hand* to the grocery store.

Hand in the cookie jar [noun phr] caught doing something wrong. Ex: That politician was caught with his *hand in the cookie jar* and is going to have to explain all his expenses.

Hand it to him on a silver platter   [verb phr]   something attained with little or no effort because someone favored you. Ex: He got that job *handed to him on a silver platter* because his father is Vice-President of the company.

Hand it to you   [verb phr]   paying someone a compliment. Ex: I've got to *hand it to you.* That is a good idea.

Hand-me-downs   [noun]   used clothing. Ex: Poor children sometimes wear *hand-me-downs*.

Hand over fist   [adv phr]   reach a goal rapidly. Ex: The new company is making money *hand over fist*.

Handful   [noun]   child who is unruly. Ex: Joyce's two year child is a *handful*.

Handle it   [verb]   take care of it. Ex: "Are you going to put the snow tires on the car?" "Yes, I will *handle it.* "

Handle with kid gloves   [verb phr]   treat gently or carefully. Ex: We have to *handle Jill with kid gloves* because she is so sensitive.

Hands down   [adv]   win by a large margin. Ex: He won the contest *hands down.*

Hands off   [verb]   Don't touch or mess with. Ex: That's my project. *Hands off!*

Hands on   [adj]   learn by actually doing. Ex: Many people learn computer programs by *hands-on* experience.

Handwriting is on the wall [noun phr] easy to predict. Ex: I think we are going to have snow today. The *handwriting is on the wall* since the temperature has dropped to freezing.

Handy dandy [adj] useful. Ex: That's really a *handy dandy* screwdriver.

Hang a BA [verb phr] (crude) pull down your pants and bend over, exposing your buttocks to someone. Done as a joke.

Hang a left/right [verb phr] turn left/right when driving a car. Ex: *Hang a left* at the next stop light and you will be at Norm's house.

Hang by a thread [verb phr] barely functioning. Ex: The climber is *hanging by a thread* on that precipice.

Hang in the air [verb phr] leave undecided. Ex: The decision has been left *hanging in the air*.

Hang in the balance [verb phr] waiting to be finished. Ex: The rest of the project is *hanging in the balance* while we wait for more funding.

Hang in there [verb phr] do not give up. Ex: *Hang in there*. You will have a better day tomorrow. (See *Tough it out*)

Hang it up [verb phr] give something up. Ex: I'm going to have to *hang it up.* I can't play tennis since I broke my shoulder.

Hang loose [verb phr] be flexible and relaxed; ready for any situation. Ex: Let's just *hang loose* and see what happens.

Hang on [verb phr] please wait - sometimes said during a phone conversation. Ex: *Hang on.* I think someone is at my door.

Hang on for dear life [verb phr] grip very tightly. Ex: When you ride the roller coaster, *hang on for dear life.*

Hang out [verb] group of people enjoying one another. Ex: Let's *hang out* at Tim's tonight and play pool.

Hang out to dry [verb phr] Ex: He left me to *hang out to dry* on that business deal. (See *Left in the lurch*)

Hang the moon [verb phr] (2013 slang) worship someone. Ex: She *hangs the moon* whenever Jim talks to her.

Hang tough [verb phr] (See *Hang in there*)

Hang your hat on [verb phr] an idea or plan you can support. Ex: Now that's a theory that you can *hang your hat on.*

Hangin' by your toenails [verb phr] in a tough situation and trying to handle it the best you can. Ex: He has been *hangin' by his toenails* since he got lung cancer.

Hanky panky [noun] improper activity. Ex: The teenagers were involved in some *hanky panky.*

Happen upon [verb phr] find unexpectedly. Ex: If you *happen upon* my ruler, will you put it back in my desk?

Happy as a clam [adj phr] carefree with no worries. (See *Hakuna Matata*)

Happy go lucky [adj phr] carefree. (See *Hakuna Matata*)

Happy hour [noun phr] usually between 5:00 P.M. to 7:00 P.M. when a bar will serve alcoholic drinks for half price. Ex: Are you going to *Happy Hour* tonight at the club?

Happy hunting ground [noun] Heaven (Indian phr) Ex: His father went to the *happy hunting ground* last year.

Happy medium [noun] an agreement or compromise. Ex: They reached a *happy medium* and decided to meet at Bill's house.

Harbors a grudge [verb phr] (See *Holds a grudge*)

Hard act to follow [noun phr] someone has performed brilliantly. The next person will have a difficult time exceeding that performance. Ex: That comic is a *hard act to follow*.

Hard and fast rule [noun] a rigid procedure with no room for flexibility. Ex: It is a *hard and fast rule* that you have to be at school by 8:00 A.M.

Hard as a rock [adj phr] incredibly hard. Ex: When Jean left the baking powder out, her biscuits were *hard as a rock*.

Hard copy [noun] (business) paper copy of a document.

Hard headed [adj] stubborn. Ex: The boy is *hard headed* and will not put his toys away. (See *Hardnosed*)

Hard nut to crack [noun phr] person who is difficult to communicate with. Ex: I would talk to him more but he is a *hard nut to crack*.

Hard on someone [adj phr] critical and unforgiving. Ex: You are always *hard on your first born child*.

Hard pressed [adj] have difficulty. Ex: If Brian leaves, I'll be *hard pressed* to find anyone as skilled to replace him. (See *Hard put*)

Hard put [adj phr] (See *Hard pressed*)

Hard row to hoe [noun phr] a difficult situation to overcome. Ex: He's had a *hard row to hoe* since his mother died.

Hard to defrost [verb phr] unresponsive; unfeeling. Ex: That new girl is *hard to defrost*.

Hard to digest [verb phr] difficult to accept. Ex: It's *hard to digest* that Phil is a big success.

Hard to place [adj phr] difficult to remember. Ex: I know I've seen you before, but you're *hard to place*.

Hard to swallow [adj phr] difficult to believe. Ex: It is *hard to swallow* that he really got all A's.

Hard up [adj] accept something of lesser value because you are desperate. Ex: He will date any girl because he is *hard up*.

Hardnosed [adj] stubborn. (See *Hard headed*)

Harp on [verb] scold or nag someone continuously. Ex: His Mom has to *harp on him* to do his homework.

Harshed out [verb phr] really disappointed over an event. Ex: He was *harshed out* over losing his game. (See *Bummed out*)

Has his head on backwards [verb phr] not thinking clearly or rationally. Ex: I must have *had my head on backwards* when I left my lights on in my car this morning.

Has his ups and downs [verb phr] good days and bad days. Ex: He has his *ups and downs* since he got cancer.

Has his work cut out for him [verb phr] facing a difficult job. Ex: He *has his work cut out for him* since they doubled production.

Has no backbone [verb phr] without courage. Ex: He *has no backbone* and will agree to anything.

Has the floor [verb phr] authority to speak in a meeting. Ex: Excuse me. *I have the floor* now.

Has the jitters [verb phr] nervous, apprehensive. Ex: I *have the jitters* every time I have to give a speech.

Has the world by the tail [verb phr] confident. Ex: He *has the world by the tail* since he won the lottery.

Has to do with [verb phr] related. Ex: Getting your allowance *has to do with* how well you do on your report card.

Has your name on it [verb phr] something suits your personality perfectly. Ex: Samantha, that coat *has your name on it.*

Hashtag [noun] (2013 slang) # turns any word or words that follow it into a searchable link. Used on social media sites and TV. Simply put a hashtag (#) before a word or words.

Hasn't a clue [verb phr] out of touch with the situation, or with reality. Ex: He *hasn't a clue* as to where he put the keys.

Hasn't got a prayer [verb phr] futile. Ex: I'd take the proposal to the building committee, but it *hasn't got a prayer* of acceptance.

Hat trick [noun] (sports - soccer, hockey) one player scores 3 goals in a game. Ex: My son scored a *hat trick* in his hockey game today.

Hatchet job [noun] say something bad about someone. Ex: She really did a *hatchet job* on the new secretary.

Hatchet man [noun] #1 (business) someone who cuts costs, usually by laying off people. #2 in organized crime, the *hatchet man* kills people the mob wants eliminated.

Hater [noun] (2013 slang) someone who is extremely negative. Ex: Don't associate with her. She's a real *hater*.

Haul ass [verb phr] work or move quickly to meet a schedule. Ex: We better *haul ass* or we won't get this project done. (said by men)

Have a ball [verb phr] having fun. Ex: We *had a ball* at the party last night.

Have a complex [verb phr] have a problem with. Ex: He *has a complex* about wearing the color pink.

Have a cow [verb phr] be upset. Ex: Just because you missed your bus, don't *have a cow*. (See *Have a to-do*)

Have a feel for [verb phr] have an aptitude for. Ex: She really *has a feel for* jazz music.

Have a field day [verb phr] latitude to do or say almost anything. Ex: The press found out the candidate had an affair. They will *have a field day* with that information.

Have a fling [verb phr] indulge in a romantic affair. Ex: Jess and I *had a fling* about three years ago.

Have a good one [verb phr] (goodbye expression of well wishing)

Have a heart [verb phr] be merciful or forgiving. Ex: *Have a heart*, Mom! All the guys are counting on me to go on the camping trip.

Have a hissy fit [verb phr] throw a temper tantrum. (See *Have a to-do*)

Have a nose for it [verb phr] a knack for finding things. Ex: He *has a nose for* finding strange items in the encyclopedia.

Have a sweet tooth [verb phr] like sweet foods, such as chocolate. Ex: I *have a real sweet tooth* and love chocolate cake.

Have a to-do [verb phr] throw a tantrum. Ex: Don't have a *to-do* just because you can't go to the movie. (See *Have a cow*)

Have a yen for [verb phr] a desire. Ex: I *have a yen for* Italian food.

Have at it [verb phr] attack or start to work on. Ex: The invoices have arrived so I'll *have at it* and get the checks prepared.

Have cuts [verb phr] let someone go in front of you in a line when many people are waiting. Ex: Can I *have cuts?* The lunch line is too long.

Have designs on someone [verb phr] want to become romantically involved with that person. Ex: She *has designs on* her friend's brother.

Have enough sense to come in out of the rain [verb phr] not sensible. Ex: I don't think he *has enough sense to come in out of the rain.*

Have for a song [verb phr] buy inexpensively. Ex: I think you can *have that dress for a song* at the thrift shop.

Have half a mind to [verb phr] considering doing something unreasonable or unacceptable or out of character. Ex: I *have half a mind to* take the rest of the day off and drive up in the mountains.

Have his head examined [verb phr] be checked for mental competency, usually an exaggeration when someone makes a decision that seems unreasonable. Ex: He should *have his head examined* for taking the boat out in this weather.

Have his wits about him [verb phr] mentally alert. Ex: Be sure you *have your wits about you* when you go to buy a car.

Have it in for him [verb phr] hold a grudge and wait for an opportunity to retaliate. Ex: She's *had it in for him* ever since he got the promotion and she didn't.

Have something up your sleeve [verb phr] keep a secret or advantage from others until the right moment to reveal it. Ex: I think Bob *has something up his sleeve* and will reveal it at just the right time.

Have the blues [verb phr] be depressed. Ex: I *have the blues* today. It is raining again.

Have the courage of your convictions [cliché] do what you think is right regardless of what anyone else thinks. Ex: Be sure you *have the courage of your convictions* when you go to that meeting.

Have the devil to pay [verb phr] retribution. Ex: If you kids wreck my car, you will *have the devil to pay.*

Have the jump on him [verb phr] have an advantage. Ex: He *had the jump on* the other fellow in the race.

Have the runs [verb phr] have diarrhea. Ex: When I was in Mexico, I *had the runs* from eating the fruit there. (See *Montezuma's Revenge)*

Have the world by the tail [verb phr] confident of your success. Ex: He *has the world by the tail* since he started his own business.

Have two strikes against you [verb phr] be unattractive and not bright or articulate. Ex: She already *has two strikes against her* and will probably not get the job.

Have words with [verb phr] exchange angry words with someone. Ex: I *had words with* him over my dented fender on my car.

Have you got a second? [noun phr] ask to talk with someone for a very short time. Ex: *Have you got a second*? I need to ask you what time the meeting starts.

Have your back to the wall [verb phr] no choices left. Ex: My *back is to the wall* on this vote. I have to return a favor from Tim.

Have your cake and eat it too [verb phr] lucky. Ex: John has two girlfriends; one is a wonderful cook and the other is beautiful. He *has his cake and eats it too!*

Have your hands full [verb phr] be busy and challenged. Ex: You really *have your hands full* with working full time and taking care of your children.

Have your nose in the air [verb phr] act snobbish. Ex: I passed Rod today and he really *had his nose in the air.*

Have your sights set on [verb phr] count on something. Ex: He *has his sights set on* going to college out of state.

Have your work cut out for you [verb phr] There will be a great deal of responsibility in the project you are undertaking. Ex: We really *have our work cut out for us* building our new home by ourselves.

Haven't a clue [verb phr] don't know. Ex: I *haven't a clue* where George put the checkbook. (See *Haven't the foggiest*)

Haven't an inkling [verb phr] don't know. Ex: I *haven't an inkling* when he will finish raking the leaves. (See *Haven't a clue)*

Haven't had so much fun since the hogs ate my little brother [1960's country western] having a great time.

Haven't heard the last of it [verb phr] something more will happen. Ex: I know the company slowed their layoffs when they got a new order, but I'm sure we *haven't heard the last of it* yet.

Haven't the foggiest [verb phr] don't know. (See *Haven't a clue)*

Having a falling out [verb phr] a disagreement. Ex: We *had a falling out* and have not spoken since.

He can dish it out, but he can't take it [noun phr] tease others, but not want to be teased yourself.

Head and shoulders above someone [noun phr] much more talented than someone else. Ex: We hired him because he *stood head and shoulders above everyone else.*

Head for the hills [verb phr] leave. Ex: I am going to *head for the hills* tomorrow for the holiday. (See *Head out*)

Head honcho [noun] the boss. Ex: You need to ask the *head honcho* for permission. (See *Big Enchilada*)

Head hunters [noun] employment agency personnel who locate jobs for people. Ex: The *head hunters* found him a great job.

Head in the clouds [noun phr] feeling ecstatic. Ex: She has her *head in the clouds* ever since she got engaged.

Head in the sand [noun phr] unaware. Ex: You didn't hear me because you had your *head in the sand*.

Head is on the chopping block [noun phr] in danger of being fired or dismissed from your job. Ex: Your *head is on the chopping block* if you come in late again.

Head out [verb] leave. Ex: I'm going to *head out* now. (See *Shove off*)

Head over heels in love [noun phr] completely and totally in love with someone. Ex: I think Susie is *head over heels in love* with him.

Head screwed on backwards [noun phr] not thinking rationally. Ex: I had my *head screwed on backwards* when I loaned him my car.

Head them off at the pass   [noun phr]   divert someone's
attention. Ex: *Head them off at the pass* before they
discover the fresh baked cookies.

Heads are going to roll [noun phr] people are in serious trouble
and may be fired. Ex: *Heads are going to roll* if we go
over budget on the project.

Heads up [noun phr] pay attention. Ex: *Heads up!* Your Mom
is coming.

Heart is in the right place   [noun phr]   make an emotional
decision instead of a logical one. Ex: I know she can't
afford to keep the baby, but her *heart is in the right
place.*

Heart like a wheel [noun phr] fall in love many times. Ex: He
has a *heart like a wheel* and is always in love.

Heart of gold [noun phr] generous person. Ex: He has a *heart
of gold* and would help anyone out.

Heart of the matter   [noun phr] (See *Get to the heart of the
matter*)

Heart set on [noun phr] want desperately. Ex: He has his *heart
set on* a bicycle for Christmas.

Heart throb [noun] (1950's slang) a person who romantically
excites lots of people - usually a movie star. Ex: Elvis
Presley was my *heartthrob.*

Heart to heart talk [noun] share inner feelings and desires with
someone else. Ex: We need to have a *heart to heart
talk* about your career goals.

Heartfelt thanks [noun phr] sincerely grateful. Ex: He gave me
his *heartfelt thanks* for saving his life.

Heaven forbid [expression of disapproval] (said sarcastically) implies that a person's behavior could not even be changed by Heaven. Ex: *Heaven forbid* that Pam should ever get to school on time.

Heavy cross to bear [noun phr] difficult burden. Ex: She has a *heavy cross to bear* having to raise three children all by herself.

Heavy duty [adj] #1 of a very serious nature. Ex: Decisions about divorce are *heavy duty*. #2 sturdy and durable. Ex: I bought a *heavy duty* washing machine.

Heavy hitters [noun] people with great influence on a situation. Ex: The *heavy hitters* will approve the funding.

Heavy-handed [adj] strict and unyielding. Ex: He took a very *heavy handed* role in the raising of his children.

Hedge your bet [verb phr] cover your bet. Ex: When we play poker I always *hedge my bet.*

Heebie-jeebies [noun] spine-tingling feeling. (See *Case of the Heebie-jeebies)*

Held kangaroo court [verb phr] a mockery of justice. Ex: Many people *hold their own kangaroo courts* before a person is tried by a real jury.

Helicopter mom [noun] (2013 slang) overbearing and over-protective mother.

Hell on wheels [noun] wild and uncontrolled person. Ex: Joe's son is *Hell on wheels.*

Hella [adj] (2013 slang) really. Ex: "Did you like that movie?" "Hella yes".

Help yourself [verb phr] serve yourself. Ex: *Help yourself* to more snacks.

Helpless as a hog on ice [verb phr] (1960's country western) not in control. Ex: He's as *helpless as a hog on ice* in that situation.

Hem and haw [verb] grumble. Ex: Don't *hem and haw*. Just take out the garbage.

Hen pecked [adj] nagged. Ex: The husband was *hen pecked* by his wife.

Herb [noun] (1970's slang) undesirable person. (See *Gomer*)

Here goes nothing [expression indicating a lack of confidence] trying something and you think you can't do it well. Ex: "Are you going to dive into the water?" "Well, *here goes nothing.*"

Here's your hat; what's your hurry? [noun phr] sarcastic comment made when you want someone to leave immediately. (See *Take a flying leap in a rolling doughnut)*

Hey [hello greeting] 2014 slang - very popular.

Heyday [noun] in his prime. Ex: He was a great runner in his *heyday*.

Hidden agenda [noun] (business) not disclosing what your real motive is, but subtly manipulate people. Ex: Warren has a *hidden agenda* for this meeting.

Hide nor hair [adj] have not seen anywhere. Ex: I have not seen *hide nor hair* of Desi since last week.

High and dry [adj] without any support. (See *Left high and dry*)

High and low [adv] in all places. Ex: I have looked *high and low* for that boy.

High falutin' [adj] snobby. Ex: Don't invite Sarah. She's so *high falutin'*.

High five [noun] (gesture) slap someone's hand, palms up, when you both are in total agreement. Ex: Give me a *high five*. We just won the game. (See *Fist bump)*

High handed [adj] a snobbish approach. Ex: Why does she take such a *high handed* approach in her dealings with people?

High mucky muck [noun] prestigious and influential person. Ex: We should invite some of the *high mucky-mucks* to the meeting. (See *Head honcho*)

High noon [noun] exactly twelve o'clock. Ex: Meet me at *high noon* at the movies.

High roller [noun] someone who spends lots of money. Ex: He acts like a *high roller* when he is in Las Vegas.

High spirited [adj] independent and strong minded. Ex: That horse is quite *high-spirited.*

High time [adv] past the appropriate time. Ex: It's *high time* you were getting home.

High water pants [noun phr] pants that are too short for you.

Higher than a kite [adj phr] drunk. (See *Three sheets to the wind*)

Hightail it [verb] move fast. Ex: The boy broke the window and *hightailed it* home.

Highway robbery [noun] excessively expensive. Ex: I wouldn't pay that much for the coat. It's *highway robbery*.

Hill of beans [noun phr] small, insignificant. Ex: That plan does not amount to a *hill of beans*.

Hindsight is 20-20 [noun phr] If you could see the future, you would probably make different choices in the present. Ex: We could have won that game, but *hindsight is always 20-20*.

Hinky [adj] (2013 slang) odd, strange. Ex: His excuse for not being in school sounded *hinky* to me.

Hippies [noun] college students in the late 1960's who advocated communal living, free love, drugs and a non-materialistic existence.

His better half [noun] usually said by a husband about his wife. Ex: I'll ask *my better half* what we are doing on Friday night.

His brother's keeper [noun] (Biblical) responsible for another's care. Ex: With the influx of refugees, we should be our *brother's keeper* and help them get homes and jobs.

His days are numbered [noun phr] your wrongdoing has been discovered. Ex: *His days are numbered* since he was accused of harassment. (See *His goose is cooked*)

His goose is cooked [noun phr] (See *His days are numbered)*

His own worst enemy [noun phr] takes actions that get him into trouble or ruins his reputation. Ex: Dave is *his own worst enemy*. He is always late to work and has poor excuses.

His right hand man [noun phr] a person who is close to you on whom you can depend. Ex: Sometimes the vice-president of a company is the President's *right hand man.*

Hissy fit [noun] temper tantrum. Ex: Her daughter threw a *hissy fit* because she couldn't buy that dress. (See *Have a to-do*)

Hit a brick wall [verb phr] stopped by an impossible (or impassible) obstacle. Ex: When I made my budget proposal to the company, I *hit a brick wall.* There were no funds available.

Hit below the belt [verb phr] be unfair. Ex: When he said I was incompetent, that really *hit below the belt.*

Hit full stride [verb phr] the ultimate of your ability. Ex: Some people do not *hit full stride* until they are in their 40's.

Hit him over the head [verb phr] make someone aware. Ex: When the test scores *hit him over the head*, he realized that he would have to study harder.

Hit home [verb phr] what someone said pertained precisely to you. Ex: It really *hit home* when the instructor said we need to study harder.

Hit it [verb phr] Let's go! Ex: The water skier said "*hit it*" and the driver of the boat pulled him up.

Hit it off [verb phr] having instant rapport with someone you have just met. Ex: I *hit it off* right away with Debbie. We both love music.

Hit like a ton of bricks [verb phr] has a deep effect on you. Ex: When he lost the race, it *hit him like a ton of bricks.* (See *Hit me with a 2 x 4*)

Hit me [verb phr] #1 (game - cards) in the game of "21" where you want the dealer to give you another card, you say, "*Hit me*." #2 being physically struck by someone. Ex: That boy *hit me* on the playground.

Hit me right [verb phr] perceive favorably. Ex: The deal *hit me right* so I invested my money in it.

Hit me with a 2 x 4 [verb phr] (See *Hit like a ton of bricks*)

Hit on [verb phr] flirting that is not mutual. Ex: He has been *hitting on* Cindy for several months, but she doesn't like him.

Hit pay dirt [verb phr] get rich. Ex: I hope I *hit pay dirt* before I am too old to enjoy it.

Hit rock bottom [verb phr] #1 be out of financial resources. Ex: I *hit rock bottom* and may have to sell my car. #2 have no more resources. Ex: He needs extra support since he *hit rock bottom* when his wife died.

Hit the books [verb phr] study. Ex: Let's *hit the books* tonight. The test is tomorrow.

Hit the bottle [verb phr] drink liquor. Ex: Haven't you been *hitting the bottle* a little heavily lately? (See *Hit the sauce*)

Hit the ceiling [verb phr] get angry. Ex: I *hit the ceiling* when I found out he had gambled away his entire paycheck. (See *Fly off the handle*)

Hit the ground running [verb phr] ready for action. Ex: We've got to *hit the ground running* tomorrow and get that water pipe fixed.

Hit the hay [verb phr] go to bed. Ex: I'm tired and am going to *hit the hay*. (See *Hit the sack*)

Hit the high points [verb phr] cover the main ideas. Ex: Just *hit the high points* in your speech.

Hit the jackpot [verb phr] #1 won lots of money. Ex: I hit the jackpot and won $100,000. #2 found a great resource. Ex: I *hit the jackpot* when I found a lumber yard where I could get free wood.

Hit the mark [verb phr] were correct. Ex: You *hit the mark* when you said he was not responsible. (See *Hit the nail on the head*)

Hit the nail on the head [verb phr] (See *Hit the mark*)

Hit the road [verb phr] leave. Ex: I'm going to *hit the road* now. (See *Shove off*)

Hit the roof [verb phr] get angry. Ex: I *hit the roof* when I found a dent in my car. (See *Lose your grip*)

Hit the sack [verb phr] go to bed. (See *Hit the hay*)

Hit the sauce [verb phr] drink liquor. (See *Hit the bottle*)

Hit the showers [verb phr] take a shower. Ex: Let's *hit the showers* and then go to the movies.

Hit the spot [verb phr] eat or drink something that satisfies you. Ex: That glass of lemonade really *hit the spot*.

Hit the wall [verb phr] (sports) out of energy when running. Ex: After I *hit the wall,* I got a spurt of extra energy and finished the race.

Hither and yon [adv] here and there. Ex: The notes got scattered *hither and yon* when the wind blew them.

Ho [noun] (2012 slang) prostitute.

Hoedown [noun] (1940's country western) gathering of country-western or hill-billy musicians, often accompanied by food and dancing. Ex: *Hoedowns* are lots of fun for everyone.

Hog heaven [noun] (1950's country western) ecstatic. Ex: He was in *hog heaven* when he got his new fishing pole.

Hog on ice [noun phr] (1950's country western) without control; acting independently. Ex: When he tried to roller skate, he was like a *hog on ice*. (See *Helpless as a hog on ice*)

Hog something [verb phr] take more than your share. Ex: Mom, Jerry *hogged* the ice cream and there's none left.

Hog tie [verb] (country western) forcibly restrain. Ex: I am going to have to *hog tie* the dog if he doesn't stay in the yard.

Hog wild [adv] crazy with excitement. Ex: He went *hog wild* when he got his new bike.

Hogwash [1950's expression of disbelief] that's ridiculous.

Hoi Polloi [noun] common folk; masses. – from the Greek.

Hold down the fort [verb phr] be responsible for. Ex: *Hold down the fort* till I return from the store.

Hold in high esteem [verb phr] admire or value highly. Ex: They *hold* their mother and father *in high esteem.*

Hold on [verb] wait a minute. Ex: *Hold on.* You have to wash the dishes before you can go to the store. (See *Hold onto your hat*)

Hold onto your hat [verb phr] (See *Hold on*)

Hold out #1 [noun] not go along with the group. Ex: The jury had one *hold out* and could not convict the person. #2 [verb] extend. Ex: *Hold out* your hand and I will give you some candy.

Hold over [noun] (business) work carried over from the day before. Ex: We need to work overtime tonight because the *hold over* is so high.

Hold your feet to the fire [verb phr] strongly persuade. Ex: We need to *hold their feet to the fire* to convince them to change the design.

Hold your ground [verb phr] not change your mind. Ex: I think he is going to *hold his ground* on that decision.

Hold your horses [verb phr] wait. (See *Hold on*)

Hold your tongue [verb phr] be quiet. (generally said to children)

Holding the bag [verb phr] taking the consequences by yourself. Ex: He was left *holding the bag* when the other boys ran off.

Holds a grudge [verb phr] unforgiving.

Holds all the cards [verb phr] has control. Ex: She *holds all the cards* in the real estate deal.

Holds down [verb] #1 works. Ex: He *holds down* a second job on the week-ends. #2 keep from moving. Ex: *Hold down* that steer while we brand it.

Hole in the wall place [noun phr] small location. Ex: The new dress shop is just a *hole in the wall place*.

Hole up somewhere [verb phr] hide out. Ex: The bandits *holed up in the mountains.*

Hollow leg [noun phr] able to eat or drink a lot. Ex: He has had four beers already. He really has a *hollow leg.*

Hollow victory [noun phr] to win, but with many negative aspects. Ex: Getting the tax increase defeated was a *hollow victory*. We don't have the funds to build our new public hospital.

Holy cow [exclamatory expression of surprise or amazement] (See *Holy smoke*)

Holy shit [crude, impolite] (See *Holy cow*)

Holy smoke (See *Holy cow*)

Home free [noun phr] certain to succeed. Ex: When our closest competitor lost his engine, we knew our racing boat was *home free.*

Home front [noun] what is happening at your house. Ex: What's happening on the *home front?*

Home grown [adj] high quality because you grew it yourself. Ex: Those tomatoes are *home grown* and very tasty.

Home stretch [noun] last part of a project or journey. Ex: We're on the *home stretch* now and will be in Seattle by noon.

Homecoming [noun] #1 a celebration in high school, taking place in the Fall when there is a school dance following a football game and a Queen of Homecoming is crowned along with 3 or 4 princesses. #2 [adj] coming back to your home town after a long absence. Ex: We're going to have a *homecoming* party for John. He will be in town next week.

Homer [noun] (sports - baseball) home run. Ex: The player hit two *homers* today.

Homlier than a mud fence [1940's country western] unattractive - usually said about a woman. Ex: She is just *homlier than a mud fence.*

Honest as the day is long [cliché] undeniably honest; trustworthy.

Honey do's [noun] list of tasks that a wife gives a husband to accomplish (such as mowing the lawn, carrying out the garbage, etc.) Ex: I'll play poker with you after I get my *honey-do's* done.

Honeymoon's over [noun phr] the illusions about marriage have given way to reality. Ex: I knew the *honeymoon was over* when he squished toothpaste all over the sink.

Hooch [noun] homemade liquor. Ex: Lloyd made his own *hooch* in the basement.

Hook up with [verb phr] romantically involved with someone. Ex: He *hooked up with* Serena last year.

Hoopla [noun] commotion. Ex: What's all the *hoopla* about?

Hoosegow [noun] (country western) prison. Ex: They won't let him out of the *hoosegow* for a long time. (See *In the slammer*)

Hooters [noun] (<u>crude</u>) women's breasts. Also the name of a chain of restaurants.

Hop, skip, and a jump [noun phr] close by. Ex: The lake is just a *hop, skip, and a jump* from my cabin.

Hop to it [verb phr] hurry up. Ex: *Hop to it.* We have to be there in 15 minutes. (See *Step on it*)

Hope springs eternal [noun phr] Always believe in better days. Ex: I will win the race next year. After all, *hope springs eternal*.

Horn in on [verb phr] force your presence on someone. Ex: Tom has to *horn in on* any party we are planning. (See *Elbow in*)

Hornswoggled [verb] (1950's country western) fooled. Ex: I was sure *hornswoggled* on that deal.

Horse around [verb phr] physically play with someone. Ex: Those two brothers always *horse around*.

Horse of a different color [cliché] something entirely different. Ex: "Would you like to go to the movies?" "No". "How about going bowling?" "Well, that's a *horse of a different color.*"

Horse pucky [exclamatory expression of disbelief] (impolite)
(See *Horsefeathers*)

Horsefeathers (1940's slang) (See *Horse pucky*)

Hose over [verb phr] badly manipulated. Ex: I got *hosed over* on that stock deal.

Hostess with the mostest [noun phr] said appreciatively about a woman who has definite talent as a hostess. Ex: Sue is really the *hostess with the mostest*. It is always a pleasure to go to her home.

Hostile takeover [noun phr] acquisition of a company against its wishes, usually through purchase of majority of stock in the company. Ex: There were many *hostile company takeovers* in the 1980's.

Hot and bothered [verb phr] angry. Ex: I get *hot and bothered* when I hear someone swearing. (See *Hot under the collar*)

Hot and heavy [adv phr] enthusiastic and plentiful. Ex: With only three months left before the elections, the campaign commercials are coming *hot and heavy* on the TV.

Hot button [noun] something that is certain to anger someone. (See *Push someone's hot button*)

Hot foot it [verb phr] hurry. Ex: *Hot foot it* down to my house. (See *Shake a leg*)

Hot off the presses [adj phr] just printed. Ex: That information is *hot off the presses*.

Hot ticket item [noun] popular and profitable. Ex: IPhones are becoming the *hot ticket* item in many stores.

_____

Hot to trot [verb phr] anxious to have sex. Ex: Let's leave the dance early. I'm *hot to trot.*

Hot under the collar [adj phr] angry. Ex: I get *hot under the collar* whenever he comes home late. (See *Frosted*)

Hot-dog skiing [noun] daredevil and dangerous tricks done while skiing. Ex: You have to be an excellent athlete to *hot dog ski.*

Hotter than blue blazes [adj phr] (weather) when the temperature gets very hot. Ex: It has been *hotter than blue blazes* this summer in Arizona.

Hotty [adj] (2013 slang) sexy and desirable person, either man or woman.

Houdini [noun] person who works like magic. Ex: He is a real *Houdini* - playing the piano at night and being a lawyer during the day.

House of cards [noun phr] unstable situation. Ex: The plans for buying a sailboat is a *house of cards.* If the financing doesn't come through, it will crumble.

Household word [noun] commonplace, easily recognizable. Ex: The Internet has become a *household word,* since so many people have computers.

Housewarming [noun] a party for people in a new house. Ex: I am having a *house warming* for Denise. I hope you come.

How are things? [Hello greeting] (See *Yo*)

How come? [noun phr] Why? Ex: *How come* you don't want to go to the beach?

How do you like them apples? [noun phr] (1960's slang) what do you think of that?

How goes it? [Hello greeting] (See *What's happenin'*?)

How sweet it is [noun phr] expression of happiness. Ex: I just got a new car. *How sweet it is!*

How would you like a knuckle sandwich? [noun phr]   How would you like to get hit? (usually said to a friend in jest, but can be serious depending on who says it)

How's that? [noun phr] What did you say?

Hullaballoo [noun] commotion. Ex: There was a lot of *hullabaloo* about the athletes using steroids. (See *Hoopla*)

Humdinger [noun] something wonderful. Ex: I just got a new fishing pole and it's a *humdinger*.

Humongous [adj] huge. Ex: The sandwiches they serve in that restaurant are *humongous.*

Hump day [noun] Wednesday- the middle of the workweek.

Hung jury [noun]   jury that cannot agree upon a verdict. Ex: That court case had a *hung jury,* so they will have to try the case over.

Hung out his shingle [verb phr]   advertised. Ex: The lawyer *hung out his shingle* in the small town.

Hungry as a horse [cliché] ravenous. Ex: When will we eat dinner? I am *hungry as a horse.*

Hunker down [verb] #1 squat on tiptoes. Ex: The small child *hunkered down* to see the flower. #2 get serious about a situation. Ex: We've got to *hunker down* and get the government deficit reduced.

Hunky-dory [adj] O.K. Ex: "How are things?" "*Hunky-dory*".

Hunt and peck [verb] type on a computer not using the correct fingering. Ex: She types by the *hunt and peck* system.

Hyped [verb] excited. Ex: He was real *hyped* about going to Mexico. (See *Revved up*)

IDK [abbrev] *I don't know.* Cell phone texting abbreviation.

IMAO [abbrev] *In my arrogant opinion*. Cell phone texting abbreviation.

I am not amused [noun phr] sarcastic comment made to someone who says something you don't like.

I bagged it [noun phr] #1 stopped doing it. Ex: "Are you still taking ballet?" "No, *I bagged it.*" #2 completed the action. Ex: I *bagged* the deer yesterday.

I could just die [noun phr] am embarrassed. Ex: Every time I have to speak in front of people, *I could just die.*

I drifted [noun phr] lost concentration on the subject. Ex: *I drifted* and did not hear the last part of the lecture.

I have had it! [noun phr] losing your temper. Ex: *I have had it!* Marv is always late and makes everyone else wait. (See *Fly off the handle*)

I have to run for now. [noun phr] have to leave. (See *Let's boogie*)

I have to see a man about a horse [noun phr] when asked where you are going, and you don't want to answer directly say, *"I have to see a man about a horse."*

I know what side my bread is buttered on. [noun phr] I know who is paying my way. Ex: Darrin is nice to the boss because he knows *what side his bread is buttered on.*

I'll be a monkey's uncle [1950's exclamatory expression] (See *Gadzooks*)

I'll be all over you like a case of the hives

I'll be all over you like a case of the hives [noun phr] an implied threat of control over someone. Ex: If you are late for dinner tonight, *I'll be all over you like a case of the hives.*

I'll eat my hat [noun phr] punishment for losing a bet. Usually said when making a bet. If I lose this bet, *I will eat my hat.*

I'll give you a piece of my mind [noun phr] telling someone exactly what you think about something they have done. Ex: I am so angry *I'll give you a piece of my mind.* (See *Have words with someone*)

I'm all ears [noun phr] anxious to hear what the other person is going to say. Ex: *I'm all ears.* Tell me what Sherry said yesterday.

I'm easy [noun phr] flexible person. Ex: "Do you want to go to the movies tonight?" "Sure, *I'm easy.*"

I'm from Missouri. Show me. [cliché] prove it. Ex: When someone says something far-fetched, you can say "I'm from Missouri. Show me."

I'm in the book [noun phr] my phone number is listed in the directory. Ex: "How can I reach you?" *"I'm in the book."*

I'm outta here [noun phr] I'm leaving. Ex: *I'm outta here.* See you tomorrow. (See *Head out*)

I've got your number [noun phr] I can predict your actions. Ex: I've got your number.

Ice water in his veins [noun phr] unfeeling and unemotional. Ex: He has *ice water in his veins.* He never accepts any excuse for people being late to work.

Icebreaker [noun] words or actions that help people relax and enjoy themselves. Ex: Starting a game at a party is a good *icebreaker.*

Idle chit chat [noun phr] meaningless conversation. Ex: Don't engage in *idle chit chat* at work. (See *Shoot the breeze*)

If I eat another bite, I will explode [noun phr] having eaten too much and feel stuffed.

If I live to be a hundred [noun phr] If you reach old age you still will be amazed by some action or behavior. Ex: *If I live to be a hundred,* I will never understand how space stations work.

If it were a snake, it would have bit you [noun phr] look for something that is close by, but not see it. Ex: I can't believe I couldn't find my keys and they were here all the time. *If they were a snake, they would have bit me.*

If it's not bolted down, it walks. [noun phr] everything is subject to being stolen.

If looks could kill [noun phr] display open hostility. Ex: Did you see how Melissa greeted Ron? *If looks could kill,* Ron would be dead.

If memory serves me right [noun phr] if I remember correctly. Ex: *If memory serves me right,* your birthday is today.

If push comes to shove [noun phr] if things become too difficult. Ex: Rick likes to support his wife, but *if push comes to shove*, she will get a job.

If the shoe fits [cliché] if it pertains to you. Ex: " The instructor says I am always late." "Well, if the shoe fits..."

If worse comes to worst [noun phr] if the most unfavorable situation occurs. Ex: *If worse comes to worst,* I will have to move out of my apartment.

If you can't take the heat, then stay out of the kitchen [cliché] if you can't handle pressure, then don't get into pressure situations.

If you snooze, you lose [noun phr] always be alert or you will miss opportunities. Ex: "I didn't know we were supposed to sign up for the class today." " Well, *if you snooze you lose.*"

If you think you can, you can [noun phr] positive thinking can accomplish anything. Ex: "I don't think I can pass that college course." "Oh, if *you think you can, you can* or if you think you can't, then you can't. Either way you're right.

If you're going to soar with the eagles, you can't hoot with the owls. [cliché] If you want to think sharply in the morning, you can't stay up all night.

Iffy [adj] uncertain. Ex: Politics in Afghanistan is *iffy*.

Ill at ease [verb phr] uncomfortable. Ex: When he stares at me I am *ill at ease.*

In a bind [prep phr] in a quandary. Ex: I am *in a bind.* My car won't start.

In a breeze [prep phr] easily. Ex: I can run five miles *in a breeze.*

In a class by itself [prep phr] distinctive, good or bad. Ex: That sports car is *in a class by itself.*

In a cloud of dust [prep phr] left in a hurry. Ex: She left him *in a cloud of dust* without saying goodbye.

In a coon's age [prep phr] (1930's country western – <u>not politically correct</u>) long time. Ex: I haven't seen you *in a coon's age.*

In a family way [prep phr] pregnant. Ex: Mary's daughter has been *in a family way* for several months. (See *baby bump*)

In a fix [prep phr] have a problem. Ex: I am *in a fix.* My car tire is flat. (See *In a jam)*

In a flash [prep phr] in a minute. Ex: I'll be with you *in a flash.*

In a jam [prep phr] (See *In a fix*)

In a jiffy [prep phr] soon. Ex: I'll be off the phone *in a jiffy.*

In a nutshell [prep phr] summing it all up. Ex: *In a nutshell,* the East coast colleges are too expensive for me.

In a pickle [prep phr] in a tough situation. (See *In a fix*)

In a row [prep phr] #1 in succession. Ex: The quarterback threw three long passes *in a row*. #2 one behind the other. Ex: The class lined up *in a row* at the drinking fountain.

In a rut [prep phr] bored with the same old routine every day. Ex: I need to take some more computer classes. *I am in a rut.*

In a spin [prep phr] state of anxiety. Ex: *I am in a spin.* I have to be downtown in 20 minutes for my class and the traffic is horrible.

In a think tank [prep phr] extremely bright people get together to share and brainstorm ideas.

In all good conscience [prep phr] honestly. Ex: I told you what my car cost *in all good conscience.*

In all my born days [prep phr] in my entire lifetime. Ex: *In all my born days I* have never seen such a big house.

In all probability [prep phr] probably. Ex: *In all probability,* Chris won't go to the movies.

In an uproar [prep phr] an upset state of mind. Ex: When he shouts, the whole class is *in an uproar.*

In and out of season [prep phr] constantly, all year long. Ex: We grow those flowers *in and out of season.*

In any case [prep phr] regardless of the circumstances. Ex: *In any case,* you need to wash your hands before dinner.

In any way, shape, or form [prep phr] static; unchanging. Ex: I am not going to change my mind *in any way, shape, or form.*

In cahoots with [prep phr] partners with someone of questionable background. Ex: The two brothers were *in cahoots with* the Mafia.

In case [prep phr] if. Ex: *In case* I am late, start dinner without me.

In cement (See *Cast in cement)*

In close proximity [prep phr] next to. Ex: He is standing *in close proximity* to his sister in the picture.

In cold blood [prep phr]   deliberate and planned, not in an emotional state of mind. Ex: The three people were murdered *in cold blood.*

In demand [prep phr]   desired. Ex: Good technicians are *in demand.*

In depth [prep phr]   thoroughly. Ex: I have to study the book *in depth.*

In due course [prep phr]   later, at the right time. Ex: He will finish reading the book *in due course.*

In fine print [prep phr]   the small printing on a document that is usually at the bottom of the page and overlooked by most people when they are reading it. Ex: It says *in fine print* that this story is copyrighted.

In for a rough landing [prep phr]   a bad outcome or unhappy end to a relationship. Ex: He is *in for a rough landing* if his girlfriend leaves him.

In for a rough ride [prep phr]   difficult situation to handle. Ex: When he married Janice, he was *in for a rough ride.*

In for it [prep phr] expecting punishment. Ex: The boy ate his mother's pie and now he's *in for it.*

In full bloom [prep phr]   looking or doing the best. Ex: My plant is *in full bloom now.*

In full glory [prep phr]   happy and proud. Ex: When our dog won the prize at the dog show, he was *in full glory.*

In his glory days [prep phr]   when he was popular or admired. Ex: John Wayne made a lot of movies *in his glory days.*

In her pocket [prep phr] has the situation mastered. Ex: She has her tennis game *in her pocket.*

In hot water [prep phr] in trouble. Ex: He is *in hot water* because he broke the window. (See *Deep do-do*)

In house [prep phr] (business) all production is done within the company. Ex: I think we should keep our video production *in house.*

In keeping with [prep phr] respecting. Ex: We buried my dad next to his mother's grave, *in keeping with* his wishes.

In la-la land [prep phr] #1 asleep. Ex: We put our child to bed and she's now *in la-la land.* #2 without a sense of reality. Ex: Sometimes Hollywood is called *La-La Land.*

In league with the devil [prep phr] actions that appear evil. Ex: He cheated the people on that land deal and appears to be *in league with the devil.*

In like Flynn [prep phr] easily accepted. Ex: "Did you get into Yale University?" "Sure, *in like Flynn.*"

In limbo [prep phr] undecided. Ex: "Are you going to the movies?" "Oh, I am *in limbo* right now. I have to wait until my brother gets home."

In living color [prep phr] for real. Ex: Here's Bob, *in living color.*

In my mind's eye [prep phr] imagining something. Ex: *In my mind's eye,* I see a split level house on that piece of land.

In name only [prep phr] related to someone but do not want to be associated with that person for a variety of reasons. Ex: I am related to Denise *in name only.*

In no uncertain terms [prep phr] permission denied. Ex: My Mom said I could not stay out after 10:00 *in no uncertain terms.*

In nothing flat [prep phr] immediately. Ex: He got dressed *in nothing flat.*

In on the ground floor [prep phr] included at the beginning of a project. Ex: We got *in on the ground floor* of the housing development plans.

In one ear and out the other [prep phr] did not remember something right after you heard it. Ex: When he said he was leaving school, it went *in one ear and out the other.*

In one fell swoop [prep phr] all at once. Ex: I changed all the computer passwords *in one fell swoop.*

In other words [prep phr] rephrasing. Ex: *In other words,* your homework must be done before you go out to play.

In over his head [prep phr] tried something too difficult. Ex: When he took that chemistry course, he was *in over his head.*

In person [prep phr] physically present. Ex: I get to talk to Tim *in person* tonight. Usually we talk over the phone.

In place [prep phr] established. Ex: We now have the procedure *in place.*

In private [prep phr] secretly or quietly. Ex: I'd like to speak with you *in private* on a personal matter.

In rare form [prep phr] at your best mentally. Ex: He was *in rare form* and his jokes were sure funny.

In recent memory [prep phr] lately. Ex: We haven't had such a storm *in recent memory.*

In red ink [prep phr] in debt, or in financial trouble. Ex: The company is *in red ink* and will have to close.

In round numbers [prep phr] estimate to the closest number ending in zero - to the nearest 100, 1000, 10,000, etc. Ex: *In round numbers*, the house costs $100,000.

In seventh heaven [prep phr] ecstatic. Ex: He has been *in seventh heaven* since he got married. (See *On cloud nine)*

In short [prep phr] summarizing. Ex: *In short,* you have two weeks to paint the house.

In short order [prep phr] right away. Ex: I'll have those groceries bagged *in short order.*

In short shrift [prep phr] scarce. Ex: I was going to plant gold dahlias this year, but the bulbs are *in short shrift.*

In spades [prep phr] finalized. Ex: The vacation plans are *in spades* now.

In stitches [prep phr] laughing hard. Ex: That joke had me *in stitches.*

In the altogether [prep phr] nude. (See Nudie kazootie)

In the bad/good graces of [prep phr] favored or not favored by someone. Ex: He is not *in good graces* with his teacher because he didn't finish his homework.

In the bag [prep phr] certain. Ex: Winning the game is *in the bag*.

In the black [prep phr] solvent financially. Ex: The company's finances were *in the black*.

In the blink of an eye [prep phr] a second. Ex: *In the blink of an eye* the child darted across the street.

In the briny [prep phr] in the ocean.

In the buff [prep phr] naked. Ex: They were in the hot tub *in the buff*.

In the cards [prep phr] inevitable. Ex: It was *in the cards* that our team would win the game.

In the clear [prep phr] innocent. Ex: The defendant is *in the clear* according to the jury.

In the clink [prep phr] in jail. (See *In the slammer*)

In the clover [prep phr] rich. Ex: A lot of movie stars are *in the clover*. (See *Moneybags*)

In the dark [prep phr] ignorant. Ex: He was *in the dark* about the status of his job.

In the deep [prep phr] in the ocean. Ex: There are many sharks *in the deep*.

In the doghouse [prep phr] in trouble. Ex: You are *in the doghouse* for coming home late. (See *Your name is mud*)

In the driver's seat [prep phr] in control. Ex: Evan is *in the driver's seat* tonight.

In the far-flung future [prep phr] distant future. Ex: I may go to Italy *in the far flung future.*

In the fast lane [prep phr] taking a lot of risks. Ex: Rob lives *in the fast lane.* He went bungee jumping the other day.

In the final analysis [prep phr] in conclusion. Ex: *In the final analysis,* our product costs are too high.

In the fine print [prep phr] small font size. Ex: It says right here *in the fine print* that you can't return it just because you don't like it.

In the flesh [prep phr] appear personally. Ex: We actually saw the CEO *in the flesh.* (See *In person*)

In the foreground [prep phr] prominent. Ex: Most recording stars like to stay i*n the foreground* to sell more records.

In the genes [prep phr] hereditary. Ex: Some people believe Alzheimer's is *in the genes.*

In the groove [prep phr] abreast of current trends. Paul is *in the groove.* He just started an international business.

In the heat of the moment [prep phr] when emotions are running high. Ex: Don't say things you will regret *in the heat of the moment.*

In the hot seat [prep phr] in trouble and have to explain some wrong doing. Ex: You are *in the hot seat* because you wrecked Dad's car. (See *Deep do do*)

In the know [prep phr] knowledgeable. Ex: My uncle is *in the know* about running a business.

In the light of day [prep phr] Many issues are more clearly analyzed in the morning when your mind is more alert. Ex: My problems didn't look so impossible *in the light of day.*

In the limelight [prep phr] (theater expression) the center of attention. Ex: Movie stars like to be *in the limelight.*

In the long run [prep phr] over a long period of time. Ex: *In the long run* this company's stock will keep improving.

In the loop [prep phr] part of the activity. Ex: We like to keep Mike *in the loop* because he knows a lot about our project.

In the midst of it all [prep phr] in the middle of what is happening. Ex: *In the midst of it all*, the dog jumped onto the couch.

In the nick of time [prep phr] just in time. Ex: I got to the store *in the nick of time* before they closed.

In the palm of his hand [prep phr] totally in his control. Ex: He's got the vice presidents in *the palm of his hand.*

In the pink [prep phr] feeling healthy and mentally alert. Ex: Ever since his operation he has been *in the pink.*

In the pipeline [prep phr] #1 in direct contact. Ex: If you want to market your new invention, you need to get *in the pipeline* with the dealers. #2 (business) queued. Ex: We can only put about five transactions *in the pipeline* before our system fails.

In the public eye [prep phr] known generally; current news. Ex: Immigration issues are currently *in the public eye.*

In the red [prep phr] have a negative cash flow. Ex: If the company operates *in the red,* its stockholders will lose money.

In the same boat [prep phr] in the same situation. Ex: I am *in the same boat* as you. I can't afford a vacation to Hawaii.

In the slammer [prep phr] in jail. Ex: If you break the law, you will be *in the slammer* for several years. (See *In the clink*)

In the small scheme of things [prep phr] from an individual perspective. Ex: *In the small scheme of things,* I think we may have to increase the school budget.

In the soup [prep phr] have money.   Ex: He is *in the soup* since he got that job on T.V. (See *On easy street)*

In the stars [prep phr] predestined, inevitable. Ex: It is *in the stars* that he will be successful.

In the swim [prep phr] join in an activity or enjoy life. Ex: We are right *in the swim* of things at the Country Club.

In the thick of it [prep phr] in the middle of something. Ex: I can't come to the phone now because I am *in the thick of it* painting the kitchen.

In the trenches [prep phr] people who are doing all the basic work on a project or idea are *in the trenches.* (used during war time to designate the ground troops who fight in the trenches).

In the twinkling of an eye [prep phr] instantly. Ex: *In the twinkling of an eye,* the small child reached for the cookie. (See *In the wink of an eye*)

In the wee hours of the morning [prep phr] about 2:00 a.m. Ex: I am not going to answer the phone *in the wee hours of the morning.*

In the wink of an eye [prep phr] (See *In the twinkling of an eye*)

In the works [prep phr] being handled now. Ex: That project is *in the works* right now.

In this day and age [prep phr] now; at present. Ex: *In this day and age,* most women work outside the home.

In view of [prep phr] because of. Ex: *In view of* recent developments, we will not be buying a new car.

In vogue [prep phr] fashionable. Ex: Your new dress is certainly *in vogue.*

In your dreams [prep phr] unlikely. Ex: If you make a comment one of your friends thinks is unlikely he/she will say "*In your dreams.*

Information superhighway [noun] transmission of information by computer, iPads, iPhones, cable and satellite T.V. and any other communications technology. Ex: There is a lot of knowledge we can gain from the *information superhighway.*

Inner city [noun] slums. Ex: Many people in the *inner city* are poor.

Innocent as a lamb [adj phr] inexperienced. Ex: She was *innocent as a lamb* when she went to work for that company.

Ins and outs [noun phr] all the details. Ex: She knew all the *ins and outs* of selling her product.

Internet [noun] (computer) a global network of linked computers that share databases, messages and other features. Ex: All kinds of information can be accessed on the *Internet.*

Into every life a little rain must fall (cliché) everyone has sad times in his/her life.

Into the melting pot [prep phr] combination of various items. Ex: Many ideas go *into the melting pot* before a good decision is made.

Into the sunset [prep phr] ended or disappeared. Ex: My car went *into the sunset* with my teenager.

Into thin air [prep phr] not visible anymore. Ex: My keys have disappeared *into thin air.*

Invade his domain [prep phr] territorial expression meaning to be in someone else's area of occupancy. Ex: The dog did not want the cat *to invade his domain*.

Invite trouble [prep phr] behavior that is likely to have bad consequences. Ex: If you play with Kenny, it will certainly *invite trouble.*

Iron hand in the velvet glove (cliché) soft-spoken and know how to control people by manipulation and not by direct force. Margaret Thatcher, former Prime Minister of England, was called the Iron Hand in the Velvet Glove.

Iron horse [noun] railroad, usually refers to a steam locomotive. Ex: The *Iron Horse* has become obsolete in the 21st century except for use on tourist railroads.

___

Iron out [verb] resolve. Ex: Let's get started with the plan and *iron out* the problems as they arise.

Irons in the fire [noun phr] activities. Ex: I have too many *irons in the fire* to handle any more projects.

It doesn't bode well [noun phr] looks bad. Ex: Global warming theories do not *bode well*.

It doesn't wash [noun phr] not credible. Ex: That's a good story, but *it doesn't wash*.

It never rains, but it pours (cliché) problems occur all at once, instead of one at a time.

It will all come out in the wash [noun phr] everything will be o.k.

It will put hair on your chest [noun phr] the experience will make you more "manly" or macho. Ex: Why don't you eat these frog legs? *It will put hair on your chest.*

It's a breeze [noun phr] easy. (See *Easy as pie*)

It's a bummer [noun phr] bad luck of some kind. Ex: "I wanted to go skiing, but I have to work." "I know. *It's a bummer.*"

It's a fight to the finish [noun phr] compete and win no matter what it takes. Ex: I can run faster than him but it*'s a fight to the finish* in every race we run.

It's a jungle out there! [noun phr] complex world. Ex: Be careful. *It's a jungle out there!* (See *It's a zoo*)

It's a shoe-in [noun phr] easy to tell who is going to win. Ex: The Congressional election is a *shoe in.*

___

It's a steal [noun phr] something is priced very cheaply. Ex: That new perfume is on sale and *it's a steal.*

It's a wrap [noun phr] (movies) the scene that was just filmed is perfect and will not have to be re-done.

It's a zoo (See *It's a jungle out there*)

It's all Greek to me [noun phr] can't understand it. *Ex:* "Do you understand the new math?" *"No, it's all Greek to me."* (See *Haven't the foggiest*)

It's always darkest before the dawn (cliché) before you have good luck, you usually have more than your share of bad luck.

It's beyond me [noun phr] can't comprehend it. Ex: I read the instructions, but *it's beyond me.* (See *It's all Greek to me*)

It's high time [noun phr] the time element has become crucial. Ex: *It's high time* you came in out of the rain or you will catch a cold.

It's history [noun phr] in the past; no longer existing. Ex: I know we did it that way before, but *it's history* now.

It's in the bag [noun phr] a certain thing. Ex: My new job is *in the bag.*

It's not a bug; it's a feature. [noun phr] (computer) sarcastic remark about some built-in mechanical problem or computer software deficiency, implying that it was made that way deliberately.

It's not as black as it's painted [noun phr] things are not in as bad a state as they appear to be. Ex: Our economy is not as *black as it's painted.*

It's not over till the fat lady sings [noun phr] sometimes a predictable outcome can change at the last moment. Ex: You think the Blazers are a cinch to win this game, but *it's not over till the fat lady sings*.

It's not rocket science [noun phr] difficult. Ex: *It's not rocket science* to put a bicycle together.

It's up to him [noun phr] his decision. Ex: "Is Bruce going to the movies?" "I don't know. *It's up to him.*"

It's your funeral [noun phr] sarcastic comment made to someone who intends to engage in risky behavior. Ex: Are you going kite surfing? *It's your funeral*.

It's your nickel [noun phr] call someone and they listen to your problem first because you took the initiative to call.

Itsy bitsy [adj] quite small. Ex: The ant is *itsy bitsy*.

JIT [abbrev] (business) *just in time*. Refers to delivery of parts and material just as they are needed to build something. Ex: We need to install a manufacturing resource planning system on our computer if we are going to go to *JIT*.

Jack frost [noun] ice. (refers to weather) Ex: *Jack frost* is really nipping at my toes this morning. It is really cold.

Jack of all trades, master of none [cliché] multi-talented; able to handle a variety of vocations, but does not excel at one. Ex: Don is a *jack of all trades, but master of none.*

Jack shit [noun] (crude) nothing. Ex: I didn't make *jack shit* in the stock market this quarter.

Jack up [verb] #1 raise with a jack. Ex: I had to *jack up* the car to change the tire. #2 increase the price. Ex: Just before Christmas, the drug store will *jack up* the price of candles.

Jam session [noun] impromptu gathering of jazz musicians to play and enjoy each other's talents. Ex: What a great *jam session* we had last night at the club.

Jammin' [verb] playing good music and enjoying it. Ex: We were *jammin'* last week at your house.

Jar your teeth [verb phr] get a surprised reaction from someone. Ex: His new hairdo will *jar your teeth.*

Jazzed up [verb] excited. (See *Hyped up*)

Jazzy [adj] colorful. Ex: That is a *jazzy* shirt.

Jelly side down [adv phr] something does not turn out the way you wanted it to. Ex: If you had an open faced jelly sandwich and dropped it, it would land *jelly side down.*

Jerk him around [verb phr] manipulate someone. Ex: That administrator *jerks the students around.*

Jet [verb] leave. Ex: Time for me to *jet.*

Jet set [noun] rich people who fly to resort places all over the world. Ex: Monaco is a great place for the *jet set.*

Jibonking [verb] riding a snowboard on surfaces other than snow, such as logs. Ex: Adventurous people love *jibonking.*

Jiminey Crickets [exclamation of surprise] (See *Good grief*)

Jockey for position [verb phr] trying to figure out how you can best compete in a group. Ex: The young graduates *jockey for position* at the company.

Joe Blow [noun] average man. Ex: Any *Joe Blow* can drive a car.

Jog my memory [verb phr] remind me. Ex: I need to *jog my memory* to remember to stop at the cleaners after work.

Johnny on the spot [noun phr] ready in a moment with a solution or some assistance. Ex: I can always depend on you to be *Johnny on the spot* when I need some help.

Jolly well better [adj phr] definite; no room for negotiation. Ex: "I don't know whether I can make it by 7:00." "Well, you *jolly well better.*"

Jot it down [verb phr] write it down. Ex: *Jot it down* so you won't forget.

Joy ride [noun] trip just for the pleasure of speed. Ex: The two teenagers took a *joy ride* in the their cars last night.

Joy stick [noun] video game control. Ex: The *joy stick* guides the figures in the video game.

Judged by the press [verb phr] receive good or bad reviews by newspaper personnel. Ex: The American President is *judged by the press.*

Judgment call [noun] arbitrary decision. Ex: The umpire called the batter "out". It was a *judgment call.*

Juggle his calendar [verb phr] rearrange appointments. Ex: I'll *juggle my calendar* so we can have lunch.

Jump at something [verb phr] accept it immediately. Ex: He will *jump at any job offer.*

Jump down someone's throat [verb phr] verbally chastise someone. Ex: Don't *jump down my throat* for forgetting your birthday.

Jump for joy [verb phr] excited and happy. Ex: I *jumped for joy* when I passed my driver's test.

Jump on [verb] scold. Ex: Don't *jump on* him. He didn't know what time it was. (See Lambaste someone)

Jump the gun [verb phr] be premature. Ex: Don't *jump the gun* and assume the weather will be nice.

Jump through hoops [verb phr] exceed any previous performance. Ex: He will *jump through hoops* to get that project finished on time.

Jump to conclusions [verb phr] come to a decision without careful study of all the facts. Ex: He *jumped to the wrong conclusion.*

Junk (my) [noun] #1 men's privates e.g. genitals. #2 items no longer wanted or needed.

Junk bonds [noun] high risk, high yield bonds that made millions of dollars during the 1980's for some people. Ex: Some people who made great fortunes in *junk bonds* ended up in jail.

Junk it [verb] destroy or discard it. Ex: *Junk that model airplane.* We will build another. (See *Deep six*)

Junk mail [noun] Advertisement brochures, newspapers, etc. you get in the mail that are unsolicited and usually quickly thrown away.

Just a kick [prep phr] amusing. Ex: You must see that new play. It is *just a kick.*

Just between you and me [prep phr] confidentially. Ex: *Just between you and me,* Darcy looked better with her hair shorter.

Just desserts [noun] get what you deserve. Ex: The bully got his *just desserts* when the two smaller kids finally beat him up.

Just like clockwork [prep phr] as scheduled; per routine. Ex: We eat dinner at 6:00 every night, *just like clockwork.*

Just like old home week [prep phr] see someone you knew well when you were younger. You say "Just like old home week."

Just off the boat

_____

Just off the boat [prep phr] inexperienced or naive. Ex: I know how to file my tax return. I'm not _just off the boat_ you know.

Just one big happy family [prep phr] can be your actual family or a group of people who are very close to each other and share a lot. Ex: The Martins are _just one big happy family_. They have six children.

Just scraped by [verb phr] barely survived financially. Ex: Andrew _just barely scraped by_ last month because he had to get new brakes for his car.

Just the other day [prep phr] within the last couple of days. Ex: _Just the other day_ I went to visit my brother.

Just the same [prep phr] nevertheless. Ex: _Just the same_ I want you to be home by 5:00.

Just the thing [prep phr] precisely the solution. Ex: This new umbrella is j_ust the thing._ It does not turn inside out in the wind easily. (See _Just the ticket_)

Just the ticket [prep phr] (See _Just the thing_)

Just under the wire [prep. phr] barely meet a time limit. Ex: She made it through the check-out line _just under the wire_.

Just what the doctor ordered [prep phr] the perfect solution. Ex: After all that overtime, a vacation was _just what the doctor ordered_.

K-pop Gangnam Style [noun phr] 2014 wildly popular song by South Korean musician Psy.

Keel over [verb] faint. Ex: He *keeled over* from exhaustion.

Keep a civil tongue in your head [verb phr] don't talk rudely or use vulgar language. Ex: *Keep a civil tongue in your head* when you talk to your Mother.

Keep a lid on it [verb phr] keep it secret. Ex: I just heard that the company is merging, but *keep a lid on it.* (See *Keep it under your hat*)

Keep a low profile [verb phr] be unobtrusive. Ex: He *kept such a low profile* that we didn't realize he was a company vice-president.

Keep a stiff upper lip [verb phr] be brave. Ex: I know you are afraid of the water, but *keep a stiff upper lip.*

Keep a straight face [verb phr] keep from laughing when something is hilariously funny. Ex: The teacher does that weird thing with his nose and I can hardly *keep a straight face.*

Keep abreast of [verb phr] stay informed. Ex: Are you *keeping abreast of* the latest developments in the famous murder case?

Keep an eye on [verb phr] observe on a regular basis. Ex: *Keep an eye on your child.* He is pushing other children.

Keep an eye out for you [verb phr] #1 will watch for opportunities for someone you know. Ex: I will *keep an eye out for you* and tell you about any available jobs. #2 You will look carefully for someone at a crowded place. Ex: I will *keep an eye out for you* at the Mall around 2:30.

Keep at arm's length [verb phr] avoid familiarity. Ex: He always *keeps his friends at arm's length,* and we never know if he has any problems.

Keep at it [verb phr] not give up. Ex: If you *keep at it,* you will become a very good piano player.

Keep body and soul together [verb phr] survive. Ex: Ever since Randy moved back in, we can hardly *keep body and soul together.*

Keep company with [verb phr] seeing someone regularly. Ex: Haven't you been *keeping company with* Beth for several months?

Keep him cooling his heels [verb phr] keep him waiting. Ex: The woman kept her boyfriend *cooling his heels* while she was shopping.

Keep his distance [verb phr] not get involved. Ex: He *keeps his distance* ever since the dog bit him.

Keep his head [verb phr] maintain control in a crisis or argument. Ex: He always *keeps his head* in an argument.

Keep his own counsel [verb phr] refuses to discuss his plans. Ex: You never know what Bob is doing because he always *keeps his own counsel.*

Keep in mind [verb phr] remember. Ex: *Keep in mind* that we must be at the Opera House by 7:00.

Keep in touch [verb phr] (goodbye expression) Ex: We'll have to *keep in touch* this summer when you are on vacation.

Keep it down [verb phr] #1 reduce the volume. Ex: Will you kids *keep it down* so I can hear the news. #2 not vomit. Ex: The food was so greasy, I don't know if I can *keep it down*.

Keep it to yourself [verb phr] keep it a secret. Ex: I think Brad is failing Math, but *keep it to yourself.* (See *Keep a lid on it)*

Keep it under your hat [verb phr] keep it secret. (See On the DL)

Keep me on my toes [verb phr] alert. Ex: That new science teacher sure *keeps me on my toes.* He is always having quizzes.

Keep on course [verb phr] maintain a schedule. Ex: *If you keep on course,* you will finish college by Spring.

Keep on trucking! [verb phr] a positive affirmation. Ex: "I'm having a hard time in Physics class." "Well, *keep on trucking."*

Keep pace with [verb phr] stay informed. (See *Keep abreast of)*

Keep tabs on [verb phr] watch carefully. Ex: I am going to *keep tabs on* my checkbook next month.

Keep the ball rolling [verb phr] continue. Ex: We need to *keep the ball rolling* on the house remodel with additional budget.

Keep the faith [verb phr] believe that good things will happen. Ex: We especially need to *keep the faith* since our home was damaged by the flood.

_____

Keep the home fires burning [verb phr] keep everything running smoothly while another person is gone. Ex: I will *keep the home fires burning* while you are at the beach.

Keep the peace [verb phr] maintain harmonious relations. Ex: I hope we can *keep the peace* until our relatives leave.

Keep the wolf from the door [verb phr] make enough money for survival. Ex: Ben made enough money fishing last summer to *keep the wolf from the door*.

Keep track of [verb phr] monitor. Ex: You need to *keep track of* your monthly expenditures.

Keep up my end [verb phr] do what was agreed. Ex: I'll keep up *my end of the bargain* if you keep up yours.

Keep up with the Joneses [verb phr] accumulate as many material items as the neighbors. Ex: Many people think they have to *keep up with the Joneses.*

Keep you on your toes [verb phr] keep you alert. Ex: He *keeps me on my toes* by his challenging questions.

Keep you posted [verb phr] keep you informed. Ex: I'll *keep you posted* of any new developments in our search for our lost dog.

Keep your chin up [verb phr] be brave. Ex: *Keep your chin up*. Don't let that bully get to you. (See *Keep a stiff upper lip*)

Keep your cool [verb phr] be calm. Ex: *Keep your cool* when talking to children.

_____

Keep your distance [verb phr] do not get emotionally involved. Ex: You need to *keep your distance* when dealing with your fellow workers.

Keep your eyes peeled [verb phr] look for. Ex: *Keep your eyes peeled* for a good restaurant.

Keep your fingers crossed [verb phr] be hopeful. Ex: *Keep your fingers crossed* that I will be accepted into the university.

Keep your hands to yourself [verb phr] #1 Don't hit each other. Ex: You kids *keep your hands to yourself*. #2 Don't touch me or my things. Ex: *Keep your hands to yourself*. I don't like anyone borrowing my cell phone.

Keep your head [verb phr] be rational. Ex: We need to *keep our heads* during a crisis.

Keep your head above water [verb phr] be solvent financially. Ex: I am barely *keeping my head above water* since our home was damaged in the fire.

Keep your nose clean [verb phr] do not get into any trouble. Ex: You boys *keep your noses clean* while I am at the store.

Keep your nose to the grindstone [verb phr] work hard. Ex: If you *keep your nose to the grindstone,* you will be successful.

Keep your shirt on! [verb phr] wait. Ex: *Keep your shirt on!* I will be there in a minute.

Kept in the dark [verb phr] kept uninformed. Ex: We are *kept in the dark* about a lot of business decisions.

_____

Kept woman [noun] a mistress. Ex: A _kept woman_ does not
     have the legal rights a wife has.

Key to my heart [noun phr] affect someone emotionally. Ex:
     She has the _key to my heart_ and I am going to marry
     her.

Keyed up [verb phr] #1 anxious. Ex: The threat of layoff has a
     lot of my co-workers _keyed up._ #2 bolster courage.
     Ex: Sam got _keyed up_ to face the audience and speak.
     #3 typed. Ex: Have you got my report _keyed up_ yet?

Kick around [verb phr] #1 discuss all aspects. Ex: The
     committee wants to _kick around_ the proposal for more
     staff before giving their recommendation.   #2
     mistreat or belittle. Ex: We won't have Coach Smith _to
     kick around_ anymore. He's retiring this year. #3 Do
     nothing important; relax. Ex: Let's _just kick_ around
     town this weekend.

Kick back [verb phr] relax. Ex: I'm going to _kick back_ and play
     golf this weekend.

Kick butt [verb phr] (impolite, but popular) take charge of a
     situation, be confident and ready to meet all
     obstacles. Ex: Our team is going to _kick butt_ this
     weekend.

Kick in [verb phr] #1 force entry. Ex: When the firemen arrived
     they had to _kick in_ the door to get to the fire. #2 start;
     energize. Ex: In the morning my brain doesn't _kick in_
     until I've had a cup of coffee. #3 donate. Ex: If your
     taking up a collection for Diego, I'll _kick in_ a couple
     dollars.

Kick in the pants [noun phr] #1 amusing. Ex: That new comedy show is just a *kick in the pants.* #2. prod. Ex: I have to give Kevin a *kick in the pants* to do his homework.

Kick into high gear [verb phr] move faster. Ex: Let's *kick this project into high gear.* We have to be finished in one month.

Kick-off [noun] start something. (as a new business program or a kick-off at a football game) Ex: We need to get there an hour before the *kick-off.*

Kick off the weekend [verb phr] begin the weekend. Ex: Let's *kick off the weekend* by going out to breakfast.

Kick the bucket [verb phr] died. (impolite to say about people) Ex: Danny's goldfish *kicked the bucket* last night.

Kick up a storm [verb phr] complain bitterly. Ex: My kids *kick up a storm* if they have to go to bed before 8:00 p.m.

Kick up your heels [verb phr] enjoy life, celebrate. Ex: The students *kicked up their heels* when they graduated.

Kick upstairs [verb phr] (business) refer a problem to higher management. Ex: We need more budget. We better *kick this project upstairs.*

Kill two birds with one stone (cliché) take care of two items with only one course of action.

Killed the goose that laid the golden eggs [proverb] destroy whatever was your source of income.

Kiss ass [verb phr] (impolite) ingratiate yourself with someone. He really *kisses ass* to get the boss's approval. (See *Suck up*)

Kiss it better [verb phr] said to a child who has hurt himself. "I'll *kiss it better.*"

Kiss it off [verb phr] forget it. Ex: You might as well *kiss off* that car since the motor blew up.

Kiss of life [verb phr] mouth to mouth resuscitation. Medical aid personnel have to give the *kiss of life* to lots of people.

Kiss that good-bye [verb phr] lost forever. Ex: After you criticized the manager's idea, you can *kiss that* promotion *good-bye.*

Kissing cousins [noun] remotely related people. Ex: I think Sophie and I are *kissing cousins.*

Kit and caboodle [noun phr] includes everything. Ex: They loaded the whole *kit and caboodle* into the car. (See *Everything but the kitchen sink)*

Kitchen cabinet [noun] (political) unofficial presidential advisors.

Knee high to a grasshopper [adj phr] (1930's country western) refers to a small person, usually a child. Ex: When you were *knee high to a grasshopper,* Grandpa used to hold you on his lap.

Kneejerk reaction [noun phr] act without thinking. Ex: Sometimes Congress has *kneejerk reactions* to issues.

Knew like a book [verb phr] completely familiar. Ex: He *knew his wife like a book.*

Knit her brows [verb phr] frown. Ex: Fran *knit her brows* while trying to think of the answer.

Knock around town [verb phr] casually drive or walk through the streets of a city. Ex: "What are you going to do tonight?" "Well, I thought we would just *knock around town* and see what happens."

Knockdown, drag-out [noun] violent, unrestrained fight. Ex: He had a *knockdown, drag-out* with his brother.

Knock 'em dead [verb phr] well wishing by a friend when you are about to undertake a challenge.

Knock for a loop [verb phr] overwhelm. Ex: That information really *knocked me for a loop.*

Knock it off [verb phr] stop it. Ex: Dad told the children to *knock it off* when they were fighting.

Knock off [verb] #1 quit doing something. Ex: Let's *knock off* for lunch and finish painting later. #2 imitation of something genuine. Ex: That watch is a *knock off* of a Rolex.

Knock on wood [verb phr] (gesture) knocking on wood for good luck. Ex: "Do you think you will get that job?" "*Knock on wood*" (actually knocking on wood). "I hope so."

Knock some sense into you [verb phr] threat to hit someone. Ex: If you behave that way again, I will *knock some sense into you.* (See *Knock the stuffing out of you*)

Knock the bottom out from under [verb phr] surprise someone with an unexpected course of action. Ex: The news about the stock market *knocked the bottom out* from under many investors.

Knock the stuffing out of you [verb phr] (See *Knock some sense into you*)

Knock your block off [verb phr] hit you in the head. Ex: The bully threatened to *knock his block off.*

Knock your socks off [verb phr] amaze you. Ex: You should see our new pitcher. He will *knock your socks off.*

Knocked into the middle of next week [verb phr] hit very hard. (See Mop up the floor with him)

Knocked the wind right out of his sails [verb phr] deflated someone's ego. Ex: When he stole Bart's idea, it *knocked the wind right out of Bart's sails.*

Knocking on death's doorstep [verb phr] close to death. Ex: My grandmother has been *knocking on death's doorstep* for several months now.

Know a thing or two [verb phr] have a certain amount of knowledge about a subject. Ex: I *know a thing or two* about fiber optic networks.

Know by heart [verb phr] memorize. Ex: I know the Pledge of Allegiance *by heart.*

Know full well [verb phr] completely understand. Ex: You *know full well* that I expected you to finish your work before going to the movies.

Know-it-all [adj] arrogant person. Ex: Adam is a *know-it-all* who gets straight A's.

Know it like the back of my hand [verb phr] completely familiar with. Ex: I *know that part of the country like the back of my hand.*

Know squat [verb phr] be completely uninformed. Ex: He doesn't *know squat* about fixing computers.

Know the ropes [verb phr] be experienced. Ex: She *knows the ropes* and will be a good team player.

Know what's what [verb phr] be knowledgeable. Ex: Scott *knows what's what* about wiring a house.

Knows his place [verb phr] realize proper or appropriate behavior. Ex: The dog *knows his place*. He doesn't come in the dining room when we are eating.

Knuckle sandwich [noun] a punch in the face with a closed fist. Ex: He gave his brother a *knuckle sandwich*.

Knuckled under [verb phr] gave in. Ex: We *knuckled under* and agreed to go to the beach.

LAN [abbrev] (computer) Local Area Network. It connects various computers and allows transmission of files from one site to another. Ex: We can use our computer software since we hooked up to the LAN.

LBD [abbrev] little black dress. Ex: Why don't you wear your LBD to the play?

LOL [abbrev] laughing out loud - Cell phone texting abbreviation.

La-la land [noun] (See In la-la land)

Labor of love [noun phr] do a task for someone you care for. Ex: Mowing his Dad's lawn was a real labor of love.

Lace into [verb] reprimand. Ex: If that boy walks in with dirty shoes, I'm going to lace into him. (See Get on his case)

Laced with [verb phr] poisoned or otherwise doctored. Ex: The deadly drink was laced with arsenic.

Lady killer [noun phr] a man who is good looking and charming, and is sought by many women. Ex: Some movie stars are real lady killers.

Lady luck [noun phr] being lucky. Ex: Lady Luck is with me tonight. I won at the casino.

Laid back [adj phr] casual, difficult to upset. Ex: Al is so laid back. He never gets upset if the traffic is bad.

Laid low [verb phr] become ill. Ex: The flu had me laid low for a week.

Laid off [verb phr] dismissed from your job. Ex: Dillon was laid off last January.

Laid to rest [verb] buried. Ex: We *laid Aunt Martha to rest* on Tuesday.

Laid up [verb] ill, helpless. Ex: I was *laid up* for two weeks with the flu.

Lollapalooza [noun] big event. Ex: The rock concert was a *lollapalooza.*

Lambaste someone [verb] chastise someone. Ex: The boy was *lambasted* for coming home late at night. (See *Read the riot act*)

Land in his lap [verb phr] opportunity materializes. Ex: That great job just *landed in his lap.*

Land of milk and honey [noun phr] country that is environmentally rich. Ex: Jordan is sometimes called the *land of milk and honey.*

Land office business [noun] profitable. Ex: We have so many new orders that we are doing a *land office business.*

Land on his feet [verb phr] recover after a setback. Ex: He always *lands on his feet* because he is confident.

Lap it up [verb phr] enjoy flattery. Ex: I told him I liked his shirt and he l*apped it up.* (See *Eat it up*)

Lap of luxury [noun phr] wealthy. Ex: Since he became a TV announcer he is sitting in the *lap of luxury.* (See *Life of Riley)*

Lardo [noun] (<u>impolite</u>) fat person. Ex: That *lardo* is taking up most of the airplane seat.

Larger than life [adj phr] An exaggeration of the real thing. Ex: That picture of a circus lion is *larger than life*.

Last but not least [adj phr] The final person or object to be included in an event, but no less important. Ex: Now, *last but not least,* is our final diver, Ginger.

Last ditch effort [noun phr] final attempt to do or accomplish something. Ex: These sales figures for the last quarter are *the last ditch effort* at getting our company back on its feet.

Last go-around [noun] give a certain situation one last try. Ex: This is my *last go-around* to try and ride that bicycle.

Last hurrah [noun] final moment. Ex: This game is not over until the *last hurrah.* (See *It's not over till the fat lady sings*)

Last round-up [noun] (country western) death. Ex: Pete's gone to the *last round-up* in the sky.

Last straw [noun] final test of patience. Ex: That is the *last straw.* You kids better do your homework now. (See *Straw that broke the camel's back*)

Latchkey [adj] describes children who return home from school to an empty house. Ex: There are a lot of children who are not getting proper supervision because they are *latchkey*.

Late bloomer [noun] #1 one that develops later than others. Ex: I know Margaret is small for her age, but I'm sure she's just a *late bloomer*. #2 talent which appears sometime late in life. Ex: His ability to write came as a *late bloomer*.

Latest and greatest [adj] anything that is current and therefore is assumed to be better than anything that came before it. Ex: This is the *latest and greatest* car that that has been designed.

Laugh all the way to the bank [verb phr] make money from an idea that others have ridiculed. Ex: They made fun of my cousin's invention, but he laughed *all the way to the bank.*

Laugh in his beard [verb phr] secretly laugh at a person or situation. Ex: When he made that last comment I just *laughed in my beard.* (See Laugh up his sleeve)

Laugh up his sleeve [verb phr] (See *Laugh in his beard)*

Laughed myself silly [verb phr] laugh uproariously. Ex: I *laughed myself silly* when I watched that new TV show. (See *Split a gut laughing*)

Law of averages [noun phr] bad behavior eventually will be punished. Ex: You can only cheat on your exams so many times and the *law of averages* catches up with you.

Lay a little rubber [verb phr] accelerate your car rapidly causing the tires to screech. Ex: Some teenagers like to *lay a little rubber* when they get a car.

Lay about [verb] be lazy. Ex: He *lay about* all summer without earning a cent.

Lay away [verb] #1 partially pay for an item and the store holds it until fully paid for. Ex: The store will *lay away* clothes for three months. #2 eat excessively. Ex: I've seen him *lay away* a whole pie after dinner.

Lay down arms [verb phr] surrender and stop fighting. Ex: The two countries agreed to *lay down arms* and stop the war.

Lay down the law [verb phr] enforce the rules. Ex: I am *laying down the law*. You kids will be in bed by 8:00 every night.

Lay it on the line [verb phr] #1 specific and honest when communicating with someone. Ex: I'll *lay it on the line* for you. I expect you home at 10:00 tonight, and there will be no exceptions. #2 take a major risk. Ex: Our servicemen *lay it on the line* every time they go out to defend us.

Lay it on the table [verb phr] share all the information you have with whoever is involved with the situation. Ex: The group *laid all the cards on the table* so they could make a good decision.

Lay it on thick [verb phr] flatter. Ex: He *lays it on so thick* it is hard to believe anything he says. (See *Suck up*)

Lay it to rest [verb phr] cease discussing a situation or problem. Ex: We have had a lot of discussion. Let's *lay this problem to rest* and discuss it again tomorrow.

Lay low [verb] be inconspicuous; hide. Ex: I think you should *lay low* until your dad calms down over the broken window.

Lay of the land [noun phr] current environment. Ex: When you go to a meeting , the first thing to do is assess the *lay of the land*.

Lay off [verb] #1 stop doing something. Ex: Why don't you *lay off* fixing your car and come help me mow the lawn? #2 [noun] (business) certain employees are dismissed by the company for cost reduction reasons. Ex: They let 2,000 people go in the last *layoff*. #3 [verb] Ex: The company will *lay off* 4,000 people.

Lay out [verb] #1 spread to view or work on. Ex: I *am laying out* the fabric on the table to pin the pattern. #2 suntan. Ex: I told her not to *lay out* more than a half hour the first day or she would sunburn. #3 explain in detail. Ex: I need to understand how it works; will you *lay* it *out* for me?

Lead footed [adj] push down hard on the accelerator of a car. Ex: Don't be so *lead footed* or I won't let you drive my car.

Lead in [noun] a sentence or phrase that enables other people to add to the conversation. Ex: That is a good *lead in* *fo*r me to tell him about my new hobby.

Leading him on [verb phr] #1 telling him something untrue. Ex: The salesman was *leading him on* when he said it was the best bargain in town. #2 pretending to be romantically involved. Ex: Sherry was *leading him on* and really was not interested in dating him.

Leading question [noun] question asked to get a certain response. Ex: "Where were you last night?" is an example of a *leading question.*

Leads a charmed life [verb phr] someone is lucky in life. Ex: Sandra *leads a charmed life.* Everything turns out well for her.

Lean and mean fighting machine [verb] intimidating. Ex: Our team this year is a *lean and mean fighting machine.*

Lean towards [verb] prefer. Ex: I *lean towards* acquiring more real estate than stocks for investing.

Leapfrog [noun] #1 playing a children's game of jumping over each other's bent back. Ex: We played *leapfrog* as children. #2 [verb] jumping from one subject to another. Ex: I can't follow his thinking because he is *leapfrogging*.

Leaps and bounds [adv] rapidly. Ex: My son's growing by *leaps and bounds*. (See *Like a weed*)

Learn by heart [verb phr] memorize. Ex: I have to *learn* the Presidents of the United States *by heart* tonight for the test.

Leatherneck [verb] tough people. Ex: Marines are *leathernecks*.

Leave a bad taste in your mouth [verb phr] negative impression. Ex: The fact that he did not wait for me *left a bad taste in my mouth*. (See *Rubs me the wrong way*)

Leave a paper trail [verb phr] create extensive documentation. Ex: The stockbroker *left a paper trail* so the investigator found the evidence.

Leave his mark [verb phr] make an impression. Ex: The railroad has *left its mark* on American business.

Leave it at the doorstep [verb phr] exclude or eliminate something undesirable. Ex: If any of you have a problem working with other ethnic groups, *leave it on the doorstep*.

Leave no stone unturned [verb phr] explore every possibility. Ex: We must find out who murdered Mrs. Wall. We must *leave no stone unturned* in our investigation.

Leave someone hanging [verb phr] (See *Left high and dry*)

Leave to his own devices [verb phr] allow him to do whatever he wants. Ex: *Left to his own devices*, Andy would stay up until midnight every night.

Leave well enough alone [verb phr] forget it. Ex: "Those sales figures are incorrect." *"Leave well enough alone."* They usually pad those figures anyway. (See *Drop it)*

Left hand doesn't know what the right hand is doing [noun phr] two groups or persons who should be working closely are duplicating efforts because of a lack of communication. Ex: John says we should proceed with the project while his assistant says we should wait. *The left hand sure doesn't know what the right hand is doing.*

Left high and dry [verb phr] relinquish support. Ex: I thought Derek was going to do half of the presentation, but he never showed up and really left me *high and dry.* (See *Left holding the bag*)

Left holding the bag [verb phr] (See *Left high and dry)*

Left in charge [verb phr] temporarily made responsible. Ex: Joan was *left in charge* of babysitting her younger brother while her Mother went to the store.

Left in the dust [verb phr] way behind in a competitive situation. Ex: The runner left his competitor *in the dust* and won the race.

Left in the lurch [verb phr] (See *Left high and dry)*

Left out in the cold [verb phr] not included in plans that others had made. Ex: Everyone went to the movies, but Jeri was *left out in the cold.*

Left to lick his wounds [verb phr] recover from a defeat by yourself. Ex: After the last election the congressman was *left to lick his wounds.*

Leg to stand on [verb phr] support for your position. Ex: Everyone supported NAFTA and I didn't have a *leg to stand on.*

Leg up [noun phr] assistance. Ex: The boss gave him a *leg up* on his new project.

Lend a hand [verb phr] help me out. Ex: I need to move my couch. Would you *lend* me *a hand?*

Lend your name to it [verb phr] support it. Ex: Would you *lend your name to my seminar idea?*

Let by [verb] #1 stand aside to allow someone to pass. Ex: I need to go in this doorway, so will you *let* me *by*? #2 allow less than expected performance. Ex: Jim got a good grade, since his teacher *let* him *by* without the final paper.

Let bygones be bygones [verb phr] (1940's slang) forgive and forget. Ex: We *let bygones be bygones* and renewed our relationship.

Let down [noun] a disappointment. Ex: Losing their last game was a real *let down* to the little leaguers.

Let 'er rip [verb phr] turn it on and see what happens. Can be said about something mechanical that is being worked on. When the work is finished the motor is turned on to see if it runs o.k. Ex: We've finished working on the motor now. *Let 'er rip.* (See *Let it fly*)

Let go [verb] #1 fire or dismiss someone from their job. Ex: The company was losing so much money, they had to *let go* about half the employees. (See *Lay off*) #2 release (feeling or object). Ex: You will never be able to be happy unless you *let go* of the past. #3 permit. Ex: I *let* Mary *go* to the pricing seminar.

Let in [verb] invite. Ex: I opened the window to *let in* some fresh air.

Let it all hang out [verb phr] relax and enjoy yourself. Ex: I didn't know Brent could dance so well. He really *let it all hang out*. (See *Let your hair down*)

Let it be [verb phr] #1 allow without argument. Ex: I didn't agree with Walt's opinion of the new employee, but I *let it be*. #2 leave something to heal without disruption. Ex: If you want that rash to heal, stop scratching and *let it be*. #3 famous song by The Beatles.

Let it fly [verb phr] (See *Let 'er rip*)

Let loose [verb phr] #1 emitted. Ex: After his team won, Howard *let loose* a deafening scream. #2 set free. Ex: When the cows were *let loose* to pasture, I had to climb the fence to get out of their way.

Let nature take its course [verb phr] don't plan the outcome. Ex: I don't know whether Troy will go to college. We are going to *let nature take its course.*

Let off [verb] #1 go without punishment. Ex: I *let* him *off* with a warning this time. #2 deliver someone. I *let* him *off* in front of the department store.

Let off steam [verb phr] yell and express your frustrations. Ex: If you have to *let off steam*, go to the basement so no one will hear you.

Let on [verb] show knowledge of. Ex: Don't *let on* that we know today is his birthday until the party.

Let out [verb] #1 loosen. Ex: You can't expect to catch a fish if you don't *let out* a little more line. #2 alter clothing to larger size. Ex: If I don't stop gaining weight, I will have to *let out* all my skirts. #3 open the door to let someone outside. Ex: The dog needs to go for a run. Will you *let* him *out*?

Let sleeping dogs lie [verb phr] don't bring up something that happened in the past. Ex: *Let sleeping dogs lie.* Don't remind her that she had anorexia last year.

Let the cat out of the bag [verb phr] disclose a secret. Ex: *Don't let the cat out of the bag,* but I heard Melinda is getting married to Bart in August. (See *Spill the beans*)

Let the chips fall where they may [verb phr] sit back and see how a situation will turn out. Ex: I gave the group my opinion and now we will just have to *let the chips fall where they may.*

Let the dust settle [verb phr] let the situation return to normal. Ex: I'm *letting the dust settle* and then I will ask for a raise.

Let the good times roll [verb phr] let's party! Ex: I'm giving a party tonight. *Let the good times roll!*

Let them eat cake [verb phr] first said by Marie Antoinette, Queen of France, when told that her subjects had no bread to eat. She replied, "*Then let them eat cake*". Generally said when someone is insensitive about the reality of a situation.

Let up [verb] cease. Ex: It rained for eight days straight without *letting up*. (See *Ease up*)

Let your hair down [verb phr] relax and have fun. (See *Let it all hang out*)

Let's boogie [verb phr] #1 Let's leave. Ex: *Let's boogie*. I've got to be home in 10 minutes. (See *Skedaddle*) #2 Let's dance.

Let's get down to business [verb phr] let's discuss the issues that are important. Ex: *Let's get down to business* now and decide where we are going for our vacation.

Let's get the show on the road [verb phr] Let's begin. Ex: If we are all packed for our vacation, *let's get the show on the road*.

Level with [verb] tell the truth. Ex: Why don't you *level with* me and tell me what really happened yesterday?

Leveraged buy-out [noun] (1980's) corporate raiders took over many companies by taking possession of the major portion of their stock. Ex: *Leveraged buy-outs* ruined many good companies.

License to steal [noun phr] unlocked and unprotected. Ex: You better put your bike lock on, or you are issuing a *license to steal*.

Lick and a promise [noun phr] do something quickly, but with the intention of doing it more thoroughly later (like house-cleaning). Ex: I'll just give it a *lick and a promise* now because I don't have much time.

Lick his boots [verb phr] flatter. Ex: If you *lick his boots,* you might get better grades. (See *Brown nose)*

Lick his chops [verb phr] anticipate eagerly. Ex: The dog *licked his chops* because he was getting a steak bone.

Lick it into shape [verb phr] under control. Ex: Once I get this project *licked into shape,* we can take a break.

Lickety-split [adj] move fast. Ex: We need to get to the store *lickety split.* (See *Shake a leg)*

Lie like a rug [verb phr] lie blatantly. Ex: You can't trust her. She *lies like a rug.* (See *Lie through his teeth*)

Lie low [verb] hide out. Ex: The robbers had to *lie low* because the sheriff was looking for them.

Lie through his teeth [verb phr] (See *Lie like a rug*)

Life is just a bowl of cherries [noun phr] everything is wonderful. Ex: Things are going great for me and *life is just a bowl of cherries.*

Life of Riley [noun phr] living comfortably. Ex: I won the lottery and am living the *life of Riley.*

Life of the party [noun phr] the center of attention and the most popular person. Ex: Bob sure is the *life of the party* tonight.

Light at the end of the tunnel [noun phr] improving situation. Ex: I got my degree, and can see the *light at the end of the tunnel.*

Light fingered [adj] likely to steal. Ex: Her son is *light fingered* so don't leave any money lying around.

Light of your life [noun phr] most important person in your life. Ex: Julie's granddaughter is the *light of her life.*

Light up [verb] #1 put a match to a cigarette. Ex: He will *light up* his cigarette. #2 exert a positive influence over. Ex: Derek just *lights up* Sarah's life.

Lighten up! [verb phr] don't be so serious. Ex: *Lighten up!* You are going on vacation next week.

Lightening never strikes twice in the same place [cliché] A misfortune is never repeated. Ex: Of course I'm parking my car where it got hit last week. *Lightening never strikes twice in the same place.*

Lights are on, but nobody's home [noun phr] not mentally alert. Ex: I gave her specific directions. I think the *lights are one, but nobody's home.* (See *One brick short of a full load*)

Like a duck to water [adv phr] adapt to an activity easily. Ex: Jimmy took to roller skating *like a duck to water.*

Like a fish out of the water [adv phr] uncomfortable and awkward. Ex: Whenever I go skiing, I feel *like a fish out of water.* I have only skied for two years.

Like a fly on a skillet [adv phr] nervous and unsure. Ex: Would you stop acting *like a fly on a skillet?*

Like a hole in the head [adv phr] totally unnecessary and
unwanted. Ex: I'm so busy. I need another
assignment *like a hole in the head*.

Like a house afire [adv phr] rapidly. Ex: She got dressed *like a
house afire,* because her Dad was taking her to the
beach.

Like a million bucks [adv phr] attractive and well dressed. Ex:
Joan looked *like a million bucks* tonight. She had a
new black dress.

Like a ton of bricks [adv phr] affected you greatly. Ex: My
brother's death hit me *like a ton of bricks*.

Like a weed [adv phr] very fast. Ex: Joey is growing *like a
weed*. I had to buy him some new pants yesterday.

Like death warmed over [adv phr] look pale and unwell. Ex:
Did you see Janelle tonight? She looked *like death
warmed over* after her illness.

Like it or lump it [adj phr] accept what is offered you with no
complaint. Ex: You're going to the dentist - *like it or
lump it*.

Like mad [adv phr] quickly or enthusiastically. Ex: We ran *like
mad* to the store.

Like magic [adv phr] miraculously. Ex: He made the
touchdown just *like magic*.

Like nailing Jell-O to the wall [adv phr] unable to define or
contain. Ex: Trying to get the two brothers to agree
on anything is *like nailing Jell-O to the wall.*

Like old home week [adv phr] something pleasant from the past. Ex: Seeing my old girlfriends was *like old home week.*

Like shooting fish in a barrel [adv phr] easily accomplished. Ex: Selling that house to the newcomers was *like shooting fish in a barrel.* (See *Easy as pie)*

Like taking candy from a baby [adv phr] extremely easy. (See *Like shooting fish in a barrel)*

Like two peas in a pod [adv phr] alike. Ex: The twins are just *like two peas in a pod.*

Like water off a duck's back [adv phr] easily accomplished. (See *Like taking candy from a baby)*

Likely as not [adv phr] could be either way. Ex: *Likely as not,* we'll catch a fish.

Likely story [noun] suspicious explanation or excuse. Ex: His excuse for being late this morning was a *likely story.*

Limp along [verb] progress slowly in spite of problems. Ex: The choir will *limp along* without its best tenor.

Line his pocket [verb phr] take advantage of an opportunity to make money. Ex: During the 1850's the gold miners *lined their pockets* with gold.

Line of baloney (malarkey) [noun phr] sales pitch or persuasive argument consisting of lies or exaggerations. Ex: How does he expect us to believe that *line of baloney* about that car?

Line of fire [noun phr] at risk or vulnerable. Ex: The Marines were in the direct *line of fire.*

Line up [verb] one person stands behind another, etc. to wait for an event to happen. Ex: Come on, *line up* here for your tickets to the opera.

Lion's share [noun phr] the biggest or most prestigious part of something. Ex: Uncle Joe got the *lion's share* of his brother's will.

Lip service [noun] praise something, but not really support it. Ex: Congress pays *lip service* to immigration reform, but they don't pass any laws backing it up.

Listen to your betters [verb phr] pay attention to people who are older or wiser. Ex: If you *listen to your betters,* you will get in less trouble.

Listen up! [command] pay close attention. Ex: *Listen up.* This is important.

Lit [verb] angry. Ex: I could tell he was *lit* by the look in his eyes. (See *Fully edged*)

Lit into him [verb phr] chastised him. (See *Chewed him up one side and down another*)

Litmus test [noun] final truth or test of being genuine. Ex: Let's give that theory the *litmus test* and see if it holds up.

Little bird told me [cliché] relate a secret from an undisclosed source. Ex: *A little bird told me t*hat you and Dean were getting married.

Little monkey [noun] active child. Ex: That *little monkey* crawled up on the counter five times yesterday. (See *Little shaver*)

Little shaver [noun] (See *Little monkey*)

Live a little [verb phr] relax and enjoy life. Ex: Your children are grown so *live a little.*

Live and learn [verb phr] comment usually said after a negative experience, indicating that you will avoid the situation in the future; you have learned by your experience. Ex: I won't make dinner for all the relatives by myself again. You *live and learn.*

Live and let live [verb phr] don't meddle in other people's business. Ex: It doesn't matter what your neighbors are doing. *Live and let live.*

Live by his wits [verb phr] be clever. Ex: He doesn't have a college degree, but he does very well *living by his wits.*

Live down [verb phr] stop being embarrassed about a certain incident or behavior. Ex: I'll never be able to *live down* acting silly when I had too much to drink.

Live from hand to mouth [verb phr] have barely enough to eat. Ex: He was getting tired of *living from hand to mouth* and never being able to save any money.

Live high on the hog [verb phr] live extravagantly. Ex: That couple really *lives high on the hog.* They bought a yacht yesterday. (See *Rolling in the dough)*

Live in an ivory tower [verb phr] removed physically or emotionally from the mainstream. (sometimes said about royalty) Ex: If you *live in an ivory tower,* you are unaware of what the ordinary people are doing.

Live in fortune's shadow [verb phr] wealth eludes you. Ex: He *lives in fortune's shadow* but so far has not been lucky.

Live in his own world   [verb phr] not relate to other people. Ex: He *lives in his own world* and spends a lot of time watching Sci-fi movies.

Live it up [verb phr] have fun. Ex: You better *live it up* now. When you get old you may not be healthy.

Live like a king [verb phr] live luxuriously as though you were wealthy and powerful. Ex: He *lives like a king* even though he is a store clerk.

Live like there's no tomorrow [verb phr] live recklessly or be a spendthrift. Ex: She *lives like there's no tomorrow* and is seen shopping every day.

Live off the fat of the land [verb phr] what can be grown in a garden. Ex: Since they have retired, they *live off the fat of the land.*

Live on her looks [verb phr] use attractiveness to manipulate people. Ex: She *lives on her looks* now, but will have to develop her mind as she gets older.

Live wire [noun] hyper person. Ex: That boy is a real *live wire.* He has been running around for two hours now.

Live with [verb] accept; become accustomed to. Ex: You have to learn to *live with* the fact that Peter is always late wherever he goes.

Live within your means [verb phr] budget your money. Ex: Some people find it difficult to *live within their means.*

Load the dice [verb phr] unfairly pre-arrange. Ex: I know he *loaded the dice* and we don't have a chance of winning.

Loaded for bear [verb phr] anticipate and be prepared for a battle or argument. Ex: The boss came to the budget meeting *loaded for bear*.

Loaf around [verb phr] lazy; not working. Ex: Ashley has *loafed around* all day.

Lock down [verb] obtain final approval. Ex: I don't think we can start to build the new office until we *lock down* the financing.

Lock out [noun] (business) management decision to keep union members from working. Ex: When the union refused to take a cut in pay, the company instituted a *lock out*.

Lock, stock, and barrel [adj phr] all of something. Ex: The new owner took over the business - *lock, stock, and barrel*. (See *Everything but the kitchen sink*)

Lock up [verb] secure. Ex: Be sure to *lock up* your house before you leave in the morning.

Lock up and throw the key away [verb phr] keep a prisoner forever. Ex: *Lock up* that criminal *and throw away the key* so he will never be free.

Locker-room language [noun] foul or vulgar words. Ex: Can you please calm down and keep the *locker-room language* out of the meeting?

Lollygag [verb] waste time. Ex: Get those dishes done now. Don't *lollygag* around, watching television.

Lone wolf [noun] person who prefers to work alone.

Lonesome George [noun] someone who prefers to be alone; unsociable. Ex: He decided to be *lonesome George* so he now lives by himself.

Long and the short of it [adj phr] #1 present both sides of a situation and say, "Well, that's the *long and the short of it*". #2 relate an unfortunate happening and end the story with "That's the *long and short of it*".

Long shot [noun] not a sure bet. Ex: It's a *long shot* that Native Sun will win the horse race.

Long walk on a short pier [noun phr] (See *Take a long walk on a short pier*)

Look at the bright side [verb phr] consider the positive aspects of a situation. Ex: *Look at the bright side.* Even though you did not get an "A" in history, you got an "A" in math.

Look at the world through rose colored glasses [verb phr] see only the good in life. Ex: My grandparents always seem so happy, but then they *look at the world through rose colored glasses*.

Look before you leap [cliché] be cautious. Ex: I know you want to wind surf, but *look before you leap*.

Look daggers [verb phr] stare at someone with hostility. Ex: Diane *looked daggers* at the woman because she didn't like her.

Look down your nose [verb phr] condescending toward someone. Ex: He *looks down his nose* at people who do not have as much education as he has.

Look for a loophole [verb phr] search for a legal way to avoid paying taxes or escape punishment. Ex: His lawyer was *looking for a tax loophole.*

Look for greener pastures [verb phr] search for new or better opportunities. Ex: She was unhappy in her job and decided to *look for greener pastures.*

Look for trouble [verb phr] invite disaster. Ex: That boy has a knife and is *looking for trouble*.

Look high and low [verb phr] search everywhere. Ex: I have *looked high and low* for my car keys and I cannot find them anywhere.

Look like a million [verb phr] dressed up.

Look like the cat that ate the canary [verb phr] look guilty. Ex: What's the matter? You *look like the cat that ate the canary.*

Look sharp [verb phr] #1 dress appropriately or be well-groomed. Ex: Jerry really *looks sharp* today with his new suit and tie. #2 pay attention and appear alert. Ex: *Look sharp* because the President is coming to visit our office today.

Look what the cat drug in [verb phr] jokingly refers to someone you know, when they show up unexpectedly. Ex: *Look what the cat drug in* George. It's your brother.

Looks all right on paper [verb phr] an idea appears to be logical as written. Ex: *It looks all right on paper.* Let's try it out and see if it works.

Looney [adj] crazy. Ex: That old woman is acting *looney.*

Looney bin [noun] mental ward. Ex: He has been in the *looney bin* for ten years.

Looney tunes [noun] crazy people. Ex: Those two drunks are *looney tunes.*

Loopy [adj] drunk. (See *Three sheets to the wind)*

Loose connection [noun] faulty thinking. Ex: He's got a *loose connection* somewhere. That idea will never work.

Lord it over [verb phr] act in a superior manner. Ex: Don't *lord it over* me just because you got an "A" on your paper.

Lord love a duck! [1940's expression of amazement] Ex: You learned to sail a boat? *Lord love a duck!* (See *Good grief)*

Lose face [verb phr] embarrassed. Ex: He *lost face* when his son won the game against him.

Lose it [verb phr] #1 become angry or irrational. Ex: If I can't find my keys, I will lose it. (See *Hit the ceiling)* #2 disassociate from. Ex: That tie is too bold for your interview. *Lose it.*

Lose sleep over it [verb phr] worry. Ex: I don't wear the latest fashions in clothes, but I am not going to *lose any sleep over it.*

Lose touch with [verb phr] no longer in contact with. Ex: I have *lost touch with* Tom since he moved to Alaska.

Lose your bearings [verb phr] get lost or bewildered. Ex: They *lost their bearings* on the hike.

Lose your cool [verb phr] irritated. Ex: I will *lose my cool* if I have to explain it to him again. (See *Lose your grip)*

Lose your grip [verb phr] (See *Lose your cool*)

Lose your head [verb phr] become irrational. Ex: Be careful that you don't *lose your head* when you fall in love.

Lose your marbles [verb phr] behaving irrationally. (See *Few screws loose*)

Lose your shirt [verb phr] lose all your money in a business venture. Ex: They *lost their shirts* and had to close their business.

Loser [noun] undesirable person. (See *Gomer*)

Losing ground [verb phr] #1 not winning in a competitive situation. Ex: I seem to be *losing ground* every time I play you in tennis. Are you practicing more?

Lost cause [noun phr] hopeless. Ex: Don't waste your time trying to teach him. He's a *lost cause*.

Lost in the shuffle [verb phr] lose track of an aspect of a situation. Ex: They hired him without knowing he had been arrested. That fact was *lost in the shuffle*. (See *Fell through the crack*s)

Lost the thread [verb phr] forgot the point of the discussion. Ex: I *lost the thread* of your last sentence. Could you please repeat it?

Lot in life [noun phr] fate. Ex: It is his *lot in life* to be unhappy.

Love conquers all [noun phr] love is a stronger emotion than others. Ex: *Love conquers all* is a positive affirmation about yourself and others.

Love handles [noun] rolls of fat around the waist. Ex: When your metabolism slows down, you have to watch your diet or you will get *love handles.*

Love is blind but the neighbors ain't [cliché] be discreet when you are in love with someone because other people are watching you.

Love me, love my dog [verb phr] if you care for me, you will also care about my pets.

Love ya! [goodbye expression] said when two friends are parting.

Low life [noun] undesirable person. (See *Hairball)*

Low man on the totem pole [noun phr] employee with no influence or position. Ex: I can't make that decision. I am the *low man on the totem pole.* (See *Peon)*

Low spirits [noun] sadness; depression. Ex: He has been in *low spirits* since he lost his job.

Lower 48 [noun] the forty-eight continental United States, not including Alaska or Hawaii. Ex: There are a few good places to hunt for cougar in the *lower 48.*

Lower Slobovia [noun] an imaginary, undesirable place. Ex: I wish I could send her back to *Lower Slobovia*.

Lower the boom [verb phr] exhibit sternness. Ex: I will have to *lower the boom.* She has not done her homework.

Luck of the Irish [noun phr] fortunate in life. Ex: He has the *luck of the Irish* and wins a lot of money when he gambles.

Luck out [verb phr] fortunate, usually in a risky situation. Ex: You *lucked out* not getting caught selling your rock concert ticket at scalper prices.

Lukewarm about it [adj phr] not enthusiastic. Ex: I am *lukewarm about* you bicycling in Europe.

Lump in my throat [noun phr] emotionally moved. Ex: I get a *lump in my throat* every time I think of my daughter's wedding.

Lump of coal in your stocking [noun phr] threat of getting nothing at Christmas. Ex: If you don't behave, you're going to get a *lump of coal in your stocking*.

Lunch bunch [noun] group that meets for lunch regularly. Ex: The *lunch bunch* is going to that new Italian cafe for lunch.

Lunch mouth [noun] someone who eats a lot of food. Ex: That teenager is a real *lunch mouth.*

Lurk around [verb phr] spying on someone. Ex: I have seen him *lurking around* the school.

MIA (acronym) [military] status of a member of the armed forces who is shot down during a war. Ex: We're still looking for *MIA*'s from the Vietnam war.

Mad as a hatter [cliché] appear crazy. Long ago, hatters (people who made hats) used mercury to seal and waterproof pieces of the hat. The mercury was so toxic that many of the hatters literally went crazy. Ex: She is screaming and looks *mad as a hatter.* (See *Go into orbit)*

Mad as a March hare [cliché] wild and unpredictable. Ex: The people in mental institutions sometimes act *mad as a March hare.*

Mad dash [noun] a quick unplanned trip. Ex: I need to make a *mad dash* to the grocery store to get some bread.

Mad money [noun] extra money you have hidden away for an extravagance. Ex: "Can you go to the movies?" "Yes, I've got some *mad money* I can use."

Mad scramble [noun phr] rushing around to accomplish something fast. Ex: It sure is a *mad scramble* trying to get all the children dressed and to church on time.

Madder than a wet hornet [adj phr] (country western) explosively angry. Ex: I was *madder than a wet hornet* when he ran into my car.

Made in the shade [verb phr] a cinch. Ex: "Do you think you can win the race?" "Sure. I've got it *made in the shade.*"

Made it by the skin of my teeth [verb phr] barely accomplish something within a specific time constraint. Ex: "Did you get that important project finished yesterday?" "Yes, I *made it by the skin of my teeth.*"

Made of money [verb phr] extremely wealthy. Ex: My son asked me for twenty-five dollars to go out on a date. He must think I'm *made of money*. (See *Rolling in the dough*)

Made out like a bandit [verb phr] get the advantage. Ex: Marcie *made out like a bandit* when she got a free trip in addition to her regular frequent flier miles.

Made up [verb] #1 invents, as a story or lie. Ex: He *made up* a story that his car broke down to cover up for being late. #2 reconciled. Ex: The young couple *made up* after their disagreement. #3 prepared. Ex: She *made up* the spare bed for guests.

Main drag [noun] main street in town. Ex: The drugstore is located right along the *main drag.*

Main man [noun] most important male figure in a woman's life. Ex: He's my *main man.*

Main squeeze [noun] serious boyfriend or girlfriend. Ex: I'm goin' out with my *main squeeze* tonight.

Mainstreaming [verb] putting disadvantaged children back into a regular classroom. Ex: We need to *mainstream* the dyslexic children in our school.

Maintain the status quo [verb phr] no change. Ex: Lots of people want to *maintain the status quo* and do not like new ideas.

Make a beeline for [verb phr] go straight for something without deterring. Ex: The small child *made a beeline for* his toys.

Make a big thing out of it [verb phr] exaggerate the importance of a problem. Ex: I know I have a sprained ankle, but let's not *make a big thing out of it.* (See *Make a mountain out of a molehill*)

Make a break for it [verb phr] attempt to escape. Ex: The convicts *made a break for it* but got caught.

Make a bundle [verb phr] make a lot of money. Ex: Did you know that George *made a bundle* off his last real estate deal? (See *Make a killing*)

Make a clean break [verb phr] end a relationship amicably, but completely. Ex: I decided to *make a clean break* with Eli and date other people.

Make a clean sweep [verb phr] start over. Ex: When Gerald was elected Mayor, he *made a clean sweep* and appointed all new officials.

Make a federal case out of it [verb phr] overemphasize a negative event. Ex: I only got a "C" in Spanish. Let's not *make a federal case out of it.*

Make a killing [verb phr] make a lot of money. Ex: Jeremy *made a killing* in the stock market last year. (See *Make a mint*)

Make a living [verb phr] be able to pay your bills. Ex: The young couple couldn't *make a living* unless they had two jobs.

Make a mint [verb phr] (See *Make a killing*)

Make a mockery [verb phr] scorn it. Ex: They *made a mockery* out of the fact that he was an environmentalist.

Make a monkey out of him [verb phr] make a fool of someone. Ex: The bully *made a monkey out of him* by ridiculing his big feet.

Make a mountain out of a molehill [verb phr] (See *Make a big thing out of it*)

Make a play for [verb phr] flirt with. Ex: Jill is always *making a play for* Steve and he is really not interested in her. (See *Make eyes at*)

Make a point of [verb phr] will accomplish. Ex: I will *make a point of* picking up some milk on my way home from work.

Make a stab at it [verb phr] attempt to do something. Ex: "Do you think that you can climb that tree?" "I'll sure *make a stab at it.*"

Make allowances for [verb phr] overlook faults or weaknesses. Ex: You have to *make allowances for* the fact that he hasn't done that type of work before.

Make tracks [verb phr] ready to leave. Ex: I've got to *make tracks* and get to football practice.

Make you an offer you can't refuse [verb phr] make the deal attractive. Ex: Bring in your old car and I'll *make* you *an offer you can't refuse.*

Make believe [verb] pretend. Ex: Why don't you *make believe* that you are rich?

Make both ends meet [verb phr] balance your budget. Ex: If I don't take that trip to Europe, I can *make both ends meet* this month.

Make do [verb] adjust. Ex: Jack is bringing guests for dinner tonight. I don't have any extra food so we'll just have to *make do*.

Make eyes at [verb phr] flirt. Ex: Did you see Mona *making eyes at* Sam today? (See *Make a play for*)

Make for the door [verb phr] prepare to leave. Ex: I'm going to *make for the door now* so I can be home at 10:00.

Make hay while the sun shines [cliché] take advantage of an opportunity.

Make heads or tails of it [verb phr] understand it. Ex: I can't *make heads or tails of* this memo Tom wrote.

Make headway [verb] make progress. Ex: At last we are *making headway* on this project.

Make him sit up and take notice [verb phr] make someone pay attention to you. Ex: If I win first prize, maybe Dad will *sit up and take notice.*

Make his mark [verb phr] succeed or gain fame. Ex: Native Dancer *made his mark* in race horse history.

Make it count [verb phr] handle it correctly. Ex: You have only one chance to impress your new client. *Make it count.*

Make it on a shoestring [verb phr] live on little money. Ex: Brian is *making it on a shoestring* with just his income alone. His wife does not work.

Make it on his own [verb phr] live independently. Ex: He *made it on his own* and bought the property without any help from his parents.

Make it snappy [verb phr] do it quickly. Ex: Please get me the sugar and *make it snappy*! (See *Chop chop*)

Make lemonade out of your lemons [cliché] take a negative situation and make it positive. Ex: Even though I got laid off from my job, I am going to *make lemonade out of my lemons* and get a better job. (See *Make the best of it*)

Make light of it [verb phr] treat a matter casually. Ex: Let's just *make light of the fact* that we are out of gas. We can walk to the gas station.

Make my day [verb phr] do something unusual to please or impress me. Ex: Go ahead, *make my day.* Take me to that concert. (Popularized by Clint Eastwood.)

Make no bones about it [verb phr] prefaces a true statement. Ex: *Make no bones about it.* I am planning to build a new home next year.

Make note of [verb phr] remember. Ex: I want you to *make note of* the fact that Sally will be out of the office on Monday.

Make or break him [verb phr] succeeding or failing. Ex: That business deal will either *make or break* Jorge.

Make out [verb phr] #1 have physical contact with someone of the opposite sex, such as kissing and petting. Ex: Evan and his girlfriend *made out* at the movies last night. #2 perform. Ex: How did you *make out* on that job interview?

Make out like a bandit [verb phr] make a lot of money, possibly unscrupulously.

Make the best of it [verb phr] be positive about bad luck. Ex: After Ron had his accident, he made the best of it and developed new hobbies. (See *Make lemonade out of your lemons*

Make the cut [verb phr] perform to a set of expectations. Ex: He did not *make the cut* and will not be on the football team. (See *Make the grade*)

Make the dust fly [verb phr] work vigorously. Ex: She really *made the dust fly* yesterday and cleaned her room in one hour.

Make the fur fly [verb phr] start an argument or fight. When those two brothers get angry, they really *make the fur fly.* (See *Raise the roof*)

Make the grade [verb phr] meet expectations. Ex: Employees who don't *make the grade* will be terminated. (See *Make the cut*)

Make tracks [verb] leave. (See *Let's boogie*)

Make up ground [verb phr] catch up to everyone else. Ex: He *made up ground* in the bicycle race and now is in first place.

Make up your mind [verb phr] decide. Ex: Why don't you *make up your mind* whether you want to go Cancun or Florida?

Make whoopee [verb phr] (1940's slang) have sex. Ex: Let's *make whoopee* tonight! (See *Get it on*)

Make your hair stand on end [verb phr] will surprise and amaze you. Ex: I've got some sales figures that will *make your hair stand on end.*

Make your mouth water   [verb phr]   desire either food or someone of the opposite sex so much that you salivate just thinking about them. Ex: Just thinking about chocolate cake *makes my mouth water.*

Make yourself at home   [verb phr]   be comfortable. Usually said when a guest arrives at your home. Ex: "Hi Greg, come in, and *make yourself at home."*

Makeover   [noun]   get a new look cosmetically. Ex: Lots of beauty shops offer free *makeovers* if you get your hair done there regularly.

Makes my blood boil   [verb phr]   makes me angry. Ex: The fact that Congress raised our taxes *makes my blood boil.* (See *Hacked off*)

Makes my heart bleed   [verb phr]   grieves me. Ex: The fact that the little boy was killed in a drive-by shooting *makes my heart bleed.*

Makes your head swim   [verb phr]   confuses you. Ex: The new tax structure is so complicated that it *makes your head swim.*

Man about town   [noun phr]   well known and self-confident person. Ex: Jack Smith is a real *man about town* and will probably be elected mayor in the next election.

Man of his word   [noun phr]   trustworthy. Ex: Patrick is always a *man of his word.* He does what he promises he will do.

Man/woman of means   [noun phr]   rich. Ex: *People of means* travel a lot. (See *Rolling in clover*)

Man on the street [noun phr] ordinary person. Ex: Let's hear from the *man on the street* about the new sales tax.

Man to man [noun phr] two people sharing a confidence. Ex: *Man to man* I'd say he's in a lot of trouble.

Managed competition [noun phr] (business) harnessing market competition among various providers to drive down prices and maintain quality.

Many happy returns [noun phr] a written expression on someone's birthday card wishing him/her well.

Marching orders [noun] directions to carry out a task. Ex: Wait till you get your *marching orders* before you clean out the garage.

Marching to a different drummer [verb phr] non-conforming. Ex: Eric is going to raft the Amazon River. He always *marches to a different drummer.*

Mark my words [verb phr] remember what I say. Ex: *Mark my words.* My brother will graduate from college next year.

Mark up [verb] #1 raised prices in stores at certain times. Ex: I know they *marked up* that blouse just because the Christmas season is coming. #2 edit material before publishing. Ex: The editor sure *marked up* his book. He will have a lot of revisions to make.

Marking time [verb phr] count the days until a certain event will happen. Ex: She is just *marking time* until the baby is born.

Married to his job [verb phr] spending too much time at work. Ex: You would think Terry is *married to his job.* He stayed at the office until 8:00 last night.

Maryjaned [verb] (1960's slang) stoned on marijuana. Ex: He got *maryjaned* and stayed at my house last night.

Matter of course [noun phr] regular routine. Ex: *As a matter of course,* we always eat dinner at 5:00. (See *Matter of fact*)

Matter of fact [noun phr] (See *Matter of course*)

Matter of life or death [noun phr] a situation of extreme importance. Ex: If he doesn't get his insulin shot, it will be a *matter of life or death.*

Matter of principle [noun phr] issue of integrity. Ex: It is a *matter of principle* that the new school superintendent got all new furniture for her office.

Matters at hand [noun phr] events that require immediate attention. Ex: *Matters at hand* require that I go home and help my invalid mother.

Maxed out [verb] gone beyond the limit. Ex: His bank account is really *maxed out.*

May the blue bird of happiness fly up your nose [1960's expression] a nonsensical well wishing to a friend.

May-September romance [noun phr] an older woman dating a younger man. (See *Cougar*)

Mean streak [noun phr] change moods and be abusive. Ex: Blake's stepfather sure has a *mean streak.*

Mean to do something [verb phr] intend. Ex: I *mean to do something* about my car brakes.

Measure up [verb] meet expectations. Ex: Can we find a programmer that will *measure up* to Alan?

Meat and potatoes person [adj phr] basic. Ex: Jerome is a *meat and potatoes* man. He doesn't like those cream sauces.

Meet your Waterloo [verb phr] fail and lose control of a situation. (from a reference to French leader Napoleon, who lost control of France at the Battle of Waterloo) Ex: If I don't get that job, I will *meet my Waterloo.*

Meeting of the minds [noun phr] powerful people gathering together. Ex: It was a real *meeting of the minds* when Roosevelt, Churchill and Stalin gathered at the Yalta Conference.

Mega-bucks [noun] lots of money. Ex: Those basketball shoes cost *mega-bucks.*

Mega-trend [noun] current fads. Ex: The grunge look is a real *mega-trend.*

Mellow out! [verb expression] don't be upset or excited; calm down. Ex: *Mellow out!* I'm sure you will find your cat tomorrow.

Melt his heart [verb phr] warms him. Ex: When his granddaughter hugs him, it just *melts his heart.*

Melt in your arms [verb phr] relax totally when someone hugs you. Ex: When her boyfriend comes, she just *melts in his arms*.

Men in blue [noun phr] Navy personnel or police. Ex: The *men in blue* were in the parade.

Mend his ways [verb phr] behave more appropriately. Ex: I know Trevor will *mend his ways* and return to school.

Mend your fences [verb phr] forgive others and ask forgiveness. Ex: I'm going to *mend my fences* with my sister.

Mentally challenged [noun] low I.Q. Ex: He is in a special education class for the *mentally challenged*.

Mess around [verb phr] playing. Ex: You kids stop *messing around* and come to dinner. (See *Fool around*)

Met a milestone [verb phr] (business) accomplished a major planned event or scheduled activity. Ex: We *met a milestone*, getting our new computers installed on time.

Meter's running [noun phr] time is passing quickly. Ex: "Can I talk to you a minute Phil?" "Well, hurry up. The *meter's running*."

Method to his madness [noun phr] a reason for unpredictable behavior. Ex: "Why is Kevin acting so weird?" "I don't know. There must be a *method to his madness*."

Mickey Mouse [adj] easy. Ex: The test on Friday was really *Mickey Mouse*. (See *Slam dunk*)

Middle class [adj phr] people who make a median income e.g. the majority of Americans. Ex: The vast majority of the *middle class* is concerned about job security.

Midnight oil (See *Burn the midnight oil*)

Midnight requisition [noun] (business) take an office item and move it to your office after hours so no one will notice. Ex: Since we didn't get any new chairs, we will have to *midnight requisition* some.

Might as well [verb phr] should. Ex: You *might as well* leave without Brad. He is late.

Milk it for all it's worth [verb expression] take an advantage. Ex: His wife does all the housework and he *milks it for all its worth*.

Mill around [verb phr] casually walk about with no purpose in mind. Ex: The cattle were *milling about* the feeding trough.

Millennials [noun] America's young adults, ages 18-33. Ex: The Millennials consider themselves politically independent.

Millstone around my neck [noun phr] heavy burden. Ex: Having to take care of my Aunt who has Alzheimer's is a *millstone around my neck*.

Mince words [verb phr] choose what you say carefully and concisely. Ex: I'm not going to *mince words*. Do your homework now.

Mind games [noun] manipulation. Ex: Lauren got to the top of the corporate ladder by playing a lot of *mind games* with her co-workers.

Mind in the gutter [noun phr] thinking obscene thoughts. Ex: That boy has his *mind in the gutter* and cannot concentrate on his school work.

Mind like a sieve [noun phr] not concentrating. (See *In one ear and out the other*)

Mind like a steel trap [noun phr] bright and quick witted. Ex: Don't tangle with Josie. She has a *mind like a steel trap*.

Mind over matter [noun phr] control your behavior through strong willpower. Ex: I am going to exercise *mind over matter* and not smoke that cigarette.

Mind your p's and q's [verb phr] (Usually said to children) behave properly. Ex: Now you *mind your p's and q's* when we go to visit Aunt Martha.

Misery loves company [cliché] a depressed person tends to associate with others who feel the same way.

Mishmash [noun] a conglomeration of things; nothing really fits with anything else. Ex: I have such a *mishmash* of tools and cannot find the one I need.

Miss know-it-all [noun phr] conceited woman. Ex: Ask *Miss know-it- all.* She has all the answers.

Miss the boat [verb phr] #1 lost an opportunity. Ex: I really *missed the boat* on that car deal. #2 misunderstood altogether. Ex: I *missed the boat* with Renee. I thought she really liked me.

Missed by a mile [verb phr] guess at something and miss the answer totally. Ex: Joe *missed by a mile* on question #2 of the exam. (See *Missed the mark*)

Missed the mark [verb phr] (See *Missed by a mile)*

Missed you something terrible [verb phr] miss someone very much. Ex: When you were gone last week, I *missed you something terrible.*

Missing link [noun] #1 supposed evolutionary link between man and ape. Ex: Scientists have discovered the *missing link* between apes and man. #2 not act or speak rationally. Ex: He really has a *missing link*. Did you hear that last remark he made?

Mix it up [verb phr] #1 fight. Ex: I know Joe and Ed will *mix it up* when they see one another. #2 dance. Ex: Let's *mix it up* on the dance floor. #3 prepare (as in cooking) Ex: Let's *mix it all up* and put it in the oven.

Mix up [verb] #1 confuse. Ex: People often *mix up* Jack with Frank, because they look so much alike. #2 be involved. Ex: Don't get *mixed up* with a gang or you might get in trouble.

Mixed blessing [noun] one that has both good and bad aspects to it. Ex: Grandpa has lived a long life, but he has Alzheimer's Disease. It is a *mixed blessing.*

Mixed company [noun] men and women together. Ex: I wouldn't tell that joke in *mixed company*.

Moan and groan [verb phr] complain constantly. Ex: He has a new TV and now is *moaning and groaning* over not having a new DVR.

Mod [adj] in style. Ex: That new velvet dress is really *mod*.

Modem [noun] (computer) a peripheral that, when connected to a computer, allows communication over telephone lines so faxes and E-mail can be sent. Ex: I just got a new *modem* so I can access the Internet with my PC.

Mom and pop store [noun phr] small grocery or drug store run by a husband and wife. Ex: Why don't you get some milk at the *mom and pop store* down the street?

Momaflauge [noun] camaflouge an item from your mother.
Ex: The *momaflauge* will keep my cigarettes hidden.

Mommy track [noun] (business) a woman has a career, has a
baby and quits work for a while to care for the child.
Then she returns to her position in business. Ex:
Women on the *Mommy track* find it difficult to get
good child care.

Monday morning quarterbacking [noun phr] action you should
have taken. Ex: We should have sold the house last
year when the interest rates were low. But that's just
Monday morning quarterbacking.

Moneybags [noun] someone who is rich.   Ex: The Sheik of
Arabia is known as old *moneybags*. (See *Gotrocks*)

Monkey on his back [noun phr] a difficult problem to solve. Ex:
Why don't you get the *monkey off your back* and give
that problem to Rob to solve?

Monkey see, monkey do [expression] copy someone's actions
or words.

Monkey suit [noun] tuxedo. Ex: I suppose we have to rent
monkey suits for the wedding.

Montezuma's Revenge   [noun]   diarrhea.   Ex: I got
Montezuma's Revenge when I drank the water in
Mexico. (See *Have the runs*)

Month of Sundays [noun phr] a long time. Ex: I haven't seen
my daughter in a *month of Sundays*.

Moon ball [noun] (sports - tennis) high arcing slow ball. Ex:
He lost the game because he couldn't return all the
moon balls.

Moola [noun] money. Ex: I don't have enough *moola* to go to the movie. (See *Dough*)

Moonlight [verb] work at a second job after your daytime eight hour a day job. Ex: I have to *moonlight* to pay my rent.

Moot point [noun] does not make any difference to the discussion. Ex: The fact that you were trying out for the basketball team is really a *moot point*. You should have studied more for the test.

More bang for your buck [noun phr] get a greater advantage with one choice than with another. Ex: If you choose to buy Brand B, you will get *more bang for your buck.*

More fish in the sea [noun phr] other people you can date. Ex: I know you miss Joan, but there are *more fish in the sea*.

More fun than a barrel of monkeys [noun phr] enjoyable. Ex: You should try hang gliding. It's *more fun than a barrel of monkeys.*

More or less [adv phr] approximately. Ex: We will be at the movies at 7:00, *more or less.*

More than he bargained for [adj phr] the situation was more difficult to handle than was anticipated. Ex: When the dog attacked the cat, he got *more than he bargained for.*

More to it than meets the eye [adj phr] A situation is more complex than it initially appears. Ex: It looks like a simple suicide, but I believe there is *more to it than meets the eye.*

Mother country [noun] homeland; place of birth. Ex: His *Mother country* is Japan.

Mother hen [noun] woman who is protective of her children. Ex: Shirley is a real *mother hen*. She won't let her children out of her sight. (See *Helicopter Mom*)

Mother of all battles [noun phr] WWII. Ex: WWII was the *mother of all battles.*

Motherhood and apple pie [noun phr] inherent values of a country. Ex: We can't take money from the Social Security benefits. That's *Motherhood and apple pie.*

Motor mouth [noun] someone who is talkative and says little of significance. Ex: He is a *motor mouth* and doesn't listen well.

Mouth full of marbles [noun phr] not enunciating clearly or distinctly. Ex: I can't understand a word you are saying. It sounds like you have a *mouth full of marbles.*

Move heaven and earth [verb phr] have to accomplish the impossible. Ex: He's going to have to *move heaven and earth* to get her to marry him.

Move in [verb] #1 locate in new surroundings. Ex: Ellen got a new apartment and I helped her *move in*. #2 Take part of someone's territory. Ex: We have a candy counter, but the new vending machines are trying to *move in.*

Move in with [verb] #1 share living space with someone. Ex: Jean's sister had to *move in with* her until her apartment was painted.

Movers and shakers [noun phr] aggressive and action-oriented people. Ex: The *movers and shakers* of the world get a lot of changes accomplished.

Mow someone down [verb phr] knock someone down, literally. Ex: Stop running so fast or you will *mow someone down.*

Mucking around [verb phr] living aimlessly. Ex: You need to stop *mucking around* and get a plan for your life.

Muddying the water [verb phr] make a situation more unclear. Ex: The politician really was *muddying the water* on that issue.

Mudslinging [verb] (political) character assassination done by one politician to another. Ex: There is a lot of *mudslinging* going on in the Senate campaign.

Muffin top [noun] (2012 slang) excess belly fat on women. Ex: We are exercising a lot to get rid of our *muffin tops.*

Mule-headed [adj] stubborn. Ex: He is so *mule headed* that he doesn't perform well as a team member.

Mumbo-jumbo [adj] not understandable. Ex: Everything the President says about health care is just *mumbo-jumbo* to me.

Munch mouth [noun] someone who likes to eat lots of snack food. Ex: We have a couple of *munch mouths* at our house.

Munchkin [noun] small child. Ex: Dress the *munchkins* warmly before they go outside. (See Pipsqueak)

Mushroomed [verb] uncontrolled growth. Ex: The population has *mushroomed* where computer companies have sprung up.

Music to my ears [noun phr] pleasant and positive news. Ex: You got a promotion today. Now that's *music to my ears.*

My cup runneth over [cliché] significantly blessed. Ex: We are having all the children home for Thanksgiving holiday this year. *My cup runneth over!*

My ex [noun] my ex-husband or ex-wife. Ex: *My ex* and I are still good friends.

My hands are tied [noun phr] can't take action. Ex: I'd like to be able to loan you the money, but *my hands are tied.*

My hat's off to you [noun phr] a compliment. Ex: You managed to win the race. *My hat's off to you.*

My heart goes out to him [noun phr] sympathize with someone. Ex: Duane lost his wife recently. *My heart really goes out to him.*

My heart was in my throat [noun phr] apprehensive and scared about a situation. Ex: I heard a strange noise in the middle of the night and *my heart was in my throat.*

My lips are sealed [noun phr] I will keep it a secret. Ex: *My lips are sealed* about the new stock deal. (See *On the DL*)

My own flesh and blood [noun phr] my children. Ex: *My own flesh and blood* will inherit our investments.

My three squares

My three squares [noun phr] refers to the three meals one should eat every day for a balanced diet. Ex: If I have *my three squares,* I feel really great.

My turf [noun phr] (business) an area you control. Ex: Managers don't want to step on *each other's turf.*

NAFTA [abbrev] (political) *North American Free Trade Agreement* - a treaty that opened up free trade between the United States and Canada and Mexico. Ex: Since *NAFTA* was enacted, many companies have been outsourcing production.

NIMBY [abbrev] *Not in my backyard.* Opposing any kind of waste dump close to your property. Ex: *NIMBY* activists get a lot of publicity.

Nailed him good [verb phr] verbally put someone in his place or embarrass him. Ex: When he tried to make an excuse, she really *nailed him good.*

Nailed him on the spot [verb phr] confront someone directly about what happened in a situation. Ex: Mike took her car keys and she *nailed him on the spot.*

Naked truth [noun] absolute truth about a situation. Ex: If I tell him the *naked truth* about it, he will be very upset.

Name dropper [noun] someone who mentions the names of famous people as if they knew them personally. Ex: Jan is such a *name dropper*, but I don't think she really knows all those people.

Name your price [verb phr] how much do you want? Ex: I'd like to buy this car. Just *name your price.*

Nannygate [noun] (politics) political scandal where Presidential Cabinet candidates were found to have evaded paying into Social Security for their nannys.

Narc [noun] tattletale. Ex: Brian is a *narc*. He told his Mother we skipped school yesterday.

Narrow it down [verb phr] eliminate some of the choices or alternatives. Ex: Well, let's *narrow it down* to going to the movies or going out to a restaurant.

Neat as a pin [verb phr] thoroughly clean and orderly. Ex: Your room is *neat as a pin.*

Necessity is the mother of invention [cliché] If you really need to, you can be creative.

Neck and neck [verb phr] equal in a race. Ex: The two skiers were *neck and neck* coming down the slope.

Need like the plague [verb phr] don't need or want. Ex: I need another problem *like I need the plague.*

Needle in a haystack [noun phr] very small item. Ex: When I dropped my contact lens, it was as hard to find as a *needle in a haystack.*

Needless to say [adj phr] obviously. Ex: *Needless to say*, I would like to get an advanced degree in journalism.

Neither here nor there [adj phr] insignificant or unimportant. Ex: The fact that he graduated from Yale is *neither here nor there.* His talents are what the company needs.

Nerves are shot [noun phr] full of anxiety. Ex: Having to take care of four children is exhausting. *My nerves are shot.*

Nervous wreck [noun] extremely anxious. Ex: I'm a *nervous wreck* driving the freeways.

Nest egg [noun] money saved for an emergency. Ex: We can use our *nest egg* to put the down payment on the new house.

Never never land [noun] a fantasy. Ex: "Do you think Emily will really go to Europe this year?" "No, she's in *never never land.* She doesn't have enough time off to go."

Never say die [verb expression] keep trying. Ex: "I can't believe you're still trying to ski." "Well you know me. *Never say die!"*

New bag of tricks [noun phr] new ways of manipulating people. Ex: What's Sean got in his *new bag of tricks?*

New kid on the block [noun phr] Any newcomer or recent arrival. Ex: Have you met the *new kid on the block* yet?

New lease on life [noun phr] energized, with a positive attitude. Ex: James sure has a *new lease on life* since he got that raise.

Next door to [adv phr] refers to your "neighbor". Ex: Do you live *next door to* Bill?

Next to nothing [adj phr] little, insignificant amount. Ex: I got *next to nothing* for my allowance this week.

Nice guys finish last [cliché] sometimes people who are agreeable and pleasant instead of ambitious and greedy do not end up rich.

Nice work if you can get it [noun phr] a coveted position. Ex: Paul is going to be a ski instructor this year. That's really *nice work if you can get it.*

Nickel and dime to death [noun phr] usually said about a child who continuously asks for small change for a candy bar, etc. Ex: I just bought you a balloon, and then candy, and now you want what? You are going to *nickel and dime me to death.*

Nicotine fit [noun] wanting a cigarette. Ex: Shelly is having a *nicotine fit*. She hasn't smoked for two days.

Nip and tuck [adj] uncertain. Ex: Keeping my daughter in college on a single income is becoming *nip and tuck*.

Nip it in the bud [verb phr] stop an activity before it becomes uncontrollable. Ex: Josie is biting other children. I will have to *nip that in the bud*.

Nitty gritty [noun] The basics of a situation. Ex: Let's get down to the *nitty gritty*. Are we going to expand the business or not?

Nix on that [verb phr] "no" to that. Ex: "Are you going bike riding today?" "*Nix on that*."

No bed of roses [noun phr] not pleasant and easy. Ex: Digging up that tree stump was *no bed of roses*.

No big deal [noun phr] easily done and did not impact anyone. Ex: "Thanks for fixing my flat tire." "*No big deal*."

No brainer [noun] an action done automatically. Ex: Solving that puzzle is a *no brainer*.

No can do [verb phr] unable to do what someone asks or requests. Ex: "Can you fix my car?" "*No can do*. You'll have to take it to the shop."

No dice! [noun] Definitely not! Ex: "Let's skip school tomorrow." "*No dice!*"

No doubt [verb expression] A certainty. Ex: "I know Rich will get a new car this year." "*No doubt*."

No holds barred [adv phr] exercising no restraint. Ex: "Do you think you will win the bicycle race this weekend?" "Sure. I am racing *no holds barred.*"

No ifs, ands, or buts about it [noun expression] no excuse. Ex: You have to do your homework and there is *no ifs, ands, or buts about it.*

No love lost [noun phr] not have friendly feelings towards someone. Ex: There's *no love lost* between Jack and his ex-wife.

No man's land [noun phr] undesirable territory. Ex: "Wow, he's really off in *no man's land*, paying so much for that antique.

No matter what [noun expression] precedes an unconditional remark. Ex: *No matter what,* you are going to school.

No pain, no gain [cliché] usually said about exercise. Ex: In order to get in shape, you must stretch your muscles till they hurt. *No pain, no gain.*

No problem [noun expression] do a favor for someone who is appreciative. You say, "No problem" because you are happy to do the favor. (See *No sweat*)

No rhyme nor reason [noun expression] illogical. Ex: There's *no rhyme nor reason* to move the company to New York.

No shit Sherlock [1960's expression] used when someone makes a statement that is obvious to everyone. Ex: "I think the gas prices are too high." "*No shit Sherlock.*"

No show [noun phr] someone with an appointment who neither came nor cancelled. Ex: I can get you in to see the dentist now since we had a *no show*.

No skin off my nose [noun expression] not my concern. Ex: "Derek should win the 10k race this year. " "Well, that's *no skin off my nose.*"

No sooner than [adv phr] no time lapse. Ex: *No sooner than* I said, "Where's Peter", then he appears.

No strings attached [noun phr] not expect to be paid back for something you've done for someone else. Ex: "How can I pay you back for all the work you've done on my yard?" "Don't worry. There's *no strings attached.*"

No sweat [noun] no problem; easy to accomplish. Ex: "Can you vacuum the house?" "*No sweat.*" (See *No problem*)

No two ways about it [noun expression] no alternative. Ex: There's *no two ways about it*; we've got to save for college if Kevin wants to be a doctor.

No way man [noun phr] emphatic no. Ex: "Are you going on to college next year?" "*No way man.* You know how much tuition is at the major schools?"

No win situation [noun] neither person will be pleased in a negotiation. Ex: That car deal's really a *no win situation.*

Nobody's fool [noun] not gullible. Ex: Denise is *nobody's fool*. She knows Harv is dating another girl also.

Nodding acquaintance [noun] a person you hardly know. "Do you know Bart?" "Not really. He's just a *nodding acquaintance* of mine."

None the less [noun expression] anyway. Ex: *None the less*, we will go to the school play tonight.

Nooks and crannies [noun phr] odd places to keep things. Ex: Did you look in all the *nooks and crannies* for your baseball glove?

Normal wear and tear [noun phr] refers to clothes. They should last a certain length of time, given the usual activities of a person. Ex: This shirt should last you a year given *normal wear and tear*.

Nose to the grindstone [noun phr] work hard without stopping. Ex: Leroy is really a workaholic. He keeps his *nose to the grindstone* every day.

Not a happy camper [noun phr] unhappy about a turn of events. Ex: Jack is *not a happy camper* since he lost that big contract.

Not a kernel of truth [noun phr] total lie. Ex: There is *not a kernel of truth* in what she told me.

Not a kick left [noun phr] #1 dead. Ex: That horse does *not have a kick left* in him. #2 defeated. Ex: The runner had *not a kick left* and so lost the race.

Not a living soul [noun phr] no one. Ex: Now do *not* tell *a living soul* what I've just told you.

Not a peep out of you [noun phr] (usually said to children) be quiet. Ex: It's time for you to go to bed and *not a peep out of you*.

Not a pretty sight [noun phr] embarrassing. Ex: It was *not a pretty sight* when I dropped my notes and forgot the end of my speech.

Not a red cent [noun phr] not receive a single penny. Ex: The minister did *not get a red cent* for his talk to the students.

Not a second to spare [noun phr] no extra time to waste. Ex: We must rescue the climber and there is *not a second to spare.*

Not about to [noun phr] unlikely. Ex: I'm *not about to* loan you $5,000.

Not by a long shot [noun expression] highly unlikely. Ex: Are you going to take history next term? "*Not by a long shot.*"

Not cricket [adj] not honest. Ex: Cheating on the test was *not cricket.*

Not enough hours in the day [noun phr] too much to do and too little time. Ex: With a full-time job, two kids, and a house to clean, there are just *not enough hours in the day*.

Not enough room to swing a cat [noun expression] cramped quarters. Ex: This closet is so small there is *not enough room to swing a cat.*

Not far off [adv phr] close. Ex: The day is *not far off* when I can retire.

Not for love nor money [prep phr] be unwilling to do what someone asks no matter what the consequences. Ex: I won't lie for you *for love nor money.*

Not give someone the time of day [verb phr] unwilling to communicate with someone. Ex: I wanted to talk to the boss, but he *won't give me the time of day.*

Not going to touch it with a ten foot pole [verb phr] avoid it. Ex: "Who wants to tell Bill that those sales figures are not correct?" "Not me! I *wouldn't touch that with a ten foot pole.*"

Not his long suit [noun phr] not a strength. Ex: I'd ask Brett to help me, but plumbing is *not his long suit.*

Not in a hundred years [prep phr] never. Ex: I wouldn't buy one of those cars, *not in a hundred years.*

Not in my bailiwick [prep phr] area of responsibility. Ex: "Are you going to prepare that report?" "No. It's *not in my bailiwick.* Kathie should do it."

Not in my lifetime [prep phr] not ever. Ex: "Do you intend on speaking to her again?" *"Not in my lifetime."*

Not just whistling Dixie [affirmative expression] Ex: "Rita sure is a beautiful girl." *"You're not just whistling Dixie!"*

Not know him from Adam [verb phr] not recognize someone at all. Ex: "Did you know that guy who just spoke to you?" "No, I did *not know him from Adam.*"

Not missing a beat [verb phr] move quickly on to another challenge with no time in between. Ex: He just moved on to make another movie *without missing a beat.*

Not my cup of tea [noun phr] not something you choose to do or are interested in. Ex: "Do you want to play golf with me?" "No, it's *not my cup of tea.*"

Not on speaking terms [prep phr] upset with someone and not talk to him/her. Ex: Molly and her Mother are *not on speaking terms* after their last disagreement.

Not playing with a full deck [verb phr] mentally unstable. Ex: I think she has a real problem and is *not playing with a full deck.*

Not the only fish in the sea [noun phr] not the only available person. Ex: I really liked Ramona, but she's *not the only fish in the sea.*

Not too shabby [verb phr] look at something or someone with appreciation. Ex: "I got a B in the test today." "That's *not too shabby."*

Not up to snuff [prep phr] not good quality. Ex: This new watch does not keep good time. It is *not up to snuff* with my old one.

Not worth a dime [verb phr] worthless or useless. Ex: His directions to get to the fair are *not worth a dime.* (See *Not worth a plugged nickel*)

Not worth a plugged nickel [verb phr] worthless. (See *Not worth a dime*)

Not worth his salt [verb phr] working below capacity. Ex: Philip was *not worth his salt,* so I had to fire him.

Not worth the paper it's written on [verb phr] a contract that is not enforceable. Ex: You know that restraining order is *not worth the paper it's written on.*

Nothing between the ears [noun phr] unintelligent. Ex: Don't give the directions to Liz. There's *nothing between the ears.* (See *Airhead*)

Nothing doing! [noun expression] Absolutely not! Ex: "Can I borrow your new car tonight?" *"Nothing doing!* Use your own."

Nothing in particular [noun phr] not specific. Ex: I have *nothing in particular* planned for Sunday afternoon.

Nothing to sneeze at [noun phr] has value or importance. Ex: Mary's promotion to director is *nothing to sneeze at.*

Now you've gone and done it [expression of disappointment] made a big mistake. Ex: *Now you've gone and done it.* It will be impossible to get that ink out of your shirt.

Nudie kazootie [noun] (1950's slang) naked. Ex: Close the door so the neighbors won't see you *nudie kazootie.* (See *In the altogether*)

Number crunching [noun] (business) manipulation of figures. Ex: Let the accounting department do the *number crunching* on our new product.

Numero uno! [noun] Spanish expression meaning "number 1" e.g. the best. Ex: You are *numero uno* in my book.

Nursing a grudge [verb phr] angry and unforgiving about some past experience. Ex: Are you still *nursing a grudge* about not getting that job?

Nutmeg [noun] #1 a spice. #2 [verb] (sports - soccer) kick the ball between a player's legs to keep it away from him. Ex: The player made a goal after he *nutmegged* his opponent.

Nuts and bolts [noun phr] the basics. Ex: Let me show you the *nuts and bolts* of the operation.

Nuts to you [expression of disgust] forget it. (See *Stuff it*)

Nutty as a fruitcake [verb phr] acting crazy. Ex: Sherry's grandmother is *nutty as fruitcake.*

O.D. [abbrev] overdose of a drug. Ex: He *O.D.*'d on sleeping pills last night.

O.K. [adj phr] all right. Ex: "What do you think of Steven?" "He's *O.K.* in my book."

OMG [abbrev] *Oh my God.* Cell phone texting abbreviation.

O.S. [abbrev] (computer) *Operating System*. Ex: We have the Windows 8 Operating System.

O.T. [abbrev] (business) overtime. Ex: How many hours of *O.T.* did you put in this week?

Obamacare [noun] new comprehensive government health plan that aims to insure everyone medically.

Odd man out [noun phr] person who does not fit into a group. Ex: Why is Drew always the *odd man out*?

Odds and ends [noun phr] things that are random and do not match. Ex: This drawer is just full of *odds and ends.*

Off base [prep phr] inaccurate or inappropriate. Ex: You're totally *off base* with that remark.

Off color [adj] with sexual innuendos. Ex: Don't tell *off color* jokes to the ladies.

Off his rocker [prep phr] not behaving rationally. Ex: Old man Wilson went *off his rocker* yesterday. I think he bumped his head when he fell last week.

Off in the ozone [prep phr] out of touch with the real world. Ex: Is Charlie *off in the ozone* again? I have asked him the same question twice.

Off into the great unknown [prep phr] undertake a trip or adventure that has uncharted territory. Ex: We're going to take a bike trip *off into the great unknown.*

Off line [[adv phr] (business) #1 not located where the main
business office is. Ex: Our Toronto office is *off line*. #2
another time and place. Ex: Let's not discuss it in this
meeting. We'll discuss it *off line*.

Off shore [adv] (business) on foreign soil. Ex: The airplane
parts will be manufactured *off shore*.

Off the beaten path [prep phr] stray from the known and
familiar. Ex: Columbus went *off the beaten path,* but
discovered a great new country.

Off the cuff [prep phr] remark said without thinking. Ex: You
hurt my feelings with that *off the cuff* remark. (See
Shoot from the hip)

Off the deep end [prep phr] do something totally irrational. Ex:
He went *off the deep end* when Marge divorced him.

Off the hook [prep phr] free from responsibility. Ex: I will take
over the account and let you *off the hook*.

Off the record [prep phr] not quotable officially. Ex: Lots of
politicians make remarks that are *off the record*.

Off the top of my head [prep phr] give a spontaneous answer.
Ex: *Off the top of my head*, I would not advise you to
go to Dominican Republic now.

Off the wall [prep phr] unconventional. Ex: Her remarks are *off
the wall*.

Off your hands [prep phr] no longer your responsibility. Ex:
Here, let me take this child *off your hands* so you can
take a nap.

Offer an olive branch [verb phr] apologize; try to reconcile. Ex:
She *offered her husband an olive branch* after their
disagreement.

Offload [verb] delegate. (business) Ex: Why don't you *offload* Project X?

Oil and water [noun phr] opposites. Ex: Mary and Jack are like *oil and water*. She likes the opera and he likes to play poker.

Okie-dokie [expression of agreement] (country western) all right. Ex: *Okie-dokie*, let's go to the movies tonight.

Old as the hills [adj phr] ancient. Ex: That black rotary dial phone is *old as the hills.*

Old bag [noun] (impolite) derogatory term referring to an old woman. Ex: That *old bag* needs to move, because we are going to tear down her apartment.

Old ball and chain [noun] men refer to their wives as the *old ball and chain* when they place too many restrictions on the men. (not in the presence of the wives!) Ex: I can't play pool because the *old ball and chain* has me moving furniture.

Old boy network [noun phr] (business) men who are good friends in the business world and support each other. Ex: It's impossible for a woman to get promoted here – the good *old boy network*, you know.

Old codger [noun] (impolite) old man. (1940's slang) Ex: That *old codger* has lost all of his teeth. (See *Old coot*)

Old coot [noun] (See *Old codger*)

Old duffer [noun] (See *Old codger*)

Old geezer [noun] (See *Old codger*)

Old guard [noun] (See *Old boy network*)

Old habits die hard [cliché] A habit is difficult to break or change.

Old hand at it [noun phr] experienced. Ex: Jim is an *old hand at carpentry* and built his children a tree house.

Old hat [adj] obsolete, unfashionable. Ex: Computers are *old hat* now. IPads and iPhone are more popular.

Old home week [noun phr] a reunion of people who went to school together.

Old school of thought [noun phr] outdated. Ex: Using a typewriter instead of a computer is *old school of thought.*

Old stick in the mud [noun phr] conservative; unwilling to try new ideas. Ex: Our boss is just an *old stick in the mud.* You can't introduce any new way of doing things.

Old wives tale [cliché] a story that has been passed down by several generations and which may or may not be true. Ex: The story that cats smother babies is an *old wives tale.*

Old wrinkled prune face [noun phr] (impolite) an older person.

Oldie but goldie [noun phr] something old, but really valuable. Ex: Many comic books that were published in the 1950's have become oldies, but goldies, worth a lot of money. (e.g. Batman, Little Lulu)

Oldie moldy [adj] (1950's slang) something that is old. Ex: That antique clock is an *oldie moldy.*

On a roll [prep phr] continuing good luck. Ex: I won again at poker. I'm *on a roll.*

On a shoestring [prep phr] living on a limited budget is "*living on a shoestring.*"

On a silver platter [prep phr] referring to the best of treatment. Ex: He wants everything served to him *on a silver platter* .

On a wing and a prayer [prep phr] undertake a task with little knowledge of how to proceed. Ex: "Have you ever built a garage before?" "No, I'll just do it *on a wing and a prayer."*

On account of [prep phr] because. Ex: *On account of* Rory being late, we missed the bus.

On approval [prep phr] buy something, but with the option to return it if it is unsatisfactory. Ex: I will buy that dress *on approval* and see if I like it.

On board [prep phr] (business) newly hired. Ex: Darien is now *on board* at the company.

On borrowed time [prep phr] about to die. Ex: Matt's dad is living *on borrowed time* these days. He has cancer.

On call [prep phr] ready and responsible if a problem arises. Ex: The doctor is *on call* 24 hours a day.

On cloud nine [prep phr] ecstatic. Ex: Christina is *on cloud nine* since Brent asked her to marry him.

On deck [prep phr] ready for action. Ex: Our first baseman is *on deck* and will be the next batter.

On easy street [prep phr] live comfortably, having plenty of money. Ex: Troy is living *on easy street* since winning the lottery.

On edge [prep phr] anxious. Ex: He was *on edge* since he had so many projects to finish.

On good/bad terms with [prep phr] have either a positive or negative relationship with a person. Ex: She is *on bad terms with* her sister. They haven't spoken in four years.

On hand [prep phr] available. Ex: We have plenty of food *on hand* for the picnic.

On her broom [prep phr] irritable. Ex: Miss Jones is really *on her broom* today.

On his best behavior [prep phr] act appropriately for a period of time. Ex: Eric has been *on his best behavior* today because he wants to go to the movies tonight.

On his case [prep phr] keep nagging someone until a task is done. Ex: I'm going to be *on your case* until you get your room cleaned.

On his coattails [prep phr] use someone else's influence to gain position. Ex: Brian followed *on the coattails* of Mr. Watkins and is now Vice President.

On his ear [prep phr] humble someone. Example: I set him *on his ear* today.

On his high horse [prep phr] behaving arrogantly. Ex: Bodie was *on his high horse* today and refused to speak to us.

On his last legs [prep phr] exhausted. Ex: Ray was *on his last legs* as he crossed the race finish line.

On his own [prep phr] independently. Ex: The child tied his shoelaces all *on his own.*

On his own accord [prep phr] independent decision. Ex: Jorge left the party *on his own accord.*

On his soapbox [prep phr] believe strongly in a cause, sometimes political, and let everyone know how you feel about the situation. Ex: Carl is *on his soapbox* again about job security.

On hold [prep phr] delay in an activity. Ex: The new project is *on hold* until more studies are completed. (See *On ice*)

On ice [prep phr] put an activity *on hold* or discontinue doing it temporarily. (See *On hold*)

On one hand…and on the other [prep phr] weigh both sides of an argument. Ex: *On one hand* she has good computer skills, but *on the other hand* she works very slowly.

On pins and needles [prep phr] anxious with anticipation. Ex: I am *on pins and needles* and can hardly wait for the race to begin.

On purpose [prep phr] deliberately. Ex: He pushed the other boy *on purpose*.

On sight [prep phr] immediately. Ex: If you see the escaped criminal, shoot him *on sight*.

On-site meeting [noun] (business) located at a building where all the meeting attendees normally work. Ex: The meeting will be *on-site* in Room 32.

On the average [prep phr] most of the time. Ex: *On the average* he is a good baseball player.

On the back burner [prep phr] postpone something. Ex: We'll put the Thompson project *on the back burner* for now.

On the ball [prep phr] alert. Ex: Larry is always *on the ball*.

On the bandwagon [prep phr] join popular opinion. Ex: A lot of people jumped *on the bandwagon* when they passed the gun law.

On the bleeding edge of technology [prep phr] past the "leading edge" of technology, where you are taking too high a risk or you are not calculating the risk correctly. Ex: The company was *on the bleeding edge of technology* and went bankrupt.

On the blink [prep phr] broken. Ex: The toaster has been *on the blink* for two weeks. We need to buy a new one. (See *On the fritz)*

On the board [prep phr] (sports) The Hawks are *on the board* with one minute to go in the first half of the game.

On the brain [prep phr] thinking about something continuously. Ex: My algebra test is *on the brain.*

On the cutting edge [prep phr] forerunner in new technology. Ex: The new airplane technology is *on the cutting edge.*

On the DL [prep phr] (2014 slang) On the down low. Something you want to keep secret. (See On the QT)

On the double [prep phr] quickly. Ex: James, get over here *on the double.*

On the face of the earth [prep phr] in the whole world. Ex: He is the smartest person *on the face of the earth.*

On the fast track [prep phr] (business) climbing the corporate ladder quickly. Ex: Jody is *on the fast track* and is now Vice President.

On the fence [prep phr] indecisive. Ex: Joel is always on the fence when we have to make a decision.

On the fritz [prep phr] broken. (See *On the blink)*

On the house [prep phr] free of charge. Ex: Drinks are *on the house* tonight.

On the lam [prep phr] a fugitive. Ex: He is one of the ten most wanted criminals and has been *on the lam* for four years.

On the leading edge [prep phr] current technological leader who has advanced development of a product. Ex: Our company is *on the leading edge* with that new app we developed.

On the level [prep phr] truthful. Ex: Alex has been named Vice-President of the company, and that's *on the level*.

On the line [prep phr] #1 Used in a risky or vulnerable situation. Ex: I am going to lay it *on the line*. Either you guys produce more or you're fired. #2 used in a telephone/cell phone conversation. Ex: I'll be with you in a minute; I'm *on the line* right now.

On the make [prep phr] looking for a sexual encounter. Ex: He is *on the make* since his divorce.

On the mend [prep phr] get well after an illness. Ex: Alice is *on the mend* after her bout with the flu.

On the money [prep phr] accurate. (See *Right on the money*)

On the move [prep phr] #1 gaining training or qualities for promotion. Ex: The new sales representative is definitely *on the move*. He wants the CFO spot. #2 migrating. Ex: The ducks are *on the move* going South. #3 gaining momentum. Ex: The idea of electing a woman president is *on the move*.

On the off chance [prep phr] an unlikely possibility. Ex: We have prepared an alternative plan *on the off chance* that our first plan cannot be carried out.

On the QT [prep phr] secretly. Ex: The teenager was smoking *on the QT*. (See *On the DL*)

On the rag [prep phr] <u>impolite</u> reference to a woman having her monthly period.

On the ragged edge [prep phr] tired and exhausted. Ex: She was *on the ragged edge* after tending those children all day.

On the rebound [prep phr] end a relationship and be looking for someone new. Ex: Sierra is *on the rebound* and wants to go out.

On the record [prep phr] Your response can be shared with the public. Ex: *On the record*, he voted for Sam Smith.

On the rocks [prep phr] #1 to order a drink with ice. Ex: I'd like a scotch *on the rocks*. #2 in a ruined condition. Ex: His career is sure *on the rocks* since he was transferred.

On the same page [prep phr] having similar ideas and thoughts. Ex: We need to get *on the same page* before we write our goals and objectives as a company. (See *On the same wave length)*

On the same wave length [prep phr] (See *On the same page*)

On the side [prep phr] #1 used when ordering food in a restaurant. Ex: I'd like my salad with the dressing *on the side*, meaning in a separate dish. #2 used when you have a business that is in addition to your regular eight hour a day job. That business is *"on the side"*.

On the sidelines [prep phr] out of the main activity. Ex: The two football players had to sit *on the sidelines* because they had injuries.

On the sly [prep phr] secretly. (See on the DL)

On the stick [prep phr] (See *Get on the stick*)

On the spot [prep phr] confronted. Ex: The teacher put me *on the spot* when she asked the capitol of Pennsylvania.

On the spur of the moment [prep phr] unplanned decision. Ex: We decided to go bicycling *on the spur of the moment*.

On the straight and narrow [prep phr] honest and respectable. Ex: Rod's behavior is *on the straight and narrow.* He always tells the truth.

On the tip of my tongue [prep phr] trying to think of an answer to a question and you can't quite think of it. Ex: "What is the capital of Massachusetts?" "It's right on the *tip of my tongue.* "

On the up and up [prep phr] honest. (See *Above board*)

On the wagon [prep phr] abstaining from alcohol. Ex: She has been *on the wagon* for four months.

On the warpath [prep phr] in an angry mood. Ex: Mother is *on the warpath* since you got mud on the living room carpet.

On the whole [prep phr] all things considered. Ex: *On the whole*, he is really a nice guy.

On the wrong side of the tracks [prep phr] the poorer or tougher side of town. Ex: He lives *on the wrong side of the tracks* and does not have new shoes for school this year.

On top of everything [prep phr] in addition to. Ex: *On top of everything* he wants me to make him coffee every morning.

On top of the world [prep phr] happy. Ex: She is *on top of the world* since she won that vacation.

On your head [prep phr] unforgiveable mistake. Ex: If you cheat on the test and get caught, you will have that *on your head* for the rest of your life.

On your honor [prep phr] behave correctly when an authority figure is not present. Ex: You kids need to be *on your honor* while I go to the store.

On your lips [prep phr] drunk. (See *Snockered*)

On your plate [prep phr] business assigned to you. Ex: I have too many projects *on my plate* now.

On your toes [prep phr] alert. Ex: Better be *on your toes* when the teacher quizzes you today.

Once in a blue moon [adv phr] infrequently. Ex: I only see Tiffany once in a blue moon. (See *Once in a while*)

Once in a while [adv phr] infrequently. (See *Once in a blue moon*)

One-armed bandit [noun] slot machine at a casino. Ex: The *one-armed bandits* in Las Vegas bring in a lot of money.

One fell swoop [noun phr] all at once. The eagle dove and got the fish all in *one fell swoop*.

One foot in the grave [noun phr] appear dull and lifeless. Ex: He is so low key it seems he has *one foot in the grave*.

One for the books [noun phr] unusual occurrence that is noteworthy. Ex: George hit a home run. That's *one for the books.*

One good turn deserves another [cliché] return a favor someone has done for you.

One horse town [noun phr] (country western) small town.

One in a million [noun phr] someone special. Ex: You are *one in a million*. (very complimentary)

One-night stand [noun phr] have sex with someone for only one night. Ex: You don't get involved emotionally in a one-night stand.

One on one [noun phr] #1 (sports-basketball) two players playing against each other. Ex: Let's play a game of horse. #2 teaching or training a single student at a time. Ex: I can learn better in a *one on one* learning environment. #3 communication taking place between two people. Ex: I understand his point of view after talking to him *one on one*.

One shot deal [noun phr] one chance for this to happen. Ex: Let's buy that stock now. This is a *one shot deal.*

One step forward, two steps back [noun phr] not making any progress. Ex: I just got the siding up on the new house and it rained – *one step forward, two steps back*.

One stop shopping [noun phr] go to one store and buy food, clothes, toys, etc. Ex: Walmart is good for *one stop shopping*.

One track mind [noun phr] think about one subject all the time. e.g. sex.

One up on [noun phr] out-smart someone. Ex: I got *one up on* Randy. When he arrived home late, I locked him out.

One way ticket to nowhere [noun phr] send someone away permanently. Ex: I'm going to buy you a *one-way ticket to nowhere.*

Only game in town [noun phr] only activity worth doing. Ex: Poker is the *only game in town*.

Onward and upward [noun phr] renewed energy after a setback. Ex: I know we lost the last game, but next week it's *onward and upward*.

Oorah [expression of excitement] Marine rally cry.

Open and shut case [noun phr] outcome has been previously determined. Ex: That murder case is an *open and shut case.*

Open Pandora's box [verb phr] discover more than anticipated. Ex: Why did you *open Pandora's box* by asking him about his experiences in the war? (See *Open up a can of worms*)

Open up a can of worms [verb phr] (See Open Pandora's box)

Operating on one cylinder [verb phr] not using all your mental capacity. (See *Operating with one oar in the water*)

Operating with one oar in the water [verb phr] (See *Operating on one cylinder*)

Order of the day [noun phr] agenda of activities. Ex: When you get to camp, they will tell you the *order of the day.*

Other fish to fry [noun phr] have other things to do. Ex: I'd like to go with you, but I have *other fish to fry.*

Our fearless leader [noun phr] usually said in jest about someone's boss. Ex: *Our fearless leader* is coming in at 9:00 today.

Out and about [adv phr] not at home. Ex: I went over to see Bud, but he was *out and about*.

Out in left field [adj phr] different from the rest of the group. Ex: Sarah is really *out in left field*. Her ideas are so strange.

Out in the boondocks [adv phr] in the wilderness. Ex: We're going camping *out in the boondocks*.

Out in the boonies [adv phr] (See *Out in the boondocks*)

Out in the bush [adv phr] (See *Out in the boondocks*)

Out in the sticks [adv phr] (See *Out in the boondocks*)

Out in the toolie-berries [adv phr] (See *Out in the boondocks*)

Out in the toolies [adv phr] (See *Out in the boondocks*)

Out like a light [adj phr] fall asleep right away and sleep soundly. Ex: The baby is really *out like a light*.

Out of circulation [prep phr] not dating. Ex: Gary got married and is now *out of circulation*.

Out of commission [prep phr] broken. Ex: My TV set is *out of commission. (See On the fritz)*

Out of hand [adj phr] a situation has become unpredictable or uncontrollable. Ex: The drive-by shootings in our neighborhood are getting *out of hand*.

Out of here [adv phr] leaving immediately. Ex: The game is over and I'm *out of here*.

Out of his league [adj phr] beyond his expertise. Ex: He is playing on the professional team this year and is *out of his league.*

Out of his mind [adj phr] crazy. Ex: Dale nearly went *out of his mind* when he thought his son was lost.

Out of his tree [adj phr] act in an irrational manner. (See *Out of his mind)*

Out of it [adj phr] depressed and not functioning normally. Ex: I have been *out of it* ever since Derek moved away.

Out of line [adj phr] a remark or behavior that is inappropriate to the situation. Ex: Sean said something really *out of line* to Taylor.

Out of my hands [adj phr] no longer under my control. Ex: I sent the package yesterday and it is *out of my hands.*

Out of my league [prep phr] out of my area of capability or expertise. Ex: Tony wanted me to be President, but it was way *out of my league.*

Out of practice [prep phr] not having practiced an activity. Ex: I can't play that piano piece any more. I am *out of practice.*

Out of print [prep phr] no longer available from the publisher. Ex: That book has been *out of print* for two years.

Out of shape [prep phr] not athletically fit. Ex: Since I work in an office all day, I am really *out of shape.*

Out of sorts [prep phr] cranky. Ex: The baby was *out of sorts* because it was teething.

Out of step [prep phr] non-conforming. Ex: Harold is *out of step* with the rest of the team.

Out of the blue [adj phr] not relevant to the discussion. Ex: We were talking about politics and *out of the blue* Dick said that he is going to Hawaii this summer.

Out of the box thinking [noun phr] using your creativity. Ex: We need more *out of the box thinking* to redesign the that app.

Out of the frying pan, into the fire [cliché] volatile situation explodes. Ex: When Josh didn't get the promotion he deserved, he was angry. Then he found out that his best friend got the promotion instead. It was *out of the frying pan and into the fire f*or Josh.

Out of the loop [adj phr] (business term) not included. Ex: The President claimed he was *out of the loop* on the international terrorist affair.

Out of the picture [adj phr] not to be considered. Ex: I think Shelly is *out of the picture* for a promotion.

Out of the question [adj phr] impossible. Ex: We can't consider your idea. It is *out of the question*.

Out of the running [adj phr] will not be among the choices. Ex: He will be *out of the running* for Vice-President in 2016.

Out of this world [adj phr]   fantastic.   Ex: The scenery in Australia is *out of this world.*

Out of whack [prep phr] not performing as expected. Ex: My hairdryer has been *out of whack* lately.

Out like a light [adj phr] fall asleep immediately and sleep soundly. Ex: The children are tired from playing all day and were *out like a light* when I put them to bed.

Out on a limb [adj phr] vulnerable. Ex: When you didn't show up for the party, it left me *out on a limb*.

Out on the town [adv phr] having a good time partying. Ex: My friends and I are *out on the town* tonight.

Out the door [prep phr] totally removed from a situation. Can refer to being fired from your job.   Ex: "What happened to Ed?" "He's *out the door*."

Out the window [prep phr]   gone; disappeared. Ex: That deal just flew *out the window* when you refused to negotiate.

Out to lunch [prep phr] #1 not tuned in mentally to what others are doing. #2 actually being at lunch.

Over a barrel [prep phr] having the edge in negotiations. Ex: The salesman had his customer *over a barrel* and the customer didn't get a good deal.

Over easy [adv phr]   way of cooking eggs, turning them over once and leaving the yoke runny. Ex: The waitress asks you how you like your eggs. You reply "*Over easy*".

Over his head [prep phr] beyond his capabilities to handle. Ex: I don't think Joel belongs in our Calculus class. It is *over his head*.

Over the edge [prep phr] greatly stressed. Ex: I am just about *over the edge* on this car deal.

Over the hill [prep phr] anyone over 40 is jokingly referred to as *"over the hill"*.

Over the top [prep phr] exaggerate beyond expectations. Ex: That movie we saw yesterday was *over the top*. It was so funny.

Overstay your welcome [prep phr] stay longer than the hostess anticipated. Ex: Ex: Let's not *overstay our welcome* at Lucy's house.

Owe you one [verb phr] acknowledge you owe a favor to someone. Ex: Thanks for fixing my car. I *owe you one*.

PC [abbrev] #1 *personal computer*. Ex: I got a new PC this year. #2 *politically correct*. Ex: It is *politically correct* not to smoke.

Pack it in [verb phr] give up. Ex: I'm too tired to finish this report, so I'll *pack it in* for today.

Pack it into [verb phr] #1 carry something. Ex: Take that bag of groceries and *pack it into* the house. #2 prepare for shipping. Ex: I'll *pack it into* some bubble wrapping to protect it from breaking.

Pack of lies [noun phr] totally untrue. Ex: Everything Mitch said about my sister is a *pack of lies*.

Packed in like sardines [verb phr] in an extremely crowded situation. Ex: They were all *packed in like sardines* on the crowded bus.

Packs a powerful wallop [verb phr] strong minded and powerful people exerting their influence. Ex: The mayor's vote *packs a powerful wallop.*

Paid off [verb phr] #1 investment was successful. Ex: Buying that stock really *paid off.* #2 pay the rest of the money you owe on a loan. Ex: I'm sure glad we got the car *paid off.*

Pain in the butt [noun phr] (impolite) act irritating. Ex: He is a *pain in the butt,* but I like him anyway. (See *Pain in the neck*)

Pain in the neck [noun phr] (See *Pain in the butt)*

Paint a pretty picture [verb phr] describe a situation positively. Ex: She *painted a pretty picture* of her life at college.

Paint the town red [verb phr] celebrate by stopping at several bars or restaurants. Ex: Come on. Let's *paint the town red* tonight to celebrate your promotion.

Pansy ass [noun] (impolite) coward.

Paper copy [noun] (business) the version printed or written on paper. Ex: I need a *paper copy* of that memo. (See *hard copy*)

Paper pusher [noun] someone who handles lots of paper in an office. Ex: Our secretary is a *paper pusher*.

Paper thin [adj] extremely skinny. Ex: Laura sure is *paper thin* since she went on a diet.

Par for the course [noun phr] a usual or expected course of behavior or actions for someone. Ex: Is Larry late again? That's *par for the course*.

Pare it down to size [verb phr] (business) reduce the scope of a task. Ex: Let's *pare this project down to size* and decide who is going to work on each phase of it.

Park your bod [verb phr] (informal) sit down. Ex: Come on in and *park your bod*.

Part and parcel [noun phr] most essential part. Ex: Over-seeing the water district is *part and parcel* of his job on the city council.

Parting of the ways [noun phr] #1 going different directions. Ex: There was *a parting of the ways* of the two friends. #2 difference. Ex: There was a *parting of the ways* on how this problem would be resolved.

Party animal [noun] one who loves to drink and celebrate. Ex: Tom is a real *party animal*. He left at 3:00 A.M.

Party hardy [verb phr] have a lot of fun at a party. Ex: *Party hardy* for me. I have to work tonight.

Party line [noun] #1 (business) expected company "brainwashing" in the company philosophy. Ex: Have you heard the latest *party line* on employee empowerment? #2 more than one person on a telephone line. Ex: We have a *party line* and others can listen in on our conversations.

Party on! [verb phr] continue on with whatever you are doing. Ex: *Party on!* I'll join you later.

Party's over [noun phr] the fun is ceasing. Ex: The *party's over.* Time to get back to work.

Pass off [verb] #1 (sports) give the ball to another player. Ex: Jeff *passed off* the ball to Tim and he made a basket. #2 delegate responsibility. Ex: You should *pass off* that project to Alicia. #3 pretend authenticity. Ex: He tried to *pass off* the coins as solid gold.

Pass on [verb phr] #1 relate. Ex: I need to *pass on* Jim's directions to get to his house. #2 decline. Ex: I'll have to *pass on* going out for drinks after work. #3 die. She may *pass on* any day now.

Pass out [verb phr] #1 faint. Ex: She *passed out* from the heat. #2 distribute. Ex: Eugene, would you please *pass out* the papers?

Pass the buck [verb phr] (See *Don't pass the buck*)

Pass the hat [verb phr] collect a monetary donation from people. Ex: They *pass the hat* in church every week.

Pass the test of time [verb phr] endure. Ex: That car battery sure has *passed the test of time.*

Pass the time [verb phr] relax. Ex: My friends and I *pass the time* by talking.

Pass up [verb] decline or miss. Ex: I hate to *pass up* an opportunity to go to the ball game.

Passed away [verb] (polite) died. Ex: My Aunt Sophie *passed away* on Friday.

Pat on the back [noun phr] a compliment. Ex: I gave him a *pat on the back* for completing his assignment.

Patch things up [verb phr] reconcile. Ex: The young couple *patched things up* after their quarrel.

Paternal leave [noun] time off from work for the father of a new-born child. Ex: *Paternal leave* is three weeks in our company.

Patience of Job [noun phr] (biblical) endless patience. Ex: He takes care of his three children and has the *patience of Job.*

Pattern after [verb phr] copy. Ex: Peter built his model plane *patterned after* a real jet.

Paved the way [verb phr] encouraged acceptance. Ex: Randy really *paved the way* for his son's success in the company.

Pay lip service [verb phr] (See *Lip service*)

Pay the piper [verb phr] accept the consequences of your actions. Ex: If you misbehave, you will *pay the piper* eventually.

Pay through the nose [verb phr]   pay more for an item than what it was worth. Ex: I had to *pay through the nose* for my new table saw.

Pay your dues [verb phr] gain experience. Ex: You need to *pay your dues* and then you can get a raise.

Pay your respects [verb phr]   attend someone's funeral. Ex: We *paid our respects* to Aunt Martha on Tuesday.

Payback [noun] your reward for doing a task well. Ex: He got an award as *payback* for his excellent work on the project.

Peabrain [noun] nitwit. (See *Dimwit)*

Peach of a guy   [noun phr]   well respected because he is interested in others. Ex: Chester is just a *peach of a guy* and has lots of friends.

Peaches and cream   [adj] a woman's flawless complexion. Ex: What a beautiful *peaches and cream* complexion you have.

Peanut-buttered [verb] (business) spread evenly across. Ex: The corporate overhead expenses are *peanut-buttered* over the division budgets.

Peanut gallery [noun] kibitzers. Ex: No comments from the *peanut gallery* please.

Pecking order [noun]   line of authority. Ex: The man kicked the dog because he was angry at his boss. That's an example of the *pecking order*.

Peel out [verb phr] accelerate your car rapidly, causing the tires to screech. Ex: When he first got his car, he *peeled out* to impress his friends.

Peer pressure [noun] influence from your friends. Ex: *Peer pressure* caused him to drink the beer.

Pen is mightier than the sword [cliché] the written word is more powerful than guns and force.

Penny for your thoughts [cliché] tell me what you are thinking about.

Penny-pincher [noun] miser. Ex: Don't ask Rick to contribute. He's a *penny-pincher*.

Penny wise and pound foolish [proverb] stingy with small amounts of money and spend large amounts of money foolishly.

Peon [noun] (business) ordinary employees of a company. Ex: The *peons* don't make as much money as management. (See *Rank and file*)

People who live in glass houses shouldn't throw stones [cliché] Don't criticize others when you act in a similar manner.

Perish the thought [verb phr] forget it. Ex: *Perish the thought.* I don't want to wash the windows.

Pester me to death [verb phr] aggravate continuously. Ex: Those kids are going to *pester me to death* until I fill their swimming pool.

Petered out [verb] fatigued. (See *All tapped out*)

Phase in [verb] start using slowly. Ex: We're going to *phase in* the new product line as soon as we can.

Phase out [verb] eliminate slowly. Ex: We better *phase out* those old style boots.

Phony as a three-dollar bill [adj phr] obvious fake. Ex: Vera's diamond necklace was as phony as a *three-dollar bill*.

Phony baloney [noun phr] something you are skeptical about. Ex: That story about her diamond ring is *phone baloney.*

Photo finish [noun phr] too close to be able to determine by sight. Ex: The hundred yard dash was a *photo finish* and showed that Frank won.

Physically challenged [noun phr] disabled. Ex: Many war veterans become *physically challenged* from war injuries after they return home.

Pick and choose [verb phr] make a selection. Ex: There are so many toys. It is hard to *pick and choose.*

Pick at [verb] #1 eat slowly and with little bites. Ex: He just *picked at* his beans. #2 nagged at. Ex: His Mother *picked at* him to clean his room.

Pick his brain [verb phr] ask specific questions to gain knowledge that another person has. Ex: You need to *pick his brain* to see what he thinks of that idea.

Pick me upper [noun] anything that makes you feel excited and improves your state of mind. Ex: The afternoon break at work is a *pick-me-upper.*

Pick of the litter [noun phr] the best - refers to puppies born at the same time. Ex: We got the *pick of the litter* and he is easy to train.

Pick off [verb] #1 (sports – baseball) get tagged out. Ex: The baseball runner led too far off second base and got *picked off.* #2 Pull off. Ex: *Pick off* all the old flowers from the bouquet.

Pick on [verb] tease. Ex: Don't *pick on* your little brother.

Pick out [verb] select. Ex: Why don't you *pick out* your dress now?

Pick over [verb] sort through. Ex: These sale items sure have been *picked over*.

Pick to pieces [verb phr] criticize unmercifully. Ex: She *picked* his term paper *to pieces*.

Pick up [verb] #1 clean. Ex: *Pick up* your room   #2 [verb] understand. Ex: He really *picks up on* the new procedure quickly. #3 [noun] a woman who gives sexual favors. Ex: The girls on that street corner are *pick-ups*. #4 buy. Ex: When you go to the store, please *pick up* some oranges.

Pick up speed [verb phr] gain momentum. Ex: The anti-drug campaign will *pick up speed* at the elementary school level when they broadcast anti-drug cartoons.

Pick up the pieces [verb phr]   recover from an emotional setback and function normally again. Ex: It took six months for him to *pick up the pieces* after his father died.

Picture of health [noun phr] in good shape, physically and mentally. Ex: She is the *picture of health* and exercises regularly.

Picture perfect [adj] without fault. Ex: That mountain scene is just *picture perfect*.

Pie in the sky [adj phr]   unrealistic; wishful thinking. Ex: Thinking you will buy a Mercedes is a *pie in the sky* wish.

Piece of cake [noun phr] easy. Ex: That math problem is a *piece of cake.* (See *Easy peasy*)

Piecemeal [adv] in sections or parts. Ex: We received the information *piecemeal.*

Pig in a poke [cliché] (country western) out of place. Ex: Jeb is a *pig in a poke* as a state senator.

Pig out [verb] eat too much. Ex: The small child *pigged out* on candy.

Pig-headed [adj] stubborn and difficult. Ex: The child was so *pig-headed* and would not do his homework.

Pillar of society [noun phr] well respected and well known person in the community. Ex: Mrs. Jones is a *pillar of society.*

Pilot to bombardier [noun phr] Are you listening? (See *Earth to Mars*)

Pin down [verb] #1 determine exactly. Ex: We need to *pin down* the cause of our overstock. #2 (sports - wrestling) don't let the person move. Ex: Paul had to *pin down* his opponent in less than three minutes to beat Sam's record.

Pin him to the wall [verb phr] demand a commitment. Ex: *Pin him to the wall* and get his decision today.

Pin it on him [verb phr] blame him, usually unjustly. Ex: When he broke the glass, he *pinned the blame on his brother.*

Pin up [noun] #1 picture of a pretty girl. Ex: He has a *pin up* of Marilyn Monroe in his locker. #2 [verb] secure. Ex: I need to *pin up* your hem before I sew it.

Pin your hopes too high [verb phr] wish for something nearly impossible. Ex: Don't *pin your hopes too high*. The Army may not let your husband come home for Christmas.

Pinch pennies [verb phr] frugal with money. Ex: We need to *pinch pennies* so we can save for vacation.

Pink collar [noun] women clerical workers who receive low wages. Ex: The *pink collar* workers only got a 3% raise.

Pink slip [noun] notice that you are fired or laid off from your job. (See *Laid off*)

Pipe down [verb] be quiet. Ex: *Pipe down*. Your Mother is sleeping. (See *Simmer down*)

Pipe dream [noun] wishful thinking. Ex: I'd like to go to Hawaii, but it is only a *pipe dream*.

Pipsqueak [noun] child. Ex: That *pipsqueak* took my doughnut. (See *Small fry*)

Piss someone off [verb phr] (Crude, but commonly used) irritate. (See *Tick someone off*)

Pit stop [noun] #1 go to the bathroom. Ex: I gotta make a *pitstop*. Be back in a minute. #2 a place where speedboats or race cars in a race are refueled. Ex: The race car made a *pit stop* and got behind in the race.

Pitch a fit [verb phr] throw a temper tantrum. Ex: That child *pitched a fit* when he couldn't have any candy. (See *Have a hissy fit*)

Pitch black [adj] totally dark. Ex: It was *pitch black* in the cellar until I lit a candle.

Pitch in [verb] help, cooperate. Ex: Let's *pitch in*. We can get this job done in no time.

Pizazz [adj] flashy or colorful. Ex: The showgirl has a lot of *pizazz*.

Plain as day [noun phr] obvious. Ex: It's as *plain as day* that you are not to be trusted. (See *Plain as the nose on your face*)

Plain as the nose on your face [noun phr] (See *Plain as day*)

Plain Jane [noun] homely girl. Ex: His girlfriend is a *plain Jane,* but very generous.

Plank in his platform [noun phr] (politics) important idea on which he is campaigning. Ex: Immigration is a *plank in his platform*.

Plastic [noun] #1 credit cards. Ex: Are you paying with *plastic?* #2 synthetic items. Ex: The toy is made of *plastic.*

Play a long shot [verb phr] bet against the odds. Ex: *Play a long shot* and you win more money.

Play a part [verb phr] act. Ex: He *played the part* of a doctor in the school play.

Play a waiting game [verb phr] patient. Ex: We will *play a waiting game* and hope your illness gets better.

Play all your aces [verb phr] not keep anything in reserve. Ex: He *played all his aces* because the stakes were high. (See *Play his last trump*)

Play around [verb] #1 flirt. Ex: Don't *play around* with my girlfriend. #2 manipulate. Ex: Don't *play around* with the video equipment.

Play ball [verb phr] #1 cooperate in a business venture. Ex: If you *play ball* with me, we can double our money in six months. #2 begin a game, such as baseball. Ex: The umpire said "*Play ball*".

Play both ends against the middle [verb phr] take both sides in a discussion. Ex: You could get burned *playing both ends against the middle*.

Play by ear [verb phr] play a musical instrument without taking any lessons or without knowing how to read music. Ex: I can play *Happy Birthday* by ear on the piano.

Play close to the vest [verb phr] secretive. Ex: He *plays so close to the vest* that we are always surprised by his actions.

Play dumb [verb phr] pretend to be totally ignorant. Ex: If Mary asks you how late I came in last night, just *play dumb*.

Play fast and loose [verb phr] take uncalculated risks. Ex: He *played it fast and loose* and won lots of money in Las Vegas.

Play footsie [verb phr] flirt by rubbing your foot against someone's leg when you are sitting. Ex: *Playing footsie* is lots of fun.

Play for keeps [verb phr] serious about your competition. Ex: When he plays rugby, he *plays for keeps.*

Play hardball [verb phr]   be tough and aggressive in all situations. Ex: By *playing hardball* he got a good deal on his new car.

Play his last trump [verb phr] have nothing left in reserve. Ex: He *played his last trump* on the real estate deal and lost.

Play into his hands [verb phr] gullible. Ex: He *played into my hands* and it was easy to convince him to sell the property.

Play it by ear [verb phr] spontaneous. Ex: I don't have any plans for tonight. Let's *play it by ear.*

Play it cool [verb phr] poised and in control. Ex: *Play it cool* and do not let her know you are upset.

Play it safe [verb phr] not take any risks. Ex: *Play it safe* and take your umbrella in case it rains.

Play it up [verb phr] exaggerate a certain point. Ex: He *plays up* his college degree on his resume.

Play on words [noun phr] a double meaning for a word or phrase. Ex: The Peacekeeper Missile is a *play on words.*

Play the cards you are dealt [verb phr] use your talents well. Ex: You can be successful if you *play the cards you are dealt.*

Play the devil's advocate [verb phr] take an opposing point of view in a discussion just for the sake of arguing. Ex: He likes to *play the devil's advocate* just to keep the discussion lively.

Play the field [verb phr] date many people. Ex: He *played the field* in high school and had many girlfriends.

Play up to [verb phr] flirt with. Ex: She *played up to* the football player.

Play with fire [verb phr] take an uncalculated risk. Ex: He is *playing with fire* investing his money in those junk bonds.

Play your cards right [verb phr] wisely. Ex: If you *play your cards right,* you can sign that contract for a lot of money.

Playing catch up [verb phr] learning certain information quickly. Ex: I am *playing catch up* since I was on vacation when the business plan was introduced.

Playing possum [verb phr] pretending to be asleep. Ex: The boy was *playing possum* so his mother would think he was asleep.

Pleased as punch [verb phr] (1950's slang) delighted, happy. Ex: I am *pleased as punch* you are coming to the party. (Usually said by women)

Pleasingly plump [adj phr] slightly overweight. Ex: Even though she is *pleasingly plump*, she exercises regularly.

Plenty good enough [adj phr] sufficient. Ex: These cupcakes are *plenty good enough* for the party.

Plow through [verb phr] work diligently and steadily. Ex: I'd like to go out with you tonight, but I need to *plow through* all these homework papers and get them graded.

Plum tuckered out [verb phr] completely exhausted. Ex: The two children played so hard all day that they were *plum tuckered out* by evening. (See *All tapped out*)

Podunk [adj] substandard. Ex: Those houses really are *podunk*.

Poetic justice [noun] receive treatment you deserve. Ex: It was *poetic justice* that he forgot his lines in the play after he made fun of others for forgetting their lines.

Poetic license [noun] stretch the rules to allow for creativity. Ex: The author granted a lot of *poetic license* with his play when it was made into a movie.

Point by point [adv phr] (business) one detail at a time. Ex: Let me address the recovery plan *point by point*.

Point of no return [noun phr] irreversible position. Ex: We are at a *point of no return*. We have invested heavily and cannot recover our losses.

Point of order [noun phr] (business) protocol needs to be followed. Ex: As a *point of order*: the motion must be seconded before a vote can be called.

Point out [verb] direct attention to. Ex: Let me *point out* that I made three "A"s on my report card last term.

Points up [verb] demonstrates. Ex: The number of people in our society that cannot read *points up* the failure in our education system.

Poke fun at [verb phr] ridicule. Ex: The two boys *poked fun at* the blind man.

Poke his nose into [verb phr] investigate. Ex: Why does she always *poke her nose into* other people's business?

Poke holes in [verb phr] find errors or deficiencies. Ex: He *pokes holes in* that argument every time.

Poker face [noun phr] not show any expression on your face. Ex: Darren has such a *poker face* we don't know what he is thinking.

Pokey [noun] #1 prison. (See *Slammer*) #2 [adj] slow. Ex: He is so *pokey* he will never make it to school on time.

Polish off [verb] #1 devour. (as a meal) Ex: We *polished off* all the mashed potatoes tonight. #2 defeat. Ex: We really *polished off* the team from Jefferson High School.

Politically incorrect [noun] behavior that is not acceptable by the majority. Ex: It is *politically incorrect* to smoke in public.

Polluted [verb] #1 drunk. (See *Three sheets to the wind*) #2 having waste material in it. Ex: The water got *polluted* when the river flooded.

Pond scum [noun] insignificant person. Ex: Don't invite that boy. He is just *pond scum.*

Pony up [verb] admit responsibility. Ex: We know who painted on the ballpark walls, and we hope he will *pony up* to it.

Pool all our resources [verb phr] combine our assets. Ex: If we *pool all our resources*, we can buy an IPad.

Pooped out [verb phr] exhausted. Ex: I am *pooped out* after babysitting for those four children. (See *Done in*)

Poor as a church mouse [cliché] extremely poor. Ex: The family was *poor as church mice* but honest.

Pop for it [verb phr] pay for it. Ex: If we ask Dean to take us out for dinner, he may even *pop for it.*

Pop his cork [verb phr] become angry. Ex: Jim *popped his cork* when they dropped his favorite project. (See *Flip his lid*)

Pop in [verb] visit unexpectedly. Ex: I think I'll *pop in* at the hospital and see how Darren is doing.

Pop loose [verb] donate. Ex: I think we can get Dad to *pop loose* with a few dollars for the movie.

Pop out [verb] leave for a short time. Ex: The session lasts all morning, but I can *pop out* and call you.

Pop the clutch [verb phr] release the clutch too fast in your car, causing the car to lurch forward. Ex: Be careful that you don't *pop the clutch* when you drive the car.

Pop the question [verb phr] ask someone to marry you. Ex: I think I'll *pop the question* to Renee tomorrow.

Pop-up [noun phr] #1 unplanned event. Ex: I didn't know about the meeting until this morning since it was a *pop-up*. #2 [adj] 3D figures in a book. Ex: I got a *pop-up* Mother Goose book for my granddaughter.

Poppycock [1940's expression of disbelief] Ex: *Poppycock*! I don't think you can run that fast.

Pork barrel [noun phr] money from the Federal Treasury that legislators use for favorite projects for their home states. Ex: There are too many *pork barrel* projects in the Senate.

Pork out [verb] overeat. Ex: I really *porked out* this Thanksgiving.

Porker [noun] person who eats a lot and usually is overweight. Ex: Dan is getting to be a real *porker*. I'll bet he weighs 300 pounds.

Possession is nine tenths of the law [cliché] you own any object you possess regardless of how you got it. Ex: Since you left your jacket at my house for six months it is mine. *Possession is nine tenths of the law.*

Potbelly [noun] fat stomach (generally not desired by anyone!) Ex: The older he gets the more of a *potbelly* he gets.

Pot calling the kettle black [cliché] accusing someone of faults which you also display.

Pound of flesh [noun phr] #1 degrading term for prostitute. #2 extortion. Ex: The Mafia demanded their *pound of flesh*, even though the man could not pay up.

Pound out [verb phr] #1 use a tool to hit an object to change its shape. Ex: Did you *pound out* the dent in your car? #2 determine or decide. Ex: We have to *pound out* the responsibilities for each task on the project.

Pound the pavement [verb phr] looking for a job. Ex: I *pounded the pavement* for two hours yesterday and did not get an interview.

Pour it on [verb phr] kid someone. Ex: Everyone likes to *pour it on* Ted, but he has a good sense of humor and takes it well.

Pour oil on water [verb phr] things that will not mix well. Ex: When Jack started dating Emily, it was like *pouring oil on water.*

Pour on the coal [verb phr] speed up when driving. Ex: *Pour on the coal.* We have to be at the wedding by 4:00.

Pour salt in the wound [verb phr] criticizing someone who has already been injured or shamed. Ex: It was cruel of him to pour *salt in the wound* when he knew her brother was arrested for drug dealing. (See *Add insult to injury*)

Poured cold water on it [verb phr] negative about an idea. Ex: At first I *poured cold water on that idea,* but on second thought I like it.

Poured out her heart [verb phr] confide in someone. Ex: She *poured out her heart* to him and he was sympathetic.

Pouring good money after bad [verb phr] put additional money into a bad investment. Ex: Let's not invest any more money. We would be *pouring good money after bad.*

Pouring it on thick [verb phr] flatter someone in an exaggerated way. Ex: Roy was really *pouring it on thick* last night, and I did not believe half of what he was saying. (See *Lay it on thick*)

Pow - right in the kisser [expression from the old TV show starring Jackie Gleason] said in jest and accompanied by a hand gesture, when someone says something you do not agree with.

Powder my nose [verb phr] go to the restroom. (said only by women) Ex: Excuse me, while I go *powder my nose.*

Powder room [noun] ladies bathroom or restroom. Ex: She went into the *powder room* and will be back in a minute.

Powder the ball [verb phr] (sports - baseball) hit a baseball very hard. Ex: Jose *powdered the ball* and made a home run.

Power base [noun]   the extent of your sphere of influence. Ex: The governor has quite an extensive *power base.*

Power breakfast [noun] (business) going to breakfast for business reasons only. Ex: The organization *power breakfast* is at 6:00 A.M.

Powers that be [noun phr]   head decision makers. Ex: The *powers that be* said that we could have a day care center. (See *Head honchos*)

Prairie-dogging [verb] (business) (2011 slang) Peering out over cubicles in the workplace.

Preaching to the choir [verb phr] lecturing to convince those who already believe in the idea. Ex: I would tell you more about empowering employees but I am *preaching to the choir.*

Precious few [adj] not many. Ex: There are *precious few* years that your children are small.

Pregnant pause [noun phr]   a moment when there is no conversation. Ex: There was a *pregnant pause* while he got ready to give his speech.

Press on [verb] persevere. Ex: Let us *press on* to the top of the mountain.

Press the flesh [verb expression] shake hands. Ex: Politicians love to *press the flesh* when they are campaigning.

Press your luck [verb phr] request more than is reasonable. Ex: I already gave you two weeks allowance in advance. Don't *press your luck*!

Pretty as a picture [adj phr]   good looking; often said about women. Ex: She is as *pretty as a picture*.

Pretty penny [noun] lots of money. Ex: This diamond ring will cost you a *pretty penny*.

Price adjustment [noun) common term for "price increase". Ex: There will be a *price adjustment* in the product.

Prick up your ears [verb phr] listen closely. Ex: I *pricked up my ears* when he said he was going to go get ice cream.

Pride and joy [adj phr] something you value a great deal. Ex: My new sports car is my *pride and joy*.

Prides himself on [verb phr] is proud of. Ex: He *prides himself on* always being on time.

Prime the pump [verb phr] made an effort to get an action started. Ex: You may have to *prime the pump* with a few dollars to get a new campaign started.

Probable cause [noun] most likely motive. Ex: The police arrested him once they determined he had *probable cause* for doing the crime.

Proof is in the pudding [cliché] if someone says he/she has a certain skill, wait until they have specifically demonstrated that skill. Ex: I've never seen her play the piano. The *proof is in the pudding.*

Prophet of doom [noun phr] take the negative point of view. Ex: Sam is always the *prophet of doom.* He thinks the economy will never recover.

Pros and cons [noun phr] review both sides of a situation; the *pros* (all the reasons for) and the *cons* (all the reasons against) a course of action. Ex: I'll take a look at all the *pros and cons* and then make my decision.

Pull a fast one [verb phr] fool someone. Ex: Rick really *pulled a fast one* on his brother. He got him to loan him $5,000 with no interest!

Pull a rabbit out of your hat [verb phr] successful at the last possible moment. Ex: I am going to have to *pull a rabbit out of the hat* to get this contract signed by Tuesday.

Pull any punches [verb phr] be deceptive. Ex: Go to bed at 8:00 tonight. Don't *pull any punches.*

Pull in your horns [verb phr] do not be aggressive. Ex: *Pull in your horns.* I was not talking about you.

Pull it off [verb phr] accomplish something successfully. Ex: The two robbers *pulled off the robbery* very smoothly.

Pull out all the stops [verb phr] pursue something with all your energy and determination. Ex: When he *pulled out all the stops,* he was elected governor.

Pull strings [verb phr] influence important people. Ex: If I *pull some strings,* I can get you into the Club.

Pull the plug [verb phr] #1 relinquish support. Ex: Management *pulled the plug* on the extra budget for product development. #2 disconnect lifesaving apparatus. Ex: She is brain dead and it is time to *pull the plug.*

Pull the rug out from under [verb phr] leave someone with all the responsibility for a project. (See *Leave someone hanging*)

_____

Pull the wool over his eyes [verb phr] fool someone. Ex: He thought he could _pull the wool over my eyes,_ and I would not know he had not done his homework, but I found out. (See _Pull a fast one_)

Pull your weight [verb phr] do your share on a project. Ex: If you're working with me, you have to _pull your weight._

Pull yourself together [verb phr] compose yourself. Ex: _Pull yourself together._ The funeral is tomorrow.

Pull yourself up by the bootstraps [verb phr] recover from a setback. Ex: _Pull yourself up by the bootstraps_ and get back on your horse.

Pulling my hair out [verb phr] worried. Ex: I am _pulling my hair out_ because my son is late again.

Pulling your leg [verb phr] kidding someone. Ex: Don't you know that he is just _pulling your leg?_

Pump iron [verb phr] exercise by lifting weights. Ex: Scott _pumps iron_ for 30 minutes every day.

Pump up [verb] motivate, energize. Ex: The coach _pumped up_ his players and they won the game.

Punch drunk [adj] acting silly. Ex: We stayed up all night studying, and were _punch drunk t_he next day because we were so tired.

Punch holes in [verb phr] find fault. Ex: I suppose Congress will _punch holes in_ the new gun law proposal.

Punch the clock [verb phr] (business) put a time card in a slot each day when you come and leave work that records the times you arrived and left.

Punk rocker [noun] musician who plays a certain style of music. Ex: Sid Vicious was a famous *punk rocker.*

Puppy love [noun] teenage love. Ex: They thought they were really in love, but their parents thought it was *puppy love.*

Pure and simple [adj] no frills. Ex: That's the plan, *pure and simple.*

Pure as the driven snow [adj phr] innocent. Ex: Jessica is *pure as the driven snow* and would never embarrass her parents.

Push someone's hot button [verb phr] say something that will anger another person. Ex: *If you push his hot button,* he might hit you.

Push the panic button [verb phr] over react. Ex: Don't *push the panic button* when the fire alarm goes off.

Pushing up daisies [verb phr] dead and buried. Ex: My uncle will be *pushing up daisies* by the time he turns 90.

Pussy foot [verb] walk lightly. Ex: We have to *pussy foot* around Liz. She is so sensitive you know.

Pussy whipped [adj] man who is intimidated by his wife. Ex: He is so *pussy whipped* that he can never play pool with us in the evening.

Put 2 and 2 together [verb phr] figure out the solution to a problem. Ex: She *put 2 and 2 together* and figured out her son had not done his homework.

Put a bag on it [verb phr] forget it. (See *Stuff it*)

Put a bug in his ear [verb phr] reminder or warning. Ex: You'll have to *put a bug in his ear* that practice time was changed to 7:00 on Thursdays.

Put a damper on it [verb phr] not be enthusiastic. (See *Rain on my parade*)

Put a little body English on it [verb phr] (sports) hit it hard. Ex: If you *put a little body English on your tennis serve,* you will get it over the net.

Put a muffler on it [verb phr] be quiet. (See *Simmer down)*

Put a nix to that [verb phr] prohibit or prevent something from happening. Ex: The kids think they're going to stay out past midnight, but I'll *put a nix to that*!

Put all his eggs in one basket [verb phr] put all your energy into one plan. Ex: Don't *put all your eggs in one basket* or you will be disappointed.

Put all the cards on the table [verb phr] tell everything you know about a situation. Ex: Let's *put all the cards on the table* so we can make the right decision.

Put away food [verb phr] eat a large quantity of food. Ex: He *puts away* six pancakes every morning!

Put back for a rainy day [verb phr] save for hard times. Ex: Let's *put at least $100 back for a rainy day.*

Put down [verb] belittling someone. Ex: Donna is always *putting down* her husband.

Put forth [verb] offer. Ex: He *put forth* $5,000 for the used car.

Put hair on your chest [verb phr] said in jest about any task that would be "macho" to undertake. Ex: You're going to hike up Mount Rainier? That will *put hair on your chest.*

Put his foot down [verb phr] unwavering. Ex: Dad *put his foot down* and said the kids could not borrow his car.

Put his foot in it [verb phr] #1 make a mistake. Ex: He *put his foot in it* when he let his wife know he had played poker the night before. #2 interfered in someone's business. Ex: Don't *put your foot where it doesn't belong.* Let the couple solve their own problems.

Put his lights out [verb phr] knock someone out. Ex: The heavyweight champion *put his opponent's lights out* in the fourth round.

Put in a good word [verb phr] say something complimentary. Ex: I'll *put in a good word* for you so you can get the job.

Put in charge [verb phr] having power to make decisions. Ex: The boss *put* Derek *in charge* when he was on vacation.

Put in my two cents [verb phr] give my opinion. Ex: I *put my two cents worth in* about the coal trains.

Put it behind you [verb phr] forget it. Ex: The sooner you *put it behind you,* you can move ahead with your life.

Put it to bed [verb phr] (business) complete a project. Ex: Let's *put this project to bed* before Friday.

Put it to you [verb phr] ask for your decision or opinion. Ex: I *put it to you.* Did I do the right thing or not?

Put it where the sun don't shine [verb phr] (<u>impolite</u>) refers to putting something up someone's ass.

Put me on your list [verb phr] invite me. Ex: If you decide to have the Christmas party, *put me on your list*.

Put on airs [verb phr] be snobby. Ex: She has *put on airs* since moving to that exclusive neighborhood.

Put on hold [verb phr] delay or cancel. Ex: The project has been *put on hold* until more funding can be approved.

Put on the dog [verb phr] try to impress someone. Ex: Get dressed up. We are going to *put on the dog tonight* and impress the boss. (See *Dressed to the Nines*)

Put on your thinking cap [verb phr] use your brain. Ex: *Put on your thinking cap* and tell me how we can solve the problem of the rising water.

Put our heads together [verb phr] collaborate. Ex: If we *put our heads together*, I am sure we can solve the problem.

Put out to pasture [verb phr] retire. Ex: Uncle Tim was *put out to pasture* last year, and he is enjoying himself.

Put some teeth into it [verb phr] make it more solid. Ex: If you would *put some teeth into* that proposal, I would accept it.

Put spin on it [verb phr] your personal touch. Ex: He will *put his spin on the plans* for the new library.

Put that in your pipe and smoke it (1940's slang) accept what was said. Ex: I said you couldn't go back East to school. *Put that in your pipe and smoke it.*

Put the bite on him [verb phr] #1 put pressure on someone. Ex: Better *put the bite on him* to return your new sweater. #2 borrow or beg money from someone. Ex: I need to *put the bite on my brother* for a loan of $100. (See *Put the squeeze on*)

Put the brakes on [verb phr] stop what you are doing. Ex: *Put the brakes on* until we read the next instruction.

Put the cart before the horse [cliché] (See *Don't put the cart before the horse*)

Put the pedal to the metal [verb phr] speed up when driving. Ex: *Put the pedal to the metal*. We want to get to the store before it closes.

Put the squeeze on [verb phr] pressured for payment. Ex: The bank *put the squeeze on* their creditor who was 30 days late with the payment.

Put to shame [verb phr] humiliate. Ex: He was *put to shame* by lying to his brother.

Put under a microscope [verb phr] examine. Ex: We need to *put* his motives *under a microscope*.

Put up a good front [verb phr] #1 pretend to be happy or well, when actually upset or ill. Ex: She *put up such a good front* that I did not know her husband had cancer. #2 successfully hide the actual status or nature of something. Ex: The mob put *up a good front* in that dry cleaners. They have gambling in the back room.

Put up a smokescreen [verb phr] confuse the issue. Ex: When you ask him a direct question, he will *put up a smoke screen*.

Put up or shut up [verb phr] (<u>impolite</u>) help correct a problem or accept it without complaint. Ex: Here is what we can do about the ant problem. *Put up or shut up.*

Put your best foot forward [verb phr] do your best. Ex: *Put your best foot forward* when you go to the interview.

Put your finger on it [verb phr] identify it. Ex: I can't *put my finger on it,* but I think Trevor is taking drugs.

Put your foot down [verb phr] be strict about the rules. Ex: Parents have to *put their foot down* on many issues with their children.

Put your money where your mouth is [verb phr] support financially whatever you have supported verbally. Ex: The millionaire *put his money where his mouth was* and built a school in Africa.

Put yourself out [noun phr] (See *Don't put yourself out*)

Puts his pants on one leg at a time [verb phr] people who are well-known have common traits also. Ex: The President "*puts his pants on one leg at a time*, just like us."

Put the screws to him [verb phr] put pressure on someone. Ex: *Put the screws to him* to have the project done in a week.

Putting on the Ritz [verb phr] act like you have lots of money. Ex: When she married a rich man, she started *putting on the Ritz.*

QT [abbrev] quirky abbreviation for "quiet". Ex: If someone gives you information "on the QT", it means that it is secretive and not to be shared.

Quantum leap [noun] greater than normal accomplishment. Ex: Every home will have an IPad in the future, but that is really a *quantum leap.*

(The) Queen's English [noun phr] proper use of English, not using slang. Ex: Few people actually use the *Queen's English.*

Queued up [verb] ready and waiting. Ex: The document is *queued up a*nd will print in a few minutes.

Quick and dirty [adj] done quickly, but not thoroughly. Ex: Here is a *quick and dirty* memo about the picnic.

Quick as a blink [adv phr] extremely fast. Ex: The rabbit disappeared into the hole *quicker than a blink*. (See *Quicker than greased lightning)*

Quick fix [noun] not permanent, but gets something functioning quickly. Ex: It's only a *quick fix,* but the lawnmower will work today.

Quicker than greased lightning [adv phr] (See *Quicker than a blink*)

Quickie [noun] have sex that only lasts few minutes. Ex: He went home for lunch and had a *quickie* with his wife (See *Slam bam, thank you ma'am)*

Quit the dance [verb phr] gave up; conceded defeat. Ex: He *quit the dance* and got a regular job when he couldn't sell his paintings.

Quit the racket

Quit the racket [verb] retire. Ex: He will *quit the racket* next
year and travel around the world.

Quit while you're ahead [verb phr] stop an activity before your
luck changes. Ex: I better *quit while I'm ahead.* I have
won the last two horse races.

Quite the thing [adj phr] fashionable. Ex: Wearing neck scarves
around your shoulders is *quite the thing* these days.

R&B [abbrev] *Rhythm and Blues*, a popular style of music.

R&D [abbrev] (business) *Research and Development*. Ex: The *R&D* Department does not have enough budget for new product development.

R&R [abbrev] *rest and relaxation.* Ex: We need to go to Hawaii for some R&R.

ROFLOL [abbrev] *Rolling on the floor laughing outloud* – cell phone texting abbreviation.

R.P.M. [abbrev] *revolutions per minute*. Ex: Most cars have a tachometer with an R.P.M. reading.

R.S.V.P. [abbrev] *Repondez s'il vous plait* , a French phrase meaning "Please respond to the invitation". This abbreviation is put at the bottom of an invitation to a wedding, party, etc. because you want the invitee to let you know if he/she is coming.

Rabbit ears [noun] an indoor television antenna that sits on top of the T.V. Outdated since satellite TV has become popular.

Rabbit food [noun] lettuce, carrots, radishes. Ex: A certain amount of *rabbit food* is good for you.

Ratchet up [verb] increase speed. Ex: Better *ratchet up* the project because we are behind schedule.

Rack and ruin [noun] total destruction. Ex: The Company would not deal with the union so it came to *rack and ruin*.

___

Rack my brain [verb phr] try to remember. Ex: I *racked my brain,* but I can't remember my English professor's name.

Rack up [verb] injure. #1. Ex: The fall really *racked up* his leg. #2 accumulate. Ex: I *racked up* a big score the last time I bowled. #3 (playing pool) *Rack 'em up.* I will win this time.

Rad [adj] (1990's slang) cool; fabulous. Ex: That new outfit is *rad.* (See *Groovy*)

Rag on someone [verb phr] criticize someone. Ex: She is always *ragging on* her husband.

Railroad it through [verb phr] get your plans or ideas accepted through intimidation and quick decision making. Ex: They *railroaded the plan through* even though it was unsound.

Rain check [noun] (See *Take a rain check)*

Rain coming down in buckets [noun phr] raining hard without ceasing. Ex: The *rain has been coming down in buckets* all day and I forgot my raincoat. (See *Raining cats and dogs)*

Rain on my parade [verb phr] dampen someone's enthusiasm. Ex: Every time I want to do something fun, you *rain on my parade.*

Raining cats and dogs [verb phr] heavy rain that continues for a length of time. (See *Rain coming down in buckets***)**

Raise a ruckus [verb phr] create a noisy disturbance. Ex: Every July Fourth, the neighbor kids *raise a ruckus* in the park. (See *Raise Cain*)

___

Raise Cain [verb phr] be rowdy. (See *Raise a ruckus)*

Raise it to a higher level [verb phr] #1 make it more important. Ex: If you don't think getting good grades is important, maybe you better *raise it to a higher level.* #2 (business) pass to upper management for decision. Ex: If we can't get funding for the project, we'll *raise it to a higher level.*

Raise the roof [verb phr] #1 be extremely loud. Ex: The band practiced in my garage and *raised the roof* last night. #2 construction on a new building. Ex: We had a party to celebrate *raising the roof* on our new church.

Rake him over the coals [verb phr] make negative comments. Ex: When Colin failed math, his classmates *raked him over the coals.*

Rake in the chips [verb phr] make lots of money. Ex: With the sale of their new invention, they *rake in the chips* now.

Ramble [verb] (1990's slang) leave. Ex: Got to *ramble.* I have a class now. (See *Shove off*)

Ramp up [verb] (business) hire more people and get resources ready for more projected business. Ex: We better *ramp up* for the new product line.

Ran amuck [verb] go awry. Ex: We had planned to sail through the San Juan's, but our plans *ran amuck.*

Ran into a roadblock [verb phr] an obstacle. Ex: We tried to get a loan, but *ran into a roadblock.*

Ran it into the ground [verb phr] #1 ruin. Ex: It was a money-making business, but he *ran it into the ground*. #2 do or use excessively. Ex: I did believe his excuse the first couple times, but he ran *it into the ground* by trying it again.

Rank and file [noun] ordinary people. Ex: The *rank and file* will vote the candidate out of office. (See *Peons*)

Rap [verb] talk with someone. Ex: The two gang leaders need to *rap* instead of fighting. (See *Gangsta Rap*)

Rare breed [noun] unique person. Ex: He is really a *rare breed*; always kind and thoughtful.

Raring to go [verb phr] excited and anxious to start something. Ex: The dog is *raring to go* for a walk.

Rat hole [noun] small unpleasant place. Ex: This apartment is just a *rat hole.*

Rat race [noun] everyday competition in the work place. Ex: It is hard to relax after the everyday *rat race.*

Rat's Ass [noun] (Impolite, but commonly used) (See *Don't give a rat's ass*)

Rat's nest [noun] mess. Ex: My hair looks like a *rat's nest* today. (remark made by women)

Rattle his cage [verb phr] upset him. Ex: If you criticize his wife, it will *rattle his cage.*

Rattled off [verb] list in rapid succession. Ex: He *rattled off* the names of all the Presidents of the United States.

Raw deal [noun] unfair. Ex: I got a *raw deal* on that piece of property.

Raw nerve [noun] #1 courage. Ex: He's got *raw nerve*, scaling that mountain in the middle of winter. #2 anxious and fearful. Ex: His *nerves were raw* after losing a lot of sleep and working hard.

Razzamatazz [noun] nonsense word for something that dazzles. Ex: I want a new boat and all the *razzamatazz* that goes with it.

Razzed [verb] tease. Ex: Hank *razzed* me about my new haircut.

Read between the lines [verb phr] understand the subtleties in communication. Ex: You need to *read between the lines* to know how he stands on the issues.

Read it and weep [verb expression when playing a card game] My good news is bad news for you. Ex: I have two Aces. *Read it and weep. (*See *One up on)*

Read my lips [verb phr] listen to what I say and believe it. Ex: *Read my lips.* I don't want you to go to the Mall today.

Read the handwriting on the wall [verb phr] perceive what will happen next. Ex: I can *read the handwriting on the wall.* There will be more international trade next year.

Read the riot act [verb phr] chastise someone. Ex: The policeman *read him the riot* act for driving without a license. (See *Give him what for)*

Read you like a book [verb phr] understand someone and can predict their behavior. Ex: He *read her like a book* since they had been married 20 years.

Real life-saver [noun] helpful person or tool. Ex: That generator has been a *real life-saver* whenever the electricity goes off.

Real McCoy [noun] authentic. Ex: That painting is the *real McCoy.*

Real trouper [noun] courage in the face of adversity. Ex: Kaitlyn is a *real trouper.* She ran for re-election even though her life had been threatened.

Reality check [noun] (business) revisit original goals in the middle of a project to see if you are on target. Ex: Let's do a *reality check* before moving on to Phase 2.

Reality impaired [noun] unaware. Ex: *Reality impaired* is a politically correct term these days.

Really swift [1950's expression] said sarcastically, meaning dumb or silly. Ex: That was *really swift* - forgetting my doctor appointment.

Red carpet treatment [noun] special treatment given to important people such as Presidents and movie stars. Ex: The Pope is coming to town on Friday and will get the *red carpet treatment.*

Red letter day [noun] an important day, such as your birthday. Ex: I wouldn't forget your *red letter day* tomorrow.

Red line it [adj] (business) edit it; correct any errors. Ex: I will *red line* your memo and get it back to you tomorrow.

Red shirt freshman [noun phr] practice with the varsity football team in college but not play. Ex: If you are a *red shirt freshman*, you still have four years of eligibility to play the sport.

Redneck [noun] conservative people from the South. Ex: The TV show "Duck Dynasty" portrays typical *rednecks* from the South.

Regular channels [noun] following established procedures. Ex: I followed *regular channels* with no success.

Reinvent the wheel [verb phr] Re-write or re-do a procedure or process when one is already in place. Ex: We can't *reinvent the wheel* on this project. Let's use our old artwork.

Remember the Alamo [verb phr] [expression of retribution or retaliation] refers back to the Mexican attack of the Alamo Mission in 1836, when all defenders were killed.

Reputation precedes you [noun phr] someone has heard about you (good or bad) prior to meeting them. Ex: Your *reputation has proceeded you.* I have heard good things about you.

Rest assured [verb expression] convince someone of a certain fact. Ex: *Rest assured* he can climb the mountain.

Resting on his laurels [verb phr] rely on past successes. Ex: He is *resting on his laurels* since his promotion.

Revenue enhancement [noun] higher taxes. Ex: The government is talking about new *revenue enhancement.*

Revenue excess [noun] profit. Ex: With the *revenue excess* we can give a raise to our workers.

Revved up [verb] excited. Ex: I'm all *revved up* about my new sports car. (See *Stokin'*)

Ride herd on [verb phr] supervise. Drew, *ride herd on* those kids before they break something.

Ride in on his white horse [verb phr] someone from the outside who takes a position of importance and changes things for the better. Ex: The marketing director *rode in on his white horse* and made some positive changes.

Ride out of town on a rail [verb phr] (country western) misbehave badly and be forced to leave town. Ex: The town had to *ride the child molester out of town on a rail.*

Ride roughshod [verb] dominate and be aggressive with someone. Ex: He *rides roughshod* over his employees, and they are afraid of him.

Ride shotgun [verb] (2013 slang) sit next to the driver in a car.

Riding a tiger [verb phr] take lots of risks. Ex: If we can *ride the tiger* the next three months, the company will show a profit.

Riff [noun] An extemporaneous musical or verbal interlude.

Right and left [adv phr] everywhere. Ex: I looked *right and left* for my book, but I can't find it. (See *Turn the house upside down*)

Right as rain [adj expression] entirely correct. Ex: You are *right as rain* about that golf course. It is really a tough one.

Right back at you [adj expression] the same to you. Ex: When someone pays you a compliment you say, "*Right back at you.*"

Right hand man [noun] person who helps you the most. Ex: The Vice-President is usually the President's *right hand man.*

Right off the bat [adv phr] to begin with. Ex: *Right off the bat* they hired some good players.

Right on [expression of agreement] that's right. Ex: "I love chocolate". "*Right on!*"

Right on the dot [adv phr] exactly. Ex: We are eating *right on the dot* at 6:00.

Right on the money [adj phr] correct. Ex: Your advice is *right on the money.*

Right on the nose [adv phr] accurately. He predicted the score of the game *right on the nose.*

Right smack in the middle of [adj phr] intensely involved. Ex: They were *right smack in the middle of* a big disagreement.

Right under your nose [adv phr] obvious location. Ex: Your car keys are *right under your nose.*

Right up your alley [adj phr] perfect for your interests and talents. Ex: I've come across a job that is *right up your alley.*

Right Wing [adj] ultraconservative people who are members of the Tea Party. (See Tea Party)

Rightsizing [verb] (business) another term for downsizing; laying off employees to cut costs. Ex: *Rightsizing* has caused a lot of people to sell their homes.

Ring a bell [verb phr] triggers a memory. Ex: When she said she was from Colorado, it *rang a bell.* I knew I had gone to school with her.

Ring a ding a doo [1950's expression] (said sarcastically) meaning "so what?"

Ring me up [verb] call me on the phone. Ex: *Ring me up* tomorrow at 3:00.

Ring true [verb] sound correct. Ex: Those figures on the account *ring true.*

Ringing off the hook [verb phr] ringing incessantly. Ex: I might get some work done if this telephone would stop *ringing off the hook.*

Rip off [noun] unfair. Ex: That price is a *rip off.* I saw that item next door for $5.00 less.

Ripped [verb] drunk. (See *Three sheets to the wind)*

Ripple effect [noun] (business) results will trickle down. Ex: When 400 people were fired from the company, the *ripple effect* was seen in all the companies they do business with. (See *Domino effect*)

Rise above it [verb phr] forgive an injustice. Ex: I know that driver flipped you off, but just *rise above it.*

Rise and shine [early morning greeting] time to get up.

Rise from the ranks [verb phr] (business) begin in a low paying position and obtain an executive position. Ex: The President of the company *rose from the ranks.*

Road hog [noun] aggressive driver. Ex: He won't let us pass him. He's such a *road hog.*

Road kill [noun] #1 chemical spray used to kill plants along the highway. Ex: The *road kill* is going to seep into our rivers. #2 dead animals along the highway. Ex: Possums are a common *road kill*.

Road rage [noun] driver of a car becomes extremely agitated with another driver. Sometimes he cuts him off, honks at him/her, makes obscene hand gestures, or shakes his/her fist. Ex: *Road rage* is causing more accidents on the highways.

Road show [noun] (business) giving a presentation to people in different locations. Ex: Tomorrow the *road show* begins. My first presentation is in Seattle.

Rob Peter to pay Paul [cliché] lack the money to pay two creditors, so you only pay one, thereby "robbing" the other creditor.

Robo [noun] (political) form letter sent to people who write to their congressman. It even has the congressman's facsimile signature.

Robocall [noun] phone call solicitation that is unwanted by most people. Ex: I got five *robocalls* this morning. An important call could not get through.

Robust [adj] (business) of good quality. Ex: The new car design is quite *robust*.

Rock and rubber [noun] (1990's slang) grilled cheese sandwiches, especially those served in cafeterias.

Rock bottom [adv] exhausted all your resources. Ex: We are at *rock bottom* since Darren got laid off.

Rock the boat [verb phr] not conforming to the status quo. Ex: If you bring up that new idea, it will *rock the boat*.

Rocks in his head [noun phr] dense; stupid. Ex: He parked too close to the railroad tracks. He must have *rocks in his head*.

Roll in the aisles [verb phr] laugh uncontrollably. Ex: The movie was so funny that we *rolled in the aisles.*

Roll in the clover [verb phr] enjoy being rich. Ex: If that stock splits, we will be *rolling in the clover*. (See *Rolling in the dough*)

Roll in the hay [verb phr] have sex. (See *Make whoopee)*

Roll off your back [verb phr] not let what someone says bother you. Ex: Jack is sharp tongued today. Just let it *roll off your back.*

Roll off your tongue [verb phr] something that was easy to say. Ex: "How did you pronounce his name correctly?" "Easy. It just *rolled off my tongue."*

Roll out the red carpet [verb phr] honor an important person when he/she arrives. Ex: We *rolled out the red carpet* for the CEO's visit.

Roll over and play dead [verb phr] concede. Ex: I know our competitor would like us to *roll over and play dead*, but we plan to expand our discount business.

Roll over in her grave [verb phr] event would shock the deceased person. *Ex:* If Aunt Sally knew her children wasted all her money, she would *roll over in her grave.*

Roll up the streets [verb phr] clean up after a party. Ex: Let's *roll up the streets*-- time to go home.

Roll up your sleeves [verb phr] get involved and work hard. Ex: *Roll up your sleeves*. We have a lot to do today.

Roll with the punches [verb phr] be flexible. Ex: You have to *roll with the punches* to be successful in life.

Roll your eyes [verb phr] (a gesture) not believe someone and <u>literally</u> roll your eyes.

Rolling in the dough [verb phr] having lots of money. Ex: Ever since Stan started his own business, he is *rolling in the dough. (See Roll in the clover)*

Rolling right along [verb phr] living life smoothly without any disturbances. Ex: I saw Larry yesterday and he is *rolling right along.*

Rolling stone gathers no moss [cliché] active people will never be bored.

Rookie [noun] (sports) first year player in a sport. Ex: The *rookie* signed a great contract.

Root of the matter [noun phr] source. Ex: If we can get to the *root of the matter* we can solve this problem. (See *Heart of the matter)*

Rope necktie [noun] noose. Ex: We watched the Western movie on TV. They tied the *rope necktie* on the horse thief.

Rotten egg [noun] disreputable person. Ex: That *rotten egg* did not finish his part of the project we were working on.

Rotten to the core [verb phr] being disreputable. (See *Rotten egg)*

Rough housing [verb] wrestling. Ex: The two boys were *rough housing* in their room.

Round file [noun] the wastebasket. Ex: You can put those papers in the *round file.*

Round peg in a square hole [noun phr] not fit into a group. Ex: She is not a team player. She's a *round peg in a square hole.*

Round robin [adj] (sports) in succession. Sports tournaments in which teams rotate playing each other.

Round trip [noun] travel to a destination and then back to the home destination. Ex: We're planning a *round trip* to Portland and back to Seattle.

Router [noun] allows multiple computers to join the same network. In order for devices on the network to connect to the Internet, the router must be connected to a modem. (See Modem)

Rub elbows with [verb phr] associate with. Ex: It's nice to *rub elbows with* the movie stars when they go to the ski resorts.

Rub him the wrong way [verb phr] make him irritated. Ex: If you use generalizations, you will *rub him the wrong way.*

Rub it in [verb phr] exaggerate someone else's mistake. Ex: You don't have to *rub it in.* I know I should have studied more for the test.

Rub off [verb] acquire by proximity. Ex: If Jim plays with Harry a lot, I hope his good manners will *rub off* on Harry.

Rubber neck [verb] turning your neck frequently to look at something interesting. Ex: You are *rubber necking* too much while driving.

Rubber stamp approval [noun] (business) automatic acceptance. Ex: You will get *rubber stamp approval* on that memo from the Vice President.

Rude awakening [noun] future enlightenment of an unpleasant nature. Ex: You'll have a *rude awakening* when you discover you should have put gas in the car.

Ruffle her feathers [verb phr] upset her. Ex: It *ruffled her feathers* when you criticized her child.

Rug rats [noun] children. Ex: The *rug rats* can stay up until 9:00 P.M. (See *Crumb snatchers*)

Rule of thumb [noun phr] general guideline. Ex: It is a *rule of thumb* that you wear a raincoat when it rains.

Rule the roost [verb phr] dominant and bossy. Ex: He *rules the roost* at work, but is not aggressive at home.

Rumble [verb] fight. Ex: I hear there's going to be a *rumble* at the football field tonight.

Rumble seat [noun] (1940's slang) extra seat behind the driver. Ex: You can put the luggage in the *rumble seat*.

Rumor mill [noun] gossip. Ex: The *rumor mill* says the company will be downsizing.

Run a railroad [verb phr] (See *That's no way to run a railroad*)

Run across [verb] encounter. Ex: If you *run across* Bill, tell him "Hi".

Run around   #1 [verb] be promiscuous. If you *run around* on your wife you will get in trouble. #2 [noun] avoid someone. Ex: He gives me the *run around* every time I ask him how the project is going.

Run around like a chicken with its head cut off   [verb phr] scatterbrained. Ex: You can think more clearly if you don't *run around like a chicken with its head cut off.*

Run circles around   [verb phr] act energetic. Ex: She *runs circles around* me. She gets up at 5:00 A.M. and runs five miles.

Run deep [verb] in football, it is a command to run to the far end of the field in order to catch a long pass thrown by a quarterback. Ex: If Bart *runs deep*, I can complete the pass for a touchdown.

Run down [adj] #1 shabby. Ex: That house we looked at was awfully *run down.* #2 [adv] tired. Ex: I am feeling so *run down* since I got the flu. #3 [verb] hit with a car. Ex: The teenager has *run down* a boy on a bicycle. #4 [verb] locate. Ex: I'll see if I can *run down* those old files.   #5 [verb] needs rewinding (as a clock) Ex: The clock has *run down* so I will wind it again. #6 [verb] degrade. Ex: Do not *run down* your sister. She is as talented as you.

Run for cover [verb phr] hide. Ex: Let's *run for cover* before it starts raining.

Run for your money   [verb phr]   challenge from tough competition.   Ex: Whenever I compete against Freeman, he gives me a run for my money.

Run his legs off [verb phr] involved in a frenzy of activity. Ex: He *ran his legs off* trying to get all the errands done today.

Run in [noun] #1 unpleasant encounter. Ex: He had a *run-in* with the police. #2 enter. Ex: Will you *run in* the store and get some milk?

Run in circles [verb phr] busy, but not accomplishing much. Ex: You have to be organized or you just *run in circles*.

Run into [verb] chance meeting. Ex: Did you *run into* Sam yesterday?

Run it by him [verb phr] get his opinion. Ex: *Run it by him* and if he approves, we will go ahead with the idea.

Run it by me again [verb phr] repeat it. Ex: I didn't hear what you said. Please *run it by me again*. (See *Grind it up a little finer*)

Run it into the ground [verb phr] belabor a point or subject. Ex: You've *run it into the ground*. Let's change the subject.

Run it up the flag pole [verb phr] make it a priority. Ex: We need to *run that problem up the flagpole* so it will get some attention.

Run its course [verb phr] complete an event. Ex: Let the storm *run its course* before you go outside.

Run of bad luck [adj phr] experiencing negativity in life. Ex: First he lost his wife; then he was in an auto accident. What a *run of bad luck*.

Run of the mill [adj phr] common, ordinary. Ex: His job at the newspaper was just *run of the mill*.

Run off at the mouth [verb phr] talk incessantly. Ex: Diana *runs off at the mouth* frequently.

Run on empty [verb phr] fatigued. Ex: I have a lot to do, but I am *running on empty*. *(See Done in)*

Run out of time [verb phr] exceed the time limit to accomplish something. Ex: We've *run out of time* and will be late to the ballgame.

Run over by a Mack truck [verb phr] fatigued. Ex: I stayed up till 3:00 a.m. to study and then got up for work. I feel like I've been *run over by a Mack truck*. (See *Rung through a wringer)*

Run the trap line [verb phr] overcome the obstacles. Ex: After I *run the trap line,* we can begin work on the project.

Run through it [verb phr] practice. Ex: Let's *run through the play* one more time.

Run true to form [verb phr] as expected. Ex: The horse ran *true to form* and finished second.

Run up [verb] accrue. Ex: He *ran up* a large debt at the Casino.

Run up against [verb phr] encounter. Ex: He *ran up against* some tough opposition in the election.

Run with it [verb phr] take charge of a situation. Ex: Go ahead and *run with it* Drew. I know you will do a good job.

Run with the wrong crowd [verb phr] associate with people who are of questionable character. Ex: I wish Alex would not *run with the wrong crowd.* I am afraid he will get into trouble.

Run through a wringer [verb phr] (See *Run over by a Mack truck)*

Running with your hair on fire [verb phr] erratic in personality.
Ex: She would be a good worker if she didn't *run around with her hair on fire* all the time.

Runs hot and cold [verb phr] act in opposite ways.   Ex: His enthusiasm for the project runs *hot and cold.*

Runs in the family [verb phr] hereditary or a family trait. Ex: Red hair *runs in the family.*

Russian roulette [noun] gamble where the stakes are very high (usually for your life). Ex: Some of the soldiers in Vietnam played *Russian roulette.*

Rustle up some grub [verb phr] (country western) fix a meal. Ex: I think it's time to *rustle up some grub.*

SME [abbrev] *subject matter expert.* Ex: Ask Alan about Java programming. He is the local *SME* on that topic.

S.N.A.P. [acronym] *Supplemental Nutrition Assistance Program* i.e. the Food Stamp Program.

SOP [abbrev] *Standard Operating Procedure.* (Business routine) Ex: The *SOP* is that we have an executive officer meeting every Friday at 10:00.

SOS [abbrev] *Save our ship.* Used during World War II when a ship was in danger of sinking. An "SOS" radio message would be sent to the head command. #2 (crude) *Same old shit* – means everything is status quo. Said when someone asks, "How are things?"

SSDD [abbrev] (crude response to "How are you?") literally, *Same shit, different day.*

Sack out [verb] go to sleep. Ex: I'll *sack out* at Donna's place if it gets too late.

Sacred cow [noun] (business) highly valued by some. May be unworthy of value. Ex: Project X is a *sacred cow.* The boss likes it even though it is way over budget.

Saddled with the responsibility [verb phr] responsible for something unpleasant or tedious. Ex: He was *saddled with the responsibility* of watching his little brother every day after school until his parents came home.

Safe and sound [adj phr] O.K. Ex: Have you seen Johnny? Yes, he is *safe and sound* in the playroom.

Salt of the Earth [noun phr] someone who is stable and reliable. Ex: Ted is the *salt of the earth.* You can always depend on him.

Same bat time, same bat channel [1960's goodbye expression] said to indicate that you will be seeing the person again at the same day and time.

Same o, same o [response to "How are you?"] the same old routine.

Samolean [noun] money. (See *Dough*)

Sandman's coming [noun phr] said to sleepy children so they will relax and go to sleep.

Sandwich generation [noun] people in their 40's and 50's who have both children and parents to care for.

Saturday night special [noun] handgun. Ex: The teenager was killed with a *Saturday night special.*

Sauce [noun] liquor. Ex: He's on the *sauce* again.

Save for a rainy day [verb phr] save for a time when you are in dire need of it. Ex: "Why don't we spend your money in your piggy bank?" "No, let's *save it for a rainy day.*"

Save your bacon [verb phr] saved from embarrassment or failure. Ex: Thank you for *saving my bacon* when I forgot my notes.

Save your breath [verb phr] don't try to convince someone. Ex: Justin will not change his mind on that subject so *save your breath.*

Saved by the bell [verb phr] intervening circumstance keeps you safe. Ex: The boy was about to be beat up by a gang when he was *saved by the bell*. A policeman rescued him.

_____

Saving grace [noun] what makes a situation salvageable. Ex: I know he is always late, but the *saving grace* is that he is always prepared when he gets here.

Sawing logs [verb] sleeping. Ex: "What were you doing at 9:30 last night?" "I was *sawing logs*. I had to get up at 4:00 in the morning."

Scalawag [noun] (1950's slang) ruffian. Ex: Those boys in the gang are sure *scalawags*.

Scarce as a two-dollar bill [verb phr] limited supply of something. Ex: Those new leather jackets are scarce as a *two dollar bill.*

Scare up [verb] produce. Ex: I'll *scare up* some girls for us to take to the movies tonight.

Scare up some food [verb phr] obtain food by resourceful means, such as digging for clams, etc.

Scared me to death [verb phr] (See *Scared spitless*)

Scared spitless [verb phr] apprehensive. Ex: He was *scared spitless* that the teacher would call on him for the answer. (See *Scared stiff)*

Scared stiff [verb phr] (See *Scared spitless*)

Scarf it up [verb phr] eat fast. Ex: Wow, he really *scarfed up* that hamburger.

Scattered to the four winds [verb phr] widely dispersed. Ex: "Where did the boys go?" "I don't know. They *scattered to the four winds.*"

School of hard knocks [noun phr] learn by experience. Ex: He learned how to defend himself through the *school of hard knocks.*

Schmooze [verb] talk casually. Ex: The two friends had a good time *schmoozing.* (See *Chit chat*)

Scope it out [verb phr] check it out. Ex: I'll have to *scope out* that ad in the newspaper and see if I really want that job.

Scorched earth [noun] totally destroy everything before rebuilding. Ex: The lumber companies have a *scorched earth* policy regarding our forests.

Scrape by [verb] live on little money. Ex: They barely *scraped by* last month because Matt lost his job.

Scrape through [verb] barely escape failure. Ex: He barely *scraped through* the test.

Scraping the bottom of the barrel [verb phr] using the last of your monetary resources. Ex: I was really *scraping the bottom of the barrel* last month before I got paid.

Scratch [noun] a small amount of money. Ex: How do you expect to play poker tonight? All you've got is *scratch.*

Scratch my back; I'll scratch yours [verb expression] repay a favor to someone. Ex: *If you scratch my back, I'll scratch yours.* Help me get into that Club and I will help you with your income tax.

Scratching their heads [verb phr] perplexed. Ex: They were *scratching their heads* because they could not find a solution to the problem.

Screaming like a banshee [verb phr] (See *Scream bloody murder*)

Screw loose [noun] not competent mentally. Ex: I think Sam has a *screw loose*. I have explained the instructions to him repeatedly. (See *Few bricks short of a full load*)

Screw up [verb]   make a mistake. Ex: I always *screw up* the directions for putting together the kids' toys. (See *Goof up*)

Screwball [noun] an eccentric or unconventional person. Ex: He is such a *screwball,* and I would never try his ideas.

Screwed up [verb]   confused, misguided. Ex: He is really *screwed up*. I think he is on drugs.

Scrub down [verb]   washing your hands and arms before an operation. (done by doctors, nurses) Ex: Be sure and *scrub down* before you enter the E.R.

Scuttlebutt [noun] gossip. Ex: What's the *scuttlebutt* you hear about the union going on strike?

Search me! [verb expression] I don't know. Ex: "Is the teacher going to give a final exam?" "*Search me!*"

Second class citizens [noun phr] a group of people treated as if they have lesser importance than others. Ex: Some black people have been treated like *second class citizens* for many years.

Second guess [noun phr]   anticipate someone's actions. Ex: I try to *second guess* him, but I am still surprised at what he does.

Second hand [noun] #1 through or by another person. Ex: I didn't hear the speech but I got the main points *second hand* from John. #2 the long hand or pointer on the face of a clock or watch which ticks off the minutes. #3 used. Ex: I often go to the thrift store and buy *second hand* clothes.

Second nature [noun] do something so many times that you can do it without thinking. Ex: Riding a bike is *second nature* to him.

Second to none [adj phr] person or object of top quality. Ex: My watch is *second to none.*

Second wind [noun] a sudden burst of energy. Ex: She got her *second wind* and won the race.

Security blanket [noun] a physical item that represents security to someone. It can be a job, a house , a car or a blanket for a child.

See eye to eye [verb phr] agree. Ex: They are a happy couple even though they don't always *see eye to eye*.

See him off [verb phr] bid farewell to someone leaving on a trip. Ex: We're going to *see him off* at 6:00 A.M. at the airport.

See how it flows [verb phr] see whether it is smooth. Ex: Let's *see how the dialogue flows* in your new book.

See how it goes [verb phr] wait for the outcome. Ex: Let's try plan A and *see how it goes. (See how it jells)*

See how it jells [verb phr] try something and see if it works. *(See how it goes)*

See how the land lies [verb phr] take a close look at a situation before you make any permanent decisions. Ex: I'm going to make a trip to Wisconsin and *see how the land lies* before I make a permanent decision to move there.

See it in the stars [verb phr] predict with accuracy something that would happen. Ex: I could *see it in the stars* that he would become famous.

See stars [verb] losing consciousness. Ex: After he hit his head on the corner of the table, he *saw stars.*

See the big picture [verb phr] understand the vision. Ex: Once the employees *saw the big picture*, they supported the plan.

See the color of your money [verb phr] prove that you have money or ability to pay. Ex: "I want to play poker with you." "Let's *see the color of your money* first."

See the fur fly [verb phr] see the fighting begin. Ex: Just get those two together and *see the fur fly*.

See the light [verb phr] understand. Ex: He finally *saw the light* and passed his Algebra test.

See through him [verb phr] evaluate someone's hidden motives. Ex: Brandy finally *saw through Joe* and broke up with him before she got hurt.

See what you can make of it [verb phr] here are the facts of a certain situation. What is your understanding of it?

See which way the wind blows [verb phr] see if the majority agree or disagree with you. Ex: Well, I am going to propose this plan and then *see which way the wind blows*.

See you in the funny papers [goodbye expression of the 1950's]

See you later alligator [part of a teen song of the 1950's used as a "goodbye" expression] The rejoinder to the first part is, "After a while crocodile." This song was written and recorded by Robert Guidry, and later recorded by Bill Haley and the Comets.

Seeing is believing [noun expression] doubt what someone says until you actually see it for yourself. Ex: I didn't think he could swim across the river, but *seeing is believing*.

Seeing red [verb] angry. (Red is a color associated with anger) Ex: When he belittles me, I *see red*. (See *Fully edged*)

Seize the ball and run with it [verb phr] take the initiative. Ex: You need to *seize the ball and run with it* to be proactive.

Selfie [noun] (2013 slang) A picture of yourself that is taken by yourself on a cell phone and uploaded to Facebook.

Self-fulfilling prophesy [noun] cause something to happen through your own actions. Ex: It was a *self-fulfilling prophesy* that he turned out to be a thief just like his brother.

Sell down the river [verb phr] betray someone. Ex: He *sold his partner down the river* before he declared bankruptcy.

Sell it to the guys upstairs [verb phr] (business) convince upper management of the worth of your idea. Ex: We need more budget for the project, and you need to *sell that idea to the guys upstairs.*

Selling like hotcakes [verb phr] sell rapidly. Ex: Those environmental T shirts are *selling like hotcakes.*

Selling snake oil [verb phr] selling a product that cannot deliver what it promises. Ex: Selling thigh cream to lose weight is like *selling snake oil.*

Send him packing [verb phr] persuade someone to leave. Ex: When I found out he was lying to me, I *sent him packing.*

Send out a posse [verb phr] look for someone deliberately. Ex: If Darrell doesn't come home soon, we'll have to *send out a posse* to find him.

Send up the river [verb phr] put in jail. Ex: For stealing from the bank, he was *sent up the river* for 20 years.

Separates the men from the boys [verb phr] a certain action will determine who has courage and daring. Ex: The climb up Mt. Everest *separates the men from the boys.*

Served his time [verb phr] #1 A criminal has *served his time* when he has completed his sentence. #2 In the business world, you have *served your time* when you have worked for the company for many years and deserve a good position.

Serves him right [verb phr] someone got their comeuppance and deserved it. Ex: It *serves him right* that he didn't make the team since he missed a lot of practices.

Set an example [verb phr] be a model to follow. Ex: Why don't you *set an example* by always washing your hands before dinner?

Set 'em up [verb phr] order a round of drinks for a group of people. Ex: Tell the bartender to *set 'em up* for my friends.

Set in cement [verb phr] unlikely to change. Ex: The politician's ideas were *set in cement*. (See *Etched in stone)*

Set in your ways [verb phr] rigid and inflexible. Ex: The old man was *set in his ways* and would not move to a retirement home.

Set me back [verb phr] cost. Ex: You'll never guess what that new car *set me back*.

Set the record straight [verb phr] correct a misunderstanding. Ex: Let me *set it straight*. I did not use up all the gas in the car.

Set sail [verb] leave to go sailing. Ex: We will *set sail* at 5:00 p.m.

Set store by [verb] depend on. Ex: You can *set store by* what Jose says. He is very reliable.

Set the world on fire [verb phr] make an impression. Ex: Brad is likely to *set the world on fire* with his new business.

Set up [noun] pre-arranged: Ex: It was a *set up* to catch the drug dealer.

_____

Set your hair on end [verb phr] scare you. Ex: Those movies
will *set your hair on end.*

Sets my teeth on edge [verb phr]   irritating to me. Ex: When
Gerald snores, it really *sets my teeth on edge*.

Settle down [verb] #1 get into a routine. Ex: Paul and Sadie
have really *settled down* since they returned from
their honeymoon. #2 don't be rowdy. (usually said to
children) Ex: *Settle down* or you will have to go to
your room.

Settle once and for all [verb phr] finalize something. Ex: I'm
going to *settle this once and for all*. We are going
camping for our vacation.

Settle the score [verb phr] #1 pay off debts. Ex: I need to
settle the score with Dan. He still owes me money. #2
get revenge. Ex: The small child *settled the score* by
hitting his brother back.

Seven-year itch [noun]   restless. Ex: I think he has the *seven
year itch* and wants to move to a new town.

Seventh Heaven   [noun] ecstatic. Ex: She is in *Seventh Heaven*
since she was accepted at that prestigious university.

Sexting [verb] (2013 slang) cell phone texting with sexual
innuendoes.

Shacking up [verb] living with someone of the opposite sex
without being married.   Ex: Many couples are
shacking up now rather than getting married.

Shades [noun] sunglasses. Ex: Where did you get your *shades*?

_____

Shadow of his former self [noun phr] weak emotionally. Ex: Jack is only a *shadow of his former self* since he lost his job.

Shady business [noun] #1 dishonest enterprise. Ex: He owns a *shady business* involving drug dealing. #2 immoral behavior. Ex: Getting Todd to take your college exam for you is *shady business* .

Shake a leg! [verb expression] hurry up. Ex: *Shake a leg!* We need to leave now. (See *Chop chop*)

Shake in your boots [verb phr] frightened. Ex: He yelled so loud I was *shaking in my boots.*

Shake the dust off your boots [verb phr] stay a while. Ex: Why don't you come in and *shake the dust off your boots?*

Shake your booty [verb phr] (2013 slang) shake your butt while dancing.

Shall we dance? [verb expression] begin an activity.

Shape up [verb] #1 behave. (said to children) Ex: *Shape up*! We are in church. #2 tone your body through exercise. Ex: We are going to *shape up* with this exercise class.

Shape up and fly right [verb expression] behave in an appropriate manner. (said to small children) (See *Shape up or ship out)*

Shape up or ship out [verb expression] either behave in a situation or leave. (said to small children) (See *Shape up and fly right*)

Shareware [noun] (computer - business) free software for use by all computer users in a group. Ex: There's some new *shareware* available.

Sharp as a tack [adj expression] mentally quick. Ex: He is *sharp as a tack* and a good person to have on your team. (See *Sharp as a whip*)

Sharp as a whip [adj expression] (See *Sharp as a tack*)

Sharpen his wits [verb phr] think quickly. Ex: Jason *sharpens his wits* by debating.

Shell out [verb] pay for. Ex: He *shelled out* $14.00 for the shirt.

Shindig [noun] party. Ex: Are you going to the *shindig* on Friday night? (See *Whingding*)

Ship shape [adj] organized and clean. Ex: I want to see this house in *ship-shape* condition when I come back.

Ships that pass in the night [noun phr] people who do not relate to one another intimately, but just have a passing acquaintance. Ex: He wanted to get to know her better, but they were just *ships that passed in the night.*

Shirts and skins [noun] (sports) when two teams play informally, one team will wear their shirts and the other team will remove their shirts and be bare-chested (men's teams only!!)

Shit for brains [noun phr] (underline)crude(/underline) act in a stupid manner. Ex: Do you have *shit for brains?*

Shit happens [noun phr] (underline)crude(/underline) unpleasant situations happen to everyone.

Shoot from the hip [verb phr] act or make a statement impulsively. Ex: If you *shoot from the hip*, you won't be very credible.

Shoot off his mouth [verb phr] brag. Ex: He is *shooting off his mouth* about his new car.

Shoot the breeze [verb phr] talk casually. Ex: Mary and her friend were *shooting the breeze*. (See *Chit chat*)

Shoot the chutes [verb phr] ride the roller coaster at an amusement park. Ex: Let's *shoot the chutes* today and go skating later.

Shoot the messenger [verb phr] (See *Don't shoot the messenger*)

Shoot the works [verb phr] gamble on one idea or choice. Ex: Let's *shoot the works* and expand our business in California next year.

Shoot your wad [verb phr] spend all your money. Ex: George *shot his wad* on his new car.

Shoot yourself in the foot [verb phr] do or say something that lessons your credibility or undermines your plan. Ex: When he criticized the boss, he *shot himself in the foot.*

Shop talk [noun] words or phrases common to your business which others may not understand. Ex: He talks *shop talk* with his friends at work.

Short and sweet [adj] concise and brief. Ex: Let's make that report *short and sweet.*

Short changed [adj] not the full amount of money back from a store clerk. Ex: I was *short changed* by $2.00 at the check-out counter.

Short end of the stick [noun phr] not get a fair deal. Ex: Jasmine got the *short end of the stick* when she went to buy a new car.

Short fuse [noun] quick to anger. Ex: Mac sure has a *short fuse.* He gets angry so easily. (See *Short tempered*)

Shorthanded [adj] not enough people to adequately complete a task. Ex: We're *shorthanded* today so we will have to work overtime to get the project done.

Short lived [adj] of slight duration. Ex: My bonus was *short lived* when I saw my car repair bill.

Short of it [noun] relate a plan briefly. Ex: That is the *short of it.*

Short order [noun] a brief period of time. Ex: I want you to clean your room in *short order.*

Short-order cook [noun] a cook whose specialties are hamburgers, hot dogs and french fries. Ex: There is an opening at MacDonald's for a *short-order cook.*

Short sighted [adj] unable to see the general or long term advantages or gains. Ex: The company was *short sighted* on its business predictions.

Short stuff [noun] small child. Ex: Hey *short stuff,* go get your coat. (See *Half pint*)

Short tempered [adj] quick to anger. (See *Short fuse*)

Short-timer [noun] person who will quit working soon. Ex: He has lost his enthusiasm to work since he is a *short timer.*

Shot in the arm [noun phr] motivated or energized. Ex: When Don got his new job, it sure was a *shot in the arm* for him.

Shot in the dark [noun phr] a guess which may or may not be correct. Ex: I think the race track is this way, but that's just a *shot in the dark.*

Shotgun wedding [noun] the bride-to-be is pregnant and has to get married fast. Ex: We had to have a *shotgun wedding* for Dave and Brenda.

Shove in the right direction [noun phr] encourage someone towards a certain action. Ex: He didn't want to go to college, so I had to give him a *shove in the right direction.*

Shove off [verb] leave. Ex: Well, I've got to *shove off* now. I must be home by 5:00. (See *Ramble*)

Show him around [verb phr] Guide someone through a house and/or property. Ex: This is our new house Josh. I'll *show you around.*

Show him the door [verb phr] usher someone outside. Ex: Will you *show him the door?* He is yelling loudly and disturbing the other guests.

Show him the ropes [verb phr] show someone a daily routine. Ex: This is our new employee. Don, will you please *show him the ropes?*

Show his true colors [verb phr] real nature. Ex: Give him a challenge so he can *show his true colors.*

Show your hand [verb phr] let everyone know what your motives are. Ex: Be careful not to *show your hand* to your opponent.

Shred [verb] (sports - snowboard) ride fast and hard. Ex: Those guys are *shredding* the mountain.

Shuffle off to Buffalo [verb expression] leave. Ex: Gotta *shuffle off to Buffalo*. See you in the morning. (See *Shove off*)

Shut the door in his face [verb phr] close off a person from further communication. Ex: He *shut the door in the salesman's face* because he did not want to buy the product.

Shut your trap [verb phr] (<u>impolite</u>) be quiet, don't talk. Ex: *Shut your trap.* Everyone can hear you. (See *Zip your lip*)

Sick and tired [adj] extremely tired and irritated. Ex: I am *sick and tired* of telling you kids to clean up your room.

Sick as a dog [verb phr] ill. Ex: I got *sick as a dog* after eating that salad.

Side tracked [adj] distracted from the matter at hand. Ex: The group got *side tracked* and forgot their agenda.

Sight for sore eyes [noun phr] be glad to see a friend you haven't seen for a long time. You say, "You sure are a *sight for sore eyes.*"

Sights set on [noun phr] an expectation or desire. Ex: I have my *sights set on* going to Greece this year.

Sign of the times [noun phr] an indication of what is currently happening. Ex: It is a *sign of the times* that people are re-financing their homes.

Sign off [verb] #1 A deejay finishes his/her radio program. Ex: Trevor Smith *signs off* at 10:00 P.M. #2 Signature of approval. Ex: Be sure you get the Vice President to *sign off* on that memo.

Sign on the dotted line [verb phr] sign your name in the place appropriately marked on a document. Ex: After you read the document, please *sign on the dotted line.*

Silence is golden [cliché] sometimes it is better not to talk.

Simmer down [verb] be quiet. Ex: You kids *simmer down* and go to bed.

Sink or swim [verb expression] succeed or fail. Ex: I did not know anything about the business, so it was *sink or swim.*

Sit a spell [verb phr] (1940's slang) come in and stay a while in my home. Ex: Come in and *sit a spell* and I'll get you some coffee.

Sit around [verb] relaxing and not doing anything. Ex: Let's just *sit around* and listen to the newest Justin Bieber CD this afternoon. (See *Veg out*)

Sit-down dinner [noun] formal dinner at which participants all sit on chairs around a table. Ex: Is Ben having a sit-down dinner or bar-b-que outside?

Sit tight [verb] wait. Ex: *Sit tight.* The movie will start soon. (See *Hold on*)

Sit well with [verb phr] not feel comfortable with. Ex: That new math does not *sit well with* me.

Sitcom [noun] comedy shows on TV. Ex: The TV *sitcoms* are really funny.

Sitting duck [noun] an obvious target. Ex: He wasn't prepared in the meeting and was a *sitting duck.*

Sitting like a bump on a log   [verb phr]   doing absolutely nothing. Ex: He was *sitting like a bump on a log* and not getting his chores done. (See *Veg out)*

Sitting on the fence [verb phr] can't make up your mind. Ex: They are *sitting on the fence* and don't know whether to buy the new house.

Sitting pretty [verb] circumstances are very favorable for you. Ex: I am *sitting pretty* since Grandma left me $10,000.

Six feet under [noun phr] dead and buried. Ex: You will be *six feet under* if you don't get the fence painted!

Six of one and half a dozen of the other [noun phr] either choice is equal in a situation. Ex: I can either go to the beach or play golf. It's *six of one and half a dozen of the other*.

Six pack [noun] (2012 slang) #1 well toned abs (said about men) #2 Six bottles of beer in a cardboard container.

Sixteen ax handles across [noun phr] (country western) wide hips. (usually said about women) Ex: Wow, she must be *sixteen ax handles* across.

Sixty-four dollar question [noun phr] a very important question needed to solve a problem. The term originated from a television game show called the $64,000 question. Ex: How much should our budget be for promotion of the new product? That's the *sixty four dollar* question.

Size up [verb] determine the strengths of an opponent. Ex: He *sized up* the person who was running the race against him.

Skanky [adj] (1970's slang) ugly. Ex: That is a really *skanky* skirt.

Skedaddle [verb] leave. Ex: Better *skedaddle* before your Mom catches you playing around instead of doing your homework. (See *Make tracks*)

Skeleton in the closet [noun phr] unsavory past action you want to be kept secret. Ex: Most political candidates have a few *skeletons in their closets.*

Sketchy [adj] [2013 slang] something that has a certain risk to it. Ex: That rocky path is really *sketchy.* (See *Dicey*)

Skinny as a rail [adj phr] thin person. Ex: He is *skinny as a rail.*

Skinny dip [noun] swim naked. Ex: We used to *skinny dip* at that lake when we were kids.

Skip a beat [verb phr] #1 have a shock. Ex: When I thought my child was lost, my heart *skipped a beat.* #2 mental lapse. Ex: Whenever Beth asks me the name of one of the managers, I *skip a beat* and can't recall any of them. #3 delay between activities. Ex: When he lost his job, Ben didn't *skip a beat*; he started building houses.

Skipped town [verb] left town. Ex: He *skipped town* when I caught him cheating on his wife.

Skosh [adj] little bit. Ex: "Would you like some pie?" "Just a skosh." (From the Japanese word for "little bit" - sukoshi) (See *Tad*)

Sky high [adv] the highest. Ex: When he lost his wallet, he blew *sky high.*

_____

Sky is the limit [noun phr] no obstacles or barriers to what you want to do. Ex: I think you can be a world-class athlete. Remember, the *sky is the limit.*

Skype [noun] A VOIP service and instant messaging client allowing video and voice calls to phones and mobiles with Skype. (See VOIP)

Slam bam, thank you ma'am [verb expression] sex lasting only a few moments. (See *Quickie*)

Slam dunk [noun] #1 (sports) dunk a basketball through the hoop without touching the rim. #2 easy. Ex: The test was a *slam dunk.*

Slammer [noun] jail. (See *In the clink*)

Slap happy [adj] acting silly. Ex: He got *slap happy* after winning the game.

Slap in the face [noun phr] insult. Ex: The fact that someone less qualified got the job is a *slap in the face.*

Slap you silly [verb phr] said in jest when someone you know says something that is mildly irritating. Ex: Watch out! I'm going to *slap you silly!*

Slash burn [noun] burning the undergrowth of a forest after the trees are harvested. Ex: *Slash burning* can eliminate bugs that are a threat to the forest.

Sleep around [verb] is promiscuous. Ex: I wouldn't date that girl. She *sleeps around.*

Sleep in [verb] sleep past your usual time of rising. Ex: Since it is Saturday tomorrow, I am going to *sleep in.*

_____

Sleep it off [verb phr] de-toxicate. Ex: After I *sleep it off* I will feel better.

Sleep like a log [verb phr] sleep soundly. Ex: I *slept like a log* last night.

Sleep on it [verb phr] wait overnight to make a decision. Ex: Let's *sleep on it* and make the decision in the morning.

Sleep with [verb] have sex with. Ex: Are you going to *sleep with* Lou tonight?

Sleeping sickness [noun] mononucleosis. Ex: If you have *sleeping sickness,* you are bedridden.

Sleepy-head [noun] someone who has a hard time waking up. Ex: Wake up *sleepy-head*. The school bus will be here in a half-hour.

Slick operator [noun] smooth talking con artist. Ex: He was a *slick operator* and talked the old woman into putting her savings into a bad investment.

Slicker than a whistle [adj phr] efficient. Ex: My new power saw is *slicker than a whistle*.

Slim pickins' [noun] scarcity of something. Ex: We did not get a bonus this year, so Christmas will be *slim pickins'*.

Sling some hash [verb phr] (1950's country western) prepare a meal. Ex: The cowboys are ready to *sling some hash* before they rope steers.

Slip him a mickey [verb phr] put liquor in someone's drink without them knowing it. Ex: If you *slip him a Mickey*, he will pass out.

Slip into [verb]   put on.   Ex: Let me *slip into* something comfortable.

Slip my mind [verb phr] forget something. Ex: I was going to buy pickles at the store, but it *slipped my mind.*

Slip of the tongue   [noun phr]   say something you did not intend. Ex: I'm sorry. That was a *slip of the tongue.*

Slip through your fingers [verb phr]   let an opportunity get away from you. Ex: It was a good interview, but the job *slipped through my fingers.*

Slip up [verb] make a mistake. Ex: Don't *slip up* when you are operating the rivet gun. (See *Goof up*)

Slipped away [verb] disappear unobtrusively. Ex: She *slipped away* from the party because it was boring.

Slippery as a greased pig [adj phr] (1940's country western) hard to pin down. Ex: The politician and his promises are *slippery as a greased pig.*

Sloshed [verb] drunk. (See *Pickled*)

Slow as a snail [adj phr] extremely slow. Ex: Serena is *slow as a snail.* I think she will miss the bus this morning. (See *Slower than a seven year itch)*

Slow burn [noun] anger slowly. Ex: I did a *slow burn* when I discovered he had been lying to me.

Slower than a seven year itch [cliché]   exaggerated way of explaining how slow someone is. Ex: Frank is *slower than a seven year itch.* It takes him an hour to get his shoes on. (See *Slower than molasses)*

Slower than molasses [verb expression]   (See *Slower than a seven year itch*)

Smack-dab [adv]   exactly.   Ex: The line is *smack-dab* in the middle of his property.

Small fry [noun]   children.   Ex: The *small fry* can't reach the doorknob.   (See *Half pint*)

Small potatoes [noun] insignificant. Ex: The amount of money I make on my second job is *small potatoes.*

Small talk [noun] trivial conversation. Ex: The school children engaged in *small talk* during recess.

Small ticket item [noun]   inexpensive.   Ex: That department store is having a sale on quite a few *small ticket items*.

Smaller than your average bear   (1950's expression) said in an amusing way about a person who is small.

Smart aleck [noun]   boastful person.   Ex: *Smart alecks* think they know everything about a subject.

Smart as a whip [adj phr] intelligent. Ex: She is *smart as a whip* and gets straight A's.

Smart money [noun]   intelligent investment.   Ex: The *smart money* is on ABC company.

Smell a rat [verb phr] a situation appears suspicious. Ex: He was supposed to pay me the money for the car two days ago. I *smell a rat.*

Smelling like a rose [verb phr] unscathed. Ex: The suspect came through the interrogation *smelling like a rose*.

Smile pasted on her face [noun phr] smile just to be polite. Ex: She always *pastes a smile on her face*, but I know she is unhappy.

Smoke and mirrors [noun] obfuscation; trying to obscure or distort the facts. Ex: The candidate's talk about revitalizing the economy was all *smoke and mirrors.*

Smokin' hot [adj] [2013 slang] guy or girl who looks sexy and fabulous.

Smooch [verb] (1930's slang) kiss. Ex: The newly married couple *smooched* in the car. (See *Suck face)*

Smoosh [verb] squash something. Ex: He *smooshed* the ant all over the ground.

Smooth move (1950's expression.) said sarcastically. Ex: When a person does or says something that embarrasses himself or others, you say "*Smooth move*" or "Smooth maneuver Hoover."

Smooth sailing [adj phr] no problems. Ex: When I open my wine shop, it will be *smooth sailing*.

Smoothie [noun] #1 someone who is suave and debonair. Ex: Don't be fooled by an old *smoothie.* #2 a drink with fruit, juice and yogurt mixed in a blender. Ex: I'll have a *smoothie* for breakfast.

Snagged him [verb] caught him. Ex: "When did you snag that fish?" "I *snagged him* last night."

Snake eyes [noun] roll two "ones" with dice. Ex: What are the chances of rolling *snake eyes*?

Snake in the grass [noun phr] sneaky and cannot be trusted. Ex: That car salesman is a *snake in the grass.*

Snap (2013 slang) #1 expression of surprise or amazement. #2 government food stamp program (See S.N.A.P.)

Snap out of it [verb expression] act decently. Ex: You've been in a bad mood all morning. *Snap out of it.*

Snap to it [verb phr] pay attention. Ex: *Snap to it* and wash the car.

Sneaking suspicion [noun] hunch. Ex: I have a *sneaking suspicion* Amy has been dating Joel.

Sneeze your brains out [verb phr] sneeze repeatedly. Ex: Having hay fever causes you to *sneeze your brains out.*

Snickelfritz [noun] small child. Ex: Hey *snickelfritz*, time to get ready for dinner. (See *Rug rats)*

Snipe hunt [noun] fooled into looking for something that doesn't exist. Ex: The cub scouts took the new boy on a *snipe hunt.*

Snockered [verb] drunk. (See *Three sheets to the wind*)

Snow job [noun] fool someone. Ex: Ryan is always giving someone a *snow job.*

Snowball's chance in Hell [noun expression] no chance. Ex: They don't have a *snowball's chance in Hell* of getting that contract.

Snowbirds [noun] retired people who spend the winter in warm climates such as Arizona and Florida. Ex: My parents became *snowbirds* when they retired.

Snowboarding [noun] similar to surfboarding, only done on snow. Ex: *Snowboarding* is great at Whistler Resort.

Snug as a bug in a rug [verb expression] (1940's slang) cozy and comfortable. Ex: He is *snug as a bug in a rug* in his new sleeping bag.

So far, so good [adv expression] cautiously optimistic. Ex: " How is your broken leg coming along?" *"So far, so good."*

So what? [sarcastic expression] means "who cares?" Ex: "I'm going to the dance Saturday." "So what?"

Soak him [verb] take advantage of someone financially. Ex: The IRS *soaked him* plenty for his new business.

Sob story [noun] get sympathy by dramatizing a sad story about your life. Ex: She told such a *sob story* that everyone felt sorry for her.

Sock it to you [verb phr] gain the advantage. Ex: His partner *socked it to him* on that new land deal.

Socked away [verb] hidden. Ex: I've got $1000 *socked away* for my vacation.

Soft hearted [adj] empathetic and understanding. Ex: His mother is *soft hearted* and let him stay up late to watch the fireworks. (See *Softy*)

Soft touch [noun] generous. Ex: Ask Ginger for a loan. She is a *soft touch*.

Softy [adj] (See *Soft hearted*)

Sold a bill of goods [verb phr] taken advantage of. Ex: He was *sold a bill of goods* on that used car.

Sold him short [verb phr] not recognize someone's true ability. Ex: His teacher *sold him short* and did not recommend him for a scholarship.

Sold out [verb] #1 no more tickets available. Ex: The Lady Gaga concert *sold out* the first day tickets went on sale. #2 betrayed. Ex: We would have had the contract if the chairman hadn't *sold out* and given it to his brother-in-law.

Solid as a rock [adj phr] dependable and trustworthy. Ex: Hire Ted. He is *solid as a rock.*

Solid gold [adj] genuine, valuable. Ex: Hal is a *solid gold* supporter for women's rights.

Some of the mud will stick [noun phr] when derogatory comments are made about someone, some of them will be believed whether or not they are true.

Something the cat drug in [noun phr] appearing bedraggled. Ex: It must be raining very hard. You look like *something the cat drug in.*

Something to wet my whistle [noun phr] quench my thirst. Ex: In this desert country I need *something to wet my whistle.*

Something's cooking [noun phr] something is happening. Ex: Did you see all the activity at the neighbor's house? *Something's cooking.*

Son of a buck [exclamatory expression of amazement] (See *Son of a gun)*

Son of a gun [exclamatory expression of amazement] (See *Good grief)*

Song and dance [noun phr] persuasive but suspicious story. Ex: Did he give you that *song and dance* about having money in a Swiss bank?

Soul mates [noun] two people who feel very close emotionally and mentally. Ex: Some people search a lifetime and never find a *soul mate.*

Souped up engine [noun] increased engine power. Ex: He has a *souped up engine* in his old car.

Sour grapes [noun] negative attitude. Ex: Just because you lost the race you don't need to act like *sour grapes.*

Southpaw [noun] #1 left handed person. Ex: Scott is a *southpaw* and has a special set of golf clubs. #2 [adj] identifies a left handed pitcher in baseball. Ex: Alex is a great *southpaw* pitcher.

Space cadet [noun] person who is not concentrating on what is being said. Ex: Didn't you hear what the teacher said? You are a real *space cadet.* (See *Space case*)

Space case [noun] (See *Space cadet*)

Space out [verb] daydream. Ex: Darryl *spaced out* when he was supposed to be listening to the teacher.

Spaz [noun] clumsy person. (1960's slang)   Not Politically Correct and not used anymore.

Speak his piece [verb phr] give his opinion. Ex: Let's give him a chance to *speak his piece* before we decide how to handle this problem.

Speak of the devil [verb phr] talk about someone and the person appears. Ex: *Speak of the devil* - here comes Harl.

Speak the same language [verb phr] have common interests. Ex: Ned knows a lot about computers too. We *speak the same language.*

Speak up [verb] talk louder. Ex: *Speak up.* I cannot hear you.

Spell it out [verb] explain it more, be more specific. Ex: Let me *spell it out* for you. Either you study hard or you can't go to the movies.

Spick and span [adj] very clean. (usually refers to housecleaning) Ex: Her house is always *spick and span.*

Spill the beans [verb phr] tell a secret. Ex: Don't *spill the beans* about our trip. (See *Let the cat out of the bag*)

Spit and polish [adj] (military) present a perfect appearance. Ex: He was all *spit and polish* when they had the inspection.

Spit and vinegar [adj] lots of spunk. Ex: She's just full of *spit and vinegar.*

Spit in the wind [verb phr] aimless talking. Ex: That's just *spitting in the wind.*

Spit it out [verb] tell me. Ex: Come on. *Spit it out.* Do you know where my car keys are?

Spitting image [noun] look exactly like someone else. Ex: He is the *spitting image* of his brother.

Split [verb] #1 leave. (1950's slang) Ex: I'm going to *split* now. #2 [verb] divide something. Ex: We have to *split* the candy bar into two pieces. #3 [noun] a bowling term. Ex: When 2 pins are left standing on opposite sides of the alley after throwing the ball, it is called a *split.*

_____

Split a gut laughing [verb phr] laughed very hard. Ex: I nearly split a gut laughing when I watched that comedian. (See *Laughed myself silly*)

Splitting hairs [noun] too finicky. Ex: Do you think that correcting his grammar is *splitting hairs?*

Spoil sport [noun] someone who dampens the enthusiasm or fun of the group. Ex: Don't be a *spoil sport.* Come hiking with us. (See *Wet blanket*)

Spoiled rotten [verb] so indulged that you become totally self-centered and self-serving. Ex: That child is *spoiled rotten* and cries whenever he does not get candy.

Spot check [noun] intermittent check. Ex: Let's do a *spot check* on the baggage.

Spout off [verb] be outspoken. Ex: I am going to *spout off* about the bad service in this restaurant.

Spread it around [verb phr] tell everyone. Ex: *Spread it around* that there is a big department store sale today.

Spread like wildfire [verb phr] spread rapidly. Ex: That rumor *spread like wildfire.*

Spread yourself too thin [verb phr] have too many activities at the same time. Ex: Bart is *spreading himself too thin* lately. I am worried because he looks so tired.

Spring chicken [noun] (country western) young inexperienced person. Ex: Why, he's just a *spring chicken* and not wet behind the ears yet!

Spring fever [noun] feeling restless. Ex: I get *spring fever* in April and want to quit my job and travel around the world.

Spring for it [verb phr] pay for it. Ex: I'll *spring for lunch* today.

Spuds [noun] potatoes. Ex: How many *spuds* do you want with your steak?

Spur of the moment [noun phr] without planning. Ex: We went to Mexico on the *spur of the moment* because Jim got a bonus.

Square accounts [noun] pay up what you owe someone. Ex: I'm glad I have a job now so I can *square accounts* with everyone.

Square meal [noun] good, nutritious meal. Ex: Three *square meals* a day provide good nutrition.

Square peg in a round hole [noun phr] not fit into a situation or group; to be different from others in appearance or actions. Ex: Everyone in the Smith family likes to ski except Joyce. She is the *square peg in a round hole.*

Squared away [verb] settle everything so matters are running smoothly . Ex: Once I get things *squared away,* we can go to the Florida Keys.

Squatter's rights [noun] arrive someplace first so you have ownership. Ex: You could sit down at a restaurant table before someone else, get a seat on the bus before someone else, or claim land in certain parts of the country (Alaska for instance).

Squeaky clean [adj] extremely clean. Ex: When I wash my hair it is *squeaky clean.* (you can actually hear the hair squeak when you put your hand through it)

Squeaky wheel gets the grease [noun phr] whoever complains the loudest gets the most attention. Ex: Marlene is always complaining, so her needs are met before those people who are quieter. She is the *squeaky wheel who gets the grease.*

Squealer [noun] someone who tells secrets. Ex: That *squealer* will tell anything if you pay him a few dollars.

Squirrely [adv] irresponsible, taking bad risks. Ex: Don't act *squirrely* or you will get in trouble.

Squishy [adj] soft and pliable. Ex: This pie dough sure is *squishy.*

Stack the deck [verb phr] manipulate a situation to your advantage. Ex: When you *stack the deck,* you are sure to get what you want.

Stack up against [verb phr] measure. Ex: How does your ability to play tennis *stack up against* mine?

Stand around [verb] mill about at random. Ex: The group was *standing around* waiting for the coach to get there.

Stand by [verb] wait. Ex: *Stand by* for the show to begin.

Stand-in [noun] take the place of someone, as in a theater play. The main actor was ill, so the *stand-in* took his place.

Stand on ceremony [verb phr] do things according to a set protocol. Ex: We always eat dinner at 5:00. We *stand on ceremony* here.

Stand on his principles [verb phr] act according to his beliefs. Ex: The mayor is known for *standing on his principles.*

Stand on your own two feet [verb phr] independent and self-sufficient. Ex: The boy moved into his own apartment and got a job. He was *standing on his own two feet* without help from his parents.

Stand pat [adv phr] don't change. Ex: The politician will *stand pat* on his decision not to support higher taxes.

Stand-up comedy [noun] impromptu entertainment by anyone who wants to tell jokes. Ex: They have a lot of *stand-up comedy* spots downtown.

Stand up for [verb] support someone's point of view. Ex: Are you going to *stand up for* Jordan on this issue?

Standard of living [noun phr] quality of your life. Ex: A high *standard of living* equates to being rich; a low *standard of living* is being poor.

Stands out like a sore thumb [verb phr] obvious. Ex: One rooster is white and the others are brown. He *stands out like a sore thumb.*

Stands to reason [verb phr] prefaces a logical statement. Ex: It *stands to reason* that the Seattle Seahawks will win the game.

Start from scratch [verb phr] start from the beginning. Ex: They *started from scratch* on the project.

State of the art [noun phr] something that is the most up-to-date and latest fad. Ex: The computer equipment we have is *state of the art.*

Stay out of my face [verb phr] (impolite) leave. Ex: *Stay out of my face* so I can get my homework done.

___

Stay put [verb] do not move. Ex: *Stay put* while I go get the hamburgers.

Staycation [noun] (2013 slang) Spend your vacation at home.

Steal away [verb] sneak away without anyone noticing. Ex: Let's *steal away* and go swimming.

Steal his thunder [verb phr] take credit for something someone else has done. Ex: Better tell the teacher you thought of the idea or Bob will *steal your thunder.*

Steamroller [noun] aggressive, insensitive person who forces his/her opinion on others. Ex: She would be more popular with the boys if she weren't a *steamroller*.

Steer clear of [verb phr] avoid. Ex: *Steer clear of* that boy. He has the flu.

Step down [verb] resign. Ex: The head of the committee was asked to *step down* today.

Step on his toes [verb phr] offend someone. Ex: I am for school bussing, but I don't want to *step on anyone's toes.*

Step on it! [verb phr] hurry! (See *Make it snappy)*

Step on your toes [verb phr] crowd your area of responsibility. Ex: I'll take Team 2, but I don't want to *step on your toes* if you want Team 2.

Stew in your own juice [verb phr] feel sorry for yourself. Ex: If you *stew in your own juice* you won't be able to contribute something positive to the team.

Stick in the mud [noun phr] boring person. Ex: He such a *stick in the mud* that he always watches TV every night.

Stick it in your ear (verb expression) forget it. (See *Stuff it*)

Stick it to him [verb phr] treat someone badly. Ex: You should *stick it to him* for putting a scratch on your car.

Stick to your guns [verb phr] do not give in. Ex: *Stick to your guns* and don't buy that stock at such a high price.

Stick to your ribs [verb phr] eat hearty food so you feel full for a long time. Ex: That meat and potatoes will *stick to your ribs*.

Stick your neck out [verb phr] take a risk. Ex: *Stick your neck out* and let's buy that new car.

Stickler for [noun] particular about. Ex: My teacher is a *stickler for* detail.

Sticks in my craw [verb phr] saying words that are difficult. Ex: Every time I have to be nice to that egotistical person, the words just *stick in my craw.*

Sticky fingered [adj] inclined to steal things. Ex: The boy liked candy and was *sticky fingered* every time he was in the store.

Sticky wicket [noun] difficult situation with several different sides. Ex: The issue of whether to wear jeans to work is a *sticky wicket.*

Stiffed him [verb] not pay money owed. Ex: When he left the restaurant, he *stiffed the waiter.*

Still and all [adverb expression] nevertheless. Ex: *Still and all,* it would be a good idea to wear a coat today.

Still waters run deep [cliché] be quiet and reserved, but have deep feelings and emotions.

Stinks like a dead dog

Stinks like a dead dog [verb phr] undesirable. Ex: That plan *stinks like a dead dog*. (See *Stinks to high Heaven*)

Stinks to high Heaven [verb phr] (See *Stinks like a dead dog*)

Stir crazy [adj phr] in one place for too long. Ex: It has snowed for five days and I am *stir crazy* in the house.

Stir up the pot [verb phr] cause dissension. Ex: Bringing up that issue will just *stir up the pot*.

Stokin' [verb] excited. (1970's slang) Ex: He was *stokin'* after being accepted into the university. (See *Revved up)*

Stole the show [verb phr] outshined everyone in the production. Ex: When Ethel Merman went on stage, she *stole the show*.

Stomach is tied up in knots [noun phr] upset or nervous. Ex: I have to take the test tomorrow and my *stomach is tied up in knots*.

Stomping mad [adj] so angry you could stamp your feet. Ex: I am *stomping mad* that I didn't win that race.

Stone cold [adj] extremely cold. Ex: If you don't eat your dinner right now, it will be *stone cold*.

Stone's throw away [noun phr] short distance away. Ex: Our house is a *stone's throw away* from Julia's house.

Stoned [adj] feeling the effects of taking drugs. Ex: He lost his job because he was *stoned* most of the time.

Stood up [verb] have a date with someone and the person does not show to keep the date. Ex: I was *stood up* by Mike last night. I am never going to see him again.

Stool pigeon [noun] one who gives information to the police, usually when they are also involved. Ex: The police got the *stool pigeon* to talk and then they caught all the criminals.

Stop at nothing [verb phr] persistent. Ex: He will *stop at nothing* to win the election.

Stop bugging me [verb phr] stop irritating me. Ex: My little brother should *stop bugging me.*

Stop by [verb] visit. Ex: After baseball practice, *stop by* my house for dinner. (See *Stop in)*

Stop in [verb] visit. Ex: You are always welcome to *stop in* at my house. (See *Stop by)*

Stop off [verb] visit on your way to somewhere else. Ex: Be sure to *stop off* at my place before you go home. (See *Stop by*)

Stopped dead in his tracks [verb phr] stop immediately and not move at all. Ex: The deer *stopped dead in his tracks* when he saw the hunter.

Straight and narrow [adj] being conservative. Ex: If you walk the *straight and narrow,* you probably are self righteous.

Straight answers [noun] honest. Ex: I asked him for some *straight answers* about where he was last night.

Straight arrow [noun] person who is honest and trustworthy. Ex: Put Amber in charge of the project. She is a *straight arrow* and will get it done right.

Straight from the horse's mouth   [cliché] hear a rumor or information from the main person involved.

Straight laced [adj] prim and proper. Ex: Acting *straight laced* means not going bare-footed in the park!

Straight scoop [noun] the truth about a situation. Ex: Jack will always give you the *straight scoop*.

Straight up [adv] #1 without ice. (how a drink is served in a restaurant or bar) Ex: Would you like your drink *straight up*? #2 rigid. Ex: Simone sat *straight up* in her chair.

Straighten up and fly right [verb phr] behave yourself. (said to children) Ex: You better *straighten up and fly right* or you won't get to go to the zoo tomorrow. (See *Shape up or ship ou*t)

Straw that broke the camel's back [noun phr] the latest in a series of incidents that cumulatively make you very angry and you lose your temper. Ex: When he completely changed his mind and said something entirely different from what he said yesterday, it was the *straw that broke the camel's back.*

Street smarts [noun] have common sense and know how to get along in most environments. Ex: People with *street smarts* can adapt very well to a variety of environments.

Stretch a point [verb phr] exaggerate a point in a discussion. Ex: Do you think you *stretched a point* when you kept saying that your car gets better gas mileage than anyone else's?

Strike a balance [verb phr] not excessive in one direction or another. Ex: Perhaps we can *strike a balance* by having both of you help wash the car. (See *Strike a happy medium)*

Strike a bargain [verb phr] come to an agreement. Ex: The two competitors struck a bargain and will share the cost of the new product.

Strike a happy medium [verb phr] (See *Strike a balance)*

Strike it rich [verb phr] gain sudden wealth. Ex: Many people *struck it rich* during the gold strike of the 1850's.

Strike out on his own [verb phr] become totally independent and provide for oneself. Ex: He *struck out on his own* when he was only 17.

Strike up the band [verb phr] begin to play. Ex: *Strike up the band*. Here comes the flag.

Strike while the iron is hot [verb phr] take advantage of an opportunity. Ex: Better *strike while the iron is hot* to get that job offer.

String along with [verb phr] go along with, cooperate with. Ex: *String along with me* and we will make a great team.

String him up [verb phr] hang him. Ex: Let's *string him up* from the highest tree.

String him along [verb phr] date someone you are not really interested in until someone else more interesting comes along. Ex: Don't *string him along* for too long if you are not serious.

Stroke of luck [noun phr] lucky moment. Ex: It was a *stroke of luck* that Ted found just the fishing pole he wanted at the department store.

Strong as an ox [cliché] quite strong. Ex: That horse is *strong as an ox*. It can carry a heavy load.

Struck oil [verb phr] became lucky. Ex: He *struck oil* with that last deal.

Strung out [verb phr] #1 tense, overworked. Ex: Take a vacation when you get *strung out.* #2 acting high from drug use or reacting to drug withdrawal. Ex: It was hard for Anita to think clearly because she was so *strung out* by drugs.

Stubborn as a mule [adj phr] difficult to persuade. Ex: It is hard to get him to do anything new because he is *stubborn as a mule.*

Stuck on him [verb phr] infatuated with someone. Ex: Sarah has been *stuck on* Ed since the 4th grade.

Stuck up [adj] snooty. Ex: That cheerleader is so *stuck up* that she hardly speaks to anyone.

Stuff it [verb expression] forget it. Ex: *Stuff it* Max. You've already said enough. (See *Give it a rest)*

Submarine sandwich [noun] a long bun sliced lengthways that has pickles, meat, lettuce, tomato and mayonnaise on it. Ex: Let's look for a place that has *submarine sandwiches.*

Suck face [verb] kiss someone. Ex: Look at those two older people *sucking face.* (See *Smooch)*

Suck it up [verb phr] bear a disappointment without complaint. Ex: He just *sucked it up* and went on with his life when his sister died.

Suck up [verb] ingratiate yourself with someone. Ex: To get a good grade in that class you have to *suck up* to the teacher. (See *Brown nose)*

Sugar coat [verb] make something appear desirable and attractive. Ex: He *sugar-coated* that new design proposal.

Sugar daddy [noun] rich older men who appeal to younger women because of their money. Ex: She married a *sugar daddy* when she grew up.

Suicide squeeze [noun] (baseball) there is a runner at third base. The batter tries to bunt the ball while the runner is running to home plate.

Suit yourself [verb phr] do what you want. Ex: "I am going to the store." "*Suit yourself*. I am going to the movies."

Sun rises and sets on him [noun phr] a popular person whose opinion is highly respected. Ex: The boss always asks Jerry's opinion. The *sun rises and sets on him.*

Sunny side up [adv] the way eggs are cooked with the yokes showing. Ex: You order eggs in a restaurant "*sunny-side up*" or "*over easy*" .

Super duper [expression of excitement] cool. (See *Wow*)

SuperPACs [noun] (political) independent political action committees which may raise unlimited sums of money from corporations, unions and individuals, but cannot contribute to or coordinate directly with parties or a candidate. Ex: The Crossroads superPAC is affiliated with Republican strategist Karl Rove.

Sure fire [adj] certain to succeed. Ex: That is a *sure fire* product for sunscreen.

Surf the web, surf the Net [verb phr] (computer) skim the information available on the Internet. Ex: My son *surfs the web* every night. He got some good information for his term paper that way.

Surf's up [noun phr] the water is perfect for surfing. Ex: Grab your board. *Surf's up*.

Swallow his pride [verb phr] be humble. Ex: He *swallowed his pride* and told his sister he was sorry.

Swan song [noun] confessing to something before you die. Ex: The serial murderer did a *swan song* before he was executed.

Sweat blood [verb phr] worry. Ex: I am *sweating blood* over the test in physics.

Sweep it under the rug [verb phr] forget it. Ex: Any problem you have you just *sweep it under the rug*. (See *Stuff it)*

Sweet nothings [noun] (1940's slang) Ex: The couple whispered *sweet nothings* in each other's ear.

Sweet tooth [noun] desire for food that is sweet, such as chocolate. Ex: I have a *sweet tooth* especially for jelly beans.

Sweeten the pot [verb phr] make something more attractive or desirable. Ex: If we *sweeten the pot,* I am sure Dave will come work for our company.

Sweetie pie [noun] (1940's slang) term of endearment. Ex: Thank you for making those cookies for me. You're a *sweetie pie*.

Swept off your feet [verb phr] infatuated with someone. Ex: She was *swept off her feet* because he was so polite and charming.

Swim against the tide [verb phr] work against the current or popular ideas or opinions. Ex: If you *swim against the tide,* you won't get far in the corporate world. (See *Buck the trend*)

Swing a deal [verb phr] negotiate something. Ex: If we can *swing that deal*, I can get you a new car.

Swing it [verb] accomplish something successfully. Ex: I will buy that boat, if I can *swing it.*

T.D. [abbrev] (football) touchdown. Ex: The Seahawks made three *T.D.'s* today.

T.G.I.F. [abbrev] *Thank goodness it's Friday*. Ex: I'm looking forward to going out tonight. T.G.I.F.

TLA [abbrev] (business) *Three Letter Acronym*. Every business uses *TLA*'s to describe their processes, like JIT (just in time) in manufacturing companies.

TMI [abbrev] *too much information.* Cell phone texting abbreviation. Said by one person to another when the subject matter is questionable or one person wants to talk at length about something personal.

TTYL [abbrev] *talk to you later*. Cell phone texting abbreviation.

Tables have turned [noun phr] reverse of luck. Ex: The *tables have turned* since he got his promotion.

Tacky [adj] not trendy or popular. Ex: Bell bottomed pants are *tacky.*

Tad [adj] small amount. Ex: "Do you want some peas?" "Just a *tad.*" (See *Skosh*)

Tadpole [noun] small child. Ex: He has loved the water since he was a *tadpole*. (See *Pipsqueak*)

Tail between his legs [noun phr] leave in shame or disgrace. Ex: He left the company with his *tail between his legs* after embezzling company money.

Tail end [noun] the last part. Ex: I missed most of the movie, all but the *tail end.*

Tail wagging the dog [noun phr] reverse of what it should be. Ex: I think by planning the new courthouse before we had the funds available was like the *tail wagging the dog*.

Tailgate party [noun] spectators at a football game who arrive early and drink and eat in their cars, trailers or vans in the parking lot before the game. If they have trucks, they put the "tailgates" down on the trucks and put the food and drink on the tailgate; hence the name "*tailgate party*".

Take a back seat to [verb phr] relinquish position, importance, or control. Ex: The President *takes a back seat* to his wife sometimes.

Take a bed check [verb phr] check on children who are in bed. Ex: Will you *take a bed check* and see if Tommy is asleep yet?

Take a break [verb phr] rest for a short period. Ex: Let's *take a break* and finish painting the living room after lunch. (See *Take a breather*)

Take a breather [verb phr] (See *Take a break*)

Take a chill [verb phr] get sick. Ex: If you don't wear your raincoat, you might *take a chill*.

Take a chill pill [verb phr] (1980's slang) relax and calm down. (See *Chill out*)

Take a clue [verb phr] follow a suggestion. Ex: *Take a clue* and do not criticize his work.

Take a crack at [verb phr] attempt. Ex: I'll *take a crack at* re-writing the document. (See *Take a stab at*)

Take a dim view of [verb phr] does not approve of. Ex: Mother t*akes a dim view* of smoking.

Take a flying leap in a rolling doughnut [verb phr] go away. (sometimes said in jest to friends) (See *Take a long walk on a short pier)*

Take a hike [verb phr] (impolite) leave. Ex: Why don't you *take a hike?*

Take a leak [verb phr] (impolite in mixed company) (phrase used by men) go to the bathroom. (See *Go to the John*)

Take a liking to [verb phr] become fond of. Ex: He *took a liking to* the puppy. (See *Take a shine to)*

Take a long walk on a short pier [verb phr] (1990's slang) leave. (When you want someone to go) (See *Take a flying leap in a rolling doughnut)*

Take a nose dive [verb phr] (sports) lose the game/race/contest on purpose. Ex: The boxer was paid to *take a nose dive.*

Take a potshot [verb phr] make a critical remark about someone. Ex: That was a nasty *potshot you took* at Andrew.

Take a powder [verb phr] disappear. Ex: You better *take a powder* before your dad sees the dent in that fender.

Take a rain check [verb phr] #1 when someone wants to see you and you are busy, but want to spend time with them so you promise to get together later on. Ex:" I can't go to the movies with you tonight, but I'll *take a rain check* and go with you tomorrow night." #2 a sale item at a store is gone when you arrive to buy it, but the store has guaranteed that you will receive the sale price when the next shipment comes in. The store clerk gives you a piece of paper called a "raincheck" to present at a later time in exchange for the item at the sale price.

Take a shine to [verb phr] fond of. Ex: He has *taken a shine* to the new baby. (See *Take a liking to*)

Take a stab at [verb phr] attempt. (See *Take a crack at*)

Take a turn for the worse [verb phr] become sicker. Ex: Overnight, Mother has *taken a turn for the worse.*

Take after [verb] look or act like. Ex: He *takes after* his mother. They both have blue eyes.

Take care [goodbye expression] Ex: *Take care.* See you soon.

Take cuts [verb] get in front of someone in a line when a friend lets you in. Ex: *Taking cuts* is not fair.

Take early retirement [verb phr] retire at age 55. Ex: I hope I have enough money saved to *take early retirement.* (See *Golden handshake)*

Take five [verb] break an activity for five minutes. Ex: *Take five* and we will practice more when we come back.

Take great pains [verb phr] be exacting or meticulous. Ex: He *took great pains* to draw every detail of the portrait.

Take heart [verb] have hope. Ex: *Take heart.* I'm sure we will find your kitten.

Take him at his word [verb phr] believe what he said. Ex: We *took him at his word* and thought he would be here at 7:00.

Take him down a peg [verb phr] humble an arrogant person. Ex: That remark sure *took him down a peg.*

Take him to the cleaners [verb phr] cheat someone out of money. Ex: That furniture salesman really *took him to the cleaners.*

Take his bearings [verb phr] stop and figure out where you are. Ex: After several wrong turns, he decided to *take his bearings.*

Take his belt in a notch [verb phr] lose weight. Ex: I had to *take in my belt a notch* after losing 10 pounds.

Take his side [verb phr] agree with a certain person against all opposition. Ex: You always *take your brother's side*.

Take home pay [noun] what is left of your paycheck after taxes are taken out. Ex: My *take home pay* is less each year.

Take into account [verb phr] consider. Ex: I will *take into account* the fact that you have worked every summer at the grocery store.

Take issue with [verb phr] dispute or are insulted. Ex: I *take issue with* your saying that I am not working hard enough.

Take it easy [verb phr] relax. Ex: *Take it easy* and let me get
dinner. (See *Veg out*)

Take it for a spin [verb phr] go for a car ride. "Your new car is
beautiful!" "Want to *take it for a spin*?"

Take it from the top [verb phr] start over. Ex: That idea didn't
work. We'll have to *take it from the top*. (See *Back to
square one*)

Take it hard [verb phr] upset over some news or event. Ex:
James will *take it hard* when he finds out his dog was
hit by a car.

Take it in stride [verb phr] relaxed and accept whatever
happens to you gracefully. Ex: There have been some
major changes in his life but he *takes it in stride.*

Take it in the shorts [verb phr] be embarrassed or humiliated.
Ex: He *took it in the shorts* on that car deal.

Take it lying down [verb phr] accept criticism without
defending yourself. Ex: I'm not going to *take those
accusations lying down.*

Take it on the chin [verb phr] absorb a blow, not necessarily
physical. Can be emotional or even financial. Ex:
Evan's father lost a lot of money in the stock market
last week. He really *took it on the chin.*

Take it out on [verb phr] angry with one person, but express
that anger to another. Ex: If you get angry with your
boss, sometimes you *take it out on* your wife.

Take it with a grain of salt [verb phr] accept what you heard as
inaccurate or incomplete. Ex: "I heard that stock is
going down." "Yes, but you should *take that with a
grain of salt.*"

Take my hat off to him [verb phr] admire him. Ex: I have to *take my hat off to him* for the way he got that contract signed.

Take my word for it [verb phr] believe me. Ex: *Take my word for it*. We will win our football division next year.

Take off on [noun phr] do a good imitation of someone or something. Ex: He does a good *take off on* that comedian.

Take out of context [verb phr] quote only part of a statement, thereby giving it a different meaning. Ex: The speech has a different meaning when you *take those phrases out of context*.

Take over the helm [verb phr] (sailing) #1 assume responsibility for steering a ship. Ex: *Take over the helm* since we are hitting rough water. #2 assume responsibility for leading a company, usually as president or chairman of the board. Ex: The company will do much better if Tom will *take over the helm*.

Take part [verb] participate. Ex: She wanted to *take part i*n the school play.

Take place [verb] happen. Ex: What is *taking place* is that interest rates are going up.

Take potluck [verb] eat whatever is available or offered. Ex: We're *taking potluck* for dinner tonight.

Take root [verb] become established. Ex: Our family *took root* in this country a hundred years ago.

Take stock [verb] analyze your assets. Ex: He *took stock* of all his investments.

Take the bull by the horns [verb phr] take charge of a situation. Ex: It is time to *take the bull by the horns* and make a decision.

Take the chair [verb phr] lead a meeting. Ex: You *take the chair* for the next two months.

Take the edge off [verb phr] lessen. (as hunger) Ex: I ate a morning snack to *take the edge off* my hunger.

Take the gloves off [verb phr] do not be combative or aggressive. Ex: I am not disagreeing with you, so you can *take the gloves off.*

Take the high road [verb phr] most admirable way to accomplish something. Ex: We *took the high road* and came in under budget.

Take the law into his own hands [verb phr] act as though you were a policeman. Ex: Citizens want to *take the law into their own hands* so they won't become victims.

Take the mountain to Mohammed [verb phr] if you can't get a written response from someone, go directly to them in person.

Take the plunge [verb phr] try something new or risky. Ex: *Take the plunge* and sign up for scuba diving lessons.

Take the reins [verb phr] (business) take control. Ex: Frank will *take the reins* of the company next week.

Take things at face value [verb phr] analyze situations superficially. Ex: Never *take things at face value.* People will surprise you.

Take to heart [verb phr] #1 be emotionally moved. Ex: He *took* the plight of the homeless *to heart.* #2 consider seriously. Ex: I will *take your proposal to heart* and give you my decision soon.

Take to his heels [verb phr] escape. Ex: The thief *took to his heels* and we couldn't catch him.

Take to task [verb phr] reprimand. Ex: She *took* the small child *to task.* (See *Called on the carpet*)

Take turns [verb] rotate. Ex: Let's *take turns* at jumping rope.

Take under his wing [verb phr] be his mentor. Ex: He *took the boy under his wing* and taught him all he knew about fly fishing.

Take wings [verb] disappeared. Ex: My keys *took wings* and I can't find them.

Take you up on that [verb phr] agree to be a part of someone's idea or plan. Ex: I'd *take you up on that,* but I have other plans for Saturday.

Take your best shot [verb phr] #1 give me your best estimate Ex: *Take your best shot* and give me the figures tomorrow. #2 challenge to someone to try and get the best of you, either physically or mentally. Ex: Go ahead, *take your best shot.* I can return anything you throw out.

Take your breath away [verb phr] something so spectacular it literally leaves you unable to breathe. Ex: The Grand Canyon will *take your breath away.*

Take your time [verb phr] do not hurry. Ex: I like to *take my time* when sewing.

Taken aback [verb] shocked and embarrassed. Ex: I was *taken aback* by his negative attitude.

Taken for a ride [verb phr] fooled by someone. Ex: We got *taken for a ride* and lost a lot of money.

Takes all kinds [verb phr] a comment made about someone's bizarre behavior. Ex: *Takes all kinds* to make a world.

Takes the cake [verb phr] behavior that disgruntles someone. Ex: Well, that *takes the cake*. He told me he would be on the team yesterday, and today he changes his mind.

Talk a blue streak [verb phr] speak incessantly. Ex: She *talks a blue streak* and you can hardly get a word in. (See *Talk a mile a minute)*

Talk a mile a minute [verb phr] (See *Talk a blue streak*)

Talk behind his back [verb phr] say negative things about someone without their knowing it. Ex: It is not good manners to *talk behind his back*.

Talk big [verb] boast or brag. Ex: He *talks big* whenever the boss is around.

Talk is cheap [noun phr] planning or discussing something is easy, but doing it is difficult or expensive. Ex: He campaigns that he'll rebuild our inner-cities, but *talk is cheap*.

Talk out of both sides of his mouth [verb phr] advocate different points of view depending on who you are talking to. Ex: You never know exactly where that politician stands. He *talks out of both sides of his mouth*.

Talk to the wall [verb phr] be ignored. Ex: I felt like I was *talking to the wall* when I told James I wanted him to study his lessons more.

Talk turkey [verb] speak candidly. Ex: The two brothers *talked turkey* about the status of the business.

Talk up a storm [verb phr] talking continuously with much animation. Ex: Those girls can sure *talk up a storm.* (See *Talk a mile a minute*)

Talk your ear off [verb phr] talk incessantly. Ex: Uncle Ted will *talk your ear off.* (See *Talk up a storm*)

Talk your way out of a paper bag [verb phr] verbally adept. Ex: Max can *talk his way out of a paper bag.*

Talking in circles [verb phr] not making any sense. Ex: He *talks in circles* and gets distracted easily.

Talks through his hat [verb phr] pretend to have knowledge. Ex: Bob *talks through his hat* about stock futures, but he has never invested.

Tan his hide [verb phr] (country western) spank someone, usually a child. Ex: If he doesn't behave, I will *tan his hide.*

Tanked [verb] drunk. (See *Three sheets to the wind*)

Tar and feather [noun] years ago when someone behaved badly, he was literally covered with *tar and feathers* and forced to leave town.

Tasty bits [noun] best parts of something. Ex: All the *tasty bits* in the play were gone when I went to audition.

Tea bagger [noun] Tea Party supporter.

Tea Party [noun] ultra conservative wing of the Republican Party.

Teach him a lesson [verb phr] make someone pay the consequences for some action. Ex: Let's *teach him a lesson* and not invite him to the next party since he drank too much at the last party.

Team player [noun] one who cooperates with the group. Ex: We've got great *team players* in our work group.

Tear-jerker [noun] event evoking tears (play, book, movie) Ex: The movie about the Holocaust is a real *tear jerker.*

Tears me up [verb phr] upsets me. Ex: It just *tears me up* that Jack decided not to go to college.

Technical [noun] (mountain biking) a difficult route to ride with lots of obstacles. Ex: That course is *technical,* but a lot of fun.

Teeny weenie [adj] extremely small. Ex: The clothes for that doll are *teeny weenie.*

Teed off [verb] irritated. Ex: I am really *teed off* that Mark decided to play poker tonight. (See *Ticked off)*

Teeny bopper [noun] (1990's slang) teenager who embraces all the latest fads. Ex: Those two *teeny boppers* go in for the grunge look.

Telecommuters (noun) (business) company employees who work at home. Ex: Many companies are letting employees *telecommute,* because it is cost effective to the company.

Teleconferencing

Teleconferencing [noun] (business) a company meeting in which several people in different places are connected by phone.

Telephone tag [noun] (business) trade telephone messages with someone without actually talking person-to-person with them. Ex: We have played *telephone tag* all morning. I'm glad I got hold of you.

Tell it like it is [verb phr] speak frankly. Ex: I am *telling it like it is*. The business is losing money this year.

Tell tales out of school [verb phr] repeat what you overheard, but can't confirm. Ex: I don't want to *tell tales out of school*, but I think the Smiths are buying a new house.

Test the waters [verb phr] try something on a small scale to see if it will work on a large scale. Ex: Let's *test the waters* by making an electric motor for this small car.

Than all get out [adv phr] better than all others.   Ex: He can run faster *than all get out.*

Than you can shake a stick at [adj phr] than you can count. Ex: You've got more shoes *than you can shake a stick at.*

Thank your lucky stars [verb phr] good fortune happens because of luck rather than skill. Ex: You should *thank your lucky stars* that you won that trip to Bermuda.

Thanks a bunch [verb expression] another form of "thank you".

That's about the size of it [noun phr] ends the telling of a story. Ex: We had to hike to town to get some gasoline. *That's about the size of it.* (See *That's all she wrote*)

That's all she wrote [noun phr] (See *That's about the size of it*)

That's all well and good [noun expression] have good intentions. Ex: *That's all well and good* to want to go to college, but you need to start by saving for your tuition.

That's half the battle [noun phr] partially influence a situation to your advantage. Ex: I got Barry to eat his cereal this morning. *That's half the battle.* Now if I can get him to eat a decent lunch.

That's no way to run a railroad [cliché] critical of the way a business practice or other situation is being handled.

That's the ticket [noun phr] that solution will work. Ex: *That's the ticket.* Be sure you follow through when you hit the ball.

That's the way the cookie crumbles [1960's slang] a response after someone tells you about a situation that did not turn out as expected. "Well, *that's the way the cookie crumbles"* e.g. that's the way life goes.

The faster I go, the behinder I get [cliché] Work is piling up faster than I can get it done.

The high sign [noun] hand signal motioning you to come. Ex: I just got *the high sign* that my wife wants to talk to me.

The more, the merrier [cliché] welcome to join someone. Ex: Why don't you come with us to the movies - *the more the merrier.*

The morning after the night before [noun phr] do something wild and crazy at night and wake up the next morning feeling guilty or remorseful. Ex: *The morning after the night before* is awful.

The pits [noun] a depressing or negative situation. Ex: I did awful on my test. It was *the pits.*

The pot calling the kettle black [cliché] someone criticizes a certain kind of behavior that they engage in also. Ex: Jenny criticizes me for having a messy house. That is really the *pot calling the kettle black.* Her house is messier than mine.

The shit hit the fan [noun phr] (<u>impolite</u>) something bad has happened.

Theater in the round [noun phr] a theater on a round platform with the audience surrounding it. Ex: You can see really well at a *theater in the round.*

Then it hit me [noun phr] realize the main point of a situation. Ex: *Then it hit me.* We should be selling that old dining set since we have a smaller house now.

There are plenty of other fish in the sea [cliché] usually said when you break up with a boyfriend/girlfriend. It means there are plenty of available people around to date.

There's a sucker born every minute [cliché] Sarcastic remark when a sales pitch for a worthless or frivolous article or activity is given, knowing that some foolish people will buy.

There's more than one way to skin a cat [cliché] there is more than one way to solve the problem or handle the situation.

Thick as pea soup [adj phr] fog that is low and heavy. Ex: It is *thick as pea soup* out there tonight. I can hardly see the car ahead of me.

Thick as thieves [adj phr] close friends. Ex: Carol and Lee are *thick as thieves.*

Thin skinned [adj] overly sensitive. Ex: She's so *thin-skinned* she cries if her husband tells her the coffee's too hot.

Thing-a-ma-bob [noun] silly word for an object you can't recall the name of. Ex: Where did you get that *thing-a-ma-bob?* (See *Thingy*)

Things are going downhill fast [noun phr] deteriorating. Ex: *Things are going downhill fast* since the company takeover.

Thingy [noun] silly word for something when you have forgotten the correct word. (See *Thing-a-ma-bob*)

Think along the same lines [verb phr] identical. Ex: We *think along the same lines*. I like those sports cars too.

Think better of it [verb phr] reconsider what you are going to say. Ex: I was going to tell Joan that I thought she had gained some weight, but I *thought better of it.*

Think nothing of it [verb expression] a casual reply to "thank you" meaning the favor you did for someone was no problem. (See *No problem*)

Think tank [noun] group of highly intelligent people who meet to share new ideas about a product or course of action. Ex: The *think tank* meets on Thursday night at 7:00.

Think up [verb] invent. Ex: Troy sure *thinks up* some creative ideas.

Thinks he's hot stuff [verb phr] acting arrogant. Ex: He *thinks he's hot stuff* since he got his new car.

Third party [noun] someone unbiased in a situation. Ex: Let's ask a *third party* to settle this argument.

This is my put [noun phr] (business) my opinion. Ex: *This is my put.* I think we should delay investing in this stock.

Thorn in his side [noun phr] irritating to someone else. Ex: She is a *thorn in her husband's side* and won't let him have a night out with the other guys.

Thrashed [verb] (1990's slang) tired. Ex: I'm *thrashed* and am going home now.

Three martini lunch [noun] (business) business associates who have several drinks at lunch while discussing business. A popular practice during the 1980's, less popular now. Ex: We don't get many of those *three martini lunches* anymore.

Three R's [noun] refers to reading, writing and arithmetic.

Three sheets to the wind [noun phr] drunk. (See *Tanked*)

Three times around the barn to close the door [noun phr] (country western) make a task much more complicated than it is.

Three-ring circus [noun] surrounded by constant activity. Ex: It's a *three-ring circus* around here when I come home. The neighbor kids and our own really make a lot of noise.

Three's a crowd [cliché] said when you don't want a third person to join you and a friend.

Threw them for a loop [verb phr] confused them.

Thrilled to death [verb phr] excited. Ex: I'm *thrilled to death* that you will be going with us to Hawaii.

Through rose-colored glasses [prep phr] looking at life positively. Ex: Jean always looks at life *through rose-colored glasses*.

Through the back door [prep phr] not the standard method of accomplishing something. Ex: We got our new computer software *through the back door*, by appealing to our customers for support.

Through the grapevine [prep phr] (business) hear information on promotions, etc. from your co-workers. Ex: We find that hearing news *through the grapevine* lets us know what is happening.

Through the mill [prep phr] experienced a variety of situations and problems. Ex: I have been *through the mill* with that child and will be glad when he is grown up.

Through the roof [prep phr] so angry you are ready to explode. Ex: I could go right *through the roof*. Bill is late getting home from school again.

Through thick and thin [prep phr] steadfast through good times and bad. Ex: *Through thick and thin* we have always been friends.

Throughput [noun] (business) volume of work that can be accomplished during a given period of time. Ex: We've got pretty good *throughput* in our Arizona store.

Throw a curve [verb phr] an unexpected development. Ex: He really *threw a curve* when he quit the company.

Throw a dirty look [verb phr] frown. Ex: If I criticize his plan, my husband will *throw a dirty look* in my direction.

Throw a hissy fit [verb phr] (See Throw a temper tantrum)

Throw a monkey wrench in the works [verb phr] provide an obstacle. Ex: Every time we have our plan ready, he *throws a monkey wrench in the works.*

Throw a temper tantrum [verb phr] become so angry you scream and cry and throw your body around (usually done by small children) Ex: I told Katy she couldn't have any candy and she *threw a temper tantrum.* (See *Throw a hissy fit)*

Throw caution to the wind [verb phr] take a risk. Ex: Oh, *throw caution to the wind* and go bungee jumping with me.

Throw him off track [verb phr] purposely mislead , usually to hide something. Ex: Let's *throw the other team off track* by changing our tactics.

Throw his weight around [verb phr] #1 be bossy and aggressive. Ex: He thinks he can *throw his weight around* just because he is bigger than his classmates. #2 use a position of wealth to influence decisions. Ex: The senator *threw his weight around* and got the bill passed.

Throw in the sponge [verb phr] give up. Ex: I'm going to *throw in the sponge* in the game. (See *Throw in the towel)*

Throw in the towel (See *Throw in the sponge)*

Throw it in my face [verb phr] remind someone of an unpleasant occurrence. Ex: Don't *throw it in my face* that I am older than you.

Throw money down a rat hole [verb phr] spend money foolishly.

Throw of the dice [verb phr] gamble on an outcome. Ex: Sometimes you have good luck by the *throw of the dice.*

Throw the baby out with the bath water [cliché] (See *Don't throw the baby out with the bath water)*

Throw the book at him [verb phr] when the police charge someone with the maximum penalty. Ex: When they caught the arsonist, they *threw the book at him.*

Throw to the wolves [verb phr] not protect someone from opportunistic people. Ex: I don't think you should just *throw him to the wolves.* He is not aware of how the stock market really operates.

Throw your hat in the ring [verb phr] decided to participate in the activity. Ex: He decided to *throw his hat in the ring* and run for governor.

Throwback [noun] #1 a relative who looks like you. Ex: Rob is a *throwback* to his Uncle Jed. #2 an ugly person, who looks like a caveman. Ex: He sure is a *throwback to* his ancestors. #3 a fish that is too small to keep legally. Ex: This trout is only 4 inches long - just a *throwback.*

Thumb his nose [verb phr] snub someone. (Can be an actual physical gesture) Ex: Vicki *thumbed her nose* at me today.

Thumbed a ride [verb phr] hitchhike. Ex: *Thumbing a ride* is very dangerous these days.

Thundering herd [noun phr] a loud noisy group of people. Ex: Here comes the *thundering herd*. I better make some more sandwiches.

Tick someone off [verb phr] irritate someone. Ex: It really *ticked me off* when he said he could not finish the work by the end of the month. (See *Piss someone off*)

Tickle the ivories [verb phr] play the piano. Ex: There is a good pianist who will be *tickling the ivories* at the club tonight.

Tickle your funny bone [verb phr] make you laugh. Ex: That joke *tickled my funny bone.*

Tickle your ribs [verb phr] cause you to laugh. Ex: If you don't smile for the picture, I'll *tickle your ribs*.

Tickled pink [verb] delighted. Ex: I am *tickled pink* that you are coming for dinner tonight. (Said by women) (See *Tickled to death*)

Tickled to death [verb phr] thrilled. (Said only by women) (See *Tickled pink*)

Tide him over [verb phr] sustain him. Ex: An extra $100 will *tide him over* until payday.

Tidy sum [noun] lot of money. Ex: She made a *tidy sum* on that real estate deal.

Tie in knots [verb phr] upset; nervous. Ex: Until I get the results of the test, my stomach will be *tied in knots*.

Tie one on [verb phr] get drunk. (See *Snockered*)

Tie the knot [verb phr] get married. Ex: We are going to *tie the knot* next February.

Tie up the loose ends [verb phr] complete a project. Ex: We need to *tie up the loose ends* before we begin the next project.

Tied to his mother's apron strings [verb phr] dependent on his mother. Ex: Trent doesn't have his own apartment, because he is still *tied to his mother's apron strings.*

Tiger by the tail [noun phr] (See *Got a tiger by the tail)*

Tight as a drum [verb phr] airtight. Ex: That scuba diving suit is *tight as a drum.*

Time after time [adv phr] repeatedly. Ex: *Time after time* I have to tell you kids to clean your rooms.

Time and a half [noun phr] work overtime and get paid regular wages plus 1/2 of your regular hourly wage. Ex: When I work on Saturday I get *time and a half.*

Time and tide wait for no man [cliché] time passes regardless of any other circumstance.

Time and time again [adv phr] repeatedly. Ex: *Time and time again* I have cleaned up after the kids.

Time flies [noun] passes by quickly. Ex: *Time flies* by fast when I am riding my bike.

Time for an attitude adjustment [noun phr] "happy hour" in a bar or restaurant. (See *Happy hour)*

Time has come and gone [noun phr] opportunity for action has passed. Ex: The *time has come and gone* for you to learn how to ski, now that you have had that knee operation.

Time on his hands [noun phr] a lot of free time. Ex: You can paint the house since you have a lot of *time on your hands*.

Time out [noun phr] #1 stop the action for a short period of time. (can be accompanied by a hand gesture) Ex: *Time out.* We need to think through these ideas before we decide on a solution. #2 [noun phr] when a small child misbehaves, he gets a "*time out*" and must go and face the wall for several minutes by himself.

Time's running out [noun phr] little time left to complete something. Ex: *Time's running out.* We need to put the plan into action now.

Tiny tots [noun] small children. Ex: The *tiny tots* were all asleep in their beds. (See *Pipsqueak*)

Tip his hand [verb phr] relate plans or information before intended . Ex: We got the new director to *tip his hand* about his reorganization plans.

Tip of the iceberg [noun phr] superficial look at a problem which is really complex. Ex: Capturing the drug lord is just the *tip of the iceberg*. There are lots of drug runners still left to apprehend. (See *Scratched the surface*)

Tip the scales [verb phr] #1 weigh, usually more than expected. Ex: The boxer *tips the scales* at 203 pounds. #2 give more weight to. Ex: He will *tip the scales* in their favor.

Tip your hat [verb phr] when a lady walks by, a gentleman can acknowledge her in greeting by *tipping his hat.*

Tipped him off [verb phr] let someone know what is going to happen next. Ex: I'm sure glad Bob *tipped me off* that the new project will be due earlier than we expected.

Tits up [noun phr] (crude) not operable. Ex: I can't use that old radio, because it's gone *tits up*. (See *On the fritz*)

To a man [prep phr] without exception. Ex: *To a man* they all voted for the incumbent.

To beat the band [prep phr] participate strenuously in an activity. Ex: He is running *to beat the band*.

To boot [prep phr] an addition to. Ex: She has a home in Florida and a home in Palm Springs *to boot*.

To cap it off [prep phr] prefixes the final point you are going to make. Ex: *To cap it off* we will be moving by July.

To coin a phrase [cliché] prefaces a popular saying that you wish to emphasize. Ex: *To coin a phrase*, a penny saved is a penny earned.

To die for [prep phr] something or someone is so fantastic, popular, good looking, desirable, etc. that you would "figuratively speaking" *die for it*. Ex: That red sport car is *to die for*.

To-do [noun] throw a temper tantrum. (See *Hissy fit*)

To end all [prep phr] the greatest. Ex: This sun roof on my new car is *to end all*.

To go [prep phr] order food in a restaurant to take somewhere else to eat. Most "fast food" restaurants have food *to go*.

To his face [prep phr] openly, regardless of reaction. Ex: I told him what I thought of his idea *to his face.*

To save face [prep phr] keep from being embarrassed. Ex: He left the party early *to save face.*

To say the least [verb expression] as a minimum. Ex: I think Joe should graduate from college, *to say the least.*

To the bitter end [prep phr] unpleasant finish. Ex: Their relationship was difficult *to the bitter end*.

To the can [prep phr] (<u>impolite</u> – used by men only) to the bathroom. Ex: I am going *to the can.* (See *To the John*)

To the ends of the earth [adv phr] exhaust every effort to accomplish something. Ex: I looked all over *to the ends of the earth* but I did not find any green sweaters. (See *To the far corners of the earth)*

To the far corners of the earth [adv phr] (See *To the ends of the earth)*

To the john [prep phr] to the bathroom. (said only by men)

To the max [prep phr] the ultimate. Ex: He turned up his stereo *to the max.*

To the nth degree [prep phr] the highest. Ex: He had his shoes polished *to the nth degree.*

To the ripe old age [prep phr] becoming elderly. Ex: I hope I live *to the ripe old age* of 90.

To the victors belong the spoils [cliché] those who lose leave and the winners get everything left behind.

To your heart's content [prep phr] as much as you want. Ex: You can eat candy *to your heart's content,* but you will be sick tomorrow.

Toast [noun] #1 (biking) wiped out. Ex: If I had taken that trail I would have been *toast.* #2 Put bread in a toaster or under the oven broiler until it is browned and makes *toast.*

Toe the line [verb phr] behave properly. Ex: You better *toe the line* or you will get in trouble. (See *Toe the mark*)

Toe the mark [verb phr] (See *Toe the line*)

Told a fish tale [verb phr] related a story that probably was not true. Ex: I think Pam *told you a fish tale.*

Tongue in cheek [noun phr] jokingly. Ex: He said he wanted to go bungee jumping, but he said it *tongue in cheek.*

Tongue lashing [noun] reprimand. Ex: She gave the child a *tongue lashing* for running into the street.

Tongue tied [adj] so shocked that you are unable to talk momentarily. Ex: When she told me she was pregnant, I was *tongue tied.*

Tongue-twister [noun] a poem or saying that has much alliteration in it, so it becomes difficult to repeat verbally. Ex: Peter Piper picked a peck of pickled peppers. If Peter Piper picked a peck of pickled peppers, where are the pickled peppers that Peter Piper picked?

Too big for his britches [adj phr] too self-assured. (usually said about children) Ex: I don't know why he made that remark. He is getting *too big for his britches.*

Too many irons in the fire   [adj phr]   involved in too many activities.   Ex: I would like to be a member of the team, but I have *too many irons in the fire* already.

Too much for me [adj phr] overwhelming. Ex: Working an 80 hour week is *too much for me.*

Too much of a good thing [adj phr] nothing is good for you if it is overdone. Ex: I would like to eat chocolate every day, but it would be *too much of a good thing*.

Too rich for my blood [adj phr] too expensive. Ex: I would like to eat at that restaurant, but it is *too rich for my blood.*

Toodle-oo [goodbye expression] (1940's slang - said by women or girls)

Took the words out of my mouth [verb phr] say something that someone else was going to say. Ex: I was going to say that I saw Jerry, but you *took the words right out of my mouth.*

Took to his heels [verb phr] escape a situation by running away from it. Ex: I tried to talk to him, but he *took to his heels.*

Tool [noun] #1 penis. #2 item used to fix things or construct things. Ex: What *tools* are you going to need to fix the washer?

Toolin' around [verb] driving around town aimlessly. Ex: We were just *toolin' around* the town until 11:30 tonight.

Top banana [noun] the boss.   Ex: The *top banana* will be in town today. (See *Head honcho*)

Top dog [noun] (See *Top banana*)

Top dollar [noun] the best price. Ex: He got *top dollar* for his gun collection.

Top drawer [noun] the best. Ex: That new play in town is *top drawer*. (See *Top notch*)

Top notch [noun] (See *Top drawer*)

Topsy-turvy [adj] discombobulated, disoriented. Ex: Everything is *topsy-turvy* since my aunt arrived.

Toss up [noun] can go either way. Ex: "Do you think our team will win this Saturday?" "I don't know. It's a *toss-up*."

Toss your cookies [verb phr] throw up. Ex: I ate too much junk food yesterday and *tossed my cookies*.

Totaled out [verb] drunk. (See *Ripped*)

Totally tubular [adj] (1990's slang) awesome. Ex: That R&B group is *totally tubular*.

Touch and feel [noun phr] functionality and visual properties. Ex: These two computer software systems are hard to learn since they don't have the same *touch and feel*.

Touch and go [noun phr] questionable. Ex: It was *touch and go* as to whether we would win our tennis match.

Touch base with [verb phr] contact someone. Ex: I'll *touch base with* you tomorrow.

Tough act to follow [noun phr] the performer following someone brilliant. Ex: I hope I get to speak before Ray. He is a *tough act to follow*.

Tough cookies

Tough cookies [1950's expression of regret] (See Tough toenails)

Tough it out [verb phr] have courage in the face of adversity. Ex: We'll have to *tough it out,* but good times are ahead.

Tough row to hoe [noun phr] difficult situation. Ex: He has a *tough row to hoe* after the accident left him paralyzed.

Tough times [noun] financial or emotional difficulties. Ex: I went through some *tough times* after I lost my job.

Tough toenails [noun] (1950's expression of regret) See Tough cookies)

Track record [noun] how someone or something has performed. Ex: Seattle's *track record* is better than San Francisco in football.

Trade-in [noun] an older model item that you trade for credit towards a newer product. Ex: My 1980 car will be the *trade-in* towards my new car.

Trade upon [verb] use to your advantage. Ex: He *trades upon* the fact that he is friends with John Travolta.

Train of thought [noun phr] sequence of thoughts. Ex: I'm not following your *train of thought.*

Trash something [verb phr] mess it up. Ex: Those renters *trashed the house.*

Trash talk [noun] (sports – football) chippy. Ex: The referees are going to keep a close watch on *trash talk.*

Trashed [verb] drunk. (See *Snockered*)

Treading on thin ice [verb phr] at risk of offending someone. Ex: You are *treading on thin ice* when you say I am fat.

Treading water [noun] #1 maintaining the status quo. Ex: We are just *treading water* and not replacing our roof now. #2 [verb] moving your arms and legs slowly in the water to stay afloat.

Trendy [adj] popular. Ex: Wearing 501 jeans is *trendy* with the teenagers.

Trial and error [noun] try many solutions to a problem. Ex: By *trial and error* they developed a new design for the car.

Trials and tribulations [noun] problems, usually exaggerated. Ex: I've just been talking with my daughter about the *trials and tribulations* of raising a two-year-old.

Trickle-down economics [noun] decisions made in the government have long time consequences. Ex: President Reagan was famous for his *trickle-down economics.*

Tricks of the trade [noun phr] how to operate successfully. Ex: He seems to know all the *tricks of the trade* and has more customers than anyone else in the business.

Tried and true [adj] reliable method. Ex: I think we ought to stick with the old *tried and true* way of building a deck.

Trigger happy [adj] #1 talk or act before you think. Ex: If you are *trigger happy,* you may regret it. #2 quick to shoot a gun.

Trip someone up [verb phr] confuse someone or put a roadblock in their way. Ex: When I saw the Detour sign, it *tripped me up* and I got lost.

Trip the light fantastic [verb phr] (1930's slang) dance. Ex: I thought we were going to *trip the light fantastic* Saturday night.

Trouble is his middle name [noun phr] take foolish risks. Ex: That child was caught stealing again. *Trouble is his middle name.*

True blue [adj] loyal to someone. Ex: His employees are *true blue* and really enjoy working for him.

Truthiness [noun] (political) not entirely true, but having the appearance of being true. Ex: *Truthiness* was coined by President George Bush during the Iraq war.

Try standing in my shoes [verb phr] try exchanging places with me. Ex: *Try standing in my shoes* the next time I have a tough customer.

Try this on for size [verb expression] what do you think of this opinion or idea?

Trying to make a living [verb phr] trying to keep up with daily expenses. Ex: The middle class of America is just *trying to make a living.*

Tub of lard [noun phr] (underlined)(impolite) someone who is fat. Ex: I don't want that *tub of lard* on our team.

Tuck him in [verb phr] put someone to bed, usually a small child. Ex: Will you *tuck Cindy in* tonight?

Tune in [verb] #1 receive. Ex: I tried to *tune in* the Canadian channel on my TV. #2 gain an understanding. Ex: A good counselor will *tune in* to your conflicts quickly.

Tune out [verb] not pay any attention. Ex: Whenever my kids get with their friends, they *tune out* any advice I have.

Turf wars [noun] (business) political games played by managers within a company who desire to increase their power. They try to acquire many people who report to them and protect information they have.

Turkey [noun] #1 a rascal. Ex: That *turkey* stole my idea. #2 animal. Ex: We eat *turkey* at Thanksgiving.

Turn-about's fair play [cliché] Retaliation in a similar manner is fair. Ex: I know I used your bicycle without asking, but you took my sweatshirt without asking. *Turn-about's fair play.*

Turn beet red [verb phr] become embarrassed. Ex: She *turned beet red* when she tripped and fell down.

Turn down [verb] #1 reduce in volume. Ex: Will you kids *turn down* the DVD player? #2 decline. Ex: I'll have to *turn down* your offer for lunch today. #3 fold back. Ex: My mother used to *turn down* my bed covers every night.

Turn green with envy [verb phr] be jealous. Ex: I *turn green* when I see him drive by in his new car.

Turn his back on [verb phr] ignore or disassociate from. Ex: How can he *turn his back on* the needs of the street people?

Turn his head [verb phr] attract him. Ex: Any girl will *turn his head.*

Turn his head around [verb phr] redirect or correct behavior. Ex: When my brother started selling drugs, I had to *turn his head around*.

Turn in [verb] #1 deliver. Ex: Please *turn in* your homework to the teacher. #2 go to bed. It's getting late, so I guess I'll *turn in* now.

Turn inside out [verb phr] #1 search everywhere. Ex: If I can't find your book in my office, I'll *turn* the house *inside out* until I find it. (See *Turn the house upside down*) #2 reverse. Ex: *Turn* your socks *inside out* before you put them in the washer.

Turn into [verb] #1 become something else. Ex: Will you *turn* these groceries *into* supper? #2 enter. *Turn into* my driveway to park.

Turn off [verb] #1 disconnect. Ex: Please *turn off* your cell phone and get to sleep. #2 eliminate sexual desire. Ex: Sloppy sweatsuits are a real *turn off* for most people.

Turn on [verb] #1 start. Ex: Please *turn on* the TV. #2 excite sexually. Ex: Tight jeans are a *turn on* for Eric. #3 take drugs. Ex: Greg *turned on* to marijuana last night.

Turn on a dime [verb phr] turn very sharply. Ex: My new truck can *turn on a dime*.

Turn on my heel [verb phr] leave. Ex: She *turned on her heel* and left him standing there.

Turn out [verb] #1 result. Ex: I hope the party will *turn out* to be a success. #2 attendance. Ex: There was a good *turnout* in church today. #3 reject, send away. Ex: I had to *turn out* my renters because their dogs were ruining the rugs.

Turn over [verb] #1 relinquish. Ex: The football team had to *turn over* the ball on the 40-yard line. #2 change physical position. Ex: *Turn over* and tan the other side of your legs too. #3 contemplate. Ex: Gordon has to *turn over* a new idea in his mind for a while before accepting it. #4 succession of new employees. Ex: The *turnover* in that department has been too high.

Turn over a new leaf [verb phr] begin anew. Ex: He *turned over a new leaf* when he got out of prison. (See *Turn over a new page*)

Turn over a new page [verb phr] (See *Turn over a new leaf*)

Turnover in his grave [verb phr] disapproval by one who is dead. Ex: If Grandpa knew what you were doing with your inheritance, he would *turn over in his grave*.

Turn state's evidence [verb phr] culprit who bargains with the prosecutor by agreeing to testify against his accomplices. Ex: When he *turned state's evidence,* he got a lighter sentence.

Turn tail [verb] run away, especially in fright. Ex: If you ask Carrie to speak to a crowd, she will *turn tail* and disappear.

Turn the heat on [verb phr] pressure someone. Ex: We need to *turn the heat on* our opponents or we won't win.

Turn the house upside down [verb phr] search diligently. (See *Leave no stone unturned*)

Turn the other cheek [verb phr] forgive. Ex: I know George hurt your feelings, but things will be better if you *turn the other cheek.*

Turn the tide [verb phr] change the direction or outcome. Ex: That intercepted pass will *turn the tide* of this football game.

Turn to [verb] go for advice. Ex: After my wife left me, I had to *turn to* my sister for advice.

Turn under [verb] till the soil. Ex: I have to *turn under* my garden by hand each spring.

Turn up [verb] #1 appear. Ex: I lost my glasses, but they'll *turn up* wherever I left them. #2 become better. Ex: Things will *turn up* as soon as the new government is in power.

Turn up your nose [verb phr] refuse to eat. Ex: Don't *turn up your nose* at those beets. They are good for you!

Turn your stomach [verb phr] make you sick. Ex: Don't these child abuse cases *turn your stomach*?

Tweet [verb] A short message that you send over the computer or IPad on a site called Twitter.

Twerking [verb] sexually suggestive dance popularized by Miley Cyrus in 2013.

Twist in the wind [verb phr] leave someone hanging, waiting for a decision. Brenda left us *twisting in the wind*, and now she's on vacation.

Twist your arm [verb phr] persuade you. Ex: I am going to *twist your arm* until you agree to come to the movies with me.

Twit [noun] scatter-brained person. (See *Ditsy*)

Twitter [noun] A social networking and microblog service that enables users to send and read each other's "tweets".

Two cents worth [noun phr] an opinion. Ex: Let me give you my *two cents worth* on the subject.

Two heads are better than one [cliché] two people can think of ideas and solutions to problems better than one.

Two jumps ahead of him [noun phr] anticipate what someone will do. Ex: You have to be *two jumps ahead of that child.*

Two plankers [noun] (sports) snowboarder's term for a skier. Ex: Those *two plankers* are ruining our fun.

Two-timing [noun] unfaithful. Ex: Sandra stopped dating Kurt when she discovered he was *two-timing* her.

U.S.A. [abbrev] United States of America.

Ugly mug [noun] (<u>impolite</u>) unattractive face. Ex: He sure has an *ugly mug.*

Umpteen [adj] indeterminate amount. Ex: I hit *umpteen* tennis balls today.

Uncle Sam [noun] symbol for the U.S.A.

Under a magnifying glass [prep phr] closely watched or scrutinized. Ex: I could have more fun if my brother didn't keep me *under a magnifying glass.*

Under cover [prep phr] secret. Ex: He was an *undercover* policeman and investigated drug dealing.

Under false pretenses [prep phr] deceiving. Ex: He was arrested *under false pretenses.*

Under fire [prep phr] #1 (military) being attacked. Ex: The platoon was *under heavy fire.* #2 pressured to complete something. Ex: The group was *under fire* to complete the project in 30 days.

Under her wing [prep phr] under her guidance. Ex: I was *under Aunt Sue's wing* while she taught me how to cook.

Under his belt [prep phr] An accomplishment of some type. Ex: He has 5 gold medals *under his belt.*

Under his skin [prep phr] irritating someone. Ex: When you whine, you get *under my skin.*

Under his thumb [prep phr] under his control. Ex: Dad has his small child *under his thumb.*

Under it all [prep phr] behind his facade. Ex: *Under it all* he is a good person.

Under lock and key [prep phr] secured or protected. Ex: She keeps her jewelry *under lock and key*.

Under the counter [prep phr] illegal. Ex: They ran an *under the counter* business.

Under the covers [prep phr] in bed. Ex: The two teenagers were *under the covers* when her parents discovered them.

Under the gun [prep phr] pressured to finish a task quickly. Ex: We are *under the gun* to design a new car in thirty days.

Under the impression [prep phr] thought. Ex: I was *under the impression* that we were going to the beach.

Under the table [prep phr] secretly. Ex: He passed his wife $5.00 *under the table,* without anyone else being aware of it.

Under the umbrella of [prep phr] grouped together. Ex: All those guidelines *fall under the umbrella of* security.

Under the weather [prep phr] not feeling well. Ex: Liz is *under the weather* today and will be staying home.

Under wraps [prep phr] a secret plan or idea you haven't disclosed yet. Ex: We're keeping the new advertising product *under wraps* for now.

Under your nose [prep phr] obvious or immediately close by. Ex: They were making fun of you *right under your nose*.

Unfriend someone [verb phr] pertains to the social networking site of Facebook. If you "*unfriend*" someone, that person no longer can access or make comments in your account.

Unimpeachable character [noun] totally honest and forthright. Ex: I would believe anything he says, since he is of *unimpeachable character*.

Until the end of time [prep phr] infinitely. Ex: *Until the end of time* I will be your friend.

Up a blind alley   [prep phr] searching for someone and go up and down streets. Ex: We have been *up one blind alley* after another and we can't find your cat.

Up a creek without a paddle [prep phr] in trouble. Ex: We are *up a creek without a paddle,* because we forgot to bring the camping stove on our trip.

Up a storm [prep phr] furiously or frantically. Ex: Whenever we have company, Aunt Betty cooks *up a storm*.

Up a tree [prep phr] stymied. Ex: I am *up a tree* and can't see an answer to the problem.

Up and about [prep phr] regain energy and walk around after an illness or hospitalization. Ex: My grandmother is already *up and about* after her knee surgery.

Up and at 'em [expression of greeting] morning greeting that tells someone to get out of bed and face the day with enthusiasm.

Up and coming [adj] the current fad; what is popular. Ex: The *up and coming* movie star was nominated for an Academy award.

Up and running [adj] (business) get a business going successfully. Ex: The new grocery store has been *up and running* for six months.

Up front [adj] open and honest. Ex: She was *up front* with me and said she did not want to join the health club.

Up in arms [prep phr] upset. Ex: The neighborhood was *up in arms* because the new sewer system cost so much.

Up in smoke [prep phr] lost, wasted. Ex: The plans for the executive suite have just gone *up in smoke*. The contractor left town.

Up the corporate ladder [prep phr] (business) secure an executive position with a company. Ex: There's not much room at the top for people who go *up the corporate ladder.*

Up the ying- yang [prep phr] excessive amount. Ex: We've got apples *up the ying-yang* this year.

Up to date [prep phr] current, timely. Ex: That flyer is not *up to date*. The information is old.

Up to his ears [prep phr] have plenty. Ex: My garden has grown so well, I'm *up to my ears* in carrots and green beans now.

Up to it [prep phr] ready to do something. Ex: I'd like to climb Mt. Rainier. Are you *up to it?*

Up to snuff [prep phr] feeling good. Ex: I am now feeling *up to snuff* after a bout with the flu.

Up to speed [prep phr] (business) having all current knowledge about a project. Ex: Will you bring Ellen *up to speed* on the project? She has been on vacation a week.

Up to your eyeballs [prep phr] have so much work to do that it is piling up. Ex: Phillip is *up to his eyeballs* in paperwork and has to work late.

Up your alley [prep phr] suited to your talent. (See *Right up your alley*)

Up your nose with a rubber hose [1950's teen expression] said as a retort to any comment that needs a quick caustic reply.

Up your sleeve [prep phr] concealed. Ex: I know Bill has something *up his sleeve,* but I don't know what.

Uphill battle [noun] challenge. Ex: We might convince your dad to let us go to Florida, but it will be an *uphill battle.*

Upper crust [noun] rich, wealthy people. Ex: The *upper crust* vacation in Cancun. (See Upper echelon)

Upper echelon [noun] (See *Upper crust*)

Upper hand [noun] advantage. Ex: She has the *upper hand* in that relationship.

Upset the apple cart [verb phr] ruin carefully planned actions or schedules. Ex: Don't *upset the apple cart* and decide not to come to my party.

Upshot [noun] final outcome. Ex: The *upshot* of the whole deal was that they decided to go to the game.

Upsy daisy [expression said to a child when he/she falls down to minimize the pain of the fall]

Upward and onward [adv phr] tackle a challenge. Ex: I didn't do too well last time I tried the high jump, but *upward and onward*!

Use it or lose it [verb expression] refers to skills or body parts. If you do not exercise them regularly, you will be unable to skillfully use them.

Use the restroom [verb phr] polite way of saying you are going to the bathroom at a restaurant. Ex: Excuse me. I have to *use the restroom*.

Use your head [verb phr] think reasonably and logically. Ex: *Use your head* and don't go outside without a coat.

User friendly [adj] (business) easy to operate. Ex: That new program I bought for my computer is very *user friendly*.

User hostile [adj] (business) The opposite of user friendly; hard to use.

VOIP [abbrev]   *Voice Over Internet Protocol* – allows you to make telephone calls over the internet and online calls to phones and mobiles.

Vacate the place [verb phr] leave. Ex: It's quitting time. Let's *vacate the place*. (See *Vamoose*)

Valley girl [noun] affluent teenager in southern California. Ex: The *Valley girls* live in Beverly Hills.

Vamoose [verb] leave. (from the Spanish word "vamos") Ex: *Vamoose*. I want to study now.

Vanity plate [noun] license plate with a customized name that you pay extra for. Ex: *Vanity plates* can be very creative.

Veggies [noun] vegetables. Ex: Be sure to eat your *veggies*.

Veg out [verb phr] relax. Ex: I *vegged out* on Saturday and laid in the sun. (See *Take it easy*)

Vent his anger [verb phr] release bad feelings. Ex: Don't *vent your anger* at me.

Viable option [noun] alternative that has a chance of success. Ex: It is a *viable option* to go skiing.

Vicious circle [noun] pitfalls keep reappearing.   Ex: I have been going in a *vicious circle* trying to get registered for that class.

Videoconferencing [noun] (business) business meetings among various sites that you can view the participants through video hook-ups.

View from a knothole [noun phr] limited vision or knowledge. Ex: With my *view from a knothole*, I think the schools need more computers.

Virtual reality [noun] computer generated environments with which humans can interact as if the computer generated objects were real. Viewers step "inside the action" and walk, talk, commit violence, make love - whatever their pleasure.

Vital signs [noun] indications of life check in medical emergencies: breath, pulse, heartbeat, color of skin. Ex: We have just brought him in with a gunshot wound. What are his *vital signs?*

Vital statistics [noun] #1 count of births, deaths, marriages, etc. by a government bureau. #2 the office that records the count of births, deaths, etc. #3 a woman's bust, waist and hip measurements.

Voluntary simplicity [noun] choosing to live a less expensive lifestyle. Ex: Because of downsizing, couples are forced into *voluntary simplicity*. (See *Downshifting*)

Voodoo economics [noun] (political) lower taxes while raising spending. Ex: President Reagan was a master at *Voodoo Economics.*

WTF [abbrev] *what the f...?* Cell phone texting abbreviation.

WWW [abbrev] (computer) *World Wide Web* – part of the address of a website. A typical internet address would be: www.google.com

WYZYWIG [abbrev] (computer) *what you see is what you get.* What is on the screen prints exactly the way you see it.

Wait and see [verb phr] be patient. Ex: Let's *wait and see* if it stops raining.

Wait on someone hand and foot [verb phr] of service to someone constantly. Ex: She *waited on the child hand and foot* when he was sick.

Wait up [verb] stop and wait for someone to catch up with you. Ex: *Wait up.* I want to go with you.

Waiting for the other shoe to drop [verb phr] wait for something unfavorable to happen. Ex: The company told us there would be downsizing and now we're *waiting for the other shoe to drop* - who will be laid off.

Waiting in the wings [verb phr] (theater) the understudies for a star wait right next to the stage in case they are needed. Ex: Many stars were understudies *waiting in the wings* for their chance.

Wake up and smell the bacon/coffee [verb phr] pay attention to reality. Ex: *Wake up and smell the coffee.* It's going to snow tomorrow.

Walk into a trap [verb phr] be deceived. Ex: The animal *walked into a trap* and was killed by the hunter.

Walk off with [verb phr] steal. Ex: The small boy *walked off with* the candy from the store.

Walk out [verb] #1 union strike. Ex: The machinists walked out on Nov. 3. #2 leave a relationship. Ex: Ellen *walked out* on Dan last weekend.

Walk the fine line [verb phr] handle a situation with finesse. Ex: You have to *walk a fine line* when you are dealing with diversity issues.

Walk a mile in his moccasins [verb phr] (Indian saying) have empathy for others. Ex: If you could *walk a mile in his moccasins ,* you would know why he acts that way.

Walking on air [verb phr] euphoric. Ex: She was *walking on air* after winning the swimming race.

Walking on egg shells [verb phr] be cautious around overly-sensitive people. Ex: You have to *walk on egg shells* around Shelly because she cries easily.

Wall-to-wall [adj] a rug that covers the entire floor. Ex: We have wall-to-wall carpeting in our home.

Wallflower [noun] girl who is unpopular with boys. Ex: The *wallflowers* at a dance do not get asked to dance.

Walls have ears [noun phr] others may be listening to a secret being told. Ex: Lower your voice. The *walls have ears.*

Wandering eye [noun] look at persons of the opposite sex with interest. Ex: He has a *wandering eye* so his wife is jealous.

Wanna get hitched [verb phr] (country western) Do you want to get married?

Wannabees [noun] dress or act like someone famous. Ex: She is a Lady Gaga *wannabee* and has dyed her hair blonde.

Warm the bench [verb phr] (sports) be on a team, but not play in the game. Ex: He has *warmed the bench* for three seasons in a row.

Washed up [verb] destroyed. Ex: My business is all *washed up.* I am going bankrupt.

Washing my hands of this mess [verb phr] leaving an unpleasant situation. Ex: I am *washing my hands of this mess* and will talk to you tomorrow.

Waste not, want not [cliché] use your resources wisely.

Wasted [verb] drunk. (See *Snockered*)

Watch him like a hawk [verb phr] keep careful track of everything someone does. Ex: *Watch him like a hawk.* I think he is stealing from the store.

Watch out [verb] be careful. Ex: *Watch out* when you go into the wilderness.

Watch your step [verb phr] #1 be cautious. Ex: *Watch your step* before getting into the car. #2 a warning to someone who is irritating you. Ex: You better *watch your step* because I am getting angry.

(A) watched pot never boils [cliché] something or someone who is scrutinized carefully can't perform.

Water under the bridge [noun phr] in the past and should be forgotten. Ex: That incident is *water under the bridge* and I want to forget it. (See *Water over the dam*)

Water over the dam [noun phr] (See *Water over the bridge*)

Watered down version [noun] not the original; controversial issues are left out. Ex: Is that the *watered down version* of the new book?

(The) wave [noun] (sports) spectators at a sports event stand up one after the other, creating a "wave" effect.

Wave a red flag [verb phr] anger someone. Ex: If you tell Mom you spent all your allowance already, it will be like *waving a red flag* in front of her.

Way cool [adj] wonderful. (See *Rad*)

Way down the food chain [verb phr] (business) non-management. Ex: They won't listen to her because she is *way down the food chain.*

Way to go [expression of enthusiasm] Ex: So you made the team. *Way to go!*

Ways and means [noun phr] methods and resources to accomplish something. Ex: We have *ways and means* of motivating people.

Weak [verb] not motivating. Ex: That history class is really *weak.*

Weak kneed [adj] ready to collapse. Ex: I felt *weak kneed* after winning the race.

Weakest link in the chain [noun phr] most vulnerable place or part. Ex: Phillip's proposal is the *weakest link in the chain.*

Wear a cement overcoat [verb phr] dead. Ex: The politician is lucky he's not *wearing a cement overcoat* with the remarks he's been making.

Wear out your welcome [verb phr] visit someone so often that the other person gets tired of you. Ex: You will never *wear out your welcome* at my house.

Wear the pants in the family [verb phr] make most of the decisions in a family. Ex: My uncle *wears the pants in his family.*

Wear two hats [verb phr] have two entirely separate roles or sets of responsibilities. Ex: She *wears two hats.* She is a busy executive and a Mother.

Wear your heart on your sleeve [verb phr] not hiding your emotions. Ex: The teenager *wears her heart on her sleeve.* It is easy to see she is in love.

Weasel out of [verb phr] get out of an uncomfortable situation. Ex: Don' t try to *weasel out of* doing your homework.

Wedgie [noun] pull someone's underwear up from the back (as a joke). Ex: When his buddy gives him a *wedgie,* everyone laughs. [immature behavior]

Weigh both sides [verb phr] consider opposing viewpoints. Ex: I have to *weigh both sides* before I can make a decision.

Well and good [adj] (See *That's all well and good)*

Well-fixed [adj] wealthy. Ex: He is *well fixed* since he inherited that money from his parents. (See *Well heeled)*

Well heeled (See *Well fixed)*

Well off (See *Well fixed*)

Well to do (See *Well fixed)*

Well-wisher [noun] someone who is positive and wants the best for you. Ex: Did all the *well-wishers* send you "Get Well" cards after your operation?

Went at it tooth and nail [verb phr] aggressive and intense in whatever you are doing. Ex: The two boxers *went at it tooth and nail.*

Went haywire [verb] needs to be fixed.   Ex: My toaster *went haywire* yesterday. (See *Went kablooie)*

Went kablooie [verb] (See *Went haywire)*

Went over like a lead balloon [verb phr] was rejected. Ex: That suggestion *went over like a lead balloon.*

Went to Hell in a handbasket   [verb phr]   deteriorate considerably. Ex: When the new President took over, the Company *went to Hell in a handbasket.*

We're talking apples and oranges here [noun phr] (business) non-compatible ideas that cannot be compared together. They do not logically fit together. Ex: *We're talking apples and oranges here.* Let's discuss issues that are similar.

Were you born in a barn? [verb phrase] Insinuation that you are sloppy. Usually follows instructions to a child, such as "shut the door " or "pick up this mess."

Wet behind the ears [verb phr]   inexperienced. Ex: He is so *wet behind the ears* that he did not make two copies of the information for his supervisor.

Wet blanket   [noun]   person who is negative and ruins everyone's fun. Ex: Come to the movies with us. Don't be a *wet blanket. (*See *Spoil sport)*

Wet your whistle [verb phr] quench your thirst. Ex: Here's some water to *wet your whistle* before you give the speech.

Wet willie [noun] wet your finger and stick it in someone's ear. Ex: He gives his friends *wet willies* and grosses them out. [immature behavior]

What a hoot [noun phr] how funny!

What are you driving at? [noun expression] What is your point? What purpose do you have? (See *What are you getting at*?)

What are you getting at? [noun expression] (See *What are you driving at*?)

What do ya say? [noun expression] What do you think about this idea? Ex: What *do ya say* we go bowling Friday night?

What gives?   [noun expression]   What is happening? Ex: Someone switched all the name tags. *What gives?*

What goes around, comes around [noun expression] When you treat someone in a certain manner, sometime in your life you will get treated the same way.

What is good for the goose is good for the gander [cliché] What is good for the husband of the house is also good for his wife.

What is your beef? [noun phr] (from a 1970's commercial) what is your problem?

What makes him tick? [noun expression] What does he respond to? What type of person is he?

What tomorrow has in store [noun phr] what's happening tomorrow. Ex: We don't know *what tomorrow has in store* for us. Maybe we will win the game!

What with [noun phr] as a result. Ex: We should all get raises, *what with* the profits the company made this year.

Whatchamacallit [noun] when you can't think of a name for something, you say "whatchamacallit". Ex: I need that whatchamacallit to help build your treehouse.

Whatever [noun] (said sarcastically) to not agree with what someone said, but will have to comply. Ex: "You're grounded for three days." "Whatever."

What's eating you? [noun phr] Why are you upset?

What's happenin'? [a familiar hello greeting]

What's her face [noun phr] said when you can't remember someone's name. Ex: "Who is going to the movies?" "Oh, *what's her face* and Ginger."

What's in it for me? [noun phr] what is the advantage for me?

What's it to you? [noun phr] sarcastic query. Ex: "What do you want to know for? *What's it to you?*

What's the catch? [noun phr] said when a plan sounds too good to be true.

What's the point? [noun phr] #1 what is the main idea? #2 statement of defeat. Ex: I haven't got a good grade in this class yet. *What's the point?* I might as well drop out.

What's the scoop? [noun phr] What is happening; what is going on? (See *What's the skinny?*)

What's the skinny? [noun phr] (See *What's the scoop?*)

What's up? [noun phr] What is happening? Pronounced "*Whazup?*"

What's your pleasure? [noun phr] What can I do for you?" Waitress or waiter comes to serve you in a restaurant and wants your order. She says, "*What's your pleasure?*"

Whatchamacallit [noun] when you can't think of a name for something, you say "whatchamacallit". Ex: I need that *whatchamacallit* to help me build your treehouse.

Whatever floats your boat [noun phr] whatever makes you happy. Ex: "I think I will have a chocolate ice cream cone today." "*Whatever floats your boat.*" (See *Whatever turns you on*)

Whatever happens, happens [noun phr] relax and do not worry. Ex: I don't know if I passed the test today. Oh well, *whatever happens, happens.*

Whatever turns you on [noun phr) whatever makes you happy. Has more of a sexual connotation. (See W*hatever floats your boat)*

Whee! [exclamation of excitement] Can be yelled while riding a roller coaster!

Wheeler dealer [noun] clever person. Ex: Better watch Sam. He is a real *wheeler dealer* and can take advantage of you.

Wheels [noun]   a car. Ex: My *wheels* are old but run pretty good.

Wheels are turning [noun phr] thinking.   Ex: Does George have the answer to the math question? I don't know, but the *wheels are turning*.

Wheelie [noun] (bicycling) go up on one wheel while cycling on a two wheel bike.

When all is said and done [adv expression] in conclusion. Ex: *When all is said and done,* we had a really good time.

When he hits bottom   [adv phr]   mentally and physically destroyed. Ex: *When he hits bottom*, perhaps he will get treatment for his drug problem.

When Hell freezes over [adv phr] never. Ex: "Jack says you are going on a date with him." "*When Hell freezes over.*"

When in Rome, do as the Romans [cliché] adapt to the customs of a country you are in.

When my ship comes in [adv phr] when I get lucky and become wealthy, successful, etc. Ex: *When my ship comes in,* I will take you on a cruise around the world.

When pigs fly [adv phr] (country western) not likely. Ex: "Do you think you will get a new car next year?" " Sure, w*hen pigs fly.*"

When push comes to shove [adv phr] when I am pressured for an answer, this is what I will do.

When the cat's away, the mice will play [cliché]   when an authority figure is not present, others will do what they wish.

When the chips are down [adv phr] when life is not going well for you. Ex: *When the chips are down,* you must try to be positive.

When the dust settles [adv phr] when people become calm after being upset. Ex: *When the dust settles,* we will talk about what nursing home Mom has to go to.

When you're up to your ass in alligators, that's no time to drain the swamp [cliché] You can't solve the source of a problem or crisis while handling the crisis.

Where there's smoke, there's fire [cliché] If you suspect something is wrong, chances are you're right.

Wherewithal [noun] money. Ex: I will take a trip to Australia if I have the *wherewithal.*

Whingding [noun] a party. Ex: Who's throwing the *whingding* Friday night? (See *Shindig*)

Whip out [verb] deliver. Ex: I can *whip out* this proposal in two hours.

Whip up [verb] make in a hurry. Ex: She will *whip up* dinner right after she gets home.

Whippersnapper [noun] small child. (1940's slang) Ex: That little *whippersnapper* can sure run fast. (See *Rug rat*)

Whistle blower [noun] person who exposes unethical business practices. Ex: *Whistle blowers* are people who risk their lives.

Whistle stop [noun] short stop, usually made by a train. Ex: The train makes a *whistle stop* at Arlington.

Whistling in the wind [verb phr] making a useless effort. Ex: Trying to make him understand is like *whistling in the wind.*

White as a ghost [cliché] shocked and the blood drains from your face. Ex: When he saw the sales figures, he was *white as a ghost. (*See *White as a sheet)*

White as a sheet (See *White as a ghost)*

White collar worker [noun] office worker. Ex: The *white collar workers* do not belong to the union.

White elephant [noun] item of little worth. Ex: We are having a *white elephant sale.* Be sure to bring all the items you don't want so we can sell them.

White glove test [noun] check someone's housekeeping by running a finger over the furniture to check for dust. Ex: He does the *white glove test* every night when he comes home from work.

White noise [noun] deliberate sounds played softly to cover office noise. Ex: Some of the office music is *white noise.*

Whiteout [noun] liquid that is painted over a typographical error or written error so you can type/write over it.

Whitewash [verb] treat a serious situation lightly. Ex: Don't *whitewash* your part in the conspiracy.

Who-done-it? [noun] a murder mystery story. Ex: "I am watching *a who-done-it on* TV tonight."

Whole ball of wax [noun phr] everything. Ex: When I ordered a hamburger, I got the *whole ball of wax* – a drink and fries with the hamburger. (See *Whole enchilada)*

Whole enchilada [noun phr] everything. (See *Whole ball of wax)*

Whole fam-damily [noun] (<u>impolite</u>) corrupted version of whole damn family; everyone. Ex: The *whole fam-damily* is coming to the reunion.

Whole kit and caboodle [noun phr] everything. (See *Whole ball of wax)*

Whole nine yards [noun phr] everything. Ex: The boss expects the *whole nine yards* from you on this project. (See *Whole ball of wax)*

Whole shebang [noun phr] everything. (See *Whole ball of wax)*

Whole shootin' match [noun phr] everything. (See *Whole ball of wax)*

Whole slew [noun] quite a few. Ex: There are a *whole slew* of relatives on Mary's side of the family.

Whoop-de-do [expression] so what. (said sarcastically)

Who's going to bell the cat? [noun expression] who will take on a job for the good of many at great risk to himself?

Why's and wherefores [noun phr] reasons. Ex: There are a lot of *why's and wherefores* that keep us from going to the beach.

Wicked off [verb] irritated. Ex: Don't get so *wicked off* when you drop the ball. (See *Ticked off)*

Wiff it [verb] (sports) strike at a ball and completely miss it. Ex: Here comes Matt. I wonder if he will *wiff it* again.

Wig out [verb] become agitated. (See *Tick someone off)*

Wild goose chase [noun] be sent on a trip to find something that can't be found. (Sometimes boys will play this trick with a new boy) (See Snipe hunt)

Willy-nilly [adj] confused, disorganized. Ex: His files are all *willy-nilly.*

Wilt on the vine [verb phr] few prospects for ever getting married. Ex: Aunt Emily is 45 years old and isn't married. She is *wilting on the vine.*

Win a few, lose a few [verb expression] things generally even out; most people do not win at everything; neither do they lose at everything.

Win hands down [verb phr] win a contest by a wide margin. Ex: He won the running race *hands down.*

Win-win situation [noun] each party in a negotiation is happy with the result. Ex: We have a *win-win situation* with our new home.

Wind it down [verb phr] taper off activities; relax. Ex: It is time to *wind it down* and go to sleep now.

Wind sprints [noun] (sports) short running races to keep players in shape. Ex: If you don't do your *wind sprints,* you will get a muscle cramp.

Wing it [verb] unprepared for a situation and use your natural skills to be successful. Ex: Do you think he will *wing it* for the presentation?

Wipe the slate clean [verb phr] start all over and forget about the past. Ex: You had a bad experience and now you have to *wipe the slate clean.*

Wiped out [verb] #1 drunk. Ex: He was so *wiped out* last night that he had to call a cab to take him home. #2 exhausted. Ex: I was really *wiped out* after running six miles. #3 broke. Ex: I am *wiped out*. I have lost all my savings in the stock market.

Wiped the floor with him [verb phr] beat someone soundly in a fight.

Wired [verb] hyper. Justin is really *wired* about playing third base in the baseball game. (See *Jazzed up*)

Wiser than an owl [cliché] a sage.

Wish I were a fly on the wall [noun phr] wish I could hear what was said when I wasn't in the room.

Wishful thinking [noun] something you would like to happen, but chances are that it will not take place. Ex: I would love to go to Norway, but that is *wishful thinking*.

Wishy-washy [adj] change your mind easily. Ex: Lots of politicians are *wishy-washy*.

With a heavy heart [prep phr] feeling sadness. Ex: *With a heavy heart* he buried his pet dog.

With a poker face [prep phr] not let your facial expression betray what you are thinking. Ex: *With that poker face* of his you can never tell if he is holding all the aces.

With all my heart [prep phr] #1 in total sincerity. Ex: I promise *with all my heart* to look after your dog when you die. #2 joyfully. Ex: I accepted the tickets for my children to go to the Nutcracker Ballet *with all my heart*.

With an eye toward [prep phr] while involved in one activity, to pay attention to another. Ex: I will give the speech *with an eye toward* pleasing the audience.

With bells on [prep phr] (said by women) enthusiastic. Ex: I'll be at the play *with bells on.*

With flying colors [prep phr] accomplish something with a high degree of success. Ex: "Yes, I passed my test *with flying colors.* I got an "A".

With his tail between his legs [prep phr] leave embarrassed. Ex: When he forgot his speech, he left *with his tail between his legs.*

With open arms [prep phr] receive warmly; welcome. Ex: The long lost relative was welcomed *with open arms.*

Without a penny to his name [prep phr] with no money at all. Ex: He came back from his trip *without a penny to his name.*

Without batting an eye [prep phr] not betray any emotion. Ex: He negotiated for the car *without batting an eye.*

Without question [prep phr] undoubtedly. Ex: *Without question* she is the prettiest girl in class.

Wolf down [verb] eat very fast. Ex: Don't *wolf down* your sandwich or you will get a stomach ache.

Wolf in sheep's clothing [noun phr] men who appear to be shy and conservative, but who really are aggressive sexually.

Women's libbers   [noun]   aggressive, independent, liberal women who strive for equal rights with men.   Ex: *Women's libbers* frequently are very vocal about their beliefs.

Won a few brownie points [verb phr] gained favor.   Ex: He *won a few brownie points* with the boss when he agreed to work overtime on the holiday.

Won a new lease on life [verb phr] do bad deeds in the past, but reform and people are willing to give you another chance to prove you have changed.

Won him over [verb phr] persuade someone to change to your viewpoint.   Ex: I finally *won over* the Vice President and he will promote my idea.

Word of honor [noun phr] promise. Ex: I give you my *word of honor* that I will be there tomorrow morning.

Word of mouth   [noun phr]   information passed by people talking to each other.   Ex: He found out she was in Canada by *word of mouth.*

Word to the wise (cliché) pass along information to someone that will be helpful to them.

Words of wisdom [noun phr] good advice.   Ex: My Mother always has some good *words of wisdom* for me.

Words stuck in my throat [noun phr] too nervous to speak. Ex: When the President of the company said hello to me, the *words stuck in my throat* and I could not answer him.

Work at a snail's pace [verb phr] work extremely slowly.

Work graveyard [verb] work the night shift in your job.

Work him into a frenzy [verb phr]   get him wildly upset or disorganized.

Work like a beaver [verb phr] work hard and fast.

Work like a dog [verb phr] working very vigorously and hard.

Work out all the bugs [verb phr] correct all the errors. Ex: Let me *work out all the bugs* on this new computer program.

Work your fingers to the bone [verb phr] work extremely hard and for long periods of time. Ex: He *worked his fingers to the bone* finishing the construction of the new addition to the house.

Worked up [verb] #1 stressed.   Ex: He was all *worked up* because he had too many activities. #2 produce. Ex: He *worked up* a fine essay. #3 intense physical or mental labor that makes you hungry. Ex: He *worked up* an appetite chopping wood.

Worker bee [noun] A diligent employee. (See *Working stiff)*

Working stiff [noun] regular worker in a company. (See *Worker bee)*

World is my oyster [noun phr] everything in life is wonderful.

World on your shoulders [noun phr] have more than your share of responsibilities. Since my Mom had a stroke, I have had the *world on my shoulders* taking care of her and my own family.

Worm something out of someone   [verb phr]   persuade someone to disclose a secret.

Worn ragged [verb] totally exhausted. Ex: The twins have me *worn ragged* by the end of each day. (See *Worn to a frazzle*)

Worn to a frazzle [verb phr] (See *Worn ragged*)

Worshipping the Porcelain God [verb phr] (1960's slang) throw up, usually after drinking too much liquor.

Wouldn't give a plugged nickel for it [verb phr] totally worthless. Ex: " That's a beautiful vase in that antique shop." " I *wouldn't give a plugged nickel for it*."

Wouldn't have a leg to stand on [verb phr] someone has been gracious and supported you in an endeavor or you would have no opportunities/alternatives. Ex: If I hadn't written that recommendation letter for Robbie, he *wouldn't have a leg to stand on.*"

Wouldn't hurt a fly [verb phr] gentle. Ex: Joe *wouldn't hurt a fly*. He is such a gentle person.

Wouldn't lift a finger [verb phr] not going to help. Ex: Those kids *wouldn't lift a finger* to help me around the house.

Wouldn't touch it with a ten foot pole [verb phr] not want to become involved. Ex: "Don't you want to help raise money for the community project?" "No, I *wouldn't touch it with a ten foot pole.*"

Wow! [exclamatory expression of surprise] very popular and well used.

Wrapped around your little finger [verb phr] flatter someone until that person is willing to do almost anything for you. Ex: "I've got Sarah *wrapped around my little finger*. She fixes breakfast for me every morning."

Wring your neck [verb phr] strangle you. Ex: I am so mad at you that I could *wring your neck*. (not literally)

Write home about [verb phr] a significant event is worth communicating about. Ari won the triathlon in Hawaii. Now that's something to *write home about*.

Writer's block [noun phr] lack of creative inspiration. Ex: Some writers do not appear to ever have *writer's block*. They just keep churning out great novels.

Wrong side of the tracks [noun phr] part of town where poor people live. Ex: Darrin is my good friend even though he is from the *wrong side of the tracks*.

Wrote him off [verb phr] not want to communicate with someone any more. Ex: "Where is Peter? I haven't seen him for a while." "Oh, I *wrote him off*. He was so full of himself."

Wuss [noun] a wimpy person. Ex: Don't be such a *wuss*. Jump off the high dive with me.

XYZ [abbrev] (1950's slang) *Examine your zipper.* Said to any boy whose pants' zipper is unzipped.

"X" marks the spot [noun phr] a specific location of something. Ex: Pirate treasure was usually *marked with an "X"*.

X-rated [adj] obscene. Ex: That movie is X-*rated*. We can't take the children.

Xerox [noun] #1 A corporation that deals in computers among other items. #2 [verb] copy. Ex: Will you please *xerox* this data for me?

Ya' know [noun phr] use after a statement that you know the listener agrees with. Ex: I think we should have less government spending, *ya' know*.

Yakity yak [verb] casual talking. (usually refers to women or children) (See *Chit chat*)

Yap [verb] bark loudly. Ex: I am tired of those *yapping* dogs.

Yell at the top of your lungs [verb phr] shout loudly. Ex: If you ever get attacked, *yell at the top of your lungs*.

Yellow belly [noun] coward. Ex: That *yellow belly* was hitting my dog.

Yesterday's news [noun phr] old information. Ex: The company's announcement of a new product is *yesterday's news*.

Yo! [hello greeting] Hi! (2010 slang)

You bet your life [noun phr] agreement with what someone just said. (See *You bet your sweet bippy*)

You bet your sweet bippy! [1970's noun expression] affirmation of what the other person has just said. used a lot on the TV show Rowan and Martin's Laugh-in. (See *You bet your life*)

You betcha [noun expression] You're right. Ex: " You went to the game last night, didn't you?" *"You betcha."*

You can call me bud [noun phr] (from a 1960's commercial) said in jest to someone who asks your name.

You can dress them up, but you can't take them out [noun phr] said about someone who puts on expensive clothes or semi-formal attire, but does not have the behavior to be acceptable. (usually said in jest)

You can lead a horse to water, but you can't make him drink [cliché] You can try to suggest the correct path of behavior for someone to follow, but that does not necessarily mean he/she will follow it.

You can't imagine how little I care [noun phr] jokingly said to a friend when he/she is prolonging an explanation.

You can't take it with you [cliché] can't take money to the grave with you. Ex: You *can't take it with you*, so you might as well spend it.

You can't teach an old dog new tricks [cliché] someone who is older finds it more difficult to learn new things.

You could have heard a pin drop [noun phr] everyone was incredibly quiet. Ex: When the company announced layoffs, y*ou could have heard a pin drop.*

You could knock me over with a feather [noun phr] hear some news that really surprises you. Ex: I didn't know Mark won the golf tournament. *You could knock me over with a feather!*

You had to be there [noun phr] relating an event to someone who does not understand what happened so you say, *"you had to be there."*

You have to play the cards you're dealt [noun phr] do the best with the talents you were given. Ex: In order to be successful, *you have to play the cards you're dealt.*

You made your own bed, now lie in it [cliché] usually said when a girl marries someone her family has disapproved of. When she complains later on, her family replies, *"You made your own bed, now lie in it"* meaning you made your choice and now you have to suffer the consequences.

You must be joking! [noun expression] a comment upon hearing some astonishing news that you hope is not true. Ex: "Ted failed his final exam." *"You must be joking!"*

You only live once [noun expression] Don't miss out on fun, excitement or experiences in life, because *you only live once.*

You scratch my back; I'll scratch yours [noun expression] you do a favor for me and I will do one for you.

You snooze, you lose [noun phr] Do not let opportunity pass you by.

You'll never hear the end of it [noun phr] a mistake will not be forgotten by someone. Ex: "You forgot to lock the door last night." "I know. *I will never hear the end of it."*

You're killing me! [noun expression] Usually said to someone who has you very excited, and you are either laughing or out of breath.

You're not just whistling Dixie! [noun expression] An affirmation. Ex: "I think it is going to snow tomorrow." *"You're not just whistling Dixie.* I already put my snow tires on."

YouTube [noun] website hosting user-generated videos that are shared with others.

You wish [noun expression] someone makes a statement that will probably not come true and you reply, *"You wish"*. Ex: "I am going to the dance with the Prom Queen." *"You wish!"*

Your ass is grass and I am the mower [noun expression] in trouble. (See *Your name is mud*)

Your guess is as good as mine [noun phr] uncertain of an answer. Ex: "When is Jack coming home?" "I don't know. *Your guess is as good as mine*."

Your John Hancock [noun phr] your signature. Ex: If I can have *your John Hancock* at the bottom of the deed, the house is yours.

Your lot in life [noun phr] destiny. Ex: It is his *lot in life* to be popular.

Your mother wears army boots [1970's noun expression] children might say this as a taunt to one another to provoke a fight. It is considered an insult to your mother.

Your name is mud [noun phr] in trouble. (See *Your ass is grass and I am the mower*)

Your neck of the woods [noun phr] where you live. Ex: "Where shall we play basketball?" *"In your neck of the woods."*

Your number is up [noun phr] time for you to die. Ex: You never know when *your number is going to be up*.

Your X [noun] your signature. Ex: Put *your X* at the bottom of the form.

Yuppies

Yuppies [acronym] *Young urban professionals*, well educated and affluent, who mostly live and work in a large city. In the 1980's the acronym YUP was lengthened to *Yuppies*.

Zap [verb] administer electroshock treatment. Ex: The policeman used his Taser gun to *zap* the perpetrator.

Zero in on something [noun phr] concentrate on one thing. Ex: He *zeroed in on* the star with his telescope.

Zero point [noun] freezing. Ex: It's going to be down to the *zero point* tonight, so you better get another blanket.

Zilch [noun] nothing. Ex: "How many points did you score tonight?" "*Zilch*". (See *Zip*)

Zillion and one [noun phr] a great many. (an exaggeration) Ex: I have a *zillion and one* homework assignments.

Zinger [noun] a stinging, critical remark. Ex: That *zinger* really hurt my feelings.

Zip [noun] nothing, zero. Ex: "How many points did you score in the game?" "*Zip.*" (See *Zilch*)

Zip your lip [verb phr] be quiet. (usually said to children)

Zit [noun] a pimple, especially on your face.

Zombie [noun] acting like you are dead; no energy or feeling of life.

Zoned [verb] exhausted. Ex: I'm really *zoned* today. The party last night lasted until 4:00 a.m. (See *Done in*)

Zoned out [verb] lose concentration. Ex: I *zoned out* today and did not pass the exam. (See *Done in*)

Zonked out [verb] #1 feeling exhausted. Ex: He *zonked out* after running that race. #2 asleep. Ex: The children *zonked out* about 8:00.

Zooey [adj] crazy. Ex: Let's go. The party is getting *zooey*.

Zoom in on [verb phr] #1 use a special camera lens for focus on distant objects. #2 direct your attention to a specific point of a discussion. Ex: He *zoomed in on* the main point of the argument.

Zoot suit [noun] an expensive black and white pin stripe suit that was popular in the 1930's and 1940's.

Made in the USA
San Bernardino, CA
07 December 2015